FOUNDATIONS OF A PLANNED ECONOMY
1926–1929

A HISTORY OF SOVIET RUSSIA

The following volumes have been published:

THE BOLSHEVIK REVOLUTION			– *1917–1923*
Volume One	(1950)		
Volume Two	(1951)		
Volume Three	(1953)		
THE INTERREGNUM			– *1923–1924*
	(1954)		
SOCIALISM IN ONE COUNTRY			– *1924–1926*
Volume One	(1958)		
Volume Two	(1959)		
Volume Three	(1964)	(In 2 parts)	
FOUNDATIONS OF A PLANNED ECONOMY			– *1926–1929*
Volume One	(1969)	(In 2 parts)	
Volume Two	(1971)		
Volume Three	(1976)	(2 parts published; third in preparation)	

A HISTORY OF SOVIET RUSSIA

FOUNDATIONS OF A PLANNED ECONOMY 1926–1929

*

VOLUME THREE – I

BY

EDWARD HALLETT CARR
FELLOW OF TRINITY COLLEGE, CAMBRIDGE

First published 1976 by
THE MACMILLAN PRESS LTD
London and Basingstoke
Associated companies in New York
Dublin Melbourne Johannesburg and Madras

SBN 333 13204 1

Printed in Great Britain by
RICHARD CLAY (THE CHAUCER PRESS), LTD.,
Bungay, Suffolk

CONTENTS

PREFACE

The first volume of *Foundations of a Planned Economy, 1926–1929*, written by Professor R. W. Davies and myself, was published in two parts in 1969, the second volume in 1971. Since then I have been engaged on the third volume, designed to cover Soviet foreign relations in this period and to bring my *History of Soviet Russia* to an end. I need not repeat what I said in the preface to Volume I of *Foundations* about my choice of this concluding point. In any case, when I reach it, I shall have done my bit, and shall be content to leave other scholars to continue the work — no doubt, in quite different forms.

The third volume has, however, swelled far beyond my original intentions and expectations, and I am able to present only two parts, with a third part still to come. Some explanation or excuse is required for this prolixity. In the late nineteen-twenties diplomatic relations between the Soviet Union and the principal capitalist Powers, with the exception of the United States, were falling into a regular and conventional pattern; only with Great Britain was there a break of two years. These relations raised no serious problem either of source material or of interpretation, and could be dealt with fairly briefly. On the other hand, Soviet relations with communist parties in capitalist countries — the policies operated through the agency of Comintern — were both complex and important. These could not be analysed in any depth without a detailed study of the development of the parties themselves; and I found myself involved at greater length than I had intended in the history of the western European parties, though I have kept in mind — in so far as the distinction is valid — that my concern was with the policies of Comintern in relations to these parties, and not with their internal affairs. It will be noticed that I have not included in the present survey several parties which figured in *Socialism in One Country, 1924–1926*, Vol. 3: the Czechoslovak party (whose fate was somewhat similar to that of the German party), the Yugoslav and Bulgarian parties (which were too thoroughly crushed by police repression to pursue any significant activity in this period), and the Swedish party (which was not very important). These omissions made possible some economy of space.

In the preface to *Socialism in One Country, 1921–1926*, Vol. 3, I lamented the lack of a serious history of any major communist party. This omission has now been repaired for the German and Italian parties respectively by Hermann Weber, *Die Wandlung des Deutschen Kommunismus* (2 vols., 1969) and P. Spriano, *Storia del Partito Comunista Italiano* (3 vols., 1967–1970), to both of which I am very substantially indebted. The former is written by a non-communist, the latter by a communist; both attain a high level of scholarship and objectivity, and are based on ample documentation. The Italian party is the first to have opened its archives to full and frank use by a historian without concealment of past errors or embarrassments. The French and British parties still await comparable treatment.

A few technical points must be mentioned. In previous volumes references to Lenin's collected works were to the second edition, the latest available when I began to publish my *History* in 1950. In the present volume I have used the fifth edition, *Polnoe Sobranie Sochinenii* (1958–1965), which contains items not in the earlier editions and is more readily accessible. The choice between Russian and German editions of the proceedings of Comintern has generally been governed by practical convenience. For the first five congresses I used the German edition; of the sixth congress only the Russian edition is complete, and I have therefore used it. Of the sessions of IKKI down to and including the seventh (November–December 1926) I have used the Russian editions. But a fragmentary record of the eighth IKKI exists only in German; no proceedings of the ninth were published; and I have used the German edition of the tenth IKKI, since the Russian edition was not available to me. As before, I have used the German edition of *Internationale Presse-Korrespondez*, which is far fuller than the English and French editions, except for a few items which appeared only in the English edition. References in the footnotes to Vol. 1 or Vol. 2 are to the earlier volumes of *Foundations of a Planned Economy, 1926–1929*.

Nearly five years have passed since I wrote the preface to the previous volume in this series; and with each successive volume the advance of years has made me more conscious of how much I owe to friends, colleagues and institutions which have helped me. I hope I may be excused, for lack of space and not of appreciation, from repeating the names of my benefactors recorded in the prefaces to previous volumes, many of whom have continued to place me in their debt. But I must once more express my special thanks to my own college for its generous support of my work, and to its library staff for labouring on my behalf to locate scarce books and borrow them from other libraries. Professor Daniel Calhoun of the College of Wooster, Ohio, using unpublished TUC archives, has made an illuminating study of the Anglo-Russian trade union joint council or committee, and put at my disposal an early version of his work, which will shortly be published by the Cambridge University Press under the title *United Front: The TUC and the Russians, 1923–1928*; what I have written about the committee owes very much to his labours. I should also thank Dr Arthur Lehning of the Institute of Social History, Amsterdam, for letting me see unpublished material on the proceedings of the League against Imperialism, and Professor G. D. Jackson of Hofstra University, Long Island, N.Y., for sending me a microfilm of a rare journal of the Peasant International. The Marx Memorial Library has kindly lent scarce pamphlets of the British Communist Party; and I am indebted for similar generous help to the magnificent library of the Feltrinelli Institute in Milan and to its director, Professor Del Bo. The editor of the *Guardian* kindly investigated the story about Soviet–German arms transactions which appeared in the *Manchester Guardian* on December 3, 1926 (see p. 39 note 15), but was unable to identify the 'correspondent' who wrote it or to uncover the source of the information.

My largest obligation by far in the preparation of this volume is to Tamara Deutscher, who for three years has devoted herself untiringly to the collection and organization of the source material. This has involved much onerous research, which I should no longer have been able to undertake myself, in the British Museum, where conditions of work have become increasingly difficult, and in other libraries. She has made her contribution both to the substance and to the form of every chapter of this volume. The chapters in particular on the British, French and Italian Communist Parties are based almost entirely on her researches.

The major remaining event of the period which, on account of both its dimensions and its influence, unquestionably calls for extended treatment is the Chinese revolution of the nineteen-twenties and the part played in it by the Soviet Government and Comintern. The advance of the revolution in 1925–1927 and its recoil in 1927–1929 were dramatic, and present problems which are still open to debate. The chapter on China will occupy nearly half of the third part, still to come, of this volume. This part will also deal with the other 'semi-colonial' countries of Asia, including India, with Latin America, which began for the first time in this period to attract serious attention in Moscow, and with the treatment by Comintern of the Negro question in the United States and in South Africa. Work on this part is far advanced, and publication should not be long delayed. It will contain the index to all three parts of the volume.

E. H. Carr

May 15, 1976

PART IV

FOREIGN RELATIONS

A: *The Soviet Union and the Capitalist World*

*

CHAPTER 57

DIPLOMACY, WAR AND PEACE

THE period of stabilization and normalization of Soviet diplomatic relations with the capitalist world, which set in after the ending of the civil war,[1] lasted for five or six years. Its counterpart in domestic policy was the gradual recovery of the Soviet economy and the heyday of NEP. Its watchword in foreign policy was "peaceful co-existence". The concept was as old as the régime. A declaration of Narkomindel of November 9/22, 1917, expressed the hope for "a rapid peace on the basis of honourable co-existence and collaboration of peoples". The phrase itself seems to have been first used by Chicherin who, in a note of September 18, 1918, called for "good neighbourly relations and peaceful co-existence with Germany".[2] But not till foreign intervention in the civil war had been abandoned could much meaning be read into the phrase. Lenin, in an interview published in an American newspaper in December 1919, spoke of the granting of concessions in exchange for technical aid "during the period when socialist and capitalist states will exist side by side".[3] Chicherin in a press interview hailed the peace treaty concluded with Estonia in February 2, 1920, as "an experiment in the peaceful co-existence of the Soviet republic with bourgeois states".[4] Lenin, in what appears to have been his only certain recorded use of the complete phrase, in an interview with an American journalist on February 18, 1920, reverted to an older tradition and spoke of "peaceful co-existence", not with states, but "with peoples, with workers and peasants of all nations

[1] See *Socialism in One Country, 1924–1926*, Vol. 3, pp. 4–6.

[2] *Dokumenty Vneshnei Politiki SSSR*, i (1957), 22, 488.

[3] Lenin, *Polnoe Sobranie Sochinenii*, xxxix, 197; the text is dated September 23, 1919, but it was first published in the *Christian Science Monitor*, December 17, 1919. The English text has the word "co-existence", but the relative authority of the Russian and English texts is hard to determine.

[4] *Pravda*, February 5, 1920; for the significance of this treaty see *The Bolshevik Revolution, 1917–1923*, Vol. 3, pp. 156–157.

who are awaking to a new life, a life without exploitation, without landowners, without capitalists, without merchants".[5] But any restriction which this formula may have implied was not characteristic of the period. The principle of co-existence with capitalist states was already well established in official pronouncements. Chicherin at the same moment in a radio message to the Japanese Government proposed negotiations "to guarantee peaceful co-existence to both peoples"; and in an address to the TsIK of the RSFSR on June 17, 1920, he repeated: "Our slogan was, and still is, the same: peaceful co-existence with other governments whatever they may be."[6] And finally in November 1920 Lenin told a Moscow provincial party conference that "we have won for ourselves the conditions in which we can exist side by side with the capitalist Powers, who are now obliged to enter into trade relations with us".[7]

The quest for peace was reinforced and justified by the need for peaceful economic relations to further the work of economic reconstruction. "What we prize most is peace and the full possibility to devote all our resources to the restoration of the economy", Lenin said on the eve of the introduction of NEP;[8] and the tenth party congress in March 1921, in a resolution entitled "The Soviet Republic in a Capitalist Environment", approved "the establishment of normal trade relations between the Soviet republic and other countries".[9] Three months later, at the third congress of Comintern, Bukharin found himself obliged to defend this policy against the argument that such economic relations would help to strengthen the capitalist world and not to promote the cause of world revolution.[10] But the concept of peaceful co-existence, though not the term, appeared with great frequency in Lenin's speeches and writing in the first months of 1922 when

[5] Lenin, *Polnoe Sobranie Sochinenii*, xl, 145.

[6] *Dokumenty Vneshnei Politiki SSSR*, ii (1958), 389, 639; on the latter occasion Chicherin substituted the word *sosushchestvovanie* for *sozhitel'stvo*—the word used in all other early pronouncements, including those of Lenin and Stalin. After 1927 (see pp. 15, 106 below) *sozhitel'stvo* was generally replaced by *sosushchestvovanie*; but no significance appears to attach to these changes of style.

[7] Lenin, *Polnoe Sobranie Sochinenii*, xlii, 22.

[8] *Ibid.* xlii, 313.

[9] *KPSS v Rezolyutsiyakh* (1954), ii, 260.

[10] *Protokoll des III Kongresses der Kommunistischen Internationale* (1921), pp. 800–803.

preparations were in hand for the Genoa conference;[11] and Trotsky at the eleventh party congress in March 1922 foresaw "a long period of peaceful co-existence and of businesslike co-operation with bourgeois countries".[12] Thereafter the phrase "peaceful co-existence" seems to have fallen out of fashion, and was rarely heard in the next few years. But Stalin at the fourteenth party congress in December 1925 spoke of "the current phase of 'peaceful co-existence' between the land of the Soviets and capitalist countries", and of "a certain period of 'peaceful co-existence' between the world of the bourgeoisie and the world of the proletariat".[13]

The second half of 1926, a period of buoyant optimism in Soviet domestic affairs,[14] was marked by growing uneasiness and anxiety in Soviet international relations. An anti-Soviet bloc of western Powers under British leadership, into which Germany would be drawn, seemed to Soviet observers the essential aim of the Locarno policy. Chicherin in April 1926 saw Great Britain engaged in "a complicated game aimed at isolating the USSR and unifying all the leading governments in one form or another against this country".[15] British resentment of Soviet support for the British general strike and for the nationalist revolution in China, and the increasing virulence and evident popularity of the anti-Soviet campaign waged by the die-hard wing of the Conservative Party,[16] fanned these fears. Poland was linked with Great Britain as a major source of apprehension. The coincidence in time between the defeat of the British general strike and Pilsudski's "Fascist *coup*" in Poland had been significantly noted;[17] in the autumn of 1926 Polish intervention in Lithuania, which would

[11] In greeting the resolutions of the Cannes conference of January 1922, which paved the way for the Genoa conference, Lenin wrote of "the equality of right of the two systems of property", and the necessity for agreement between them "as equal with equal" (Lenin, *Polnoe Sobranie Sochinenii*, xlv, 192).

[12] *Odinadtsatyi S"ezd RKP (Bol'shevikov)* (1936), p. 144.

[13] Stalin, *Sochineniya*, vii, 262; the printed text in both passages has the two words in inverted commas. The "whole period of peaceful co-existence" also appeared in the resolution of the congress (see *Socialism in One Country, 1924–1926*, Vol. 3, p. 491).

[14] See Vol. 1, pp. 11–13.

[15] *Dokumenty Vneshnei Politiki SSSR*, ix (1964), 199–200.

[16] See pp. 18–23 below.

[17] *Kommunisticheskii Internatsional*, No. 4 (78), 1927, p. 5.

bring war once again to eastern Europe, seemed no remote contingency.[18] A long article by Radek on the danger of war at the end of 1926 admitted that "England cannot simply mobilize the resources of France and Germany against the USSR", but reached the conclusion that she might mobilize the Soviet Union's immediate western neighbour in support of her designs.[19]

These fears did not yet have an obsessive character. At the fifteenth party conference in October 1926 Bukharin observed that "the danger of war must by all means be emphasized, with the reservation that this is in the first place a danger of war against the Soviet Union".[20] But the resolution of the conference went no further than to note "a complication of the struggle between the capitalist states and our country".[21] Bukharin at the seventh enlarged IKKI in December 1926 attacked the social-democrats who, misled by pacifist illusions, had abandoned "the universally recognized Marxist thesis, e.g. the famous all-embracing and familiar thesis of the inevitability of wars in the epoch of capitalism". The contradictions of capitalism were increasing, its foundations were crumbling and it was seeking to save itself "with the help of extraordinary, sharply intensified methods of exploitation".[22] Šmeral offered a more sophisticated analysis:

> The first world war was, in spite of American intervention, in essence a European war. The next world war, unless it is made impossible in good time by the prior success of a social revolution, will be a world war in the proper sense of the word. A process, similar to that which was produced in Europe before the first world war through the gradually maturing disintegration of Austria–Hungary, is now beginning at a much higher stage of the spiral, on a much larger scale, through the disintegration of the British Empire in the whole world.[23]

It was Stalin who on this occasion, eager to defend "socialism in one country", sounded a note of qualified optimism for the immediate future. He quoted Lenin on the ultimate inevitability of

[18] See pp. 80–81 below.

[19] *Mirovaya Ekonomika i Mirovaya Politika*, No. 12, 1926, pp. 3–8; the article also appeared in *Izvestiya*, January 28, 1927.

[20] *XV Konferentsiya Vsesoyuznoi Kommunisticheskoi Partii(B)* (1927), p. 92.

[21] *KPSS v Rezolyutsiyakh* (1954), ii, 329.

[22] *Puti Mirovoi Revolyutsii* (1927), i, 20.

[23] *Ibid.* i, 508.

an armed clash between the Soviet republic and bourgeois states. But it was "another question whether the capitalists can at present undertake a serious intervention against the Soviet republic"; the opposition of the workers in capitalist countries to such an enterprise ensured that such a war could not be undertaken at the present time "without the danger of exposing capitalism to a deadly risk".[24] A few weeks later, however, in the Chinese commission of the seventh IKKI, Stalin reflected that "the invasion of armies does not in the least constitute the fundamental characteristic of intervention", and that in the contemporary period "intervention has a more flexible character and a more disguised form".[25]

Causes and symptoms of apprehension continued to multiply. Chicherin, in a wide-ranging press interview in Berlin on December 6, 1926, drew attention to an article in the *Fortnightly Review* from the pen of "Augur", a Russian *émigré* journalist named Polyakov, known to be in touch with Chamberlain, advocating a European united front against the USSR under British leadership.[26] Voroshilov, speaking in January 1927 at the conference called to found the military defence society Osoaviakhim, declared that the danger of war had "penetrated the consciousness of the masses", and cited the Pilsudski *coup* in Poland, and the recent Lithuanian *coup*, as the work of "English imperialists".[27] Litvinov, while purporting in conversation with the British chargé d'affaires to deprecate "this stupid war scare", none the less asserted that "Poland is fundamentally hostile and is making every preparation for aggression".[28] When the TsIK of the USSR met in February 1927, twenty-nine deputies made a request for a report on the anti-Soviet campaign conducted in Great Britain "by members of the government and Conservative circles";[29] and Litvinov denounced British hostility to the Soviet Union, which

[24] Stalin, *Sochineniya*, viii, 263–264.

[25] *Ibid.* viii, 360.

[26] *Dokumenty Vneshnei Politiki SSSR*, ix (1964), 564–566; an aggressive article by Augur in February 1926 had already excited apprehensive comments in speeches of Trotsky and Rykov and articles in *Pravda* (*Pravda*, February 23, March 5, 10, 1926).

[27] *Izvestiya*, January 27, 1927; for this conference see Vol. 2, p. 334. For the Lithuanian *coup* see p. 80 below.

[28] *Documents on British Foreign Policy*, Series I A, iii (1970), 23–25.

[29] *Izvestiya*, February 20, 1927.

"does not date from yesterday", in a speech of February 21, 1927.[30] The attack on the Soviet legation in Peking on April 6, 1927, was widely attributed to British instigation; and Humbert-Droz, the Swiss member of the Comintern secretariat, wrote in a letter a few days later that "England is doing everything possible to provoke war".[31]

In the spring of 1927 something like panic fear obsessed the Soviet leaders, and spread to large sectors of the population.[32] With the British strike movement defeated and the British Government displaying more and more open hostility to the Soviet Union, with Germany succumbing to the lure of the League of Nations and of cooperation with the western Powers, with Poland arrayed as the outpost of imperialism on the Soviet frontier, with the Chinese revolutionary movement in ruins, no light could be discerned anywhere on the horizon. Rykov addressing the fourth Union Congress of Soviets when the break with Great Britain was imminent, and after the attack on the Soviet legation in Peking, bracketed China with the USSR as "the target of imperialist aggression", and treated British agitation against the Soviet Union as "preparation for encirclement, psychological preparation for intervention".[33] The resolution of the congress invited the government "to repel all new attempts to provoke the Soviet Union to war with anyone whatever and to do everything possible to avert war".[34]

The rupture of relations with the Soviet Union by Great Britain in May 1927 gave body to these vague fears of hostile action. On June 1, 1927, the party central committee issued a proclamation on the theme that the "British imperialists" were on the way to "unleash a pan-European war". The Russian and Chinese revolutions had intensified "the deepening crisis of capitalism, and first

[30] *3 Sessiya Tsentral'nogo Ispolnitel'nogo Komiteta Soyuza SSR 3 Sozyva* (1927), pp. 659–662.

[31] J. Humbert-Droz, *Il Contrasto tra l'Internazionale e il PCI* (1969), p. 246 (Humbert-Droz archives, 0081).

[32] The cautious British chargé d'affaires, reporting to London on "the war scare", concluded that "it is not 'faked', at all events in essentials, but indeed represents the feelings and emotions of the Communist Party and the Soviet Government", and that "this state of nervousness has been successfully communicated to the people at large" (*Documents on British Foreign Policy*, Series I A, ii (1968), 716).

[33] *SSSR: 4 S"ezd Sovetov* (1927), pp. 6–7, 19.

[34] *S"ezdy Sovetov v Dokumentakh*, iii (1960), 113.

and foremost of English capitalism". This explained the British Government's menacing gestures:

> We do not and cannot know when the enemy will openly march with bayonets against the USSR. But it can no longer be doubted that English imperialism is more and more eager to hasten this moment.[35]

The assassination of Voikov in Warsaw on June 7, 1927,[36] seemed a further step on the road to war; and two days later Voroshilov made a cautious public speech which probably reflected the appreciation of the situation by his military advisers. Recent actions instigated by the British bourgeoisie, culminating in the Voikov murder, showed that "we are now entering a period of history in which our class enemies will inevitably force a war on us"; and "the relatively peaceful period of our existence is undoubtedly over". If the rupture of relations by Great Britain had not been followed by military action, this proved that "the British bourgeoisie obviously miscalculated". The interests of the capitalist countries were "too full of contradictions" to permit of the formation of a united front, and Great Britain was not strong enough to act alone. Undue optimism would, however, be dangerous:

> If I personally am of opinion that a war this year is improbable, events develop so rapidly that we cannot predict with certainty what awaits us in the immediate future.... It can come in two years or in one year, but it is possible, though not probable, that the delay might be only a few months.

Vigilance and preparedness for self-defence were, therefore, the watchwords.[37] Few sophisticated observers in Moscow at this time expected a declaration of war by Great Britain. But fears of a Polish attack on the western frontier of the Soviet Union, encouraged and supported from London, or of an organized commercial and financial blockade, were less unrealistic.[38] In a

[35] *Pravda*, June 1, 1927.

[36] See p. 82 below.

[37] *Internationale Presse-Korrespondenz*, No. 63, June 17, 1927, pp. 1319–1321.

[38] Stresemann, in a circular to German diplomats abroad on the Anglo-Soviet rupture, thought that military consequences were "unlikely", but expressed doubt "whether and in what way Great Britain will seek to incorporate other Powers in the apparently intended economic and moral

conversation with Stresemann on the day of Voikov's murder, Chicherin refused to believe in direct military intervention by Great Britain, but expressed the fear that Pilsudski, in pursuit of his territorial ambitions, would provoke a frontier incident in which the Soviet Union would be declared an aggressor, and that France would come to his aid.[39] Rykov explained to the Moscow Soviet at the beginning of July 1927 that Great Britain, faithful to her tradition, "will wage war not with her own hands, but with those of others".[40] At the end of July 1927 Stalin contributed a long article to *Pravda* on "Contemporary Themes", the first section of which was devoted to "the danger of war", further defined as "the real and actual threat of a new war in general, and of war against the USSR in particular". The Voikov murder had been organized by agents of the British Conservative Party "to play the rôle of the Sarajevo murder by drawing the USSR into a military conflict with Poland". Contradictions between capitalist Powers were multiplying; but so also were contradictions between the imperialist Powers and the victims of imperialism.[41]

When this article appeared, the party central committee had just opened a long and contentious session. The committee adopted an extensive resolution on the international situation, in which genuine fear of war blended with a politically calculated desire to appeal to pacifist sentiment abroad and to discredit the opposition at home. The situation was said to be characterized by "extremely

blockade front" (*Akten zur Deutschen Auswärtigen Politik*, Series B, V (1972), 407).

39 *Auswärtiges Amt*, 6698/105358–65.

40 A. Rykov, *Angliya i SSSR* (1927), p. 5.

41 Stalin, *Sochineniya*, ix, 322–330. Critical British and American writers commonly dismiss Soviet fears in the summer of 1927 of hostile action engineered by Great Britain not only as groundless (which they were), but as artificially worked up for internal purposes (which in this period they were not); it is interesting to compare the matter-of-fact contemporary account in L. Fischer, *The Soviets in World Affairs* (1930), ii, 741, of the "panicky" mood and "fully developed war psychosis" which he found in Moscow in June 1927 with the sour comments in the same author's *Men and Politics* (1941), written under the influence of his disillusionment with the Soviet Union. Brockdorff-Rantzau, an acute observer not easily hoodwinked, on returning to Moscow from leave in August 1927, reported that belief in an imminent danger of war was prevalent "even among cautious members of the government". He quoted the comment of a "leading member" of Narkomindel that "a war was inevitable because otherwise English policies were completely absurd"; only an attack on Russia would ensure a Conservative victory in the next election" (*Auswärtiges Amt*, 6698/106012–3, 106018–9).

strained relations between imperialist England and the proletarian USSR", leading to "the preparation of war against the USSR". The resolution contained a full description of "the system of diplomatic and military alliances against the USSR, following the line of the so-called 'encirclement' of the USSR": this comprised alliances and pacts between eastern European countries; British activities in the Baltic, Poland, the Far East and Persia; pressure on Germany to join an anti-Soviet bloc; the British attack on Arcos and pressure on France to break off relations with the Soviet Union. "The coming war against the USSR" would be, on the Soviet side, a war for "the defence of the *socialist* fatherland"; for workers in capitalist countries the correct slogan would be not merely "*defeatism*", but "*active help* for the proletarian state".[42] The opposition at the same session was keenly sensitive to any imputation of neglecting national interest. "For the socialist fatherland? Yes", exclaimed Trotsky in the peroration of his speech; and the opposition declaration of August 8, 1927, proclaimed "unconditional loyalty" to the defence of the Soviet Union.[43] The opposition platform of September 1927 took the view that "a war of the imperialists against the Soviet Union is not only probable, but inevitable".[44] A bellicose interview by Foch in the British popular press fanned the flame;[45] and Litvinov, who had hitherto taken a fairly restrained line, spoke of the French campaign against Rakovsky in September 1927 as the work of "instigators of war".[46] Kalinin, reviewing in October 1927 the experience of Soviet relations with the capitalist world over the past ten years, concluded that "conservative bourgeois elements can still not reconcile themselves in principle to the very fact of the existence of the Soviet state".[47]

The picture of an embattled capitalist world arrayed against the Soviet Union was blurred from time to time by the ambiguous rôle of the United States of America. Stalin at the fourteenth

[42] *KPSS v Rezolyutsiyakh* (1954), ii, 359–367; for this session see Vol. 2, pp. 30–33.
[43] See Vol. 2, pp. 30, 32.
[44] L. Trotsky, *The Real Situation in Russia* (n.d. [1928]), p. 140.
[45] See p. 65 below.
[46] See pp. 66–67 below.
[47] *Dokumenty Vneshnei Politiki SSSR*, x (1963), 458.

party congress in December 1925 had recognized that "the centre of financial power in the capitalist world, the centre of the financial exploitation of the whole world, has moved from Europe to America".[48] On November 1, 1926, at the fifteenth party conference, he was still more explicit:

> Now, since the imperialist war, America has run far ahead, leaving Great Britain and the other European states behind. One can scarcely doubt that this circumstance is fraught with new great conflicts and wars.[49]

A month later, the seventh IKKI elaborated the same conclusion:

> The most characteristic fact of the contemporary situation is the shift in the economic centres, and consequently in political and military power, to the extra-European countries, primarily to the United States of America, in relation to which the European states have become debtors, and to which has passed the hegemony of the world market in general. If one cannot speak of the conversion of the European economy into a component part of the economy of the North American United States, if it seems an undue exaggeration to assert that the whole of Europe is on American rations, the exclusive role of the United States is not open to any doubt.

But, continued the resolution:

> Anglo-American rivalry gives a strong definition to the regrouping of the imperialist Powers. The attempt of Great Britain with the help of the Locarno pact to win back its positions on the continent was checkmated by America.[50]

The days when the argument revolved round Trotsky's rash prediction of an imminent armed clash between the United States and Great Britain[51] were now past. But a dramatic episode like the breakdown early in August 1927 of the naval conference of Geneva between Great Britain, the United States and Japan, kept alive the vision of Anglo-American rivalry as the chief and most dangerous antagonism within the capitalist world. Trotsky himself in a letter of February 28, 1928, wrote that, while the

[48] Stalin, *Sochineniya*, viii, 266.
[49] *Ibid.* viii, 253.
[50] *Kommunisticheskii Internatsional v Dokumentakh* (1933), pp. 627–628.
[51] See *Socialism in One Country, 1924–1926*, Vol. 3, pp. 468–473.

forecast of an Anglo-American war was an "over-simplification", the rivalry between the two countries would lead to "many sharp breaks";[52] and the programme of Comintern, adopted by its sixth congress in the summer of 1928, declared that the conflict between Great Britain and the United States "is becoming the axis of world-wide conflicts between the finance-capitalist states".[53] How persistent was communist belief in the deep-seated mutual animosity between Great Britain and the United States was illustrated in a report of the central committee of the CPGB in January 1929 condemning the "jingo propaganda" of the "capitalist and capitalist-Labour press", which "invariably utilizes American colonial policy in Nicaragua, the shooting of American workers in strikes etc., in order to work up anti-American feeling", and comparing this with anti-German propaganda prior to 1914.[54] A few months later Bell still believed that "the most active sector of the war danger is the rivalry between England and America"; and the more sophisticated Rothstein, while admitting that "British imperialism does not prepare its war with the USA in the same coarse and brutal way that it works against the Soviet Union", argued that the British press was engaged in working up "'moral' indignation" against the United States as it had done against Germany before 1914.[55]

Nor was this the only antagonism within the capitalist world which stood out in the world picture as seen from Moscow. The antagonisms between the victorious and defeated Powers in Europe, between France and Italy and between the United States and Japan, continued to preoccupy the Soviet policy-makers. The seventh IKKI in November 1926, in listing these and other antagonisms, remarked that "everywhere in the globe there is an accumulation of combustible material, ready to flare up at the first spark thrown into it".[56] Bukharin at the sixth congress of Comintern in July 1928 detected "a *kaleidoscopic change in the*

[52] Trotsky archives, T 1161.

[53] *Kommunisticheskii Internatsional v Dokumentakh* (1933), p. 13.

[54] *The New Line: Documents of the Tenth Congress of the CPGB* (n.d.), pp. 28–29.

[55] *Communist Review*, No. 5, May 1929, p. 267, No. 6, June 1929, pp. 360–361; the party programme for the general election of 1929 (see pp. 387–388 below) alleged that "British capitalism and American capitalism stand in the same relation in the post-war situation as did British and German capitalism before the war of 1914" (*Class Against Class* (1929), p. 13).

[56] *Kommunisticheskii Internatsional v Dokumentakh* (1933), p. 701.

mutual relations between states", and "a constant regrouping of forces"; yet "a fundamental tendency—a grouping of forces against the USSR—runs like a red thread" through the whole process.[57] A resolution of the congress conceded that, while "the chief political front of all the imperialist Powers" was directed against the Soviet Union and the Chinese revolution, "a collision between two imperialist groups of states in the struggle for world hegemony", on the analogy of the world war of 1914–1918, was also possible.[58] But this contingency, cutting across and in part invalidating the more familiar picture of a capitalist world united against the Soviet Union, offered an opportunity and a task of manoeuvre between mutually hostile Powers or groups of Powers, which was an indispensable and time-honoured part of the foreign policy of a state in a world of states more powerful than itself. Lenin from the days of Brest-Litovsk onwards had been fully conscious that the régime owed its survival to the bitter enmity between two groups of imperialist Powers; and in one of his last writings he had wondered whether "conflicts between the flourishing imperialist states of the west and the flourishing imperialist states of the east" would offer "a second breathing-space".[59] But this conception of diplomatic manoeuvre did not fit easily into the framework of Marxist teaching, or into the policies and procedures of Comintern.[60]

The tenth anniversary of the USSR was celebrated in November 1927 with much pomp and circumstance, and in a heady atmosphere of international applause and national self-congratulation on its achievements. From the end of 1927 the anxieties of the Soviet leaders were directed to internal problems, which temporarily relegated issues of foreign policy to second place. Fear of imminent war, deadened by constant reiteration,

[57] *Stenograficheskii Otchet VI Kongressa Kominterna* (1929), i, 38.

[58] *Kommunisticheskii Internatsional v Dokumentakh* (1933), p. 796; Lozovsky a little later spoke of "the creation of a whole series of inter-state alliances in the struggle for world hegemony, like, for example, the Anglo-French and Anglo-Japanese alliances against America, Germany and the USSR" (*Vos'moi S"ezd Professional'nykh Soyuzov* (1929), p. 209).

[59] Lenin, *Polnoe Sobranie Sochinenii*, xlv, 403.

[60] For the relation of Comintern to Soviet foreign policy see pp. 118–124 below.

became less real. But nothing had occurred to shake belief in the essentially belligerent nature of imperialism. Stalin devoted the first section of his major report to the fifteenth party congress to the instability and insecurity of the international situation:

> The strengthening of interventionist tendencies in the imperialist camp and the threat of war (in regard to the USSR) is one of the fundamental factors of the present situation.

And Stalin concluded, using the phrase, so far as the records go, for the first time since the fourteenth party congress two years earlier, that "the period of 'peaceful co-existence' is receding into the past".[61] Even if one could not predict the time or occasion of its incidence, the danger of war was ever present. The attempts of Comintern and Profintern to mobilize the workers of capitalist countries against the policies of their national governments, and to incite nationalist movements of revolt in the colonial and semi-colonial countries against their imperialist overlords, were accompanied by increasingly shrill predictions of the imminence of war arising from a bellicose capitalism. From the summer of 1928 onward, the campaign against war, geared to the new line in Comintern with its uncompromising denunciation of social-democrats as "social-Fascists", became a stereotyped ingredient of Comintern propaganda, till it gradually lost all credibility and aroused only scepticism among the foreign communists to whom it was primarily addressed.[62]

Reiteration of the danger of imperialist war was, however, matched by insistence in Soviet diplomacy on the peaceful aims of Soviet policy. This too had sound warrant in Marxist doctrine, expounded in the manifesto of the First International on the Franco-Prussian war:

> In contrast to the old society with its economic penury and political madness a new society is born, the international principle of which will be *peace*, since in every nation the same principle rules, *labour*.[63]

The first public pronouncement of the new Soviet régime had been a decree on peace. When the worst perils of the civil war had

[61] Stalin, *Sochineniya*, x, 236–238.
[62] For these developments see pp. 205–206 below.
[63] Karl Marx, Friedrich Engels: *Werke*, xvii (1964), 7.

been surmounted, and peace concluded with Estonia on February 2, 1920, Lenin was moved to claim that "we represent the interest of a majority of the population of the world for peace against the rapacious militarist-imperialists"; and a few weeks later he told an American journalist that, when the power of "the exploiters and fomenters of war" had been overthrown, "wars will very soon become absolutely impossible".[64] Chicherin, speaking on foreign policy in June 1920 to the TsIK of the RSFSR, declared that "our armament is our policy of peace".[65] Peace as the unalterable goal of Soviet policy was the constant theme of official pronouncements. Lenin in his instructions to the Soviet delegates at the Genoa conference in 1922, warned them to take a pacific line, and avoid "such frightening words" as "the inevitability of new world wars".[66]

The theme was particularly apposite in moments of international tension, and enjoyed in 1927 a revival which was well calculated to appeal to the pacifist leanings of western liberals and radicals. The fourth Union Congress of Soviets in April 1927 announced that the Soviet Union was "the only state in the world to pursue a direct and open policy of peace answering to the interests of the whole of humanity".[67] Litvinov's appearance at Geneva in November 1927 with a proposal for total and universal disarmament seemed a powerful reinforcement of this claim.[68] Stalin at the fifteenth party congress in December 1927 mockingly declared that Litvinov's initiative had "reduced the League of Nations to paralysis", and once more proclaimed a "policy of peace and the maintenance of peaceful relations with capitalist countries"; and the resolution of the congress spoke of "the continued pursuit of an unswerving policy of peace, which is nothing but a policy of struggle against the danger of imperialist wars".[69] At the same time Chicherin praised "our system of non-aggression pacts establishing neutrality as a general rule", and contrasted it with alliances between capitalist states, "which conceal aggressive intentions under a show of defence"; and Shtein, a prominent Narkomindel official, referred to the policy

[64] Lenin, *Polnoe Sobranie Sochinenii*, xl, 96, 146.
[65] *Dokumenty Vneshnei Politiki SSSR*, ii (1958), 641.
[66] *Lenin, Polnoe Sobranie Sochinenii*, xlv, 63.
[67] *S"ezdy Sovetov v Dokumentakh*, iii (1960), 113–114.
[68] For this episode see pp. 107–108 below.
[69] *KPSS v Rezolyutsiyakh* (1954), ii, 436.

of bilateral non-aggression pacts as a "peaceful offensive".[70] The Soviet Government for some time maintained its preference for bilateral pacts, and deprecated multilateral pacts between groups of countries.[71] This was, however, a matter of tactics, not of principle. As the potentialities of Geneva as an international forum came to be realized in Moscow, the prejudice against multilateralism melted away; and it made something of a sensation when the Soviet Government not only decided to adhere to the Pact of Paris, but took steps to bring it into force independently in eastern Europe.[72]

In so far as the peaceful professions of the Soviet Government proceeded from a profound determination to avoid military clashes and entanglements for which the Red Army was not equipped, they were entirely sincere. The only occasion during this period when Soviet forces showed any inclination for military action was in Manchuria in the autumn of 1929; and here action was undertaken only against undisciplined Chinese levies in conditions where no opposition was likely to be encountered from any major Power.[73] Throughout this period Soviet foreign policy was essentially pacific and defensive; the Soviet Union was not the only country where assurances — and indeed the reality — of peaceful intentions were combined with vigorous assertions of the need for national defence. What was unique in the Soviet Union — though the difference may have been rather in degree than in substance — was the existence of an elaborate and much publicized institution conducting persistently subversive propaganda against potential enemies in the capitalist world. The fear and anger inspired by this propaganda in capitalist countries, genuine at first but, later, like Soviet fear of imperialist aggression, grossly inflated for political motives, proved a more disturbing factor than the propaganda itself in the course of Soviet relations with the external world. The passage of time progressively blurred these differences, and brought the purposes and practices of Soviet policy more nearly into line with those of the capitalist world.

[70] *Dokumenty Vneshnei Politiki SSSR*, x (1965), 543–544; *Izvestiya*, November 6–7, 1927.

[71] *Dokumenty Vneshnei Politiki SSSR*, xi. (1966), 249, 252–253, 256; for the Turkish treaty of December 17, 1925, which was the prototype of these pacts see *Socialism in One Country, 1924 1926*, Vol. 3, pp. 641–642.

[72] See pp. 113–115 below.

[73] This action will be described in a later section of this volume.

CHAPTER 58

RELATIONS WITH GREAT BRITAIN

THE consequences for Anglo-Soviet relations of the British general strike of May 1926 and the continuing miners' strike developed slowly. When the strike was already three days old, Hodgson, the British chargé d'affaires in Moscow, oblivious of the gathering storm, made one of his periodical pleas to the Foreign Office for "a settlement of one kind or another with Russia", and suggested an early resumption of negotiations.[1] The initial diplomatic exchanges on Soviet support for the strikers were conducted in a measured and formal style, which hardly reflected the popular excitement aroused by it. It was not till May 26, 1926, when the general strike had been over for a fortnight, that Hodgson protested to Narkomindel against the delay in loading two British ships in the port of Batum; he was told that the port workers had declared a strike of solidarity with the British workers, but that the ships had none the less been able to leave on May 29 and 30.[2] It was, however, clear by this time that the crux of the matter was the financial aid extended to the strikers by the Soviet trade unions. On June 5, 1926, Hodgson "expressed himself in very moderate terms to Chicherin", and did not appear to contest the right of Soviet trade unions to support the strikers.[3] But the tone soon became more heated. Pronouncements both from the central council of Soviet trade unions and from Comintern bitterly assailed the General Council of the TUC for calling off the strike, and loudly proclaimed their support for the heroic struggle of the miners;[4] and on the British side the Home Secretary, Joynson-Hicks, Churchill and Birkenhead led a vocal campaign for reprisals against the Soviet Government. On June 10, 1926, Joynson-Hicks incautiously stated in the House of Commons that "some money from the Russian Government"

[1] *Documents on British Foreign Policy*, Series I A, ii (1968) 724–729.

[2] *Dokumenty Vneshnei Politiki SSSR*, ix (1964), 297–298.

[3] *Ibid.* ix, 304; for Soviet financial aid to the strikers see pp. 318, 320–321 below.

[4] See pp. 323–324 below.

had been received by the strikers.[5] Two days later, the Soviet chargé d'affaires protested against the inaccuracy of this statement, and explained that the Soviet Government could not interfere with the right of Soviet trade unions to dispose of their funds.[6] On the same day the British chargé d'affaires in Moscow, describing the general strike as "an illegal and unconstitutional act", more prudently limited his protest to the permission given by the Soviet Government for the transfer of funds.[7] But this did nothing to lower the tone of mutual recriminations. *Pravda*, piqued by the allegation of Soviet interference in British affairs, mounted a campaign against British interference culminating in a leading article "Hands off the Soviet Trade Unions"; and workers demonstrated in Moscow against British diplomatic intervention in the domestic affairs of the Soviet Union.[8]

The Foreign Office, like Narkomindel, plainly desired at this time to avoid a confrontation. In a confidential memorandum it marshalled cogent arguments against proposals to denounce the trade agreement and expel the Soviet representatives;[9] even the King, in a letter to Joynson-Hicks of June 14, 1926, confessed himself "a little anxious with regard to our remonstrances to the Soviet Government about the money coming from Russia in aid of the families of miners who are on strike".[10] Joynson-Hicks was, however, imperturbable, and seized the moment to issue on June 22, 1926, a White Paper containing documents confiscated in the raid of CPGB headquarters in October 1925.[11] When Chamberlain spoke in the House of Commons on June 25, 1926, expressing copious indignation at Soviet interference, but declining to break off relations,[12] he was already fighting a rear-guard action against the party die-hards. The Soviet Government countered with a

[5] *House of Commons: 5th Series*, cxcvi, 1680.

[6] *Dokumenty Vneshnei Politiki SSSR*, ix (1964), 306; the Soviet chargé d'affaires chose this inauspicious moment to complain that the Soviet representation in London was officially referred to as a "legation" or "mission", and not as an "embassy", and was told that the time was "ill-chosen" for any discussion of this subject (*ibid.* ix, 303–304; *Documents on British Foreign Policy*, Series I A, ii (1968), 94–95).

[7] *Ibid.* ii, 85–86; *Dokumenty Vneshnei Politiki SSSR*, ix (1964), 310.

[8] *Pravda*, June 15, 18, 20, 1926.

[9] *Documents on British Foreign Policy*, Series I A, ii (1968), 622–627.

[10] H. Nicolson, *King George the Fifth* (1952), p. 421.

[11] See *Socialism in One Country, 1924–1926*, Vol. 3, p. 345.

[12] *House of Commons: 5th Series*, cxcvii, 770–778.

long statement reiterating its point of view, stressing its peaceful intentions and denouncing, in particular, the attacks of Churchill, the Chancellor of the Exchequer, the "chief instigator of the British intervention of 1918–1919", as "in the sharpest contradiction with elementary correctness in relations between states";[13] and Dzerzhinsky, the president of Vesenkha, gave an interview attacking speeches by Churchill and Birkenhead as "patently designed" to disrupt trade relations between the two countries.[14]

For the moment Anglo-Soviet relations survived the shock, and the excitement died down. Soviet diplomacy returned to its pertinacious insistence on the mutual advantages of trade between Great Britain and the USSR.[15] Krasin, arriving belatedly to take up his post in London, a very sick man, on September 28, 1926, devoted the few remaining weeks of his life to this theme. In a long interview to the press he dwelt on the peace-loving policies of the Soviet régime, but above all on its economic and financial stability which offered mutually profitable opportunities for trade.[16] A long and fruitless conversation with Chamberlain on October 11, 1926, led him to "the conclusion that the key to the situation at present lies apparently not in the Foreign Office, but in the City".[17] On October 15, 1926, he visited Montagu Norman, governor of the Bank of England, who exercised his well-known charm on Krasin, agreed with him that a full restoration of the European and the world economy was impossible without Soviet participation, but held out no prospects of a loan; and a visit on the following day to

[13] *Dokumenty Vneshnei Politiki SSSR*, ix (1964), 326–329; it was published in *Izvestiya*, June 27, 1926, with a cartoon depicting Joynson-Hicks, Churchill and Birkenhead, all leading members of the government, as "the Holy Die-Hard Trinity".

[14] *Dokumenty Vneshnei Politiki SSSR*, ix (1964), 332–334.

[15] A long and detailed memorandum by the Soviet trade delegation in London was published as a supplement to *The Soviet Union Monthly* on July 15, 1926; 7000 copies were distributed to MPs and other public figures (*Dokumenty Vneshnei Politiki SSSR*, ix (1964), 352–363, note 75). The opinion that the industrialists, who were interested in trade with the Soviet Union, were less hostile than the bankers, who represented the creditors, was recorded by Maisky, then a member of the Soviet *polpredstvo* in London (I. Taigin [I. Maisky], *Angliya SSSR* (1926), pp. 89–90). Hodgson endorsed the view that "the anti-Red campaign does positive and immediate harm which it is possible to calculate in terms of pounds sterling" (*Documents on British Foreign Policy*, I A, ii (1968), 457–459).

[16] *Dokumenty Vneshnei Politiki SSSR*, ix (1964), 461–470; for Krasin's initial impressions see *ibid.* ix, 492–494.

[17] *Ibid.* ix, 499–506.

MacKenna, a former Chancellor of the Exchequer and now director of the Midland Bank, yielded no more result.[18]

When Krasin died on November 24, 1926, all hopes of improved relations had faded. Realization of the blow dealt to British prestige and British trade by the general strike, the exasperation of the long drawn-out miners' strike, loudly acclaimed by the Soviet trade unions and the Soviet press, the attribution of British embarrassments in China to Soviet inspiration—all these played into the hands of die-hards who assiduously inflamed a hostile public opinion against the Soviet Union, and demanded a total break. A resolution in this sense had been adopted by the Conservative Party conference at Scarborough early in October 1926. A mass "Clear out the Reds" demonstration at the Albert Hall on October 15, 1926, at which Locker-Lampson, the Under-Secretary of State for Foreign Affairs, was the principal speaker, was the occasion of much violent speaking and hysterical enthusiasm.[19] Churchill, Joynson-Hicks and Birkenhead kept up the campaign; and Chicherin in a press interview in Berlin expressed alarm at Augur's militant article.[20] The issue, like the Zinoviev letter, served as a weapon in party political warfare. But trade union leaders were repelled by persistent Soviet denunciations, and embarrassed by a potentially compromising association with the Soviet Union; and Labour resistance to the Conservative onslaught was weak and hesitant. On December 1, 1926, Chamberlain told the House of Commons that "we should be justified on the facts as now known to us in breaking off, if we thought it expedient to do so"; and a week later Locker-Lampson, speaking for the Foreign Office, set up a further road-block in the way of negotiations by postulating, among other preliminary conditions for a *détente*, that the Soviet Government should "recognize in principle Russia's financial obligations".[21] Two days later, a Foreign Office departmental memorandum admitted that agitation for a breaking-off of relations "is becoming well-nigh irresistible", and cautiously balanced the pros and cons.[22] Rozengolts, the Soviet chargé d'affaires, visiting the

[18] *Ibid.* ix, 512–522.

[19] For some reports and comments from the contemporary press see W. and Z. Coates, *A History of Anglo-Soviet Relations* (1943), pp. 245–246.

[20] For the article and the Chicherin interview see p. 7 above.

[21] *House of Commons: 5th Series*, cc, 1165, 2082.

[22] *Documents on British Foreign Policy*, Series I A, ii (1968), 622–627.

Foreign Office on December 10, 1926, correctly diagnosed "a coldness and a certain worsening of relations", which he attributed to "Chinese events, the help given to the miners and, in particular, Cook's recent journey to Moscow".[23] The opponents of the break were plainly losing ground.

The conclusion was now predictable. The steps by which it would be reached were still undetermined. Litvinov, optimistic that a break could be avoided, pinned his hopes on moderate elements in the Conservative Party and in the Foreign Office, which still resisted the die-hards. In a press interview of February 4, 1927, he expressed the belief that "reasonable elements in British public opinion and the British Government will gain the upper hand over advocates of the policy of the iron fist, which never brought anything but misfortune to the peoples and, in general, to the cause of peace";[24] and a fortnight later, in a speech in TsIK, he denounced the anti-Soviet campaign, which "does not date from yesterday", and in which leading British ministers participated, and reiterated the Soviet desire for normal relations and for the discussion of conflicts and misunderstandings.[25] But this did not help. Chamberlain, in a conversation with Rozengolts on February 14, 1927, dismissed as useless, and devoid of any prospect of success, negotiations between the two governments on points of difference.[26] On February 23, 1927, a weighty note, evidently representing a substantial concession to the die-hards in the Cabinet, was addressed to the Soviet chargé d'affaires. Describing the state of Anglo-Soviet relations as "unsatisfactory", it rehearsed the assurances given by the Soviet Government in the past to abstain from hostile propaganda, and set beside them numerous recent utterances of Soviet leaders and in the Soviet press referring in opprobrious terms to the British Government and to Chamberlain himself. It ended with the solemn warning that the patience of the British Government was not inexhaustible, and that further provocation would render inevitable the de-

[23] *Dokumenty Vneshnei Politiki SSSR*, ix (1964), 576–577; for Cook's appearance at the seventh Soviet trade union congress in December 1926 see pp. 340–341 below.

[24] *Dokumenty Vneshnei Politiki SSSR*, x (1965), 42–43.

[25] For this speech see pp. 7–8 above.

[26] *Dokumenty Vneshnei Politiki SSSR*, x (1965), 638, note 57.

nunciation of the trade agreement and the rupture of normal diplomatic relations.[27] A defiant Soviet reply, handed by Litvinov to the British chargé d'affaires in Moscow on February 27, 1927, countered with quotations from speeches of Birkenhead, Churchill and other ministers, and concluded that, "if the present British Government supposes that a cessation of Anglo-Soviet trade and of other relations is called for by the interests of the British people, and will benefit the British Empire and the cause of world peace", it must take full responsibility for the consequences. Threats of a rupture would intimidate nobody in the Soviet Union. The Soviet Government, for its part, would "pursue its peaceful policy".[28] Litvinov's nonchalant attitude was shared by Stalin, who remarked, in an article dated March 1, 1927, that there would be "no war this year, not because our enemies are not prepared for war, but because our enemies fear the consequences of war more than anyone else, because the workers of the west do not want to fight the USSR".[29] Chicherin, staying abroad for the sake of his health, and rapidly losing effective control of Narkomindel to Litvinov, was by no means reassured. The British note, he wrote bitterly and ironically in a letter to Stalin and Rykov on March 11, 1927, "serves notice not only on us, but on the die-hard Conservatives, from whom it will remove the eagerness (!?) to renew the campaign in the immediate future". And he concluded:

> I protest against this naive and harmful self-complacency. Moscow should not shut its eyes to the fact that the English campaign against us is continuing, developing and going further.[30]

These diplomatic exchanges were rounded off by a discursive debate in the House of Commons on March 3, 1927. Some Liberal and Labour members advocated caution, and Lloyd George criticized the inflammatory speeches of Churchill and Birkenhead and articles in the die-hard press. But little was said to mitigate the evident eagerness of most Conservatives for a break.[31] The most significant statement in the debate was made by

[27] The note was published as a White Paper (Cmd. 2822 (1927)).

[28] *Dokumenty Vneshnei Politiki SSSR,* x (1965), 54–60; the British note and the Soviet reply appeared in *Izvestiya,* February 25, 27, 1927.

[29] Stalin, *Sochineniya,* ix, 170.

[30] Quoted by Gromyko in an article in *Izvestiya,* December 5, 1962, evidently designed as a rehabilitation of Chicherin; for Chicherin's earlier criticism of Bukharin see p. 124 below.

[31] *House of Commons: 5th Series,* cciii, 599–672.

Chamberlain, who justified delay in taking action on the plea that "a break between us and Soviet Russia should have consequences for other countries as well", and reserved "the right to judge both as to the expediency of any step that can be contemplated and the moment that step should be taken".[32] A few days later the council of the League of Nations met in Geneva; and nervous Soviet observers conjured up nightmares of a bargain between the western Powers with German participation to isolate the Soviet Union and impose a financial and economic blockade.[33] In fact Chamberlain found himself on the defensive. The German Government was profoundly disturbed by the growing deterioration of Anglo-Soviet relations, and apprehensive of the dangers of an open break.[34] Chamberlain issued a *communiqué* denying any aggressive intention against the Soviet Union, and depicted himself to Stresemann as heroically resisting pressure for a break, which was now, however, inevitable unless the Soviet Government changed its course.[35] Briand told Stresemann that he "adopted a cooler attitude" than Chamberlain on the Russian question, and "saw no reason to take any strong line".[36] Germany was in no mood to abandon the balance of her policy between east and west; and France had no desire to see an accretion of German power through the discomfiture of the Soviet Union.

This failure to win support could no longer arrest the train of events already set in motion in London. The advance of the national-revolutionary armies in China in the autumn of 1926 was an exacerbating factor in Anglo-Soviet relations; a Foreign Office official complained to the Soviet chargé d'affaires on January 14, 1927, of "an aggression against our interests ... with the assistance of Borodin and a number of Bolsheviks".[37] On April 6, 1927, Chinese police and soldiers took possession of a part of the

[32] *Ibid.* cciii, 631, 634.

[33] An article in *Kommunisticheskii Internatsional,* No. 12, (86), 1927, pp. 3–10, canvassed the hypothesis of an offer to Stresemann of the evacuation of the Rhineland and the return of Danzig as the price of German participation in an anti-Soviet bloc.

[34] For evidence from the German archives see *Akten zur Deutschen Auswärtigen Politik,* Series B, iv (1970), 274–275, 361–364, 380–384.

[35] *The Times,* March 9, 1927; *Gustav Stresemann Vermächtnis,* iii (1933), 113.

[36] *Ibid.* iii, 118.

[37] *Documents on British Foreign Policy,* Series I A, ii (1968), 737.

premises of the Soviet legation in Peking, arrested officials and seized a large mass of papers.[38] So daring an attack on the diplomatic quarter could hardly have been made without the tacit consent of the diplomatic corps, of which the British minister was the most influential member; and a hidden British hand was suspected behind the *coup*. These suspicions were reinforced when on May 12, 1927, a similar police raid was carried out by order of the Home Secretary, Joynson-Hicks, on the premises of Arcos, the Soviet trading agency in London, which worked under the close control of the Soviet trade delegation.[39] The premises were ransacked, officials and employees were ordered to hand over their keys and keep out, and a large quantity of documents was removed.[40] The haul proved sufficient for the end in view. On May 24, 1927, Baldwin informed the House of Commons that the raid had established the complicity of members of the Soviet trade delegation with "a group of secret agents" involved in acquiring confidential documents relating to the British armed forces, and accused the trade delegation and Arcos of engaging in "anti-British espionage and propaganda". On these grounds he announced the decision to cancel the trade agreement and break off

[38] This event will be discussed in a later section of this volume.

[39] Arcos (All-Russian Cooperative Society Limited) was formally a commercial firm with premises in Moorgate; the trade delegation was part of the Soviet diplomatic mission, and its premises in a London suburb enjoyed diplomatic immunity under the Anglo-Soviet trade agreement of March 1921. But the appointment as head of the trade delegation in February 1926 of Khinchuk, president of Tsentrosoyuz, emphasized the closeness of the link between them; and Khinchuk and some other officials of the delegation apparently had offices in the Arcos premises. At the time of the raid, Khinchuk was in Geneva as a member of the Soviet delegation to the world economic conference (see p. 105 below). In the recriminations following the *coup*, the British Government claimed that the Arcos premises were purely commercial, and that this was not affected by the presence there of some officials of the delegation; the Soviet Government pretended that the diplomatic immunity enjoyed by the delegation extended, wholly or in part, to the premises of Arcos. Evidence from the British archives indicates that Chamberlain was informed of the raid in advance by Joynson-Hicks, but failed to realize its diplomatic implications, and that the Foreign Office was not informed at all.

[40] The details were luridly described in a note of protest on the same day from the Soviet chargé d'affaires to the Foreign Office (*Dokumenty Vneshnei Politiki SSSR*, x (1965), 198–200); a more reasoned protest, invoking the principle of commercial secrecy as well as of diplomatic immunity, was handed by Litvinov to the British chargé d'affaires in Moscow on May 17, 1927 (*ibid.* x, 213–218).

diplomatic relations with the Soviet Union.[41] In the course of the debate the opposition half-heartedly proposed to postpone action till the matter had been fully examined by a select committee. Chamberlain had no difficulty in rejecting this demand in a speech in which he specifically reasserted the authenticity of the Zinoviev letter, and appeared to base the rupture of relations on the whole unsatisfactory past record of the régime rather than on any revelations resulting from the Arcos raid. The decision was approved by a large majority.[42] A few voices were raised in mild and ineffectual protest. The TUC wrote a letter to Baldwin on May 13, 1927, expressing "great surprise and concern" at the Arcos raid, and later issued a statement protesting against "the grave step taken by the British Government in breaking off diplomatic relations with the USSR", and drawing attention to its likely political, and especially its economic, consequences.[43]

The first reply of the Soviet Government took the form of a statement by Litvinov to the Soviet press appearing in *Izvestiya* on May 26, 1927, which declared that the Conservative government, ever since coming into power on the strength of the forged Zinoviev letter, had been determined to sever relations with the Soviet Union; it brushed aside Baldwin's charges of espionage, and the "facts" and "documents" produced to support them.[44] A statement of a similar tenour by Rozengolts was published on the same day *in extenso* in the *Manchester Guardian* and in abbreviated form in *The Times*, and was reprinted on the following day in *Izvestiya*. On May 26, 1927, an official note from the Foreign Office confirmed the rupture of relations, and requested that immediate steps should be taken to withdraw the personnel of the diplomatic mission and the trade delegation, and to facilitate the departure of British diplomatic and consular staff from the Soviet Union.[45] A formal reply from Litvinov on the following day re-

[41] *House of Commons: 5th Series*, ccvi, 1842–1849. The documents found in "Soviet House" were published as a White Paper (Cmd. 2874 (1927)); they revealed communist contacts with British trade unionists and British seamen, but no trace of military espionage or stolen documents.

[42] *House of Commons: 5th Series*, ccvi, 2195, 2204–2218, 2242.

[43] *The Fifty-ninth Annual Trades Union Congress*, 1927 (n.d.), pp. 213–215.

[44] *Dokumenty Vneshnei Politiki SSSR*, x (1965), 240–243.

[45] The note was published in Cmd. 2895 (1927), pp. 69–70. On the following day Rozengolts was entertained at lunch at the House of Commons by the all-party Anglo-Russian Parliamentary Committee; for the speech delivered by him on this occasion see *Izvestiya*, July 2, 1927.

peated previous protests and denials, and ended by expressing the hope that the time would come when "the British people would find possible the unimpeded realization of its strivings for peace and for the establishment of normal friendly relations with the peoples of the Soviet Union".[46] The eighth IKKI, then in session in Moscow, issued a protest in terms unusually violent even in such proclamations.[47] A proclamation of the party central committee referred to the breach as the culmination of "the dirty and criminal game of English Conservative diplomacy".[48] Finally, on June 7, 1927, the Soviet Government circulated to all governments with which it had diplomatic relations a memorandum recounting the chequered course of Anglo-Soviet relations since the agreement of March 1921, and placing on "the present British Government" sole responsibility for the consequences of the breach.[49]

The British Government, or at any rate Chamberlain, had counted on French and German sympathy and support. Gregory, a high Foreign Office official, perhaps incautiously told the German chargé d'affaires that the aim of the breach was "to rid ourselves of one of the obstacles to peace, this Asian menace to Locarno".[50] In the event, the British move conspicuously failed to provoke enthusiasm or to find imitators. Briand assured Chicherin in Paris on May 24, 1927, that "France is in no way bound, has her own Russian policy and does not side with Great Britain in this conflict".[51] When the foreign ministers met again at Geneva a month after the break Briand told Stresemann that he regarded it as "a great blunder of English policy". Chamberlain explained apologetically that the British Government did not seek to "involve any other country in these things". Briand remarked to Stresemann that France was too busy to engage in "theoretical arguments whether to break with Russia or not", and took the situation "very quietly"; and Stresemann thought that a crusade against the Soviet Union would "strengthen Russia and only

[46] *Dokumenty Vneshnei Politiki SSSR*, x (1965), 245–247.
[47] *Internationale Presse-Korrespondenz*, No. 57, June 3, 1927, pp. 1219–1221.
[48] *Pravda*, June 1, 1927.
[49] *Dokumenty Vneshnei Politiki SSSR*, x (1965), 280–288.
[50] *Auswärtiges Art*, 6698/105676–8.
[51] *Dókumenty Vneshnei Politiki SSSR*, x (1965), 231.

weaken Europe".[52] On the Soviet side Great Britain was cast for the role of principal villain. The resolution of the eighth IKKI in May 1927 described her as "the factor which most threatens the peace of the world at the moment", and as standing "at the head of world reaction".[53]

Charges of espionage by Soviet agents provoked no less plausible counter-charges. Rykov in a report to the Moscow Soviet produced documents, including an indiscreet letter from the British consul in Leningrad in 1924, showing that British representatives were not innocent of organizing espionage.[54] The Soviet press published for the first time the compromising depositions of the British spy Reilly, caught and executed in 1925;[55] and reports continued to appear in the summer and autumn of 1927 of persons condemned, and sometimes executed, as British agents.[56] In July 1927 much publicity was given to the trial of a spy named Druzhelovsky, who was convicted of working for the Polish general staff in conjunction with other "white" *émigrés* in Berlin, and sentenced to be shot. Specific allegations against him included the forging of a letter of instruction to the Belgian Communist Party and the sale of documents to the *Chicago Tribune* and the *New York Times*.[57] The Zinoviev letter does not seem to have figured in the proceedings. But Krylenko, who conducted the prosecution, subsequently stated in a press interview that Druzhelovsky had revealed the circumstances in which the letter had been forged by Russian *émigrés* known to him.[58]

The main practical consequence of the breach was a disruption of Anglo-Soviet trade. On the eve of the break an arrangement had been reached with the Midland Bank to advance credits on Soviet purchases in Great Britain up to a total of £10,000,000;

[52] *Gustav Stresemann Vermächtnis*, iii (1933), 145, 150–152.

[53] *Kommunisticheskii Internatsional v Dokumentakh* (1933), pp. 701, 703.

[54] *Izvestiya*, June 2, 1927.

[55] *Ibid.* June 17, 1927.

[56] For a list of such cases see *Survey of International Affairs, 1927* (1929), p. 276; Hodgson, in an interview in the *Morning Post*, June 13, 1927, described the charges against some of these persons as unfounded and "fantastic".

[57] *Izvestiya*, July 3, 9, 12, 13, 1927; according to a statement made two years earlier by Chicherin, Druzhelovsky was arrested in Berlin in May 1925 and found in possession of a mass of forged documents and printing equipment (*Dokumenty Vneshnei Politiki SSSR*, viii (1963), 440).

[58] *Izvestiya*, July 29, 1927.

these were not taken up.[59] Mikoyan, the People's Commissar for Trade, announced that the affairs of the trade delegation would be wound up, and no new operations undertaken;[60] and a decree was issued confining trade to countries with which the Soviet Government enjoyed "normal diplomatic relations" and "unimpeded and normal conduct of commercial operations".[61] Khinchuk issued a warning that Soviet orders would be transferred, as far as possible, to other countries;[62] and Chicherin told Stresemann in Geneva that "we have answered, and shall answer, England's hostile actions by a contraction of trade".[63] The anxieties of British industrialists were revealed in an attempt by some of them, reported by the secretary of the American–Russian Chamber of Commerce, to dissuade their American counterparts from taking advantage of the breach to extend their own trade with the Soviet Union.[64] In September 1927, a Swiss banker told a representative of Narkomfin that never in the past three years had the British authorities brought such strong pressure on the Swiss banks to avoid transactions with the Soviet Union.[65]

Similar apprehensions were manifested in a speech in the House of Commons on July 28, 1927, by Chamberlain, who, after defending the break with the Soviet Union in the usual terms, continued:

> But trade may go on. We will do nothing to interfere with it, and we have no desire to push, and no intention of pushing, our differences any farther.[66]

[59] *Dokumenty Vneshnei Politiki SSSR*, x (1965), 191–193; on the eve of the break Mikoyan informed the German chargé d'affaires in Moscow with great satisfaction of this credit, which was to run for a maximum of 42 months (*Akten zur Deutschen Auswärtigen Politik*, Series B, v (1972), 382). A year later it was said that it had not been taken up because more favourable terms had been obtained direct from British exporters (*Dokumenty Vneshnei Politiki SSSR*, xi (1966), 283).

[60] *Pravda*, May 25, 1927.

[61] *Dokumenty Vneshnei Politiki SSSR*, x (1965), 220–221.

[62] *Ibid.* x (1965), 259–260; a statement by Amtorg in New York to the effect that the break with Great Britain would "facilitate the effort being made by Soviet industrialists to trade directly with American firms, . . . and enter into closer relations with the American technical world" appeared in the *Soviet Review* (Washington), July–August 1927, p. 121.

[63] *Dokumenty Vneshnei Politiki SSSR*, x (1965), 308.

[64] *Ibid.* x, 334.

[65] *Ibid.* x, 375.

[66] *House of Commons: 5th Series*, ccix, 1530.

These words seem to have led to a rumour that the British Government was seeking a way to resume relations; on August 5, 1927, Chicherin described it as "a profound error" to suppose that Anglo-Soviet trade could continue on the same scale in the absence of diplomatic relations, but emphatically denied that any proposals, official or semi-official, for a resumption of relations had reached the Soviet Government from any quarter.[67] Uneasy bickering continued. Baldwin in his Guildhall speech on November 9, 1927, declared that, if the Soviet Government were prepared to "abstain from interference in our domestic affairs and from a policy of intrigue and hostility elsewhere", the British Government would "meet them in that spirit of liberality and good will which inspires our whole foreign policy". But, when Rykov a few days later at the tenth Ukrainian Congress of Soviets declared the Soviet Union ready to open negotiations on a basis of mutual non-interference,[68] Baldwin executed a retreat, and told a questioner in the House of Commons that no response had been forthcoming to his overture.[69] The first direct contact between the two parties after the break was a meeting between Chamberlain and Litvinov at Geneva, on the latter's initiative, on December 5, 1927. But Chamberlain was politely unbending, and dwelt principally on the rôle of Comintern and Soviet activities in China; the *communiqué* published next day merely recorded that no basis for an agreement had been found.[70]

The most sensational episode of 1928 was a revival of the "Zinoviev letter" scandal of 1924. Gregory, the senior Foreign Office official who had handled the affair,[71] was convicted in March 1928 of having improperly speculated in francs, and dismissed from the service. *Izvestiya* reopened the question of the Zinoviev

[67] *Dokumenty Vneshnei Politiki SSSR*, x (1965), 349–350.

[68] *Pravda*, November 25, 1927.

[69] *House of Commons: 5th Series*, ccxi, 264; a Soviet *communiqué* (*Izvestiya*, December 2, 1927) rebutted Baldwin's denial.

[70] *Dokumenty Vneshnei Politiki SSSR*, x (1965), 532–536, 657, note 113; Litvinov later observed that Chamberlain, "instead of discussing future proposals, preferred to talk of the past", and that this had made the conversation fruitless, but consoled himself with the thought that "the Soviet Government will outlive more than one British government" (4 *Sessiya Tsentral'nogo Ispolnitel'nogo Komiteta Soyuza SSR 4 Sozyva* (1928), No. 19, pp. 13–14).

[71] See *Socialism in One Country, 1924–1926*, Vol. 3, pp. 30–32.

letter in a leading article of March 7, 1928, headed "A Historic Forgery". The British parliamentary opposition, sensing an additional aura of disrepute surrounding the affair, again pressed for an independent enquiry into the authenticity of the letter. On March 19, 1928, Baldwin, in a blandly disingenuous speech, offered some fresh mysterious details about the origin of the letter, and once more refused an enquiry.[72] A scathing reply by Chicherin appeared three days later in the Soviet press. Chicherin declared that "there is not a word of truth in Mr Baldwin's explanations", and referred to "the lying character of his statements", which were inconsistent with those made in the original correspondence of 1924. The British Government had refused an enquiry into the authenticity of the document, since it knew that such an enquiry would reveal it as a forgery. Druzhelovsky, brought to trial in Moscow in July 1927, had confessed that the document had been fabricated in Berlin by three Russian *émigrés* on instructions from a Polish agent who was in touch with the British secret service. Similar evidence had been given at the trial in Leipzig of one Schrek, a German accomplice of the Polish agent, in January 1928,[73] Chicherin's statement evoked no official comment, and received only passing notice in the press. But the tergiversations of Baldwin, even more than Chicherin's counterblast, fed the already widespread scepticism about the origin of the Zinoviev letter. Its authenticity was now less firmly asserted by official spokesmen, and more confidently denied in Labour and Liberal circles.

A minor symptom, if not a contributory cause, of a milder climate in Anglo-Soviet relations, which set in during the latter part of 1928, was the definitive succession of Litvinov to the control of Narkomindel. Chicherin left Moscow for western Europe on grounds of health in August 1928, at a moment when preparations were being made for a step of which he certainly disapproved — the accession of the Soviet Union to the Kellogg pact;[74] and, though he retained for two years longer the titular rôle of People's Commissar for Foreign Affairs, it was Litvinov, as deputy commissar, who now effectively functioned in that capacity.

[72] *House of Commons: 5th Series*, ccxv, 59–72.

[73] *Dokumenty Vneshnei Politiki SSSR*, xi (1966), 189–193. For the Schrek case see *Izvestiya*, January 31, 1928; later evidence has broadly substantiated this version of the origin of the Zinoviev letter.

[74] See pp. 111–112 below.

Chicherin, though he had friendly feelings for Germany and France, was antipathetic to Great Britain, which he never revisited after his ignominious expulsion in 1917; and he was always ready to support Asian countries in revolt against British imperialism. Litvinov had lived for many years in Great Britain, had an English wife, spoke English better than any other foreign language and within the limits of Soviet policy sought good relations with Great Britain; he had little belief or interest in the potentialities of Asia. It may also be significant that Stalin detested Chicherin, and was favourably disposed to Litvinov.[75] These personal factors may have played some part in the gradual change of direction in Soviet foreign policy.

The main consideration, however, which brought about the thaw in Anglo-Soviet relations was the decline in Anglo-Soviet trade, and especially in Soviet imports from Great Britain.[76] This decline, occurring at a time when British goods were losing their predominant place in world markets, and unemployment loomed on the horizon as a major domestic problem, slowly made its impact felt. The Labour Party conference at Birmingham in October 1928 adopted a programme for the coming election which called for immediate steps to restore diplomatic and commercial relations with the Soviet Union in the interests of British trade.[77]

[75] Current gossip about the relative positions of Chicherin and Litvinov was retailed in *Sotsialisticheskii Vestnik* (Berlin), No. 4 (146), February 26, 1927, p. 14; for Litvinov's alleged indifference to China see *Socialism in One Country, 1924–1926*, Vol. 3. p. 801, note 1. Dirksen, Brockdorff-Rantzau's successor as German Ambassador in Moscow, noted that, though Litvinov was correct in his attitude to Germany, "his sympathies belong to Great Britain, where he spent his years of exile and met his wife" (H. von Dirksen, *Moskau, Tokio, London* (n.d. [1949], p. 94).

[76] The following were the official Soviet figures (in thousands of rubles at current prices):

	Exports to Great Britain	Percentage of Total Exports	Imports from Great Britain	Percentage of Total Imports
1925/26	220,869	31·4	129,549	17·1
1926/27	220,549	27·3	101,087	14·2
1927/28	155,833	19·7	47,521	5.0

(*Sotsialisticheskoe Stroitel'stvo SSSR* (1935), pp. 587–588, 591–592; for British figures see *Statistical Abstract for Each of the Fifteen Years 1924–1938*, Cmd. 6232 (1940), Tables 277, 279, 281, 282.)

[77] *Labour and the Nation* (1928), p. 47.

Later in the same month Joynson-Hicks himself invited the director of Arcos to visit him at the Home Office, and assured him that British visas would be available for Soviet engineers, commercial representatives or others travelling to Great Britain on business; this unexpected initiative was attributed to a belated desire to repair the damage done to British trade by the Arcos raid and its sequel.[78] The creation in London on October 23, 1928, of an international committee for the defence of Russian bondholders[79] was doubtless an attempt to stem or divert the newly flowing tide. But the current interests of industry and trade took precedence over the misfortunes of the creditors. A plan was now on foot to organize a large and representative delegation of British businessmen to visit the Soviet Union on a mission to secure orders for British industry. Remnant, the editor of the *English Review*, who had been charged with the organization of the expedition, discussed it with the Soviet Ambassador in Paris in September 1928, and was assured that visas would be granted.[80] But the preparations took a long time. Litvinov, in his speech at TsIK on December 10, 1928, pointed out that the British action in breaking off relations had achieved none of the purposes intended, and had merely diverted Soviet trade to other countries; and he welcomed the coming visit of British industrialists.[81] At length, on December 17, 1928, the British Government was induced to announce its approval of the project. This ensured the success of the delegation, but swelled its size,[82] so that the date of its departure was further postponed. Early in February 1929 a small committee of influential industrialists and bankers was formed to organize the proceedings.[83] An anti-Soviet outburst by Churchill a few days later was attributed to a desire to sabotage the preparations,[84] but had no effect. Final plans were approved at a large meeting on March 6, 1929; and on March 25 a party of eighty-eight, representing 230 firms, left London, travelling by special train from

[78] *Dokumenty Vneshnei Politiki SSSR*, xi (1966), 545–550.

[79] *The Times*, October 24, 1928; *Izvestiya*, October 27, 1928.

[80] *Dokumenty Vneshnei Politiki SSSR*, xi (1966), 512–514.

[81] *4 Sessiya Tsentral'nogo Ispolnitel'nogo Komiteta Soyuza SSR 4 Sozyva* (1928), No. 19, pp. 12–13.

[82] Litvinov in December 1928 had envisaged a delegation of not more than twelve (*Dokumenty Vneshnei Politiki SSSR*, xi (1966), 632).

[83] *The Times*, February 6, 1929.

[84] *Izvestiya*, February 17, 1929.

Ostend to the Soviet frontier.[85] The conclusion in February 1929 of an agreement between ROP (a British subsidiary of Neftsindikat, the Soviet oil trust) and Anglo-American Oil for the supply of a million tons of Soviet oil products a year for three years to the British market[86] was connected with the industrialists and their delegation. But this breakthrough on a hitherto closely guarded front was a significant index of the changing climate.

Pyatakov, now president of Gosbank, was appointed president of a reception committee for the delegates, and welcomed them on April 5, 1929, in a long speech. He stressed the falling-off in British trade as a result of the breach of 1927 and the corresponding increase in Soviet orders to Germany and the United States, leading up to the foreseeable conclusion:

> *Broad economic participation by England in the developing economy of the USSR is possible only through a resumption of normal diplomatic relations between our countries.*[87]

The delegates were plied with the usual mixture of hospitality and business discussions, and the visit was voted a success. Before their departure some of the leading delegates gave an interview to the press expressing their satisfaction with all that they had done and seen. Pyatakov was said to have given assurances of the willingness of the Soviet Government to discuss claims of British subjects, and "no insuperable obstacles to the attainment of full agreement between our countries" were felt to exist.[88] A report prepared for the fifth Union Congress of Soviets meeting in May 1929 struck a triumphant note. The British action of 1927 had been a failure. No other country had severed relations with the Soviet Union; attempts to organize an oil boycott and a credit boycott had broken down, Soviet exports to Great Britain had not suffered, but the British export market in the Soviet Union had been captured by Germans and Americans.[89]

The Soviet authorities were probably disappointed at the failure of the delegation to make a specific plea for a resumption of diplomatic relations. But this omission was repaired in an inter-

85 *Ibid.* March 8, 27, 1929; *Dokumenty Vneshnei Politiki SSSR*, xii (1967), 114–115, 117–120.

86 *Izvestiya*, March 1, 1929.

87 *Ibid.* April 6, 1929.

88 *Ibid.* April 25, 1929.

89 *Ot S"ezda k S"ezdu (Aprel' 1927–Mai 1929)* (1929), pp. 186–187.

view given after its return to London by Remnant, in which he described a resumption of diplomatic relations as "the unconditional pre-requisite of any significant development of economic relations".[90] This desirable consummation was now plainly in sight. In the campaign for the British general election at the end of May 1929, both Labour and Liberal parties committed themselves to a renewal of relations with the Soviet Government. The Labour party emerged as the largest single party. When Baldwin resigned, a leading article in *Izvestiya* celebrated with undisguised relief "The End of the Baldwin Government", and hailed the event as the defeat of the die-hards in foreign policy.[91] The length of time required to complete the resumption of relations showed, however, an absence of alacrity on the British side. It was not till nearly two months later that contacts were established, and not till the end of the year that normal diplomatic relations were resumed.

[90] *Izvestiya*, May 24, 1929.
[91] *Ibid.* June 5, 1929.

CHAPTER 59

RELATIONS WITH GERMANY

SOVIET–GERMAN relations for some months to come reflected mutual satisfaction with the Soviet–German treaty of April 24, 1926.[1] When it came up for ratification in the Reichstag on June 10, 1926, it was welcomed with varying degrees of warmth by spokesmen of all parties, the only opposition being registered by three dissident communists.[2] A report addressed by the German Ambassador in Moscow to Hindenburg on July 3, 1926, in vindication of the treaty, contained a uniquely penetrating analysis of the Soviet–German partnership by its principal German architect:

> I have continually striven since taking up my post here to create, through a close relationship with Soviet Russia, a counter-weight against the west, in order not to be at the mercy — the very expression is repugnant to me — of the favour or disfavour of the Entente Powers. A *pure* joy to work with these gentlemen it will of course never be. Our relation with the Soviet Union remains, as I once wrote years ago, a marriage of necessity; a marriage of inclination is not in question....
>
> Our relation to Soviet Russia, as I have conceived it since occupying my post, will always rest to a certain extent on bluff, i.e. it will be useful to create vis-à-vis our so-called *former* enemies the impression of a greater intimacy with Russia than in fact exists.
>
> Having regard to the instability and traditional unscrupulousness of the government here, it will of course always be difficult to go on spinning the thread which connects Berlin and Moscow — a wire such as formerly existed between Berlin and St Petersburg it is not; yet a good relation with Soviet Russia remains for us in my opinion the only means to win back for the German people the world authority which is due to it, and gradually to make possible an independent foreign policy.[3]

[1] See *Socialism in One Country, 1924–1926*, Vol. 3, pp. 438–439.

[2] See p. 406 below.

[3] The draft of the report is in the *Brockdorff-Rantzau Nachlass*, 9101/224038–224046; for a quotation from Hindenburg's reply of July 14, 1926,

A similar diagnosis, with perhaps less concentration on the west, but with the same conviction of the partner's unreliability and unscrupulousness, might have been made by a Soviet observer.

Few incidents disturbed the tenour of relations during the remainder of the year. Negotiations for the exchange of Skoblevsky and some other Soviet agents under sentence or arrest in Germany for Kindermann, Wolscht and a batch of other Germans detained in the Soviet Union[4] dragged on throughout the summer of 1926, provoking acute divisions of opinion in the German cabinet; Brockdorff-Rantzau at one moment advised agreement on the ground that, if the Soviet Government carried out its threat to put a German employee of Junkers on trial on a charge of bribing Soviet officers, embarrassing disclosures would result. It was not till October 1926 that the exchange finally took place.[5] In October 1926 a party of Reichstag deputies visited the Soviet Union, and on return to Germany gave an interview to the German press recording with satisfaction the improvement in German–Soviet relations since the previous year.[6]

Intermittent anxiety continued to be felt over the Soviet–German military agreements. For some time political circles in Germany had been aware of the existence of the Junkers aeroplane factory in the Soviet Union, and of German official involvement in it; it was partly for this reason that the German cover organization GEFU had been wound up, and replaced by a presumably better camouflaged successor known as WIKO.[7] The Junkers factory had been briefly mentioned in *Pravda*.[8] No German political party had sought to exploit these disclosures, and no public concern had been shown. But in the wake of Locarno, and at the height of the struggle for Germany's admission to the League of Nations,[9] the pro-western Schubert, and less decisively Strese-

see *Socialism in One Country, 1924–1926*, Vol. 3, p. 437, note 5. Hilger, *Wir und der Kreml* (1955), p. 152, recorded the view that German–Soviet relations rested "not really on mutual inclination, but on the existence of common problems and common enemies".

[4] See *Socialism in One Country, 1924–1926*, Vol. 3, pp. 268–269.

[5] *Journal of Central European Affairs*, xxi, No. 2, July 1961, pp. 196–199; K. Rosenbaum, *Community of Fate* (Syracuse, 1965), pp. 220–225; both these sources quote extensively from German archives.

[6] *Izvestiya*, October 13, December 8, 1926.

[7] See *Socialism in One Country, 1924–1926*, Vol. 3, Note A, pp. 1011, 1014–1015.

[8] See *ibid.* Vol. 3, p. 434.

[9] See *ibid.* Vol. 3, p. 435.

mann, were affected by fears of the consequences of a revelation of the secret arrangements. In such an event, wrote Schubert to Brockdorff-Rantzau on April 3, 1926, "we should lose all our political credit in the world". Past activities might be condoned, but "an extension of our activities at this point ... would be judged far more harshly".[10] This fear explained the blank official response to Unshlikht's overtures of the same month — an attitude which does not appear to have been shared by the Reichswehr.[11] It may be inferred that Gessler, the Minister of Defence, was himself less enthusiastic than the Reichswehr about this compromising collaboration; for, in the course of a stubborn argument about Skoblevsky's release, he declared himself willing to abandon German activities in the Soviet Union rather than give way on this point.[12] Even Brockdorff-Rantzau was uneasy. In a conversation with Gessler on November 19, 1926, he complained that he had never been properly informed of the Reichwehr's activities, and that disclosure would discredit his prestige. He and Gessler seem to have agreed that the arrangements should be allowed gradually to "peter out" or to return to a purely economic basis.[13]

The Reichswehr, functioning independently of the civil power when it conceived vital interests to be at stake, pursued its business in lofty indifference to these anxieties. In the autumn of 1926 the arrival of several cargoes of arms and munitions from Leningrad in the port of Stettin caused local comment, and some friction between social-democrat and communist workers.[14] The bombshell exploded on December 3, 1926, when the *Manchester Guardian* published a report from its Berlin correspondent, according to which, two days earlier, evidence had been submitted to Gessler (by whom was not stated) in the presence of Stresemann and of the Chancellor, Marx, that "Russia is involved in the illegal activities of the German monarchists and counter-revolutionaries". This was followed by an article from "a cor-

[10] *Auswärtiges Amt,* 4564/162703–8; for Schubert see *Socialism in One Country, 1924–1926,* Vol. 3, p. 255.

[11] See *ibid.* Vol. 3, pp. 436, note 2, 1015.

[12] *Auswärtiges Amt,* 4564/163632ff.

[13] The only record available of this conversation (*ibid.* 4564/163383ff.) is Schubert's note of what Brockdorff-Rantzau told him; this may be coloured by Schubert's prejudices.

[14] F. Melville, *The Russian Face of Germany* (1932), pp. 186–190; for the pamphlet from which this was translated see p. 45 below.

respondent", which dealt in some detail with the subventions paid to Junkers by the Reichswehr, cited visits of Reichswehr officers to the Soviet Union with false passports, and mentioned the agreement with a German chemical firm for the erection in the Soviet Union of a factory for the production of poison gas. The writer believed, or purported to believe, that the German Government was "genuinely concerned" about these arrangements concluded behind its back, and that "they will be terminated forthwith".[15]

On the following day most German newspapers carried a brief report of the *Manchester Guardian* allegations, together with a half-hearted denial of their authenticity from the semi-official Wolff agency. But on December 5, 1926, the social-democratic paper *Vorwärts* published a detailed account of the allegations, demanded an official explanation and bitterly enquired whether the Reichswehr rifles which had shot down German communist workers in 1921 and 1923 were loaded with Russian ammunition. The rest of the German press handled the theme more cautiously. The *Berliner Tageblatt* of December 6, 1926, admitted that German engineers had built three factories in the Soviet Union for the production of aeroplanes, shells and gas. If military supplies had been received from this source by Germany, this violation of the treaty was no worse than those committed by the Allied Powers. In any case, since the Locarno treaty, "as we are informed", no fresh order had been placed.[16] Chicherin, who happened to be in Berlin when the scandal broke, but did not mention it in a major interview to the press on December 6, 1926,[17] called

[15] The origin of the report is unknown, but it certainly emanated from persons in direct or indirect contact with Voigt, the *Manchester Guardian* correspondent in Berlin; a secret report in the German archives (*Akten zur Deutschen Auswärtigen Politik*, Series B, iv (1970), 154–155) that it was the work of a Soviet agent in London can safely be dismissed. Further details, mainly relating to the Junkers affair, appeared in the *Manchester Guardian*, December 6, 1926.

[16] Stresemann, who was at Geneva and expected to be questioned by his colleagues, had telegraphed on the previous day the line to be taken. This was to deny any secret agreements with the Soviet Government; to admit that "certain departments of the Reichswehr" had in past periods of crisis taken advantage of German relations with Soviet industry to obtain supplies of "ammunition and other defensive material"; but to add that, as soon as the German Government became aware of these transactions, it had taken steps to ensure that they should "gradually disappear" (*Auswärtiges Amt*, 6698/106234–5).

[17] For the interview see p. 7 above.

with Krestinsky on Chancellor Marx on the same day, to express his disquiet. Marx disclaimed any responsibility on the part of the German Government for the revelations, and promised to issue a soothing *communiqué* to the press.[18] Chicherin was also received by Seeckt's successor, General Heye, who cautiously sought the advice of the Foreign Office in advance of the interview.[19] It was noted with interest that one of Chicherin's engagements was a luncheon with Seeckt. His only public pronouncement on the subject was an interview in the *Rote Fahne* in which he confessed himself "not precisely informed" about these matters, but jocularly suggested that the "Soviet shells" might have been "made in England", or perhaps in the British Embassy in Berlin.[20] Pieck in a speech in the Prussian Landtag on December 9, 1926, described it as "a swindle" and "an infamous slander" to pretend that "Russia is manufacturing the weapons used by the counter-revolution in Germany against the workers". He boldly asserted that, at a moment when discussions were proceeding at Geneva on "the extent to which poison gas is to be used in the next war", the Soviet Union had every right "to prepare for its defence by similar means".[21] On December 16, 1926, *Pravda* grudgingly broke silence with an article referring to reports that German firms had built factories in the Soviet Union for the production of such things as aeroplanes, poison gas and shells "for our defence". Such reports, even if true, had no importance. The *Rote Fahne* followed this lead by asserting on December 25, 1926, that the whole production of the factories had "remained in the Soviet Union".

Meanwhile, a new dimension was added to the affair by Scheidemann's speech in the Reichstag on December 16, 1926. Beginning with a demand to "submit the Reichswehr to a *political examination*", he referred cryptically to "certain *proceedings*, certain *undertakings* of the Reichswehr", to the relations of the Sondergruppe with Junkers, to the expenditure of large sums under secret agreements, and to the cooperation of the Reichswehr with Right-wing organizations. Hitherto he had spoken amid angry protests and interruptions from the Right; at one point

[18] *Ibid.* 6698/111069–71. Chicherin, in a report to Narkomindel, pretended that the conversation with Marx had been confined to questions of credits and concessions (*Dokumenty Vneshnei Politiki SSSR*, ix (1964), 572).

[19] *Auswärtiges Amt*, 6698/106248–9, 111067–8.

[20] *Die Rote Fahne*, December 7, 1926.

[21] W. Pieck, *Gesammelte Reden und Schriften*, iii (1961), 514.

ON THIS DAY

May 23, 1928

Although the manufacture of a poison gas for military purposes was prohibited, phosgene production was permitted for the manufacture of dyestuffs and in other industrial processes.

THE POISON GAS DISASTER.

ELEVEN DEATHS.

(FROM OUR OWN CORRESPONDENT.)

BERLIN, May 22

Four of the more seriously affected patients poisoned by the escape of phosgene gas at Hamburg on Sunday have died since yesterday. This brings the total number of deaths up to 11. There remain some 250 persons under treatment and inhabitants of the stricken area have been alarmed to learn that cases at first slight have become more serious, and that one or two persons who for more than a day had apparently remained in perfect health, have had to be removed to hospital to-day. This characteristic accompaniment of gas poisoning has, according to reports received in Berlin, given the scene of the disaster something of the appearance of a plague-stricken area, where men and women, haggard from sleeplessness walk about haunted by the fear that they will yet be victims of the invisible peril.

Through the efforts of the fire brigades, the police and the technical experts summoned to Hamburg, fortunately assisted by continuous rain, the area is now safe. The gas-infected houses evacuated by their occupants have been rendered habitable again, and stocks of foodstuffs in the shops have been inspected, and when in the slightest degree suspicious seized and destroyed.

The official inquiries into the cause of the leakage and the origin of the phosgene are still in progress. Various firms concerned have issued statements. The Stolzenberg chemical works, now in liquidation, on whose premises the tanks were situated, state that they have no explanation to offer as regards the leakage, as the tanks were kept under expert supervision and had undergone pressure tests.

The authorities are investigating the circumstances in which such a large quantity of a deadly gas, sufficient probably to destroy the population of Hamburg, was stored in ordinary tanks and not, as is customary, in steel containers.

With regard to the presence of the phosgene at Hamburg, it is not necessarily contrary to the terms of the Treaty of Versailles. Under the arrangements reached between German and Allied authorities, Germany agreed to restrict her export of phosgene to 24 tons annually, for industrial purposes only. In Germany itself phosgene is required in fairly huge quantities for dyestuffs production and for this and other industrial purposes, although the manufacture of poison gases for military purposes is prohibited, it was agreed that three factories should be equipped to produce the necessary quantity. Of these three factories one is capable of producing eight tons of phosgene a day, and the other two between them can produce one ton a day. Nine tons a day is a large amount. The factories are probably not used to their full capacity but the existence of fairly large stocks of phosgene in Germany is clearly explained.

The Stolzenberg works are not among the specified manufacturers of phosgene. The gas is stated to have been bought for export abroad, principally to the United States. It is also said to have formed part of old war stocks which, incidentally were all supposed to have been reported to the Allied Control Commission and destroyed.

The experiences of the affected area are widely described in the Press as a foretaste of the fate of civilian populations in the next war, and the occasion is used as propaganda, on the one hand for pacificism and on the other hand for the movement, of Nationalist origin, in favour of militarism and civil defence measures on a large scale against gas attacks by hostile aircraft.

tion (8).

13 Leaflet — one about physiotherapists' practice (8).
15 Monster conger eel oddly depleted (4).
17 Interpret the sound made by wind instrument (4).
19 Chap with passion for publicity (8).
20 School in distress (6).

Solution to Puzzle No 20,486

T	A	K	E	N	■	A	R	A	U	C	A	R	I	A
E	■	I	■	A	■	M	■	I	■	A	■	A	■	R
S	A	N	D	P	A	P	E	R	■	L	I	L	A	C
T	■	■	■	K	■	H	■	E	■	L	■	L	■	H
F	O	R	T	I	F	I	E	D	W	I	N	E	■	■
L	■	E	■	N	■	B	■	■	■	O	■	N	■	E
I	R	A	N	■	D	I	S	S	I	P	A	T	E	D
G	■	R	■	C	■	A	■	H	■	E	■	A	■	I
H	E	A	D	H	U	N	T	E	R	■	K	N	I	T
T	■	D	■	A	■	■	■	L	■	B	■	D	■	O
■	■	M	A	I	D	S	O	F	H	O	N	O	U	R
S	■	I	■	R	■	O	■	L	■	B	■	■	■	S
T	A	R	S	I	■	L	O	I	N	C	L	O	T	H
U	■	A	■	N	■	O	■	F	■	A	■	I	■	I
D	I	L	I	G	E	N	C	E	■	T	U	L	I	P

3 Determined to produce notes on instrument (8).
4 Accompaniment disturbed Gobbi a lot (9).
5 Follow current trend (2,4,3,6).
6 Complain about a rule to the Speaker (7).
7 Reformed a region's regiment (8).
8 Section of theatre put up heartfelt valediction (8).
14 Pearls may be controlled (2,1,6).
15 Exactly where girl's marriage prospects could depend (2,3,3).
16 Rare slip could produce such an aggressive response (8).
17 Salvage most of River Tees wreck (8).
18 Lent is well on (8).
19 To hold on, to hold on — that's duplication (7).

Times Two Crossword, page 48

UK newspapers in the first half of 1996

Folkestone	2.8
Glasgow	4.2
Guernsey	11.9
Hastings	1.3
Hayling I.	0.1
Herne Bay	5.5
Hove	3.5
Hunstanton	X
Isle of Man	8.4
Jersey	8.0
Kinloss	3.4
Leeds	0.5
Lerwick	1.9

Ajaccio	21	70	s
Akrotiri	24	75	s
Alex'dria	26	79	s
Algiers	25	77	s
Amst'dm	12	54	c
Athens	28	82	s
B Aires	12	54	f
Bahrain	36	97	s
Bangkok	35	95	s
Barbados	29	84	f
Barcelona	20	68	s
Beirut	24	75	f
Belgrade	21	70	s
Berlin	10	50	c
Bermuda	23	73	f
Biarritz	20	68	s
Borde'x	20	68	c
Brussels	12	54	c
Budapst	13	55	r
Cairo	33	91	s
Cape Tn	19	66	f
Ch'church	X		
Chicago	17	63	s
Cologne	11	52	c

Ter

deputies of the National and People's Parties left the chamber. But at a later stage in the speech he turned with even more marked animosity to "the concerns of the Reichswehr in Russia", and to the *Manchester Guardian* disclosures, remarking amid interruptions from the KPD benches that Germany needed shells to deal with "communist *putsches*". He gave details of the cargoes which had arrived recently from Leningrad in Stettin, and named the Stolzenberg chemical works in Hamburg as responsible for the gas factory in the Soviet Union.[22] After the Chancellor had briefly deplored Scheidemann's speech, since the matter to which it related "lies so far back in the past", and several deputies of the Right had denounced its treasonable character,[23] Koenen made a long and rambling reply on behalf of the KPD. He complained that Scheidemann had only "dropped hints", and had not produced "real events, facts, data", denied that German workers had been shot down with Soviet rifles and ammunition and saw no reason why the Soviet Government should not have dealings simultaneously with Reichswehr officers and with communists.[24] On the following day Schwarz, a dissident communist and a follower of Korsch, made a pungent attack on the policies of the KPD and of the Soviet leaders, which provoked angry interruptions and ironical applause. He spoke of "a united front from Thälmann to Hindenburg". He quoted with indignation a speech of Bukharin at the fourth congress of Comintern in November 1922 justifying a military alliance between the Soviet Union and a foreign bourgeois state, and a speech of Zetkin in the Reichstag debates on the Locarno treaty defending the possibility of "*cooperation between the Reichswehr and Red Army men*", and he declared that Stalin and Bukharin had "long forsworn Marx and Engels". Scholem, on behalf of the Left opposition in the KPD, read a declaration dissociating it from Schwarz's views.[25] The *Leipziger Volkszeitung* of January 6, 1927, added fuel to the indignation of the Left by publishing a sensational account of Soviet–German plans and installations for the production of poison gas.

The jauntiness of Soviet reactions to the disclosures betrayed

[22] *Verhandlungen des Reichstags*, cccxci (1927), 8577–8586.

[23] *Ibid.* cccxci, 8586–8567.

[24] *Ibid.* cccxci, 18593–8602.

[25] *Ibid.* cccxci, 8636–8639. For Zetkin's comment see *ibid.* ccclxxxviii (1926), 4637; for Bukharin's speech see *The Bolshevik Revolution, 1917–1923,* Vol. 3, p. 447.

acute embarrassment. *Pravda* on December 31, 1926, poked fun at stories of "Soviet shells" and "secret cargoes", attacked the social-democrats as the principal villains of the piece, and laid down what was now the established line:

> We do not conceal, have not concealed, and shall not in future conceal, that we are ready to utilize the resources of German technology, as well as the resources of other leading countries, to improve our industry.

A further article in *Pravda* of January 5, 1927, repeated the same admission, and combined evasion with invective, denouncing the "nasty hate campaign" of "the Berlin social-Judases" designed to please the "imperialist John Bull".[26] Half the article was devoted to the "ultra-Left renegade" Schwarz, whose Reichstag speech had constituted "the most contemptible treason to the proletariat". Bukharin carried on the story in a speech to the Moscow provincial party conference on January 8, 1927:

> We had, and continue to have, a contract with the firm of Junkers, which, as *Pravda* wrote a few days ago, is engaged on the manufacture of aeroplanes and not of boiled sausages. We do not conceal, and never have concealed, that we had a contract with Junkers, that they did and do build aeroplanes; and we declare with complete frankness that we will not refuse to avail ourselves of any capitalist state whatever which will send us instructors and, for appropriate payment, produce on our territory aeroplanes and other weapons of war for the defence of our country.[27]

None of these pronouncements contained any hint of war material delivered to Germany. Krestinsky on January 5, 1927, told Stresemann that the Soviet Government disliked references in German official statements even to deliveries made in the past: this read like "a great confession". The Soviet Government thought that "these things should be flatly denied altogether".[28]

Perhaps the oddest feature of the situation was the attitude of

[26] Two days later Brockdorff-Rantzau complained to Litvinov that, in spite of his protests, the "senseless campaign" against the SPD in the Soviet press had not been discontinued (*Akten zur Deutschen Auswärtigen Politik*, Series B, iv (1970), 19–20).

[27] *Pravda*, January 13, 1927; for other repercussions of this speech, see pp. 123–124 below.

[28] *Akten zur Deutschen Auswärtigen Politik*, Series B, iv (1970), 20, note 5.

the western Powers, and especially of Great Britain. The British chargé d'affaires in Moscow recorded the impression prevailing in diplomatic circles that "the recent campaign has a certain substratum of fact, but not much", and was mainly "a journalistic *feu d'artifice*".[29] The admission of Germany to the League of Nations, and the much vaunted Thoiry conversation between Briand and Stresemann, had paved the way for reconciliation between Germany and the western Powers. Only a few days after the *Manchester Guardian* revelations, the British and French Governments had signed a protocol for the withdrawal of the Inter-Allied Military Control Commission from Germany on January 31, 1927. Unwilling to listen to voices that might disturb this beneficent policy, they were willing to be deceived. The contribution of the Soviet–German arrangements to Soviet rearmament was freely admitted, but dismissed as unimportant; their contribution to German rearmament was either specifically denied or ignored.

The German Government could scarcely believe its luck, but resolved to be more careful in future. At a meeting on January 24, 1927, between Schubert and Dirksen of the Foreign Office and two high Reichswehr officers, the latter explained that the Junkers enterprise had been wound up (this meant no further deliveries of material to Germany, such as had led to the disclosures of the previous autumn); that the Lipetsk flying school and the Kazan tank school had been converted into "private undertakings", though they were financed out of Reichswehr funds and were both "vital for the German army"; and that the gas experiments were "on a purely scientific basis", and involved no Reichswehr finance or personnel. Schubert, still uneasy about the "political risk" of an indiscretion, was assured that the Soviet Government was no less concerned than the German to preserve secrecy.[30] A week later Stresemann accepted these arrangements at a meeting with Heye, subject to the proviso that no serving Reichswehr officers were employed in the Soviet Union; this was easily arranged by transferring officers seconded for these duties to the reserve. On February 26, 1927, a protocol was drawn up

[29] *Documents on British Foreign Policy*, Series I A, ii (1968), 741–743.

[30] *Akten zur Deutschen Auswärtigen Politik*, Series B, iv (1970), 139–142; for the Lipetsk and Kazan schools see *Socialism in One Country, 1924–1926*, Vol. 3, pp. 1012–1013.

embodying these understandings.[31] An awkward corner had been turned and consciences were appeased.

Only the parties of the Left, perhaps less inured to *Realpolitik*, and eager to exploit the scandal at the expense of their rivals, Right and Left, still attempted with diminishing success to keep it alive. On February 16, 1927, a SPD deputy questioned Gessler on the subject, and was referred by him to the foreign affairs commission of the Reichstag; the report of this incident in *Vorwärts* on the following day caused acute alarm to Litvinov.[32] After negotiations with the SPD behind the scenes, Gessler made a carefully prepared statement in the foreign affairs commission on February 23, 1927. He dated back the transactions with the Soviet Union to the period of acute French hostility to Germany before the occupation of the Ruhr. To preserve the German war industry, and especially the aeronautical industry, from total destruction, it was compelled to engage in operations abroad. A sum of 75 million gold marks had been assigned for this purpose, and had now been completely exhausted. The activities of German industrialists in the Soviet Union had met with difficulties, and had now been brought to an end: "no establishments or agreements in contravention of the Versailles treaty exist". In the ensuing debate, Hilferding attacked the secret agreements and Wirth, who was chancellor at the time when they were made, defended them. Schubert, in a long statement apparently designed to divert the discussion to the general question of Soviet–German relations, declared that German policy was firmly based on the Locarno treaty and the German–Soviet treaty of April 24, 1926. Two KPD deputies, Stoecker and Rosenberg, criticized the statement as proof that, since Locarno, Germany had turned away from the Soviet Union. Gessler refused to speak again, and referred questioners to his initial statement. The participants were strictly enjoined to observe discretion about the proceedings; but little that was compromising appears to have been said. The press gave only formal reports of the session.[33]

[31] *Akten zur Deutschen Auswärtigen Politik*, Series B, iv (1970), 256–258, 420.

[32] *Ibid.* Series B, iv, 347, 365–366.

[33] For an account of the proceedings and the text of Gessler's statement see *ibid.* Series B, iv, 403–406; what purports to be a complete text in A. Anderle, *Die Deutsche Rapallo-Politik* (1962), p. 203, is a brief summary. For a few details of the session see G. Hilger, *Wir und der Kreml* (1965), p. 198.

After this session the SPD campaign against the German Government and its nationalist supporters petered out. The KPD did not escape so easily from the clutches of its rivals. In February 1927 the KAPD, which had split from the KPD at the Heidelberg party congress in 1919, and had maintained its existence as a splinter group opposed to all involvement of communists in Soviet state policy, addressed an open letter to the KPD repeating every detail of evidence of the aid furnished by the Soviet Government to the Reichswehr, exposing the lies and evasions of German and Russian communists, and challenging the KPD to publish the letter in its press.[34] Shortly after the eleventh congress of the KPD in March 1927, the SPD also published a pamphlet entitled *Sowjetgranaten*, which provided evidence of Soviet shipments of munitions for the Reichswehr, and ended with the claim that "the only German workers' party is the Social-Democratic Party".[35] These polemics of the SPD and KAPD were condemned by other German parties as treasonable scandal-mongering, or dismissed as irrelevant feuding between Left-wing groups. They did not alter the determination of the German and Soviet Governments to keep the agreements in being.

The Reichswehr, now virtually free from criticism at home, and released from the not very effective scrutiny of Allied controllers, went its own way. On April 23, 1927, Schubert was informed that "some further gas experiments" were to be conducted in the Soviet Union, that a site near Orenburg was envisaged for them, and that the Reichswehr had decided to send a serving officer to inspect the arrangements, his journey being camouflaged as leave. Schubert was "not very comfortable" about this plan, but could evidently do nothing.[36] A month later, on May 8, 1927, Stresemann and Schubert, Gessler, Heye and the head of the Truppenamt, Blomberg, were present at a general discussion of the various aspects of Soviet–German military collaboration. The only point to arouse difficulty was Gessler's announcement of an intention to

[34] The letter was published by the KAPD a few weeks later with an introductory chapter bitterly entitled "The Russian Tragedy"; the pamphlet had a cover decorated with the Hammer and Sickle and the Swastika, and bearing the title *Von der Revolution zur Kontrrevolution: Russland Bewaffnet die Reichswehr*. For the KAPD see *The Bolshevik Revolution, 1917–1923*, Vol. 3, pp. 138, 390–391, 396.

[35] The pamphlet is translated in C. F. Melville, *The Russian Face of Germany* (1932), pp. 178–204.

[36] *Akten zur Deutschen Auswärtigen Politik*, Series B, v (1972), 223.

carry out "a larger experiment near Orenburg in the practical use of gas for military purposes [*in der praktischen Gasabwehr*]". The Soviet military authorities demanded full participation in the exercise and unrestricted communication and exchange of material. Even Gessler seemed to fear that this was giving too much for too little, and suggested transferring the exercise to a secret site in Germany. Stressemann, uneasy as usual, undertook to consult Brockdorff-Rantzau, who was in Berlin.[37] Nothing more was heard of objections to the original plan. The Reichswehr followed its habitual practice of seeking the approval of the government where it was readily obtainable, and dispensing with it when it was not. Hilger, the experienced counsellor of the German Embassy in Moscow, was cynical, but not unfair:

> Berlin never thought of abandoning its policy ... It was clear that the military would continue their collaboration with the Russians openly or secretly, even if the political leaders followed a different course. But, apart from this, all concerned, from Stresemann down, were resolved not only to continue the military collaboration as before, but to intensify it, though with the greatest caution.[38]

In the British House of Commons, on June 29, 1927, Locker-Lampson, the Under-Secretary for Foreign Affairs, known, perhaps significantly in this context, for his extreme hostility to the Soviet Union, gave the whole subject its official burial. He understood that all transactions relating to the import of arms and ammunition into Germany in contravention of the Versailles treaty had now ceased. In any event the German Government could be exonerated:

> These transactions took place between subordinate departments of each of the governments. They were not official transactions between governments. The German Government has made it quite clear that it disapproved of these transactions, and they have stopped.[39]

The intense nervousness which began to affect the Soviet out-

[37] *Ibid.* Series B, v, 366–368.
[38] G. Hilger, *Wir und der Kreml* (1956), p. 198.
[39] *House of Commons: 5th Series*, ccviii, 383.

look on the world in the spring of 1927[40] soon manifested itself at the sensitive point of Soviet–German relations — the implications of the Locarno treaty. A storm of anger broke out over a statement attributed to Schubert by the French newspaper *Excelsior* on March 7, 1927, that Germany had agreed at Locarno to the passage of French troops across Germany, in case of need, to come to the aid of Czechoslovakia or Poland. It was a fortnight before Stresemann was induced by angry Soviet protests to deny the authenticity of the statement, and to reaffirm in a speech to the Reichstag the limited scope of German obligations under article 16 of the Covenant of the League of Nations.[41] The break with Great Britain in May 1927 revived the perennial fear that Germany would be drawn into an anti-Soviet bloc. Already on February 18, 1927, Chicherin, in a letter to Stalin and Rykov, had criticized Bukharin's outburst against Germany which had excited the indignation of the German Government. In a further letter of June 3, 1927, written from a German sanatorium, he protested that, at a moment when the existence of the USSR might depend on strengthening relations with Berlin, some comrades "find nothing better to do than to wreck all our work by sallies against Germany", and announced his intention to travel to Moscow and hand in his resignation.[42] These fears were partly assuaged by a long and friendly conversation between Chicherin and Stresemann on June 7, 1927, on the eve of the departure of the German delegation for Geneva.[43] Stresemann at Geneva made clear his refusal to follow the British lead;[44] and, when he spoke in the Reichstag on his return from Geneva, the Soviet press expressed satisfaction at his assurance that Germany would never participate in an anti-Soviet coalition.[45] But Chicherin still suspected Germany of a desire to exploit the Anglo-Soviet conflict in order to

[40] See pp. 8–11 above.

[41] *Dokumenty Vneshnei Politiki SSSR*, x (1965), 102–103, 116, 629, note 24; for a detailed account of this incident from the German archives see K. Rosenbaum, *Community of Fate* (Syracuse, 1965), pp. 243–246.

[42] Quoted from the archives by Gromyko in an article in *Izvestiya*, December 5, 1962. For Chicherin's criticism of Bukharin's previous outburst see p. 124 below; no specific later indiscretion to which Chicherin may have referred in his second letter has been traced.

[43] *Dokumenty Vneshnei Politiki SSSR*, x (1965), 300–308.

[44] See pp. 27–28 above.

[45] *Pravda* and *Izvestiya*, June 25, 1927.

strengthen her economic influence in the Soviet Union.[46] German hostility to Poland, both after the assassination of Voikov and at the height of the Polish–Lithuanian dispute, was felt to be less unequivocal than sincere friendship for the Soviet Union would have demanded;[47] Poland was always the nerve-centre of the Soviet–German alliance. But, on the whole, partnership with Germany was still yielding good results. The year which saw the fifth anniversary of the Rapallo treaty was the least eventful in the chequered course of the relation established by it. The fifth anniversary of Brockdorff-Rantzau's arrival in Moscow as German Ambassador, which coincided with the tenth anniversary of the revolution, was the occasion of a grand banquet at which he and Chicherin exchanged warm assurances of friendship and of hope for the future.[48]

Economic relations between the two countries, though less charged with emotion than political and military relations, were a constant theme. Germany was not only the Soviet Union's most important trading partner, but the one with whom a reasonable balance between imports and exports was most successfully maintained.[49] Discussions proceeded on export credits from the German banks, which the German Government had undertaken to guarantee up to a maximum of 300 million marks.[50] In July 1926 an agreement with the banks was announced for advances of 120–150 millions with interest at the rate of 9·4 per cent per annum, re-

[46] *Dokumenty Vneshnei Politiki SSSR*, x (1965), 333; Dirksen in a private letter to Brockdorff-Rantzau of October 18, 1927, expressed the view that the breach with Great Britain would make the Soviet Union less credit-worthy in the west, and compel her to seek "cheaper terms" in Germany (quoted from archives in A. Anderle, *Die Deutsche Rapallo-Politik* (1962), p. 208).

[47] See, for example, *Dokumenty Vneshnei Politiki SSSR*, x (1965), 306, 329–330, 486–488, 494–496.

[48] K. Rosenbaum, *Community of Fate* (Syracuse, 1965), pp. 250–253, quoting documents from the *Brockdorff-Rantzau Nachlass*.

[49] The following were the official Soviet figures (in thousands of rubles at current prices):

	Exports to Germany	Percentage of Total Exports	Imports from Germany	Percentage of Total Imports
1925/26	111,618	15·9	176,079	23·3
1926/27	175,514	21·8	161,616	22·6
1927/28	193,591	24·5	248,505	26·3
1929	215,126	23·3	194,648	22·1

(*Sotsialisticheskoe Stroitel'stvo SSSR* (1935), pp. 587–588, 591–592).

[50] See *Socialism in One Country, 1924–1926*, Vol. 3, p. 431.

payable in part in 1928 and in part in 1930.[51] Chicherin, during his visit to Berlin early in December 1926, sounded Stresemann on the chances of a long-term loan to replace the credits, but was put off on the plea that, while questions arising out of the Dawes plan were still unsettled, it would make a bad impression if Germany were seen to be in a position to make loans to foreign governments.[52] At the fourth Union Congress of Soviets in April 1927 Rykov announced that credits had been obtained from Germany to a total of 315 million marks and corresponding orders placed for German goods. He added that "our economic and cultural link with Germany grows from year to year and grows more than with any other country".[53] But further requests for credits or guarantees from the German Government fell on deaf ears. On June 9, 1927, it was announced that "the guarantee of the Reich for deliveries to Russia cannot be extended beyond the limit fixed in previous decisions", and that it must be "left to German industry alone to decide whether to engage further in Russian business without a Reich guarantee"; this was communicated to Chicherin who was in Berlin at the time.[54] The Soviet Government was, however, broadly satisfied with the results achieved. The head of the Soviet trade delegation in Berlin, in a press interview of November 1927, was at pains to emphasize that the trade agreement of October 12, 1925, had worked to the advantage of both sides.[55]

The German Government and German industrialists did not altogether share this satisfaction. It was felt that, while Germany alone had given substantial credits to Soviet importers,[56] German trade had not secured the preponderant position on which it had counted in the Soviet market. Conditions seemed unfamiliar and unpropitious. When Walroth casually suggested that the further development of trade depended on "a complete transformation of Russian economic policy—of course, without a change of

[51] *Dokumenty Vneshnei Politiki SSSR*, ix (1964), 324–325, 341–342.

[52] *Ibid.* ix, 561–562.

[53] *SSSR: 4 S"ezd Sovetov* (1927), p. 25.

[54] *Akten zur Deutschen Auswärtigen Politik*, Series B, v (1972), 584.

[55] *Izvestiya*, November 11, 1927.

[56] The only other country from which a block credit was obtained at this time was Austria, where a bank credit of 100 million schillings was guaranteed by the municipality of Vienna in October 1927 (*Dokumenty Vneshnei Politiki SSSR*, x (1965), 470, 563); only short-term credits covering individual consignments were obtainable in Great Britain and the United States.

régime", Brockdorff-Rantzau in a long reply explained that the Soviet economic system and programme were bound up with the survival of the régime, and that no fundamental changes could be hoped for. He added that blame for disappointments "does not lie exclusively on the Russian side", and that many German businessmen were not sufficiently acquainted with Soviet conditions, and "cannot or will not accustom themselves to the peculiar economic structure of this country".[57] On January 21, 1928, Schubert, as the result of consultations with German industry, handed to Krestinsky a list of points on which revision of the 1925 agreement was desired, and expressed the hope that a "responsible representative" would be sent from Moscow for negotiations to begin next month in Berlin; Walroth, head of the eastern division of the Foreign Office, would lead the German delegation.[58] A preliminary meeting was held in Stresemann's office on February 6, 1928. Rudzutak and Sheinman, who had come from Moscow for the meeting, raised their sights and offered orders to the value of 600 million marks if corresponding fresh credits were made available. Stresemann explained that Germany's economic situation was no longer as favourable as two years earlier, and professed to doubt the feasibility of further credits.[59] The formal negotiations, which began on February 11, 1928, opened with long polemical speeches by Walroth and Shleifer, the head of the Soviet delegation. Walroth complained that the intentions of the agreement of October 12, 1925, had not been carried out. It was not enough to invoke the principle of most-favoured-nation treatment. Trade relations must be based on reciprocity (*do ut des*); Soviet orders from German industry were not expanding and were even contracting.[60] Details of the subsequent proceedings were not published. But neither side seems to have been in a conciliatory mood; and the toughness of the negotiations was reflected in the press of both countries. *Izvestiya* chose the tenth anniversary of the Brest–Litovsk treaty on March 3, 1928, as the occasion for a carping article on Soviet–German relations. Recalling that the Rapallo treaty had been conceived as "an act of

[57] *Akten zur Deutschen Auswärtigen Politik*, Series B, v (1972), 71–74; for Walroth's remark see *ibid.* iv (1970), 447.

[58] *Dokumenty Vneshnei Politiki SSSR*, xi (1966), 35–38.

[59] *Ibid.* xi, 59–66.

[60] For extracts from the speeches see *ibid.* xi, 698–700, note 25.

mutual support", it complained bitterly of the grudging attitude of the German press to the trade negotiations in Berlin.

A fresh storm broke with the announcement on March 10, 1928, of the arrest of a large number of persons, including five German engineers (two of whom were quickly released), on charges of sabotage in the Shakhty mining area of the southern Ukraine.[61] The charge against the German engineers in the form in which it was couched is unlikely to have been well-founded. But German economic enterprises in the Soviet Union were described in a confidential German Foreign Office memorandum of the period as "indispensable and necessary outposts and observation-posts of Germany in Russia";[62] and the numerous German technicians employed in Soviet enterprises must often have been valuable sources of information to the German Government. Such activities were regarded by the sensitive Soviet authorities as espionage. The arrests were greeted by a wave of angry protests in Germany.[63] On March 14, 1928, Stresemann informed Krestinsky that the German industrialists were in a state of indignation, that the AEG threatened to withdraw its personnel from the Soviet Union, and that in this atmosphere a temporary "interruption" of the trade negotiations was unavoidable.[64] The suspension of negotiations was plainly unwelcome to the Soviet Government; a Tass *communiqué* attributed it to a governmental crisis in Germany.[65] Litvinov, visiting Stresemann in Berlin on April 5, 1928, on his way back from Geneva, professed inability to believe that "the arrest of the engineers, a completely private affair which might happen in any country, could influence relations between states", and could explain it only "by some deeper causes — a change of orientation, pressure from without etc."[66] But fresh offence was given by a speech of Bukharin in the

[61] See Vol. 1, pp. 584–585.

[62] Quoted from the archives in A. Anderle, *Die Deutsche Rapallo-Politik* (1962), p. 209.

[63] Many details about the case from German archives are collected in K. Rosenbaum, *Community of Fate* (1965), pp. 253–276. It seems clear that one of the Germans had given bribes to Soviet officials; the authorities suspected that these were designed to secure acceptance of defective products.

[64] *Dokumenty Vneshnei Politiki SSSR*, xi (1966), 161–162; Stresemann later told Krestinsky that Felix Deutsch, the head of AEG, which employed four of the five incriminated engineers, had been the chief instigator of the campaign, against the wishes of a majority of industrialists (*ibid.* xi, 576).

[65] *Izvestiya*, March 18, 1928.

[66] *Dokumenty Vneshnei Politiki SSSR*, xi (1966), 257–258.

party central committee, in which he spoke of a subversive organization linked with foreign capitalists, contact being maintained through foreign engineers, "some of whom turned out to be members of Fascist organizations, especially the German Stahlhelm".[67] When the trial opened on May 18, 1928, mutual exasperation had reached its highest point.

Beneath all this sound and fury, nobody really wanted a break. Soviet–German relations yielded too many advantages to both partners to be lightly jettisoned. While the trial was in progress, Kalinin, in a speech reported in the press, hinted that the action of the government, however justifiable, had been "rather incautious", and that nobody had meant to indict German industry as a whole.[68] In June 1928 a coalition government headed by social-democrats was formed in Germany; it was the first time for four and a half years that the SPD had been represented in a German Government. But Chicherin's speculation that it might now be possible to conclude a further political or economic agreement was received with scepticism by Krestinsky, and not pursued.[69] The judgment handed down on July 9, 1928, which acquitted two of the German defendants, and imposed a nominal sentence on the third, was evidence of the desire of the Soviet authorities to undo the harm that had been done. The results were not immediately apparent. The hostile campaign in the German press continued amid protests from the Soviet side.[70] When Brockdorff-Rantzau departed from Moscow on leave on July 18, 1928, Chicherin was already ill, and it was noticed that no representative of Narkomindel appeared at the railway station to bid the Ambassador farewell;[71] and on August 22, 1928, the Soviet Government refused re-entry visas to Scheffer and two other German correspondents who had been on leave in Germany.[72] But the ill-feeling generated by the Shakhty affair soon faded; and the more permanent interests of German industry in the Soviet

[67] The speech was reported in *Vechernaya Moskva*, April 17, 1928, but not, perhaps significantly, in *Pravda*; for an earlier indiscretion of Bukharin see p. 47 above.

[68] *Izvestiya*, June 8, 1928.

[69] *Dokumenty Vneshnei Politiki SSSR*, xi (1966), 386, 730, note 123.

[70] *Ibid.* xi, 381, 390.

[71] P. Scheffer, *Seven Years in Soviet Russia* (English transl. from German, 1931), p. 323.

[72] *Dokumenty Vneshnei Politiki SSSR*, xi (1966), 741, note 176.

market reasserted themselves. Schlesinger, the head of the economic department of the German Ministry of Foreign Affairs, sounded the Soviet mission about a resumption of economic negotiations, and received a positive answer, coupled with the suggestion that the negotiations should be transferred to Moscow.[73] This suggestion also proved acceptable to the German Government.

Before the arrangements could be completed, Brockdorff-Rantzau died in Berlin on September 9, 1928. Since his appointment in the autumn of 1922 he had worked unceasingly, and often with grudging support from his government, to strengthen German–Soviet relations; he was on terms of personal friendship with Chicherin, and was the only foreign envoy ever to enjoy the full confidence of the Soviet Government. The death of Brockdorff-Rantzau marked a stage in the cooling-off process. It coincided with the transfer of effective control of Narkomindel from the now chronically sick Chicherin to the Anglophile Litvinov, who had few associations with Germany.[74] In October 1928 the decision of a consortium of German bankers to join the newly formed international committee of Russian creditors in London provoked an outburst of indignation in Moscow, which was assuaged only in part by a press *communiqué* of the German Government dissociating itself from the action of the bankers.[75] The Soviet Government, understandably afraid that the German banks might be persuaded not to participate in credits to the Soviet Union, demanded a formal assurance from the German Government. Stresemann, embarrassed by the occurrence and caught between two fires, was most reluctant to make any further pronouncement, and haggled obstinately about the suggested terms;[76] and Soviet opinion was further outraged when Stresemann, in his first major speech in the Reichstag after a bout of illness, stressed the immutability of Germany's Locarno policy and did not mention German relations with the Soviet Union at all.[77]

These wrangles did not, however, prevent agreement being reached to re-open the trade negotiations in Moscow on Nov-

[73] *Ibid.* xi, 483, 738, note 162.

[74] See p. 32 above.

[75] *Dokumenty Vneshnei Politiki SSSR*, xi, 542–543; the *communiqué* was issued through the Wolf agency on October 20, 1928, and reported in *Izvestiya* on the following day. For the international committee see p. 33 above.

[76] *Dokumenty Vneshnei Politiki SSSR*, xi (1966), 567–570, 576.

[77] *Izvestiya*, November 21, 1928.

ember 26, 1928.[78] A few days later Dirksen, who had succeeded Walroth as head of the eastern division of the German Foreign Office earlier in the year, was appointed German Ambassador in Moscow in succession to Brockdorff-Rantzau. The negotiations on technical points of the trade agreement seem to have been reasonably brief and business-like. The vexed question of the right of transit was settled by an amendment of the relevant decree permitting transit of goods across Soviet territory from any country having diplomatic relations or a trade agreement with the USSR to any other country in the same situation.[79] The thorniest issue was the declaration demanded of the German Government dissociating it from the bankers' committee. By the middle of December 1928, the delegations in Moscow had agreed on a text which included an undertaking by the German Government "to strive as far as possible to prevent" any "unfavourable consequences arising from the action of the bankers". But Stresemann once more cavilled at this text, and counter-proposals were put forward.[80] In the end Litvinov was unwilling to delay signature of the agreement by insistence on this somewhat empty promise. On December 21, 1928, a protocol was signed recording agreement, in eight sections, on various points of interpretation and amplification of the treaty of October 12, 1925. One of the sections included a German declaration to the effect that the question of pre-war debts could be dealt with "only in accordance with the perfectly clear provisions of the Rapallo treaty", and that "the action of the German banks" had "decidedly nothing in common with the attitude of the German Government in relation to the Rapallo treaty or to general political relations between Germany and the USSR".[81] On January 25, 1929, a convention was signed for the appointment, year by year, of a conciliation commission to deal with disputes between the two countries.[82]

After the scandalous revelations of December 1926,[83] the joint German–Soviet military establishments in the Soviet Union

[78] *Dokumenty Vneshnei Politiki SSSR*, xi (1966), 572–573; articles welcoming the resumption of negotiations appeared in both *Pravda* and *Izvestiya*, November 25. 1928.

[79] *Sobranie Zakonov, 1928*, No. 63, art. 587.

[80] *Dokumenty Vneshnei Politiki SSSR*, xi (1966), 616, 619–623.

[81] *Ibid.* xi, 623–626; for Litvinov's explanation see *ibid.* xi, 751, note 213.

[82] *Ibid.* xii (1967), 44–47.

[83] See pp. 38–46 above.

continued to prosper to the advantage and satisfaction of both parties. The high point of Soviet–German military collaboration was marked by a long visit of Blomberg, head of the Truppenamt, to the Soviet Union, lasting from August 19 to September 17, 1928. Lunev, the Soviet military attaché in Berlin, was attached to the mission and supervised the arrangements. Blomberg visited Lipetsk, Kama and Tomka,[84] as well as an artillery establishment near Voronezh at which experiments were conducted by German units in combined operations between aircraft and ground artillery and in the use of gas shells. He met all the principal Soviet military leaders, was enthusiastically received everywhere, and attended army manoeuvres near Kiev. He passed a generally favourable verdict on the achievements and potentialities of the Red Army, and ended his report on the visit with an emphatic recommendation that the collaboration between Reichswehr and Red Army should continue.[85] One question raised by Voroshilov proved embarrassing, and was significant of Germany's ambiguous policy. He asked that, in order to facilitate the study by the Red Army of the Reichswehr and its training methods, five Soviet officers should be attached for an indefinite period to the training establishments of the general staff, and five each for shorter periods to establishments for training of "technical troops" and in the use of "major weapons" (meaning probably tanks). Apart from the impression that the Red Army was extracting more benefit from the arrangements than the Reichswehr, the Reichswehr had always been apprehensive of the sinister influence of a large number of Red Army officers, as well as of the threat to secrecy. Blomberg replied that this was a question for the German Government, and added that the activities of Comintern continually gave rise to difficulties; the Red Army should exercise its influence in the proper quarters to see that no such difficulties occurred. In his report Blomberg recommended in principle the granting of these facilities both as a "justified counterpart" of the facilities enjoyed by the Reichswehr in the Soviet Union, and because "the resultant strengthening of the Red Army is in the German interest".[86] Exactly how far Voroshilov's request was met

[84] For these establishments see *Socialism in One Country, 1924–1926*, pp. 1012–1014.

[85] For Blomberg's report see *Auswärtiges Amt* 9480/276183–236.

[86] *Auswärtiges Amt*, 9480/276193–4, 276235.

is not recorded. Cooperation between the Red Army and the Reichswehr, though exposed to many strains, survived without substantial change from the earlier period, and was further developed and organized.[87] But attempts made in 1926 to establish similar naval cooperation ended in failure, and a half-hearted renewal of them in the spring of 1929 also proved fruitless.[88]

In less conspicuous fields cooperation continued to flourish.[89] At the height of the mutual exasperation engendered by the Shakhty affair, a joint Soviet–German scientific expedition to the Pamirs, organized on the Soviet side by the Academy of Sciences, set out from Moscow in July 1928.[90] In the same month a "week of Soviet historians", following the international historical congress in Oslo, was held in Berlin and received good publicity in the Soviet press: it was noted that the three principal Soviet participants, Pokrovsky, Adoratsky and Dubrovsky, delivered their papers in German.[91] A "week of German technology" was opened in Moscow in January 1929 by Stomonyakov, formerly head of the Soviet trade delegation in Berlin, and now an official of the People's Commissariat of Foreign Affairs, and graced by speeches from Kuibyshev and Lunacharsky, as well as from the German Ambassador and a number of German scientists and engineers.[92]

[87] For a memorandum of January 21, 1929, detailing the numbers of German officers, on the active list and "retired", to be employed in various capacities in the Soviet Union see *Auswärtiges Amt*, 9480/276155–8.

[88] See Note A, pp. 629–631 below.

[89] Dirksen, then a senior official in the eastern division of the German Foreign Office, wrote in a letter of December 16, 1926, to Schlesinger, the German economic expert in Moscow: "I am concerning myself energetically with the idea of closer cultural cooperation between Germany and Russia — chiefly for political reasons. For a mutual close cultural involvement [*Verflochtenheit*] is one of the two pillars which guarantee the maintenance of mutual relations when some incident or quarrel temporarily disturbs political relations; the other permanent pillar seems to be the economic connexion." He hoped to organize visits of Soviet scholars to Berlin (*Auswärtiges Amt*, 4829/242427–433). For a review of the extensive German sources on German–Soviet cultural relations under the Weimar republic see *Voprosy Istorii*, No. 10, 1963, pp. 71–83; see also *ibid.* No. 1, 1971, pp. 176–180.

[90] *Izvestiya*, May 25, July 19, 1928; the scientific results of the expedition were eventually published by its two German leaders, H. Ficker and W. Rickmers, in *Wissenschaftliche Ergebnisse der Altai-Expedition, 1928*, 6 vols (1932).

[91] *Izvestiya*, July 7, 18, 1928; the visit was described by two participants, by Mints in *Istorik-Marksist*, No. 9, 1928, pp. 84–88, and by Pashukanis in *Vestnik Kommunisticheskoi Akademii*, xxx (6) (1928), 238–246.

[92] *Izvestiya*, January 6, 20, 1928; *Dokumenty Vneshnei Politiki SSSR*, xii (1967), 12–15.

In April 1929 a delegation of officials and industrialists from East Prussia visited Moscow to proclaim the advantages of Soviet trade with East Prussia, and especially with the port of Königsberg.[93] The visits to the Soviet Union of large delegations of German workers, which had taken place in 1925, 1926 and 1927,[94] fitted less easily into the current pattern, and were not repeated. When the Berlin police fired on a procession of communist workers on May 1, 1929, with many casualties, this outrage provoked a worker's demonstration in Leningrad and an indignant speech by the ever tactless Voroshilov. But German protests against this reaction were met by the usual bland assurance of lack of responsibility for Comintern and trade union activities; and the incident was not allowed to ruffle for long the calm surface of Soviet–German friendship.[95]

Soviet relations with Germany were closer and more intimate than with any other country. The constant acrimony of discussions and negotiations between them was the reverse side of a degree of mutual understanding which was almost completely lacking in Soviet relations with western countries, and of an underlying sense of common interest—the famous "spirit of Rapallo"—which, though challenged by Locarno and by the increasingly western orientation of German foreign policy under Stresemann, was only slowly eroded. Germany's improved relations with the western world had shifted somewhat the balance of power. During Blomberg's visit to the Soviet Union, it was Voroshilov who assured him that "*in the event of a Polish attack on Germany, Russia was ready to give every help*", and insistently demanded to know whether German support would be forthcoming "*in the event of a Polish attack on the Soviet Union*";

[93] *Izvestiya*, April 7, 1929; see quotations from the report of the delegation in A. Anderle, *Die Deutsche Rapallo-Politik* (1962), p. 221, and from Soviet and German archives in A. Yoffe, *Vneshnyaya Politika Sovetskogo Soyuza* (1968), p. 83.

[94] See pp. 400–401, 430–431 below.

[95] *Dokumenty Vneshnei Politiki SSSR*, xii (1967), 368, 372, 744, note 47, 758, note 95; for this incident see p. 458 below. Dirksen argued against "a policy of resentment towards Russia" and pointed out that the police had not been able to prove official complicity in the demonstration (quoted from the Dirksen archives in A. Anderle, *Die Deutsche Rapallo-Politik* (1962), p. 222).

it was Blomberg who evaded the awkward question by saying that this was a matter for the political authorities.[96] Germany had now the greater freedom of manoeuvre. But that freedom was still strictly limited. In June 1928 the situation was summed up in a report of the Soviet Ambassador in Paris more frankly than in any published document:

> Germany continues to sit between two chairs. However much she desires to sit more firmly on the western chair, the time for this has not yet arrived.... Eastern support is necessary to Germany both politically and economically.

But it was open to the Soviet Union to execute a corresponding manoeuvre:

> By strengthening our commercial and economic relations with Great Britain and France, we at the same time use this to give Germany an exemplary lesson and issue a warning to her.[97]

Stresemann continued to insist that Germany's "wretched situation as an unarmed country in Central Europe" obliged her to maintain friendly relations with all neighbouring states.[98]

Nevertheless the year 1929 witnessed an acceleration of the progressive decline in the ardour and exclusiveness of Soviet–German relations. In the negotiations of the first months of 1928 it had been assumed that the revision of the trade agreement would lead to the granting of further credits to cover more extensive Soviet orders from German industry.[99] When negotiations were resumed in November 1928, the technical revision of the treaty was hurried through, and the question of credits left for future settlement, though Stomonyakov, the leader of the Soviet delegation, told his German partner that it was intended to order ready-made goods in Germany for the peasant market in time for the next harvest.[100] During the first three months of the new year no progress was made. Then, on April 12, 1929, Dirksen broached the question casually with Stomonyakov, who brought Mikoyan into the conversation. Hesitations were apparent on both sides,

[96] *Auswärtiges Amt*, 9480/276191.
[97] *Dokumenty Vneshnei Politiki SSSR*, xi (1966), 393–394.
[98] Speech of January 25, 1929, in foreign affairs commission of the Reichstag quoted from archives in A. Anderle, *Die Deutsche Rapallo-Politik* (1962), p. 219.
[99] See p. 50 above.
[100] *Dokumenty Vneshnei Politiki SSSR*, xii (1967), 748, note 54.

while each blamed the other for the delay. Stomonyakov observed that the Soviet Union no longer suffered from "a thirst for credits". He complained of the high cost of the 300 million mark credits of 1926–1927, and observed that the visiting British delegation of industrialists held out hopes of more favourable terms of credit in Great Britain, and that credits were also being offered by American exporters. Soviet credit in world markets now stood higher than in 1926, and the Soviet Union was eager to escape from a position of exclusive dependence on the German connection. Germany was reluctant, at a crucial moment in the reparations negotiations for the Young plan, to be seen granting lavish loans and credits to the Soviet Union; on the other hand, the prospect of an American invasion of the Soviet market at the expense of German interests was also unattractive.[101]

A few days later Schlesinger put concrete proposals to Stomonyakov. A comprehensive loan from the banks would take the place of credits on specific orders. The German Government, which had guaranteed the earlier credits up to a limit of 60 per cent, would guarantee the loan up to the same limit; the Soviet Government was asked to guarantee 25 per cent, and the remaining 15 per cent could be easily covered. A total of 500 million marks was mentioned, but the duration of the loan was apparently undefined.[102] This provoked Soviet counter-proposals which envisaged a loan of 200 million marks and credits of 300 millions, both for ten years; the German share in the guarantee was to be increased to 75 per cent, the Soviet share reduced to 10 per cent.[103] Once again the negotiations ran into a dead end. Germany, throughout the summer of 1929, was preoccupied by the vital issues of the Young Plan. The Bank of International Settlements to be set up under the plan was suspect in Moscow as the instrument of a united financial front against the Soviet Union, into which Germany had been lured — a symptom of "the strengthening of anti-Soviet tendencies in Germany".[104] *Izvestiya* celebrated the tenth anniversary of the Versailles treaty by featuring Wilson's fourteen points, the speech which Brockdorff-Rantzau had planned to deliver in the Weimar as-

[101] *Ibid.* xii, 140–147; for the visiting British delegation see pp. 33–34 above.
[102] *Dokumenty Vneshnei Politiki SSSR*, xii (1967), 191–200.
[103] *Ibid.* xii, 236–246.
[104] *Ibid.* xii, 370, 464–465; for a retrospective review of the failure of the credit negotiations see *ibid.* xii, 645–651.

sembly rejecting the treaty, and several articles denouncing it — a silent reproach to Germany for her present docility in face of her conquerors.[105] When Stresemann died on October 3, 1929, Germany was well set on the path of reconciliation with the west, which led to the evacuation of the Rhineland by allied troops in June 1930, nearly five years before the date fixed by the treaty. Meanwhile, the world economic crisis, beginning in the autumn of 1929, swept away much of the débris of the past and opened a new period in the relations of the Soviet Union with Germany, as with other countries.

[105] *Izvestiya*, June 28, 1929.

CHAPTER 60

RELATIONS WITH FRANCE

EFFORTS continued for some time to revive the languishing Franco-Soviet negotiations on debts and credits.[1] On June 7, 1926, the Soviet delegation presented to the conference a detailed schedule of the credits which the Soviet Government hoped to receive from France in the next three years, and the corresponding orders which would be placed with French industry. Rakovsky repeated once more his plea not to allow "the dead to strangle the living, the economic development and credit of the USSR to be paralysed by the question of the debts of the former régime, our peasant masses to work for the past and not for the future". But the deadlock over the debts was unresolved. A week later it was decided formally to adjourn the conference till November, with the proviso that unofficial talks might continue in the meanwhile.[2] At this point a ministerial crisis led to a reshuffle of Briand's government which brought in the veteran Caillaux as Minister of Finance. Since Caillaux had been concerned in the flotation of some of the French loans to the Tsarist government, and had expressed himself in intransigent terms on the debt question, this did not seem a good omen; and the signature on June 10, 1926, of a Franco-Rumanian treaty, containing a mutual obligation to consult in the event of a threat to the "legitimate national interests" of either or to "the order established by treaties", furnished a fresh bone of contention.[3]

Briand clearly desired to avoid a break. At a meeting with

[1] See *Socialism in One Country, 1924–1926*, Vol. 3, pp. 424–425.

[2] *Cahiers du Monde Russe et Soviétique*, i, No. 4 (July–December 1960), pp. 593–594, based in part on the unpublished De Monzie papers; the schedule of June 7, 1926, is in *Dokumenty Vneshnei Politiki SSSR*, xi (1964), 301–303.

[3] The Soviet Government, apprised by the French Ambassador in Moscow of its terms, protested in a note of October 2, 1926, that the French Government, "by proclaiming its common interest with Rumania without any reservations about Bessarabia, supports the aggression and annexationist tendencies of the ruling circles of Rumania" (*ibid.* ix, 431–432, 472–473); when the treaty was published, the Soviet Government also published its protest (*Izvestiya*, January 22, 1927).

Rakovsky on July 13, 1926, he reviewed in a notably conciliatory spirit the outstanding questions between the two countries. He declared himself willing to negotiate a non-aggression pact, hinting that this might be the starting-point of a broader agreement to include Germany. He denied that the Franco-Rumanian treaty guaranteed possession of Bessarabia; and he once more promised the return of the fleet at Bizerta, and the liquidation of a Georgian mission in Paris, of whose activities the Soviet embassy had complained. Finally, he promised a meeting in two days' time on the debt question with himself, De Monzie and Caillaux.[4] When the meeting took place, Caillaux was less hostile than had been feared. He was willing to offer credits in return for a debt settlement, and broached the question of oil. A project was discussed under which a monopoly of the French market would be granted to Soviet oil and France would obtain oil concessions in the USSR. But this, as Rakovsky pointed out, meant a battle with Standard Oil and Shell; and it is difficult to believe that it was ever taken seriously.[5] On the following evening, July 16, 1926, Rakovsky and De Monzie met to draft an agreed protocol on debts and credits.[6] Rakovsky now left for Moscow to attend a fateful session of the party central committee;[7] and in his absence the political scene in France, dominated by the financial crisis, was dramatically transformed. The Briand government fell; and on July 20, 1926, Herriot formed a government with De Monzie as Minister of Finance. Any hopes engendered in Moscow by this exciting news were, however, premature. Herriot failed to win a majority in the Chamber, and was succeeded two days later by a ministry of all the talents under Poincaré, pledged above all to revive the flagging economy and the declining franc. Though Briand remained as the irreplaceable Minister for Foreign Affairs, the appointment of

[4] *Dokumenty Vneshnei Politiki SSSR*, ix (1964), 350. For the Bizerta fleet see *Socialism in One Country, 1924–1926*, Vol. 3, pp. 36, 38–39; Orjonikidze still complained at the fourth Union Congress of Soviets in April 1927 of the presence of headquarters of a "Georgian democratic republic" in Paris (*SSSR: 4 S"ezd Sovetov* (1927), pp. 59–60).

[5] *Dokumenty Vneshnei Politiki SSSR*, ix (1964), 363–366.

[6] *Ibid.* ix, 371–372; the draft, dated July 17, 1926, is preserved in the De Monzie papers (*Cahiers du Monde Russe et Soviétique*, i, No. 4 (July–December 1960), pp. 595–596). For a rather confused account of the events of these two days, doubtless derived from Rakovsky, see L. Fischer, *The Soviets in World Affairs* (1930), ii, 620.

[7] For this session see Vol. 2, pp. 30–33.

Poincaré, whose rôle in wrecking the Genoa conference of 1922 was well known,[8] seemed to close the prospect of Franco-Soviet accommodation.

The year which followed Rakovsky's return to Paris on August 2, 1926, was a time of steady deterioration in Franco-Soviet relations. The debts and credits negotiations, though not formally broken off, were in abeyance. Rakovsky's first interview with Poincaré on August 25, 1926, was marked by "dryness and formality"; at a second, on January 27, 1927, Poincaré was "very agreeable", but confined the discussion to such questions as the Bizerta fleet and the continued recognition by the French authorities of the Georgian mission in Paris and Tsarist consulates in various cities.[9] In October 1926 Rakovsky had told the press that the debt negotiations were so far advanced that it would be possible to take up the question of credits.[10] But, when on March 19, 1927, the conference on debts and credits at last reassembled, De Monzie threatened that, failing a better Soviet offer on debt payments, negotiations would be suspended indefinitely.[11] A revised schedule of payments submitted by the Soviet delegation to a further meeting on March 25, 1927, was pronounced by the French delegation to be no improvement on the offer of July 17, 1926; and the exchange ended with a formal letter of April 1, 1927, from Rakovsky to De Monzie, refusing to make any advance on the previous offer, but hinting that such might be forthcoming if more generous credits were available.[12]

By the spring of 1927, relations had been further clouded, and the last hopes of a settlement dimmed, by the international situation. Worsening relations between Great Britain and the Soviet Union made their impact on French policy and French opinion; and the activities of the French Communist Party provoked an increasingly sharp reaction.[13] On April 22, 1927, Sarraut, the Minister for Colonies, in a much applauded speech in the Chamber, eulogized French colonial policy as no longer a mercantile operation but "a work of humanity", and eloquently explained that, since "France represents in the world the moral force certainly most capable of

[8] *Izvestiya*, July 29, 1926, reviewed his record in despondent terms.

[9] *Dokumenty Vneshnei Politiki SSSR*, x (1965), 32–34, 624–625, note 10.

[10] *Izvestiya*, October 8, 1926.

[11] *Dokumenty Vneshnei Politiki SSSR*, x (1965), 120–121, 133.

[12] *Ibid.* x, 122–124, 132–133.

[13] See pp. 488–489 below.

resisting victoriously the world-wide enterprise of national and social disintegration out of which the leaders of Muscovite communism hope to erect the new imperialism of some immense Slav hegemony", Moscow was naturally bent on the destruction of this moral force. He concluded with the resounding cry: "Communism — there is the enemy." When Rakovsky, on June 30, 1927, requested De Monzie to reconvene the conference on debts and credits, he met with a blank refusal.[14] It was expected in some quarters, and feared in Moscow, that France, and perhaps Germany, would follow the British example in severing diplomatic relations with the Soviet Government. But, when Chicherin, who was on leave in France, visited Berthelot and Briand on May 23 and 24, 1927, both assured him that France would not participate in any aggressive action against the Soviet Union; Briand referred to divisions of opinion among British "magnates" and in the government, and thought that the British action would not be carried any further.[15] Conversations between the three Foreign Ministers in Geneva in June 1927 showed that neither Briand nor Stresemann was disposed to follow the British course.[16]

The situation was, therefore, already delicate when Rakovsky committed an indiscretion which arose from his loyalty to Trotsky and the Russian party opposition. At the session of the party central committee in Moscow in July–August 1927, the stormiest debates raged round international issues, and Trotsky faced charges of defeatism and disloyalty. Rakovsky took no part in the debate. But when the opposition, in a short-sighted attempt to appease the majority, issued on August 8, 1927, a declaration proclaiming and defining its fidelity to party and state in the sphere of international relations, Rakovsky signed with the rest. The declaration contained two particularly incriminating slogans:

> Defeat of all bourgeois states which wage war against the Soviet Union; every honest proletarian in the capitalist countries must work actively for the defeat of his government.
>
> Transfer to the Red Army of all foreign soldiers who do not wish to aid the slave-masters of their own countries.[17]

[14] Klyuchnikov and Sabanin, *Mezhdunarodnaya Politika*, iii, i (1928), 396–397.

[15] *Dokumenty Vneshnei Politiki SSSR*, x (1965), 224–235; Poincaré whom Chicherin visited on May 24, 1927, spoke much more critically of Soviet attitudes (*ibid.* x, 636, note 48).

[16] See p. 27 above.

[17] For this document see Vol. 2, p. 32.

Such routine pronouncements in the idiom of the Communist International normally aroused little attention. But a few days later the French Ambassador in Moscow registered a protest against this "inadmissible manifestation" by a diplomat accredited to the French Government; and after some argument Chicherin handed to Herbette a statement to the effect that the Soviet Government "condemns in the clearest and most formal manner the idea that one of its representatives could organize on French territory propaganda for insurrection or desertion". The French Government took note of the statement in a *communiqué* of September 4, 1927; Rakovsky in Paris made a declaration in the same sense; and the incident appeared to be closed.[18] The Italian Government had remained indifferent to the signature of the same document by Kamenev, then Soviet Ambassador in Rome.

Unfortunately this episode combined with several others to fan the mood of mutual exasperation and mistrust. In the summer of 1927 the English popular Sunday newspaper *Referee* published a series of interviews with leading Frenchmen. On August 21, 1927, it was the turn of Foch, who indulged in nostalgic recollections of February 1919, when he had told the Allied governments that, "if only the states surrounding Russia were provided with ammunition and the sinews of war", he would undertake "to stamp out the Bolshevist menace once for all". But he also looked forward to the future. A main reason for admitting Germany to the League of Nations was the belief that "she would align herself with the rest of Europe against the Bolshevists". Foch foresaw the day "when she will have to turn westward and so help us to defeat the common enemy", and urged France to follow the British example by breaking off relations with Moscow. Foch was now an old man. The scant attention paid by the rest of the press to his pronouncement suggests that it may have caused some embarrassment in official quarters. But *Pravda* on August 24, 1927, on the basis of telegraphic reports, announced that "Marshal Foch openly summons the bourgeoisie of all countries to war against the USSR", including a "hunger blockade" of its 150 million inhabitants, and in a leader on the following day treated the pronouncement as a showing up of western disclaimers

[18] *L'Europe Nouvelle*, No. 504, October 8, 1927, p. 1254; Rakovsky made a personal statement in similar terms which appeared in the *Manchester Guardian*, September 6, 1927.

of hostile intentions against the Soviet Union.[19] Marty, the French communist, wrote a letter from the Santé prison fiercely denouncing Foch as an instigator of war against the Soviet Union, which was published in *Humanité* on August 26, 1927, and led to Marty's indictment for slander. This was followed by a campaign in the French party; and memories of the incident rankled for a long time.[20] At the moment of the Foch interview, the execution of Sacco and Vanzetti provoked wild demonstrations in Paris as in other capitals.[21] A march of the American Legion through Paris was looked on as a counter-demonstration; and the occasion was chosen to expel the Tass correspondent from Paris on a charge of sending misleading reports to Moscow.[22]

In this heady atmosphere, the comparatively polite diplomatic exchanges about Rakovsky's indiscretion were succeeded by a press campaign against the person of the Soviet Ambassador so sudden and so violent as to suggest some concerted directive.[23] Briand's hand was forced, during his absence at the Assembly of the League of Nations in Geneva, by a semi-official statement issued through the Havas agency on September 17, 1927, to the effect that the council of ministers was agreed on the desirability of demanding Rakovsky's recall, though a final decision would await Briand's return.[24] While the Soviet leaders had shown some alacrity to disavow an indiscretion emanating from a member of the opposition, the forced recall of a Soviet Ambassador was an unwelcome blow. Litvinov in an interview in *Izvestiya* scouted the idea that the campaign was directed against Rakovsky personally or had anything to do with Franco-Soviet relations. It was an

[19] The reference to Foch's pronouncement as a "speech" suggests that information about it in Moscow was sketchy.

[20] At the sixth congress of Comintern in July 1928 the British delegate, reporting on the danger of war, congratulated the French communists on having "carried out a mass campaign in connexion with the notorious interview of General Foch" (*Stenograficheskii Otchet VI Kongressa Kominterna* (1929), ii, 32).

[21] See p. 277 below.

[22] *Izvestiya*, September 1, 1927.

[23] L. Fischer, *The Soviets in World Affairs* (1930), ii, 712–713, no doubt reporting Rakovsky's view, attributed the inspiration of the campaign, in part to Poincaré, in part to Deterding and British oil interests; Rakovsky had been associated with projects to capture the French market for Soviet oil (see p. 62 above). An article in *Humanité*, September 12, 1927, by M. C.[achin] described Rakovsky's expulsion as an act of revenge for the Soviet refusal to grant oil concessions to Great Britain and to Royal Dutch.

[24] *Le Temps*, September 18, 1927; *Izvestiya*, September 18, 1927. Officials of the Quai d'Orsay were at no pains to conceal Briand's annoyance (*Auswärtiges Amt*, 648/207260–2).

attempt "to destroy the argreement which was in sight, and to realize in France the anti-Soviet policy of Great Britain". Its instigators could be pilloried without qualification as "instigators of war, fomenters of a world conflagration".[25] A last-minute attempt on the Soviet side to stave off the demand by an improved offer for a settlement on debts and credits[26] was ignored; this was no longer what the quarrel was about. On October 1, 1927, Herbette presented the demand for Rakovsky's recall. Chicherin claimed that the incident had been closed by the French *communiqué* of September 4, 1927, and continued to haggle till the demand was formulated in still more categorical terms in a note of October 7.[27] The question was submitted to the Politburo on October 12, 1927, and an angry note of acquiescence handed to Herbette on the same day.[28] The Soviet Government apparently invited Rakovsky to lead the Soviet disarmament delegation at Geneva. But he preferred to keep his hands free to support the opposition in its critical hour.[29]

Only one faint gleam of hope survived the collapse of Franco-

[25] *Izvestiya*, September 16, 1927.

[26] For Rakovsky's letter to De Monzie of September 21, 1927, see *Dokumenty Vneshnei Politiki SSSR*, x (1965), 384–387. Litvinov in a statement on the following day professed to believe that agreement had been reached (*ibid.* x, 392); this provoked a sharp *démenti* from the French Government (*L'Europe Nouvelle*, No. 504, October 8, 1927, p. 1355). A paradoxical episode was the charge levelled by the opposition at the Soviet leaders of readiness to compromise on war debts: Bukharin at the presidium of IKKI on September 27, 1927, called this "a deliberate *lie*" (*Kommunisticheskii Internatsional*, No. 41 (115), 1927, pp. 8–9; for this session see Vol. 2, p. 36). For the opposition's preoccupation at this time with the debts question see a memorandum to the Politburo of October 12, 1927, signed by Zinoviev, Trotsky, Smilga and Evdokimov (Trotsky archives, T 1028).

[27] This correspondence was published in *Le Temps*, October 9, 1927, and is in Klyuchnikov and Sabanin, *Mezhdunarodnye Politika*, iii, i (1928), 405–406; for an interview given by Chicherin to a correspondent of *Le Soir* see *Izvestiya*, October 6, 1927. As Karakhan said later, Chicherin "made a show of not understanding" till the demand was made categorical (*ibid.* November 26, 1927).

[28] Klyuchnikov and Sabanin, *Mezhdunarodnaya Politika*, iii, i (1928), 407–408; none of this correspondence appeared in *Dokumenty Vneshnei Politiki SSSR*, x (1965). The atmosphere in Moscow was reflected in telegrams from Brockdorff Rantzau to Berlin, based on conversations with Litvinov and Chicherin (*Auswärtiges Amt*, 287/099449–50, 099458–9); *Le Temps*, October 15, 1927, exulting in the Soviet humiliation, printed the Soviet note, which also appeared in *Izvestiya*, October 14, 1927.

[29] L. Fischer, *The Soviets in World Affairs* (1930), ii, 708; the information must have come from Rakovsky himself. For Rakovsky's complaint that the government did not defend him strongly enough see Vol. 2, p. 45.

Soviet relations marked by Rakovsky's departure from Paris. Chicherin, in the statement which he made to the press during his visit to Paris in December 1925, stressing the unwillingness of the Soviet Union to join the League of Nations, had pointed to the alternative method of "direct and immediate agreements with other countries", and added that, "in my view, we are entering on a period of direct agreements between our government and the governments of other countries".[30] This vague pronouncement was explained and exemplified by the treaty of non-intervention and neutrality signed in Paris two days later with Turkey, which was hailed by Soviet diplomats and publicists as a model for future agreements between the Soviet Union and other countries.[31] In Europe, the Soviet–Lithuanian treaty of September 28, 1926,[32] fell into the same pattern. No formal proposal seems to have been made to the French Government till Chicherin, at the end of August 1927, parrying Herbette's protest against Rakovsky's indiscretion, dwelt on the pacific character of Franco-Soviet relations, and added that Rakovsky was empowered to enter at any time into negotiations for a treaty of friendship, non-aggression and non-intervention.[33] Rather unaccountably, the *communiqué* of the French council of ministers of September 17, 1927, foreshadowing the demand for Rakovsky's recall, welcomed the idea of "negotiations for a pact of non-aggression proposed by the Russians", pointing, however, by way of a further hint at the importance of removing Rakovsky, to the necessity of "assuring in advance the realization of all the conditions likely to make the negotiations possible". This polite response, designed perhaps to mask the harshness of Rakovsky's expulsion, was hailed by *Izvestiya* as "a victory for common sense",[34] and created some stir in German diplomatic circles. Brockdorff-Rantzau expressed his alarm to Chicherin; and Soviet assurances were received both in Berlin and by the German Embassy in Moscow that the whole proposal had been no more than a "tactical manoeuvre", and that the favourable French reply had come as a surprise.[35] This

[30] *Dokumenty Vneshnei Politiki SSSR*, viii (1963), 721; for this interview see *Socialism in One Country, 1924–1926*, Vol. 3, pp. 421–422.

[31] See *ibid.* Vol. 3, pp. 641–642. [32] See p. 79 below.

[33] For Chicherin's statement see p. 65 above.

[34] *Izvestiya*, September 18, 1927.

[35] *Dokumenty Vneshnei Politiki SSSR*, x (1965), 384; *Auswärtiges Amt*, 287/099355–8, 099435–9.

was partly, but not wholly, sincere. While the bitterness of the Rakovsky affair precluded for some time to come any fresh overture, Soviet diplomacy always kept in reserve the option of a *rapprochement* with France to balance excessive dependence on an increasingly problematical German alliance.

After the alarms and excursions of 1927, the year 1928 was a blank period in Franco-Soviet relations. The agreement on debts and credits was relegated to the limbo of discarded projects, from which it never emerged. Dovgalevsky, an old party member who had held diplomatic posts in Sweden and Japan, arrived to succeed Rakovsky early in January 1928; and Briand promised to curb the press campaign which had started against him.[36] Poincaré, when he received Dovgalevsky on January 29, 1928, firmly insisted on regarding the conference on debts and credits as ended; if the Soviet mission chose to retain its experts as members of its staff, it was free to do so.[37] Polite assurances were exchanged with Briand on the proposed non-aggression pact, but without effect.[38] The shipment to two New York banks in February 1928 of a consignment of Soviet gold to the value of $5 million led to an awkward episode. The American Treasury advised the State Department to give no assurance that "the title to Soviet gold will not be subject to attack, internationally or otherwise"; and on March 6, 1928, the French Ambassador in Washington addressed a note to the State Department supporting a claim to the gold put forward by the Banque de France, which had held bank deposits in Petrograd before 1917 amounting to 52 million francs. The American Treasury, faced with a dispute about ownership, refused to allow the Assay Office to handle the consignment.[39] The news was greeted with indignation in Moscow. Sheinman, the president of Gosbank, pointed out that Soviet gold had been shipped to New York in 1922 to pay for relief supplies, and had been received without demur; and Khinchuk drew attention to the damage which a seizure of the gold would do to Soviet–American trade.[40] On March 18, 1928, Herbette seems to have

[36] *Dokumenty Vneshnei Politiki SSSR*, xi (1966), 13.

[37] *Ibid.* xi, 49–50.

[38] *Ibid.* xi, 79.

[39] *Foreign Relations of the United States, 1928*, iii (1943), 827–831.

[40] *Izvestiya*, March 16, 29, 1928; a memorandum by Sheinman of March 12, 1928, is in the Gumberg archives.

denied to Chicherin that any such note had been sent; and five days later Chicherin made a formal enquiry of the French Government about the terms of the note of March 6. A belated and evasive reply of April 10, 1928, admitted that the Banque de France had taken legal action to establish its claim to the gold, and pretended that the French note of March 6, 1928, had been simply a request for information about the attitude of the State Department.[41] Four days later a Tass *communiqué* pointed out that the French Government had returned no direct answer to the Soviet enquiry whether it supported the bank's claim.[42] The issue of ownership went to the courts.[43] But on April 6, 1928, the banks, unwilling to put up with the delay, shipped the gold back to Germany, where it could be easily disposed of; and this bizarre episode provoked comment in American financial circles on the anomalous situation created by the non-recognition of the Soviet Government, as well as a disclaimer of responsibility from the State Department.[44] But the French Government remained unmoved, and, reported Dovgalevsky in June 1928, "continues to pass over the Soviet question in silence".[45]

Nevertheless, the climate improved somewhat during the year. Among other symptoms of a revival of interest in Franco-Soviet trade, a formal meeting between Soviet representatives and important French industrialists and financiers was held on November 22, 1928, to discuss prospects; and a further meeting was projected.[46] But French industrialists carried less weight than their

[41] *Dokumenty Vneshnei Politiki SSSR*, xi (1966), 230–231.

[42] *Ibid.* xi, 271–274.

[43] Nearly a year passed before the court finally rejected the French claim (*Izvestiya*, March 24, 1929).

[44] *Dokumenty Vneshnei Politiki SSSR*, xi (1966), 262–264.

[45] *Ibid.* xi, 392.

[46] *Ibid.* xi, 627, 742, note 215. Franco-Soviet trade tended to increase during this period, but never reached significant dimensions; the following were the official Soviet figures (in thousands of rubles at current prices):

	Soviet Exports to France	Percentage of Total Soviet Exports	Soviet Imports from France	Percentage of Total Soviet Imports
1925/26	39,752	5·7	19,323	2·6
1926/27	54,101	6·7	22,196	3·1
1927/28	40,568	5·1	35,850	3·8

(*Sotsialisticheskoe Stroitel'stvo SSSR* (1935), pp. 587–588, 591–592).

British counterparts; and this initiative appears to have had no sequel. A certain flurry of interest, apparently provoked by the disarmament discussions in Geneva,[47] marked the closing weeks of the year. *Izvestiya*, in an angry article of December 4, 1928, quoted an alleged remark of Poincaré that, if "our Soviet friends" had really agreed to universal disarmament, he pledged himself to follow their example, and taunted him with his hypocritical ignorance of the Soviet proposals at Geneva. On the same day, in a debate in the Chamber on foreign affairs, Briand, goaded by a remark of Cachin about the war being "prepared" against Russia, retorted that "Poland and Rumania are not without anxiety about Russia's intentions, and this can very well be explained".[48] Litvinov a few days later, speaking in the TsIK of the USSR, dealt polemically with Poincaré's pretences and with Briand's mention of Poland and Rumania, and expressed regret that the proposals for a non-aggression pact had apparently been forgotten.[49] But this was now routine business of no particular account. Chicherin, who found himself at this moment in Berlin, gave an interview to the press on foreign relations, in which the references to France, doubtless designed to impress a German audience, were surprisingly friendly. He thought that France had begun to "understand the international significance of the USSR", and that, though complicated economic negotiations were bound to take a long time, political relations had "become far more satisfactory".[50] Briand in conversation with the Soviet Ambassador in January 1929 abounded in expressions of good will, but had no concrete proposals to make for a non-aggression pact or a trade agreement.[51] Nothing else moved. De Monzie, since the departure of Rakovsky, had become involved in financial schemes for trade with the Soviet Union allegedly designed to break the monopoly of foreign trade; and, when early in 1929 he expressed a wish to visit the Soviet Union, Dovgalevsky spoke of him as "an unprincipled fantasist", and

[47] See p. 115 below.

[48] *Journal Officiel: Chambre des Députés*, No. 85, December 4, 1928, p. 3220; Briand, in his reply to the debate (*ibid.* pp. 3229–3236), did not mention the Soviet Union at all.

[49] *4 Sessiya Tsentral'nogo Ispolnitel'nogo Komiteta Soyuza SSR 4 Sozyva* 1928, No. 19, pp. 8–10.

[50] *Izvestiya*, December 3, 1928.

[51] *Dokumenty Vneshnei Politiki SSSR*, xii (1967), 16–19.

promised Litvinov to discourage him from making the journey.[52] Rykov, reporting on foreign affairs to the fifth Union Congress of Soviets in May 1929, described Franco-Soviet relations as being in "a state of semi-animation, a peculiar kind of prolonged sleep".[53] It required a major shift in the balance of forces in Europe, three years later, to bring them back to life.

[52] *Ibid.* xii, 64; Rykov at the fifth Union Congress of Soviets in May 1929 called him "the ideologue of the anti-Soviet bloc" (*SSSR: 5 S"ezd Sovetov* (1929), No. 1, p. 9). A letter from Trotsky in exile is preserved in the De Monzie papers, thanking De Monzie for his "special kindness to Rakovsky" (*Cahiers du Monde Russe et Soviétique*, i, No. 4 (July–December 1960), p. 598, note 39).

[53] *SSSR: 5 S"ezd Sovetov* (1929), p. 27.

CHAPTER 61

RELATIONS WITH ITALY

SOVIET–ITALIAN relations survived Mussolini's assumption of power, and received a certain fillip from Italy's *de jure* recognition of the Soviet Union, simultaneously with that of Great Britain, in February 1924. But Mussolini's hesitant decision to participate in the Locarno agreements came as a disappointment;[1] and henceforth Italy seemed to be ranged with the western Powers against the Soviet Union. On September 16, 1926, Italy concluded a treaty of friendship with Rumania. This inevitably brought up the question of the treaty of October 28, 1920, by which the Allied Powers had assigned Bessarabia to Rumania, and which had never acquired legal force owing to the failure of Italy and Japan to ratify it. A note signed by Mussolini and attached to the treaty of friendship announced the intention to ratify the Bessarabian treaty "when it becomes possible to do so without prejudice to Italy's general interests".[2] This equivocal phrase excited alarm and indignation in Moscow. A few days later, when the Soviet *polpred* submitted to the Italian Government a draft non-aggression treaty on the Soviet–Turkish model, a special clause was inserted in it by which each party bound itself not to ratify treaties or obligations inimical to the other party; and Mussolini increased Soviet mistrust of his intentions by rejecting the draft explicitly on the score of this clause.[3] The Soviet Government pursued the point with the passion which the Bessarabian question never failed to arouse. On October 6, 1926, the Soviet *polpred* in Rome protested against the assurance given to the Rumanian Government, and declared that ratification of the Bessarabian treaty would constitute "an infringement of the sovereign rights and interests of the Soviet Union". Mussolini

[1] See *Socialism in One Country, 1924–1926*, Vol. 3, p. 273.

[2] The text of the Italo-Rumanian treaty of September 16, 1926, and of the exchange of notes about Bessarabia, was printed in *Mirovoe Khozyaistvo i Mirovaya Politika*, No. 9, 1926, pp. 147–148; for the treaty of October 28, 1920, see *Socialism in One Country, 1924–1926*, Vol. 3, p. 250, note 6.

[3] *Dokumenty Vneshnei Politiki SSSR*, ix (1964), 452–453, 734, note 86.

displayed real or feigned annoyance, explained that the formula in the note to the Rumanian Government left him free "to postpone ratification to infinity", and demanded that the Soviet note should be withdrawn. The only concession he obtained was to delay its publication.[4] When the Italian–Rumanian treaty was published in January 1927, the Soviet note of October 6, 1926, appeared belatedly in *Izvestiya.*[5]

Some consternation was aroused in diplomatic circles when Italy on November 27, 1926, signed a treaty with Albania, which constituted a virtual Italian protectorate over Albania. Chicherin, however, in his far-ranging press interview in Berlin on December 6, 1926, did not mention Albania, pointedly observed that "Italy's policy in the Balkan peninsula is Italy's own affair", and added that Italy's attitude to Rumania was the one blot on Soviet–Italian relations.[6] In the winter of 1926–1927 Soviet diplomacy was obsessed by the deterioration in Anglo-Soviet relations; and it seemed clear that Italy had been wooed on to the British side. Sinister significance was seen in a meeting between Mussolini and Chamberlain at Leghorn on September 30, 1926, at which host and guest made a parade of firm friendship. A visit to Mussolini in Rome in January 1927 by Churchill, the notorious protagonist of an anti-Soviet front in Great Britain, confirmed the worst suspicions in Moscow. By the beginning of March 1927, Anglo-Soviet relations were rapidly moving towards an inevitable rupture; and, when on March 7, 1927, the Italian Government officially informed the Soviet Government that it was about to ratify the Bessarabian treaty, Kamenev, newly installed as Soviet representative in Rome, diagnosed the act as "a continuation of the policy of encirclement and of Chamberlain's revenge".[7]

Once, however, the break with Great Britain had occurred, and

[4] *Ibid.* xii (1967), 480–483.

[5] *Izvestiya,* January 27, 1927.

[6] *Dokunenty Vneshnei Politiki SSSR,* ix (1964), 570; for Chicherin's interview see p. 7 above. Some enthusiasts in Comintern apparently called for "a boycott of Italy"; but Bukharin rejected the proposal in a speech of February 26, 1927, in the political secretariat, arguing that a break with Italy would further isolate the Soviet Union (J. Humbert-Droz, *Il Contrasto tra l'Internazionale e il PCI* (1969), p. 239 (Humbert-Droz archives, 0077)).

[7] *Dokumenty Vneshnei Politiki SSSR,* x (1965), 75–76; for the Italian note of March 7, 1927, and the Soviet reply see *ibid.* x, 109–111. A leading article in *Izvestiya,* March 10, 1927, connected the Italian ratification with the Chamberlain and Churchill visits.

Italy showed no more inclination than any other European Power to follow the British example, the heat went out of Soviet–Italian relations, which assumed their unruffled and unexciting course. Trade and concessions were the most common topic of diplomatic exchanges. In the summer of 1928, when an Italian airship exploring the polar regions suffered disaster, a Soviet expedition equipped with ice-breakers and aeroplanes successfully searched for, and rescued, the missing crew — an exploit which attracted world-wide publicity, and earned much prestige for Soviet expertise in the Arctic; the leaders of the Soviet team subsequently visited Italy and were enthusiastically received.[8] During this period intermittent reminders came from the Soviet side of the proposal for a non-aggression pact, but met with no response. At length, in December 1928, Mussolini explained bluntly that "the conclusion of a political treaty with the Soviet Union signifies for Italy a completely new orientation in the east and a rupture of political and economic links with England and France", and was unacceptable on that account.[9] Italy was at this time concerned to maintain good relations with the Soviet Union, a potential supplier of oil and coal, but only within such limits as might be imposed by more essential relations with the western Powers.

[8] *Dokumenty Vneshnei Politiki SSSR*, xi (1966), 373, 432–483, 738, note 160; xii (1967), 100–102, 737, note 29.
[9] *Ibid.* xi, 612.

CHAPTER 62

RELATIONS WITH EASTERN EUROPE

THE first reactions in Moscow to Pilsudski's *coup* of May 12, 1926, in Warsaw were guardedly neutral. *Pravda* on May 14, 1926, reported "the overturn [*perevorot*] in Poland" without comment. On the following day, Radek in an article in *Pravda*, while conceding that Pilsudski was "an exponent of bourgeois democratic tendencies", ominously remarked that he had been "recently thought to be *linked with England*". Official assurances of non-interference were given by Narkomindel, and a *communiqué* denied a rumour of a concentration of Soviet troops on the Polish frontier.[1] On May 17, 1926, *Izvestiya* hopefully believed that the *coup* meant "*a serious weakening of French influence in Poland*". But disenchantment quickly set in. Pilsudski's record was Russophobe as well as anti-Bolshevik. He might in the past have shown some resentment of French military tutelage. But the British Government had reacted sympathetically to his *coup*. The reaction of the Soviet press was now unconditionally hostile. A leading article in *Izvestiya* of May 22, 1926, headed "A Legend Destroyed", regretfully recorded that "Pilsudski, who proclaimed a campaign against Fascism, has quickly sought to come to terms with it". Radek in *Pravda* on May 28, 1926, dubbed Pilsudski "Napoleon IV". A few days later *Izvestiya* pronounced the lapidary verdict: "*Polish Fascism consecrates* [obretaet] *its hero*".[2] Speeches by Stalin and Bukharin on June 8, 1926, denounced Pilsudski as the enemy of the revolution, and censured the Polish party for the temporizing attitude initially adopted towards him.[3]

Soviet–Polish relations in the first months of 1926, already disturbed by the Polish–Rumanian treaty of March 26, 1926,[4] were

[1] *Dokumenty Vneshnei Politiki SSSR*, ix (1964), 274–275; Chicherin assured the German Ambassador on May 16, 1926, that Soviet policy was one of non-intervention and that no troops had been sent to the frontier (*Auswärtiges Amt*, 2945/572253–4).

[2] *Izvestiya*, June 1, 1926.

[3] For these speeches see p. 566 below.

[4] See *Socialism in One Country, 1924–1926*, Vol. 3, p. 447; on July 19, 1926, the communist deputy Sochacki made a violent speech in the Sejm

further complicated by the conflicting attempts of both parties to draw the small Baltic countries into their respective orbits of influence.[5] One of the last acts of the outgoing Polish Government in May 1926 had been to send an official named Janikowski on a mission to Latvia, Estonia and Finland with revised proposals to secure the friendly neutrality of these countries, if not their participation, in any war between Poland and the Soviet Union. This visit coincided with Soviet notes to the Latvian and Estonian Governments of May 21, 1926, submitting the draft of a non-aggression treaty based on previous discussions. The Estonian reply of May 26, 1926, ominously suggested that it might be necessary to consult other states; the Latvian reply of May 31, 1926, merely promised detailed examination of the proposals.[6] Caught between their two larger neighbours, the small countries hesitated. It was understood in Moscow that Latvia leaned towards the Soviet, and Estonia towards the Polish, side.[7] But neither was willing to proceed alone. Detailed discussions between Narkomindel and the Finnish minister in Moscow on outstanding questions, including the status of the Aland Islands, whose transfer to Finland Soviet Russia had refused to recognize in 1921, took place in the second half of June 1926; and the Soviet Government, in a note to the Finnish Government of July 12, 1926, agreed to the opening of negotiations in Helsinki for the settlement of these questions and for the conclusion of a non-aggression treaty.[8] But this initiative proved fruitless.[9]

against the ratification of the treaty, protesting against "the policy of forming a bloc of counter-revolutionary states directed against the USSR", and asserting that Poland had become "a marionette in the imperialist plans of England against the Soviet Union" (*Dokumenty i Materialy po Istorii Sovetsko-Pol'skikh Otnoshenii*, v (1967), 22–24).

[5] See *Socialism in One Country, 1924–1926*, Vol. 3, pp. 448–449.

[6] *Dokumenty Vneshnei Politiki SSSR*, ix (1964), 280–288; for previous discussions see *Socialism in One Country, 1924–1926*, Vol. 3, pp. 448–449.

[7] *Dokumenty Vneshnei Politiki SSSR*, ix (1964), 315, 729, note 64; Birk, the Estonian minister in Moscow, resigned his post in protest against the attitude of the Estonian Government, which he accused, in letters published in *Izvestiya*, of obstruction and of "backstairs negotiations with other states and with Poland" (*Izvestiya*, July 13, August 4, 1926).

[8] *Izvestiya*, July 18, 1926; *Dokumenty Vneshnei Politiki SSSR*, ix (1964), 343–346.

[9] For the breakdown of the negotiations for a treaty, differently explained by the two sides, but evidently due to Finnish objections, see *Izvestiya*, November 30, December 1, 1926.

Meanwhile Soviet–Polish negotiations were also at a standstill. On June 2, 1926, Zaleski, the new Polish Minister for Foreign Affairs, disclaimed personal responsibility for Janikowski's mission, and emphatically assured the Soviet representative that Poland had no designs hostile to the Soviet Union, but said in substance nothing new.[10] On July 14, 1926, the Polish chargé d'affaires in Moscow formally communicated to Chicherin a proposal of the Polish Government "to resume negotiations with the purpose of solving the task of the pacification of north-eastern Europe by concluding an agreement". He made it clear that what was in view was a multilateral pact which would take into account "the relation of Poland to the Baltic states". Chicherin curtly replied that the Soviet Union was ready for negotiations with Poland, but only "about Polish–Soviet relations, not about relations with third parties".[11] The deadlock was unbroken. When in August 1926 Zaleski expressed the desire to pay a courtesy visit to Moscow in return for Chicherin's visit to Warsaw in 1925, the Soviet Government issued a warm invitation, but added that it would be desirable to take the opportunity to sign a Soviet–Polish non-aggression treaty: otherwise the significance of the visit would be "minimal". A few days later Chicherin asked for a postponement of the visit on grounds of health; and Zaleski simultaneously withdrew the proposal on the plea of preparations for the forthcoming Assembly of the League of Nations.[12] This did not deter the Soviet Government from submitting to the Polish Government, on August 24, 1926, a draft treaty of non-aggression and neutrality, on the same lines as the drafts simultaneously submitted to Latvia and Estonia, and from publishing it in the press.[13] But renewed anger was aroused in Moscow by a press report that, during the League assembly in Geneva, the foreign ministers of Poland and the Baltic countries had held a "secret conference" to discuss their relations with the Soviet Union and their attitude to negotiations for non-aggression pacts.[14] Polish ambition to assume some kind of hegemony over the Baltic countries in their

[10] *Dokumenty Vneshnei Politiki SSSR*, ix (1964), 296–297; for a fuller account of the conversation see *Dokumenty i Materialy po Istorii Sovetsko-Pol'skikh Otnoshenii*, v (1967), 14–17.

[11] *Dokumenty Vneshnei Politiki SSSR*, ix (1964), 351–352.

[12] *Ibid.* ix, 384, 389, 732, note 77.

[13] *Ibid.* ix, 404–405; it appeared in *Izvestiya*, August 28, 1926.

[14] *Dokumenty Vneshnei Politiki SSSR*, ix (1964), 733, note 82.

relations with the Soviet Union was an insuperable barrier to further progress.

Only one avenue was still open to Soviet diplomacy in this region. Lithuanian animosity against Poland, and apprehension of Polish ambitions, was deep-seated; since the seizure of Vilna in 1920 relations between the two countries had been completely severed. The Lithuanian Government was deterred from seeking closer relations with the Soviet Union only by fear of compromising itself in western eyes. Discussions had continued intermittently ever since Chicherin's visit to Kaunas in December 1925;[15] and during the summer of 1926 rumours of negotiations for a Soviet–Lithuanian pact continued to annoy the Polish Government.[16] Little transpired, however, in public till the announcement on September 28, 1926, of the signature of the pact in Moscow. It turned out to be a simple pact of non-aggression and neutrality in case either party became involved in war, in a slightly more elaborate form than the draft submitted to Latvia and Estonia in the previous May; some formulas borrowed from the Soviet–German treaty of April 24, 1926, were incorporated, including the obligation for each party not to participate in any financial or economic blockade directed against the other. By two exchanges of notes accompanying the pact, the Soviet Government reaffirmed the validity of the Soviet–Lithuanian treaty of June 12, 1920, and of the Soviet declaration of April 5, 1923, refusing to recognize the *de facto* Polish occupation of Lithuanian territory; and the Lithuanian Government declared that its obligations under the pact did not prejudice its obligations under the Covenant of the League of Nations.[17] *Izvestiya* hailed the pact as a further success for the policy of bilateral non-aggression pacts, and described it as the fourth such treaty to be concluded by the Soviet Union, its predecessors being treaties with Turkey (December 17, 1925), Germany (April 24, 1926) and Afghanistan

[15] See *Socialism in One Country, 1924–1926*, Vol. 3, p. 448.

[16] Zaleski, in conversation with the Soviet *polpred* in Warsaw on June 2, 1926 (see p. 78 above), while stoutly denying rumours of an intended Polish attack on Lithuania, remarked by way of warning that "friends of our enemies are our enemies", and expressed concern at Soviet negotiations with Lithuania.

[17] *Dokumenty Vneshnei Politiki SSSR*, ix (1964), 446–451; for the Soviet–German treaty see *Socialism in One Country, 1924–1926*, Vol. 3, pp. 437–438.

(August 31, 1926).[18] *Pravda* a few days later more provocatively described it as "a wide breach in the plans of Polish militarism", which sought to create a bloc of Baltic states against the Soviet Union.[19]

The success scored in Lithuania did little to advance the prospect of similar pacts with other neighbouring countries. Poland exhibited the expected disapproval of the Soviet–Lithuanian pact. The main points of objection were the reaffirmation of the Soviet–Lithuanian treaty of June 12, 1920 and of the Soviet refusal to recognize the Polish annexation of Lithuanian territory; these were said to contravene the treaty of Riga of March 18, 1921, fixing the frontier between Soviet Russia and Poland.[20] The Soviet draft of a non-aggression treaty submitted to the Polish Government on August 24, 1926, was subjected to a battery of criticisms, including the major one that the obligation of neutrality in case of war was potentially inconsistent with the Covenant of the League of Nations.[21] Elsewhere the deadlock persisted. The offer of a similar pact to Finland[22] was neither rejected nor accepted. Latvia seemed ready to accept, but Estonia was unlikely to agree, especially now that the prospect of a loan under League of Nations auspices had strengthened her western orientation.[23] Poland was seen in Moscow as the villain of the piece. As Chicherin in his press interview in Berlin on December 6, 1926, irritably observed:

> *Poland wishes to acquire a protectorate over the Baltic states. This is the gulf which at the present moment divides us from Poland.*[24]

In the last days of 1926 a fresh element of confusion was introduced in the form of a military *coup* in Kaunas, which overthrew the existing Lithuanian régime and installed Voldemaras as prime minister with quasi-dictatorial powers. The event inspired anxiety in Moscow, where the first puzzled reaction was to assume Polish

[18] *Izvestiya*, September 29, 1926; for the treaties with Germany and Turkey see *Socialism in One Country, 1924–1926*, Vol. 3, pp. 641–642; the Soviet–Afghan treaty will be discussed in a later section of this volume.

[19] *Pravda*, October 3, 1926.

[20] *Dokumenty Vneshnei Politiki SSSR*, ix (1964), 454–461; Chicherin denied any incompatibility between the pact and the Riga treaty, and asserted that "Lithuania has her place in the sun" (*ibid.* ix, 566).

[21] *Ibid.* ix, 528–532, 582.

[22] *Ibid.* ix, 523–524.

[23] *Ibid.* ix, 736, note 89, 584–586.

[24] *Izvestiya*, December 8, 1926.

instigation or to regard it as a prelude to a Polish attack on Lithuanian independence.[25] The imitation of the Pilsudski *coup* seven months earlier was flagrant. Anti-communist slogans were freely used; and the first act of the new régime was to hang several Lithuanian communists. In the eyes of Moscow this portended a swing in Lithuanian policy towards the west. An article in *Pravda* spoke of "a government of Fascists", and traced the threads of the conspiracy back to London; and a cartoon in *Izvestiya* showed Pilsudski and Chamberlain jointly applauding the executions.[26] Bukharin, in a speech at the Moscow provincial party conference, included Germany with Great Britain and Poland among the instigators of the affair, and held them jointly responsible for "all the Fascist misdeeds of the new-fangled Lithuanian Government".[27] But presently cooler views prevailed. If the new Lithuanian Government spoke in harsher and more self-assertive language than its predecessor, and ruthlessly suppressed Lithuanian communists, Poland remained the principal target of its animosity; and Lithuanian relations with the Soviet Union were in substance unchanged.

Nothing occurred in the next two years to introduce order into the tangled skein of international relations in eastern Europe. In January 1927 Patek, a former Polish Minister for Foreign Affairs, arrived as Polish representative in Moscow; and on February 10, 1927, Zaleski informed Voikov, the Soviet representative in Warsaw that, in spite of alarmist speeches by Bukharin, Rykov and Voroshilov, instructions had been sent to Patek to open negotiations for a pact.[28] Desultory talks proceeded for some time; and *Izvestiya*, in an impatient leading article of April 3, 1927, suggested that Poland was interested in a pact with the Soviet Union only when her relations with the west deteriorated. A few weeks later a Polish draft and a Soviet counter-draft were exchanged.[29]

[25] *Ibid.* December 19, 1926.

[26] *Pravda* and *Izvestiya*, December 29, 1926.

[27] *Pravda*, January 13, 1927; for the German protest against this and other criticisms in Bukharin's speech see pp. 123–124 below.

[28] *Dokumenty Vneshnei Politiki SSSR*, x (1965), 45; the conciliatory purpose of Patek's appointment had been stressed by Pilsudski in a conversation with Voikov on December 14, 1926 (*Dokumenty i Materialy po Istorii Sovetsko-Pol'skikh Otnoshenii*, v (1967), 88–89).

[29] *Dokumenty Vneshnei Politiki SSSR*, x (1965), 632, note 34, 205–213.

But Poland had so many reservations to make to a pact on the Soviet–Turkish, Soviet–Lithuanian model that the chances of agreement quickly faded;[30] and on June 7, 1927, the assassination of Voikov by a "white" Russian *émigré*, following the rupture of relations with Great Britain, created a state of alarm and indignation in Moscow[31] which precluded a resumption of negotiations for some time to come. When negotiations were formally reopened in the autumn, the "principal disagreement" still turned on "relations with the Baltic countries".[32]

Meanwhile some slight progress could be registered in Soviet–Latvian relations. On March 9, 1927, a draft pact was initiated by Soviet and Latvian representatives in Riga. But the Latvian Government, in its desire to offend nobody, largely nullified this step by a statement that it had been taken only because the Soviet representative had been in a hurry to leave Riga, and that the question how Latvia was to "reserve in relation to the USSR its rights and obligations as a member of the League of Nations" was still unsolved.[33] The most solid result of these proceedings was the signature in Moscow on June 2, 1927, of a Soviet–Latvian commercial treaty.[34] But, since the rupture of relations with Great Britain in May 1927, that country was more and more suspect as the hidden hand behind every anti-Soviet move. Opposition to the Soviet–Latvian commercial treaty, and the delay in its ratification till the end of October 1927, were attributed to British pressure.[35] It was pointed out that Estonia, economically and financially the most dependent of the Baltic states on Great Britain, was also the most friendly to Poland; Tallinn, the Estonian capital,

[30] See a personal letter from Patek to Zaleski of March 4, 1927, on the difficulty of reconciling his mission with hostile publicity in the Polish press and the activities of Polish diplomats elsewhere (*Dokumenty i Materialy po Istorii Sovetsko Pol'skikh Otnoshenii*, v (1967), 105–107), and a conversation of May 30, 1927, between Patek and an official of Narkomindel (*Dokumenty Vneshnei Politiki SSSR*, x (1965), 255–259).

[31] Voikov had gone to the railway station to meet Rozengolts, who was passing through Warsaw on his expulsion from London, and was shot while standing on the platform (*Izvestiya*, June 8, 1927).

[32] *Dokumenty Vneshnei Politiki SSSR*, x (1965), 372, 380–383.

[33] *Izvestiya*, April 5, 1927; the Comintern journal quoted the Latvian social-democratic newspaper as tracing back the obstacles to the pact "through our neighbour, Estonia, to England" (*Kommunisticheskii Internatsional*, No. 4 (78), 1927, p. 41).

[34] *Dokumenty Vneshnei Politiki SSSR*, x (1965), 267–279.

[35] *Izvestiya*, October 23, 1927.

was described in the Soviet press as "the central point in the Baltic, the focus through which orders emanating from London, either direct or through the transmission point in Warsaw, are carried into effect".[36]

Fresh tension was generated in this uneasy situation when the Lithuanian Government appealed to the League of Nations on October 15, 1927, with a request that the Polish–Lithuanian dispute should be placed on the agenda of the council. This brought the British, French and Italian Governments on the scene. The Soviet Government shared in the general disquiet. Chicherin told Patek on November 21, 1927, that everyone in the Soviet Union was conscious of the threat of war, and would regard any attack on Lithuania as "the first stage of an attack on us". Patek replied that Poland had no designs on the independence or present territory of Lithuania, but thought it indispensable "to make an end of the supposed state of war".[37] The Soviet Government went some way to meet this view. On November 23, 1927, it begged the Lithuanian Government in its own interest to terminate the formal "state of war" between Lithuania and Poland; this step would "strengthen the situation of Lithuania and promote the cause of peace".[38] On the following day, in a more formal note, the Soviet Government warned the Polish Government of "the immeasurable dangers of an eventual Polish attack in any form whatever on the independence of Lithuania", and expressed confidence that the Polish Government would take action to "remove the menacing danger of war"; a copy of this note was sent to the British, French and Italian Governments".[39] The confrontation of the rivals at the council of the League of Nations, which brought Pilsudski in person to Geneva for the first and last time, ended in a resolution which settled nothing, but secured a formal ending of the "state of war". Litvinov played an unexpectedly active part in the process of mediation, having long conversations with Voldemaras on December 4 and 5, 1927, and with Zaleski

[36] *Ibid.* November 17, 1927.

[37] *Dokumenty Vneshnei Politiki SSSR*, x (1965), 229–230; later the Soviet Government had information which it thought reliable of a plan of Pilsudski to occupy Kaunas and instal a pro-British Lithuanian Government (*ibid.* x, 539–540).

[38] *Ibid.* x, 490–491; the Soviet Government had informed the Latvian Government in confidence some days earlier of its intention to make this *démarche* in the hope of obtaining Latvian support (*ibid.* x, 485).

[39] *Ibid.* x, 491–493.

on the latter day.[40] It was no exaggeration when Litvinov, extolling in the preparatory disarmament commission the pacific intentions of the Soviet Union, claimed that the Soviet Government had "brought all possible arguments to bear on the Lithuanian Government to persuade it immediately to declare the cessation of the state of war between Lithuania and Poland".[41] Even after Geneva, the situation remained disquieting. A resolution of IKKI of January 27, 1928, took an intransigent line, denouncing "the hypocritical decision of the League of Nations", which had aggravated the danger of a Polish annexation of Lithuania, and expressing fear that the "Lithuanian Fascist government" would yield to "imperialist pressure" to come to an agreement.[42] But this did not prevent the Soviet Government in the first months of 1928 from continuing to counsel moderation in Kaunas.[43] Indeed, this course was so assiduously pursued that it became necessary in July 1928 to deny a press report that Moscow was acting in concert with the Locarno Powers to put pressure on the Lithuanian Government.[44] This episode significantly marked an initial stage in the slow transition of the Soviet Union from the rôle of trouble-maker — the champion of international revolution and the stormy petrel of diplomacy — to the rôle of a Great Power anxious to maintain peace and order in a world where its own position was increasingly assured and accepted.

The Polish–Lithuanian dispute nevertheless exacerbated relations between Poland and the Soviet Union throughout 1928. Early in 1928 negotiations in Moscow for a trade treaty were projected,[45] but never got under way. In May 1928 an attack on the head of the Soviet trade delegation in Warsaw recalled the assassination of Voikov almost a year before, and was said to have been the work of a "white" *émigré* implicated in the Voikov murder. Indignant notes from the Soviet *polpred* to Zaleski, and from Chicherin to Patek,[46] fanned the flames of mutual animosity.

[40] *Ibid.* x, 651, note 14; *Dokumenty i Materialy po Istorii Sovetsko-Pol'skikh Otnoshenii*, v (1967), 238–240. December 5, 1927, was also the date of Litvinov's fruitless conversation with Chamberlain (see p. 30 above).

[41] *Preparatory Commission for the Conference on the Reduction and Limitation of Armaments*, Series v (Geneva, 1928), p. 12.

[42] *Internationale Presse-Korrespondenz*, No. 3, February 10, 1928, pp. 260–261.

[43] *Dokumenty Vneshnei Politiki SSSR*, xi (1966), 16–17, 89–90.

[44] *Ibid.* xi, 432–434.

[45] *Ibid.* xi, 18–19.

[46] *Ibid.* xi, 294–297, 299–302.

Zaleski was said to have protested against a remark made by Bukharin in his speech at the sixth congress of Comintern in July 1928 that "Polish communists in time of war will perform their proletarian duty and defend the USSR as their own fatherland".[47] Neither the theses on the international situation nor those on the danger of war debated and adopted by the congress mentioned the Polish–Lithuanian conflict. But the member of the secretariat or IKKI who also did duty as Lithuanian delegate insisted that "the danger of an armed occupation of Lithuania by Poland is again becoming very acute", and that the resolution of the secretariat of IKKI of January 27, 1928, retained its force;[48] and the congress, in the course of the proceedings, approved without discussion a manifesto on the threat to Lithuania from "Polish imperialists".[49] When Blomberg, head of the German Truppenamt, visited the Soviet Union in the summer of 1928, Voroshilov offered him an unsolicited assurance of Soviet aid in the event of a Polish attack on Germany, and asked for a reciprocal assurance; when Blomberg tried to evade the issue as being political, Voroshilov insisted that it was decisive for the Soviet Union. The impression was clear that the Red Army regarded the Polish army as its "chief adversary" and was apprehensive of its strength.[50] Rivalry between the Soviet Union and Poland for a predominant influence in the Baltic states continued, and Soviet relations with these states were still deadlocked. Finland, more concerned with a Scandinavian orientation, shunned any commitment; and neither Latvia nor Estonia was eager to move.

As the year went on, tension was relieved by the realization in Moscow that the Polish Government did not contemplate military action against Lithuania, and that no explosion in eastern Europe was imminent. In this more relaxed atmosphere it proved possible to negotiate the pact, signed on February 9, 1929, by all the eastern European countries except Finland, to bring the provisions of the Kellogg Pact into immediate effect between them-

[47] *Stenograficheskii Otchet VI Kongressa Kominterna* (1929), ii, 91. The remark as it appeared in the official record referred simply to "workers who, in time of war, will fight bravely as soldiers of the revolution" (*ibid.* i, 63); but this may have been a bowdlerized version.

[48] *Ibid*, i, 554, ii, 159.

[49] *Ibid.* iii, 38, vi, 196–197.

[50] *Auswärtiges Amt*, 9480/276190–1, 276228; for Blomberg's visit see p. 55 above.

selves.[51] This was accepted by the Soviet Union as a substitute for the bilateral treaties of non-aggression originally proposed by it, and seems to have contributed to a general *détente* in the area, as well as to a certain increase in the prestige of the Soviet Government. On May 17, 1929, a trade treaty was at length concluded with Estonia.[52] In the same month a serious attempt was made to resume the long delayed negotiations for a trade treaty between the Soviet Union and Poland;[53] but this again came to nothing. Various incidents in the summer of 1929 illustrated the chronic sensitivity of Soviet–Polish relations. Early in June the Soviet representative in Warsaw protested against the presence of Polish officials at a meeting of Georgian *émigrés* in Warsaw and at memorial services for Petlyura;[54] and in the following months an indignant campaign of protest was mounted against the Polish refusal to admit Polish delegates elected in the Russian, Ukrainian and White Russian republics to attend a congress of Poles resident abroad which was organized by the Polish Government in Warsaw.[55] The involvement of the Soviet Union and Poland in one another's affairs was too close, and the clash of interests and outlook too sharp, to prevent underlying animosities from breaking through the polite surface of official relations.

[51] See pp. 113–115 below.

[52] *Dokumenty Vneshnei Politiki SSSR*, xii (1967), 284–299.

[53] *Ibid.* xii, 318–325.

[54] *Ibid.* xii, 390–392; the Polish Government had apparently for some time helped to finance a Georgian committee in Istanbul (*Dokumenty i Materialy po Istorii Sovetsko-Pol'skikh Otnoshenii*, v (1967), 32–38).

[55] A number of documents on this subject are collected *ibid.* v, 393–419; the central committee of the KPP was among the protesters.

CHAPTER 63

USSR AND USA

THE pattern of Soviet–American relations established between 1921 and 1926 was not substantially modified in the ensuing period. Formal recognition of the USSR by the United States was never seriously considered. Official representatives of the Soviet Government were strictly barred from entry to the country.[1] Even an application for a transit visa for Kollontai on her appointment as Soviet *polpred* in Mexico was refused.[2] The attitude of the United States Government, of the trade unions affiliated to the A.F. of L., and of most of the press, was uniformly hostile. Financial negotiations were barred by the uncompromising demand for the recognition of Russia's pre-revolutionary debts. No formal powers existed to prevent the granting of short-term credits for American exports to the Soviet Union, and this procedure was regularly followed. But the authorities studiously refrained from giving any public sanction or approval to the practice, and enquiries about the attitude of the State Department to credits for German industrialists to cover their sales to the Soviet Union met with strong discouragement.[3] Olds, an Assistant Secretary of State, explained in a letter of November 28, 1927, to a vice-president of the American Locomotive Sales Corporation that, while the State Department did not object to "the financing of ordinary current commercial intercourse", it continued to place a ban on "projects involving the flotation of loans in the United States" and "banking arrangements not incidental to the sale of American commodities to Russia". The copy of the letter in the archives carried the annotation: "Drafted after discussion of this matter by Secretary [of State] with Mr Mellon, Mr Hoover and the President."[4] The ban, though probably unenforceable in law, extended to all long-term, as opposed to short-term, credits.

[1] See *Socialism in One Country, 1924–1926*, Vol. 3, pp. 488–489.
[2] *Foreign Relations of the United States, 1926,* ii (1941), 910–911.
[3] *Ibid.* ii, 906–910.
[4] *Foreign Relations of the United States, 1927*, iii (1942), 653–654.

The growing interest of American industrial and commercial circles in the exploitation of Soviet markets appeared to bring with it no relaxation of official intransigence. When Prigarn, the president of Amtorg, visited the Department of Commerce and the State Department in October 1926 in an attempt to initiate a discussion of Soviet–American trade problems, he received the chilling reply that discussions unsupported by concrete proposals would be fruitless, and that any proposals could be submitted through the American Ambassador in London.[5] A year later, the atmosphere had not sensibly changed. When early in 1928 Shvirsky, the unofficial Soviet representative, paid one of his rare visits to the State Department, Kelly, the head of its eastern division and a well-known protagonist of the official anti-Soviet policy, assured him that, however much recognition might improve prospects for American trade with the Soviet Union, "America will never abandon her demand for the liquidation of the present activity of Comintern."[6] On one of the few occasions when the American Secretary of State thought it necessary to explain the refusal to recognize the Soviet Union, he ascribed it to "incessant propaganda from Moscow against the United States in North and South America and in China".[7]

Such progress as was made came entirely from private initiative. In June 1926 the American–Russian Chamber of Commerce in New York, a moribund institution dating from before the revolution, was reconstituted under new auspices. Schley, a vice-president of the Chase National Bank, and long a champion of trade with the Soviet Union, became president, and Charles Smith, another advocate of closer Soviet–American relations, secretary;[8] and Gumberg, a foremost promoter of American–Soviet trade since his original association with Robins in 1917–

[5] *Dokumenty Vneshnei Politiki SSSR*, ix (1964), 527–528.

[6] *Ibid.* xi (1966), 19–20.

[7] *Ibid.* xi, 256; Shvirsky's own published utterances were sometimes an object of protest (see, e.g., *ibid.* xi, 338, 371).

[8] The new constitution of the chamber was communicated by Smith on June 16, 1926, to Shvirsky (*Dokumenty Vneshnei Politiki SSSR*, ix (1964), 312–314); a year later Smith was received by Chicherin on his appointment as the chamber's representative in Moscow (*ibid.* x (1965), 333–334, 642, note 69). For Schley see *Socialism in One Country, 1924–1926*, Vol. 3, p. 486. Articles on the reorganization of the chamber appeared in *Izvestiya*, November 14, 1926, and in *Mirovoe Khozyaistvo i Mirovaya Politika*, No. 5–6, 1926, p. 67.

1918,[9] was one of its most active organizers. A substantial number of leading American industrial, commercial and financial corporations became members of the chamber, and were represented on its large board of directors. Its main function was to supply information to its members, and to fill the gap created by the absence of American official consular and commercial representation in the Soviet Union. It was professedly non-political, and conducted no propaganda for diplomatic recognition. But so influential a body did much to make active trading and financial relations with Soviet institutions acceptable to the American business world, and to provide a respectable cover for American firms whose interests impelled them towards markets and fields of investment in the Soviet Union. These conditions were responsible for the paradox that the one major country which still stubbornly refused recognition to the Soviet Government was the country whose trade with the Soviet Union expanded, in the years from 1926 to 1929, far more rapidly than that of any other Power, and whose engineers and technicians soon began to replace those of Germany as essential agents and promoters of Soviet industrial development.[10]

In these circumstances, Soviet reactions to the United States remained curiously ambivalent. After 1925 the United States entirely eclipsed Great Britain in the Soviet picture of the world as the dominant capitalist Power. Bukharin at the seventh IKKI in November 1926 propounded the current view when he referred to the Soviet Union and the United States as "two opposite poles ... the revolutionary and the counter-revolutionary pole", each with a sub-group labelled respectively "the East" and "Europe".[11] What significantly distinguished the United States from western

[9] See *Socialism in One Country, 1924–1926*, Vol. 3, p. 478.

[10] For statistics of Soviet–American trade see p. 92 below; for the rôle of American engineers see Vol. 1, pp. 598–601.

[11] *Puti Mirovoi Revolyutsii* (1927), i, 30–31; for earlier expressions of this idea see *Socialism in One Country, 1924–1926*, Vol. 3, p. 473. At the seventh IKKI in November 1926 Treint's favourite thesis of an Anglo-European alliance against the United States was aired for the last time, and summarily rejected (see p. 135 below); but visions of an Anglo-American armed conflict continued from time to time to inspire communist orators (see pp. 12–13 above). Bukharin at the fifteenth party congress in December 1927 called Britain "a *rentier* state, a huge parasite" (*Pyatnadtsatyi S"ezd VKP(B)*, i (1961), 627; a communist publication early in 1928 described the United States as "the sole country which has engaged victorious from the world war" (P. Braun, *At the Parting of the Ways* (CPGB, 1928), p. 17).

Europe in Soviet eyes was the pre-eminence of American economic resources and American technology, and the realization that these could contribute to the fulfilment of the grandiose projects soon to be enshrined in the first five-year plan. In November 1927 Litvinov explained the Soviet attitude with a touch of naivety:

> We generally object to trade with countries that have no relations with us such as, for example, Switzerland, Belgium etc., making however an exception for understandable reasons for such a powerful country as the United States of America.[12]

Unconcealed admiration for American economic and technological achievements, and eagerness to profit by them, contrasted with denunciations of the United States from Comintern platforms as the ringleader of the imperialist Powers and implacable enemy of the Soviet Union.

On the other hand, the policy of offering concessions to attract foreign capital was no longer consonant with growing Soviet ambitions of industrial expansion. The vision shared by Lenin and Robins in 1918 of the development of Soviet natural resources with American capital[13] had faded. The American delegation at the world economic conference in Geneva in May 1927 vainly attempted to impress on Osinsky, the leader of the Soviet delegation, that American financiers were "very interested in the question of the investment of capital in the USSR".[14] On July 7, 1927, a supplementary agreement was signed in Moscow to ease the working of the Harriman manganese concession of 1921.[15] But with the impetus of planned industrialization, the climate in Moscow was rapidly changing. The Harriman concession was wound up by mutual consent in 1928; and most of the other not very numerous American concessions were liquidated before that date or shortly afterwards. In March 1928 a representative of the American bankers, Dillon Reed, delivered to the counsellor of the Soviet Embassy in Paris a disquisition on the long views taken by

[12] *Dokumenty Vneshnei Politiki SSSR*, x (1965), 477.

[13] See *Socialism in One Country, 1924–1926*, Vol. 3, p. 475.

[14] *Dokumenty Vneshnei Politiki SSSR*, x (1965), 202; for the conference see pp. 105–107 below. H. Nicolson, *Dwight Morrow* (1935), p. 304, records a dinner given in Paris at this time by Morrow to Rakovsky and other Soviet representatives, which, like other such overtures, came to nothing.

[15] *Dokumenty Vneshnei Politiki*, x (1965), 642, note 71; for this concession see *Socialism in One Country, 1924–1926*, Vol. 3, pp. 484–485.

American bankers, who, far from always pursuing immediate profit, did not expect to reap immediate profits from American capital invested in the Soviet Union, but looked to future prospects. But a vague proposal for a delegation of American financiers to Moscow came to nothing.[16] A belated attempt to revive the concessions policy in the autumn of 1928 led to no tangible result.[17]

While no definite point in time can be fixed as marking a change in American policy and outlook, the winter of 1927–1928, which saw strong pressures in the Soviet Union for rapid industrialization, was regarded as a turning-point in the expansion of American–Soviet trade. As a Soviet commentator subsequently reported:

> Only since 1927–1928 have we been able to break through the inertia of United States industry; and to this year belong a more or less substantial number of agreements concluded with American firms.[18]

At an exhibition of Soviet products organized in New York by the Soviet Society for Cultural Relations (VOKS) in February 1928, Smith, the secretary of the American–Russian Chamber of Commerce, and Cooper, the American engineer in charge of the building of the Dnieprostroi dam, spoke favourably of the openings for American trade provided by the five-year plan.[19] The episode of the attempted French embargo on Soviet gold in the spring of 1928 ended in an atmosphere of sympathy for the Soviet case and criticism of the American authorities for their refusal to handle the gold.[20] The dramatic rescue by Soviet aviators of the Italian Polar expedition in the same year received wide and admiring publicity. Shvirsky judged it "of the highest significance" that this was recounted in the whole American press "with warm praise and without a single hostile word"; and the American–Russian Chamber of Commerce hastened to invite the heroic

[16] *Dokumenty Vneshnei Politiki SSSR*, xi (1966), 177–178, 256–257.

[17] See Vol. 1, p. 718.

[18] *Promyshlennyi Import*, ed. S. Aralov and A. Shatkhan (1930), p. 164.

[19] *Izvestiya*, February 12, 1928, enthusiastically reported that the speeches had been broadcast all over the United States.

[20] For this episode see pp. 69–70 above.

aviators to visit the United States.[21] More important perhaps, the prompt and willing accession of the Soviet Government to the Pact of Paris, though greeted without enthusiasm by the State Department, made a favourable impression on public opinion and on the Secretary of State himself.

But behind these fluctuations of a fickle mood, and behind the thick curtain of official disapproval, two hard realities were slowly reshaping the pattern of American–Soviet relations: the rapid expansion of American exports to the Soviet Union for the equipment of Soviet industry, and the extensive employment in the Soviet Union of American engineers and technicians. When the Secretary of State in the autumn of 1928 was prompted by an inquisitive Senator to define once more the official attitude to the Soviet Union, he duly reiterated the impossibility of "normal relations" in view of "the continued persistence at Moscow of a dominating world revolutionary purpose". But for the first time a defensive note crept into the communication. A lengthy array of facts and figures was cited to prove that the absence of such relations had not prevented the development of a "substantial trade" between the two countries.[22] Soviet trade with the United States had always been notably unbalanced. Soviet exports to the United States remained negligible; Soviet imports soared progressively till, at the end of the nineteen-twenties, the United States began to challenge Germany as the Soviet Union's main supplier.[23] In the spring of 1929 an enthusiastic article in *Izvestiya* recapitulated the reasons for the striking expansion in Soviet–American trade: the United States dominated the world market in raw cotton; the United States was the most advanced country in industrial tech-

[21] *Dokumenty Vneshnei Politiki SSSR*, xi (1966), 425–427, 446–447; for this incident see p. 75 above.

[22] *Foreign Relations of the United States, 1928*, iii (1943), 822–825.

[23] The following were the official Soviet figures (in thousands of rubles at current prices):

	Exports to USA	Percentage of Total Exports	Imports from USA	Percentage of Total Imports
1925/26	30,666	4·4	122,162	16·2
1926/27	23,429	2·9	145,867	20·4
1927/28	28,033	3·5	187,764	20·0

(*Sotsialisticheskoe Stroitel'stvo SSSR* (1935), pp. 587–588, 591–592).

nology, in mass production, and in standardization; the organization of American industry in large units of production brought it closest to Soviet industry; bank credits were available; and American prices were lower than European prices.[24]

From this time the big American corporations began to display an active interest in the expanding Soviet market. On October 9, 1928, Amtorg signed an agreement in New York with the General Electric Company for the supply to the Soviet Union of electrical equipment to the value of $26 million, the deal involving a five-year credit for 75 per cent of the payment; these were said to be the most favourable terms yet secured by the Soviet Union on the American market. The most vocal critic of the agreement was the A.F. of L. leader, Matthew Woll.[25] Meanwhile negotiations had been opened with Ford and with General Motors for the construction of an automobile factory in the Soviet Union. In the spring of 1929 Mezhlauk with a delegation from Vesenkha visited the United States, and signed an agreement with Ford on May 9, 1929.[26] The example of the British delegation of businessmen to the Soviet Union in the spring of 1929[27] was bound to provoke emulation. A large American delegation was due in the summer of 1929 to attend a congress in Amsterdam of the International Chamber of Commerce. At the end of April 1929 the American–Russian Chamber of Commerce sent to all the prospective American participants in the congress an invitation to proceed on a visit to the Soviet Union; and recruiting also went forward in the United States. Hoover, the new President, had no inclination to brave prejudices against political recognition of the Soviet Government. But he had always been an advocate of American commerce in the Soviet Union, and gave his approval to the delegation. A party of ninety persons, including bankers, industrialists and representatives of commerce, accompanied by a number of American correspondents, spent a month in the Soviet Union from July 15 to August 15, 1929.[28] Much hostile opinion had to be overcome, and the international scene to undergo striking changes,

[24] *Izvestiya*, April 12, 1929.

[25] *Dokumenty Vneshnei Politiki SSSR*, xi (1966), 544, 554–557, 744, note 90.

[26] *Ibid.* xi, 556, 745, note 192; Mezhlauk reported on his visit in *Izvestiya*, July 31, 1929.

[27] See pp. 33–34 above.

[28] *Dokumenty Vneshnei Politiki SSSR*, xii (1967), 247, 305–307, 753, note 79.

before the diplomatic recognition of the Soviet Union became practical politics in Washington. But by the end of the nineteen-twenties the breakthrough on the industrial and commercial front had been effectively achieved.

CHAPTER 64

RELATIONS WITH JAPAN

DETERMINATION to safeguard Soviet rights in Manchuria and over the Chinese Eastern Railway (CER) by conciliation of Chang Tso-lin, and therefore also of the Japanese Government, guided Soviet diplomacy in Tokyo in the summer of 1926.[1] Chicherin in September 1926 defined the response of the Soviet Government to Japan's ambiguous attitude:

> The Japanese Government speaks friendship, but in practice Japanese agents unofficially encourage our enemies. We must preserve with Japan friendly relations which put some restraint on the militarists.[2]

In October 1926 the Japanese Ministry of Foreign Affairs expressed satisfaction with the situation, favouring direct negotiations on railway tariffs between the CER and the South Manchurian Railway, and hoping to eliminate rivalries between the two lines, and between the ports of Vladivostok and Dairen.[3] Elsewhere prospects seemed less favourable. Disputes about Japanese concessions on Sakhalin continued.[4] The Soviet–Japanese treaty concluded in Peking on January 20, 1925, had provided for a revision of the Russo-Japanese fishery convention of 1907. A Soviet–Japanese conference convened in Moscow for the purpose held no less than five sessions between December 1925 and September 1926, but did little more than list the numerous points of disagreement between rival drafts.[5] Early in 1927 the Soviet Government registered protests about the interminable delays.[6] A further session of the conference in February 1927 pro-

[1] See *Socialism in One Country, 1924–1926*, Vol. 3, pp. 882–883.

[2] *Dokumenty Vneshnei Politiki SSSR*, ix (1964), 414–415.

[3] *Ibid.* ix, 480.

[4] *Ibid.* ix, 591–593, x (1965), 104–106.

[5] *Ibid.* ix, 163–164; for a detailed account of these proceedings drawn mainly from Japanese archives see G. Lensen, *Japanese Recognition of the USSR* (Tokyo, 1970), pp. 242–251; for the treaty see *Socialism in One Country, 1924–1926*, Vol. 3, pp. 869–870.

[6] *Dokumenty Vneshnei Politiki SSSR*, x (1965), 19–20.

duced a draft treaty with variant texts, which seems to have constituted some slight advance.[7] Political relations stagnated. Kopp left Tokyo in June 1926, and was replaced by Besedovsky as chargé d'affaires.[8] But, when in August 1926 Besedovsky proposed a Soviet–Japanese non-aggression pact on the model of the Soviet–German treaty of April 24, 1926, the offer was politely but firmly declined: the Japanese Government preferred not to go beyond the terms of the Peking treaty.[9] It came as something of a surprise in Moscow when the Japanese Minister for Foreign Affairs, in a speech in the Japanese diet on January 18, 1927, gave a notably friendly account of Soviet–Japanese relations, reporting favourable progress in the negotiations on concessions and on fishing rights, and dwelling on the continued strengthening of relations in the two years since the Peking treaty.[10] Thus encouraged, the Soviet chargé d'affaires in the following month reopened the question of a non-aggression pact, but once more received the reply that a political agreement should follow, not precede, the economic agreements foreseen in the Peking treaty — the fishery convention and a trade treaty.[11] Shortly afterwards the Soviet Government, alarmed by the prospect of Italian ratification of the Bessarabian treaty, warned the Japanese Government that ratification by it of a treaty in which it had no conceivable interest could only mean that it was taking sides with Great Britain in the struggle against the Soviet Union.[12]

The arrival in Tokyo of a new Soviet *polpred*, Dovgalevsky, at the end of March 1927, and the installation of a new Japanese Government with Tanaka as Prime Minister, might have offered prospects of a thaw. A certain discord between British and Japanese attitudes to the Chinese nationalists had been hopefully noted in Moscow.[13] At a moment of mounting British hostility to the Soviet Union, this became an obsessive factor in Soviet policy;

[7] G. Lensen, *Japanese Recognition of the USSR* (Tokyo, 1970), pp. 251–257.

[8] G. Besedovsky, *Na Putyakh k Termidoru* (Paris, 1931), ii, 23, 31; for Kopp's unpopularity see *Socialism in One Country, 1924–1926*, Vol. 3, pp. 882–883.

[9] *Dokumenty Vneshnei Politiki SSSR*, ix (1964), 735, note 88; for further particulars of this *démarche*, quoted from Soviet archives, see L. Kutakov, *Istoriya Sovetsko-Yaponskikh Diplomaticheskikh Otnoshenii* (1962), pp. 71–72.

[10] *Dokumenty Vneshnei Politiki SSSR*, x (1965), 20, 624, note 7.

[11] *Ibid.* x, 51.

[12] *Ibid.* x, 106–107, 164; for the Italian ratification see pp. 73–74 above.

[13] *Izvestiya*, January 28, 1927.

and Stalin told Wang Ching-wei, who was in Moscow early in March 1927 on his way back to China, that the Soviet Government was interested in an *entente* between the Soviet Union, China and Japan directed against Great Britain.[14] When Tanaka, in his first public declaration of policy on April 22, 1927, coupled an assurance of Japanese neutrality in the civil war in China with a statement of Japan's determination to defend her interests in China, this was thought in Moscow to foreshadow a greater readiness to act independently of Great Britain and the United States.[15] On May 28, 1927, Tanaka, who had been a professional soldier, announced that, in order to counter the threat to Japanese interests of the advance of nationalist forces in China, two Japanese battalions would be landed at the treaty port of Tsingtao in Shantung; and the troops eventually penetrated as far as Tsinan, in the interior of the province. That Japan now stood in the front rank of imperialist Powers would have been hard to deny. The alleged Tanaka memorandum, advocating the conquest of Manchuria and Mongolia as a prelude to eventual domination over China, dated from July 1927. Its authenticity was never established; but its appearance at this time was symptomatic of trends of opinion in influential Japanese circles. Throughout the summer Soviet diplomacy, now in a mood of isolation and alarm following the break with Great Britain, continued to toy with the prospect of improved relations with a Japanese Government increasingly at loggerheads with Great Britain and the United States. But three long conversations between Dovgalevsky and Tanaka, on May 24, June 16 and July 1, 1927, were confined on both sides to patient repetition of familiar expressions of good will and familiar arguments.[16] Extreme caution continued to mark Japanese foreign policy. The Japanese troops landed in Shantung in May 1927 provoked no incidents, and in September were quietly withdrawn.

At this point, a cautious initiative was taken from the Japanese

[14] T'ang Leang'li, *The Inner History of the Chinese Revolution* (1930), p. 275; Wang's rôle will be discussed in a later section of this volume.

[15] *Mezhdunarodnaya Zhizn'*, No. 3, 1928, p. 20.

[16] The conversations are summarized in *Dokumenty Vneshnei Politiki SSSR*, x (1965), 626, note 17; the summary does not include a remark later said to have been made by Tanaka (to which Dovgalevsky took immediate exception) that he would regard as "a fine idea" a policy of the open door and equal opportunities in Siberia (*ibid.* xi, 705, note 40).

side. In October 1927 an economic mission, headed by Kuhara, a prominent Japanese industrialist, set out for Moscow and Berlin. If its purpose was to secure economic concessions from the Soviet Government, its success appears to have been small.[17] It was followed by the ostensibly private visit to Moscow in December 1927 of the pro-Soviet elder statesman Goto. Goto, whose views reflected a sturdy Japanese nationalism rather than any sympathy for the Soviet régime, and whose visit showed every sign of official backing, expounded his views with considerable frankness to Dovgalevsky in Tokyo and to Chicherin, Litvinov and Karakhan in Moscow. He envisaged Japanese–Soviet cooperation in China, particularly in order to counter "the penetration into Manchuria of the British and Americans", and extensive concessions for Japan in the coastal regions of Siberia, which would help to develop this empty territory and to relieve population pressures in Japan. He attributed the Japanese refusal to conclude a non-aggression pact to fear of "spoiling relations with England and America". He was received with enthusiasm as a protagonist of Soviet–Japanese friendship, though most of his concrete proposals were unacceptable.[18] Only a few days before Goto's arrival, Bukharin had given the fifteenth party congress a melodramatic account of Japan's "Draconian demands" in Manchuria and Inner Mongolia, which would have "in practice reduced to nothing even the appearance of independence of these two countries".[19]

Goto's most important contribution was to bring about agreement on the vexed question of the fishery convention. On October 10, 1927, an agreed text had at last been initialled by Karakhan and the Japanese representative in Moscow. It seems to have been believed on the Soviet side that the issue had been clinched.[20] But

[17] For some particulars of this mission, mainly from Soviet archives, see L. Kutakov, *Istoriya Sovetsko–Yaponskikh Diplomaticheskikh Otnoshenii* (1962), pp. 81–83.

[18] *Dokumenty Vneshnei Politiki SSSR*, xi (1966), 13–15, 22–29, 693, note 3, and further material from the archives quoted in L. Kutakov, *Istoriya Sovetsko–Yaponskikh Diplomaticheskikh Otnoshenii* (1962), pp. 86–89; for Goto see *The Bolshevik Revolution, 1917–1923*, Vol. 3, pp. 542–543.

[19] *Pyatnadstayi S"ezd VKP(B)*, i (1961), 667; on the same occasion Lozovsky accused "the Japanese bourgeoisie" of seeking to "organize Asia against Europe" (*ibid.* i, 694).

[20] *Izvestiya*, October 11, 1927; *Dokumenty Vneshnei Politiki SSSR*, x (1965), 465–466.

Japanese fishery interests had not been fully appeased; and demands for further amendments were made as a condition of signature. Early in January 1928 Goto intervened, ostensibly in a personal capacity; and, after a lot of hard bargaining on both sides, the Japanese Government eventually accepted a vaguely worded Soviet declaration to the effect that the Soviet Government recognized the "great economic significance" of the Japanese fishing industry, and would see to it that "the reasonable and lawful interests of Japanese subjects may not be impaired". With this proviso embodied in an attached protocol the convention was signed in Moscow, just after Goto's departure, on January 23, 1928.[21] It was the last achievement of Soviet diplomacy in Japan for a long time to come. The convention never functioned without friction. Troyanovsky, who had just succeeded Dovgalevsky as Soviet representative, argued, in reply to Japanese protests in April 1929, that it was more favourable to Japanese fishery interests than the agreement of 1907,[22] but failed to convince the Japanese Government.

At this point Japanese internal politics and a revival of Japanese communism began to impinge disconcertingly on Soviet–Japanese relations. The first Japanese elections held under a law of manhood suffrage, which raised the number of electors from 3 to 12 millions, took place on February 20, 1928; and the Japanese Communist Party, suppressed in 1924, but illegally resurrected in December 1926, participated under instructions from Comintern, albeit in disguised forms, in the elections.[23] The Japanese authorities reacted swiftly. For the first time since 1924 the Japanese press during the election campaign printed allegations that Left parties were in receipt of funds from Moscow and from the Soviet mission in Tokyo. Troyanovsky's first extended conversation with Tanaka on March 8, 1928, included some polite, but unexpectedly frank, exchanges. An odd feature of the conversation was that Tanaka, apparently wishing to conceal the meeting from the press, came to the Soviet Embassy on foot, accompanied only by an

[21] *Dokumenty Vneshnei Politiki SSSR*, xi (1966), 20–29, 41–47; G. Lensen, *Japanese Recognition of the USSR* (Tokyo, 1970), pp. 262–269, and sources there quoted; for the English text of the convention with its attached protocols and declarations see *ibid.* pp. 271–316.

[22] *Dokumenty Vneshnei Politiki SSSR*, xii (1967), 228–229.

[23] For the activities of the revived party see pp. 620–621 below.

interpreter. Troyanovsky, having dilated on the growing friendship between the two countries, referred to "an unpleasant residue from the not remote past" and to "apprehensions regarding the real Japanese designs in relation to the USSR". Tanaka replied emphatically that all this rested on a misunderstanding, and that Japan had "no thoughts whatever of attacks on the USSR or seizures of territory". Troyanovsky asked for a speedy ratification of the fishery convention, and received diplomatic assurances. A lengthy discussion on the prospects of negotiations for a trade treaty produced nothing but unhelpful generalizations on the incompatibility of different economic systems. Troyanovsky complained of strained relations between the Chinese Eastern and South Manchurian Railways, of hostile attitudes to Soviet officials and of an attack by a Russian *émigré* on a secretary of the Soviet consulate in Dairen. When Tanaka tried to embark on a general discussion of China and of its "immense importance" for Japan, Troyanovsky avoided the issue by remarking that "we cannot resolve Chinese affairs without China". Finally, in the category of "small questions", Troyanovsky blandly denied that the Soviet Government or the Soviet Embassy had been concerned in the financing of Left parties, and asked for "an authoritative declaration" from Tanaka to put an end to the press campaign. This Tanaka promised.[24] A few days later he no less blandly informed the press that the Soviet Ambassador had denied the allegations, and that a majority of the Japanese people believed him — a form of words which Troyanovsky found unsatisfactory, and which failed to stop the campaign.[25] The rounding up of Japanese communists continued throughout March 1928,[26] to the accompaniment of noisy protests against Soviet intrusion into Japanese affairs. On March 23, 1928, youths broke into the courtyard of the Soviet embassy, let off an explosive device and nailed to a tree a manifesto which accused the Ambassador of giving money to the Japanese Communist Party, and summoned him to return to his own country. The Japanese Ministry of Foreign Affairs expressed its regrets; but this did not dispel Troyanovsky's

[24] *Dokumenty Vneshnei Politiki SSSR*, xi (1966), 137–147.

[25] *Ibid.* xi, 163, 706, note 42; Goto, back in Tokyo, gave an interview to Tass also rejecting the allegations (*Izvestiya*, March 15, 1928).

[26] See p. 621 below.

suspicion that the demonstrators had received official encouragement.[27]

Having displayed his mailed fist at home, Tanaka turned to the real target of his ambitions. While Soviet prestige in China had suffered grave defeats from the events of 1927 — Chiang Kai-shek's defection to the imperialists, the collapse of the Wuhan government and the fiasco of the Canton rising — Tanaka now developed, with less and less disguise, the forward and aggressive policy foreshadowed in his utterances of the previous year. In the sensitive and apprehensive climate of Moscow, the fleeting vision of Soviet–Japanese cooperation against Great Britain in China was revealed as an instrument for the harnessing of Soviet power to Japan's ambitious designs. Japanese encroachment might well prove a greater menace to Soviet authority in Manchuria and Soviet control of the CER than Great Britain or the United States had ever been. Stalin, in a speech of April 13, 1928, observed with heavy irony that "we could establish 'friendly' relations with Japan if we agreed to share Manchuria with her".[28] In the same month Japanese troops were once again landed in Shantung, and on May 3, 1928, attacked the Chinese nationalist army which had occupied Tsinan, by way of warning the nationalists not to proceed with their advance towards the north. The Japanese Government in a memorandum of May 18, 1928, addressed to both Peking and Nanking governments, expressed apprehension that the disorders prevailing in China might extend to the vicinity of Peking and Tientsin, and might even affect Manchuria, and declared unequivocally that it "attaches exceptional importance to the maintenance of peace and order in Manchuria". Chicherin in an interview of May 21, 1928, reacted sharply to these events, believing — or affecting to believe — that Japanese action had the full approval of "such Powers as Great Britain, the United States and France", and reaffirmed the Soviet policy of "unconditional non-interference in the internal affairs of China".[29] Meanwhile,

[27] *Dokumenty Vneshnei Politiki SSSR*, xi (1966), 240–242; three months later groups of "Fascists" presented themselves at the embassy to protest against the Ambassador's activities, and again warned him to leave Japan (*ibid.* xi, 405).

[28] Stalin, *Sochineniya*, xi, 55.

[29] *Dokumenty Vneshnei Politiki SSSR*, xi (1966), 324–325, 724, note 102. On May 19, 1928, Japanese troops occupied premises in the grounds of the Soviet Embassy in Peking; but they were withdrawn immediately and an apology tendered (*ibid.* xi, 326, 725, note 103). The Japanese memorandum of

the Japanese press raised a hue and cry about alleged Soviet designs on Manchuria, and provoked equally vigorous counter-attacks in the Soviet press.[30] The constant harassing of Soviet consular representatives in China by the Chinese authorities was attributed to joint British and Japanese instigation.[31]

Relations between the three great imperialist Powers in China remained something of a puzzle, and were variously interpreted by speakers at the sixth congress of Comintern in July 1928. A Chinese delegate contrasted the aims of Great Britain and Japan, who wanted a partition of China, with the United States policy of the open door.[32] A Japanese delegate contemplated "a military partition between the imperialists of Great Britain, United States and Japan". He observed that "the imperialists have been talking for a long time of an American–Japanese war over China and the Pacific", but that this did not prevent the three imperialist Powers from being united in their hostility to the USSR.[33] An understandably confused and cautious diagnosis of Chinese affairs by Karakhan in October 1928 depicted Japan, Great Britain and (more passively) the United States pursuing their divergent interests, with Japan determined to exploit her "monopoly position" in Manchuria in the spheres of trade and railway construction, and assumed that she would meet no "sharp or open opposition" from the other two Powers.[34] At the tenth IKKI in July 1929 the Japanese delegate insisted that the United States was now "Japan's greatest rival", and asserted that Japan had "concluded a secret treaty with England in order to be able to carry on the struggle against America".[35] The refusal of Japan to support the Chinese nationalist assault on the CER and on Soviet interests in Manchuria in the autumn of 1929[36] showed

May 18, 1928, was afterwards described as "tantamount to a claim to a Japanese protectorate over Manchuria and north China" (*Problemy Kitaya*, vi-vii (1931), 201).

[30] *Pravda*, June 16, 1928; *Izvestiya*, June 15, 16, 19, 1928.

[31] *Dokumenty Vneshnei Politiki SSSR*, xi (1966), 401.

[32] *Stenograficheskii Otchet VI Kongressa Kominterna* (1929), i, 449–450.

[33] *Ibid.* ii, 138; according to an American delegate, the American Workers' Party down to 1927 had regarded American diplomacy in China as "the tool of England", but had recently changed over to the view that the United States was "following in the wake of Japanese imperialism" (*ibid.* iv, 172).

[34] *Dokumenty Vneshnei Politiki SSSR*, xi (1966), 536–540.

[35] *Protokoll: 10. Plenum des Exekutivkomitees der Kommunistichen Internationale* (n.d.), p. 441.

[36] This will be described in a later section of this volume.

that Japanese designs on this region had not yet matured; and the vision of a future in which the Soviet Union would successfully woo American and British support in opposing a Japanese advance in Manchuria had not yet begun to dawn in Moscow.

CHAPTER 65

THE INTERNATIONAL SCENE

IN the spring of 1926 the Soviet Government, while not abating its hostility in principle to the League of Nations, had expressed its willingness to participate in international discussions on economic problems and on disarmament, provided these were not held on Swiss soil.[1] Chicherin in his press interview in Berlin in December 1926 explained that anyone who pretended that the Soviet Union would join the League of Nations "simply distorts the truth — not to employ a stronger expression".[2] But the admission of Germany to the League of Nations had ended the situation in which the Soviet Government could profess political indifference to what took place at Geneva; and the problems of economic reconstruction had begun to point to the need for closer practical relations with the capitalist world. The inconvenience and absurdity of a formal obstacle to Soviet participation in international activities had become too glaring to be tolerated, especially in view of the impending world economic conference at Geneva. On April 14, 1927, an exchange of notes was effected between the Swiss and Soviet representatives in Berlin, in which the Swiss Government condemned and regretted the "criminal actions" leading to the assassination of Vorovsky and attacks on other members of Soviet delegations, and expressed its willingness to discuss with the Soviet Government all outstanding questions, including the payment of compensation to Vorovsky's daughter; on this basis, the two governments pronounced their conflict at an end, and agreed to withdraw all discriminatory measures against each other.[3] The agreement was ratified by a decision of TsIK and Sovnarkom of April 22, 1927;[4] and the Soviet economic boycott of Switzerland was formally

[1] See *Socialism in One Country, 1924–1926*, Vol. 3, pp. 461–462.

[2] *Dokumenty Vneshnei Politiki SSSR*, ix (1964), 567–568; for this interview see p. 7 above.

[3] *Ibid.* x (1965), 161–162.

[4] *Sovetskoe Stroitel'stvo*, No. 5–6 (10–11), May–June 1927, p. 160.

ended by a decree of May 4, 1927.[5] A fortnight after the conclusion of the agreement, a large Soviet delegation under the presidency of Osinsky, which included Sokolnikov and Khinchuk, set out for Geneva in time for the opening session of the world economic conference on May 4, 1927. Passing through Berlin, the delegation assured a sensitive German press that participation in the conference did not imply any intention on the part of the Soviet Government to join the League of Nations.[6] Extraordinary precautions were taken by the Swiss police to avoid hostile manifestations. The party left the train at a station outside Geneva, and was conveyed in police cars to a hotel prepared for its reception.[7]

The conference, which lasted almost three weeks, provided the occasion for the first major appearance of a Soviet delegation on the international scene. Both Sokolnikov and Osinksy spoke on May 7, 1927, in the opening debate on the world economic situation. Sokolnikov refuted "pessimistic prophecies" about the Soviet economy, and defended the monopoly of foreign trade; the Soviet Union desired collaboration with capitalist countries, which also represented "a kind of competition between two economic systems". Osinsky later on the same day also spoke of "the co-existence of the bourgeois and capitalist systems for a limited period". But he addressed himself more provocatively to the contradictions of the capitalist world and ways of overcoming them, putting forward eleven basic proposals, which included the eight-hour day, the raising of wages, a cessation of "the economic and political boycott" of the Soviet Union, and "complete and effective disarmament".[8] Members of the Soviet delegation participated actively in the work of the three commissions on commerce, industry and agriculture. In the first of them, in an atmosphere strongly impregnated with the current campaign for the removal

[5] *Sobranie Zakonov, 1927*, No. 23, art. 253.

[6] *Novyi Mir*, No. 7, July 1927, p. 134; a manifesto of IKKI of April 15, 1927, on imperialism and the danger of war, provoked by events in China, had called the League of Nations "the most hypocritical organization of all time" (*Internationale Presse-Korrespondez*, No. 41, April 16, 1927, pp. 859–860).

[7] *Izvestiya*, May 6, 1927; a protest was registered against the degree of police supervision to which the delegates were subjected.

[8] *Report and Proceedings of the World Economic Conference* (Geneva, 1927), i, 119–122, 125–129; the speeches were published in *Izvestiya*, May 8, 10, 1927.

of trade barriers, Khinchuk and Osinsky were both engaged in warding off attacks on the monopoly of foreign trade;[9] in the commission on industry Osinsky expounded the Soviet view on the differences between capitalist and socialist "rationalization".[10] In the plenary session of May 21, 1927, Khinchuk, Sokolnikov and Varga respectively explained the Soviet reservations to the reports of the three commissions;[11] and at the concluding session Osinsky lamented that the conference desired only "minor changes in the economic and social policy of the capitalist states", and had not considered the proposals put forward by the Soviet Union.[12]

But the chief disappointment related to the formula of "co-existence". In the coordinating committee Osinsky put forward a draft resolution by which the conference "recommends to all states to develop their relations with the Soviet Union on the basis of pacific co-existence of two different economic systems."[13] This proved unacceptable to several delegations. The final resolution merely spoke of "the participation of all the countries present, irrespective of differences in their economic systems, as a happy augury for the pacific commercial cooperation of all nations". Osinsky, in his speech at the concluding session of the conference, dwelt once more on the importance of "establishing measures for the peaceful co-existence of two economic systems", but thought that "the principle has been enunciated sufficiently clearly" in the resolution.[14] The confrontation in Geneva, coinciding with the Arcos raid in London and the breaking off of Anglo-Soviet diplomatic relations, yielded few positive results. Khinchuk commented bitterly that the British action had been designed to destroy "the possibility of co-existence between two national

[9] *Report and Proceedings of the World Economic Conference* (Geneva, 1927), ii, 18–19, 21–22.

[10] *Ibid.* ii, 145; for the Soviet view see Vol. 1, p. 342, note 2.

[11] *Report and Proceedings of the World Economic Conference* (Geneva, 1927), i, 145, 148, 150.

[12] *Ibid.* i, 165–166; for a list of the resolutions of the conference, mainly technical, to which the Soviet delegation adhered, and of those to which it adhered with reservations, see *ibid.* i, 56.

[13] *Ibid.* i, 174.

[14] *Ibid.* i, 56, 165. The Soviet delegates spoke in French, and the official records were in French and English; the Soviet press reporting the conference sometimes translated "co-existence" by *sozhitel'stvo*, sometimes by *sosushchestvovanie* (for the two terms see p. 4, note 6 above).

economic systems".[15] But the Soviet delegation had broken the ice, and emerged from the ordeal with some credit.[16]

Disarmament provided a more delicate problem. Invitations to attend the earlier sessions of the preparatory commission had been declined on the plea that the Soviet Government, while always ready to discuss disarmament, could not send delegates to Switzerland.[17] Now that this bar had been removed, no further invitation arrived, apparently because the previous invitations were considered as still valid; and the suspicious Litvinov conjectured that "leading League circles" no longer wanted the Soviet presence.[18] On October 20, 1927, Chicherin informed the Secretary-General of the League of Nations by telegram that, since the settlement of the Soviet–Swiss dispute, no obstacle now existed to Soviet participation in the preparatory commission, and ten days later he received a notification that the commission would meet on November 30, 1927.[19] The appointment of a large Soviet delegation headed by Litvinov and Lunacharsky received considerable publicity in the Soviet press.[20]

Litvinov did not disappoint the widespread curiosity evoked by his first appearance at Geneva. On the opening day of the session, he submitted a proposal for "the complete abolition of all land, naval and air forces".[21] After a politely temporizing reply by Paul-Boncour, and some embarrassed comments by lesser delegates, it was agreed to postpone discussion till the next session. No attempt was made to proceed with the discussion of the skeleton draft disarmament convention which had been before the previous session of the commission in March 1927. The only

[15] *Izvestiya,* May 18, 1927.

[16] In 1928 Soviet delegates attended League conferences in Geneva on double taxation and on economic statistics, and in 1929 on measures to suppress counterfeit money; the statistical conference was reported in *Internationale Presse-Korrespondenz,* No. 34, November 30, 1928, p. 2669. For a list of all international conferences attended by Soviet delegates in this period see K. Davis, *The Soviets at Geneva* (Geneva, 1934), pp. 297–301.

[17] See *Socialism in One Country, 1924–1926,* Vol. 3, pp. 459, 461.

[18] *Dokumenty Vneshnei Politiki SSSR,* x (1965), 469.

[19] *Izvestiya,* November 2, 1927.

[20] See *ibid.* November 22, 1927, for an interview with Litvinov and photographs of the delegation.

[21] *Documents of the Preparatory Commission for the Disarmament Conference,* Series v (Geneva, 1928), pp. 9–12.

substantive decision taken was to set up a committee on arbitration and security. Litvinov did not fail to point out that this "must inevitably divert attention from the fundamental question", but agreed to the participation of a Soviet "observer". In fact, Litvinov was present at the first meetings of the committee on the two succeeding days, but did not speak.[22] Baldwin, questioned in the House of Commons on the Soviet disarmament proposals, replied that they had not been "regarded by the committee as a practical and helpful contribution to the problem", and declined to discuss them.[23] Litvinov, reporting on the proceedings to the fifteenth party congress a fortnight later, made fun of a draft disarmament convention which contained no figures, but had already provoked disagreements between the British, French and German delegations: the only decisions taken at the session had been to fix the date of the next session and to set up the security committee.[24]

The Soviet Government lost no time in pressing home its initiative. On February 15, 1928, it sent to the Secretary-General of the League of Nations a detailed draft convention to serve as a basis of discussion at the forthcoming session of the preparatory commission. This provided for total disarmament by stages, and the strictest regulation of forces required for the maintenance of order; the whole operation was to be supervised by an international control commission.[25] On the eve of the session, which opened on March 15, 1928, Litvinov learned with indignation of a plan to give the draft a quiet burial by referring it to a subcommission. But the proposal came to nothing owing to the unwillingness of the leading delegates to serve on such a body.[26] Litvinov's presentation of the Soviet draft on March 19, 1928, was followed by the somewhat inhibited comments of a number

[22] *Ibid.* Series V, pp. 19, 36–54.

[23] *House of Commons: 5th Series,* ccxi, 973.

[24] *Pyatnadtsatyi S"ezd VKP(B),* ii (1962), 1060–1070.

[25] *Dokumenty Vneshnei Politiki, SSSR,* xi (1966), 90–111; *Documents of the Preparatory Commission for the Disarmament Conference,* Series VI (Geneva, 1928), pp. 324–339. It was printed in full in *Izvestiya,* February 21, 1928.

[26] *Dokumenty Vneshnei Politiki SSSR,* xi (1966), 76; the dilemma was explained by the United States delegate in a telegram to the State Department, which replied that "the proposals are not of primary interest to this government, and we should not assume a leading role in the discussions under any circumstances" (*Foreign Relations of the United States, 1928,* i (1942), 250–251).

of delegates. The Turkish and German delegates alone expressed some mild sympathy for the boldness of the Soviet plan. One of the few to display no embarrassment was the British delegate, Cushenden, whose rambling, but unrestrained invective drew the sharpest rapier-thrusts in Litvinov's reply.[27] When a resolution was submitted which amounted to a shelving of the Soviet draft, Litvinov countered by the announcement of yet another Soviet draft convention for a reduction, no longer a total abolition, of armaments, which was being sent to the secretariat for immediate distribution. He protested vigorously against a proposal to postpone its consideration till the next session.[28] But on the following day, the commission adopted a resolution declaring that the first Soviet draft "cannot be accepted as a basis for its work", and referring to the second draft to the next session of the commission, for which, however, no date was fixed; and, after a further protest from Litvinov, the session ended.[29] In April 1928 Litvinov made an ironical report to TsIK on the proceedings of the preparatory commission, and received a vote of confidence for his policy.[30] An official report indicated the advantages which the Soviet Government hoped to reap from its activities at Geneva: the Soviet disarmament proposals, it declared, "attracted the sympathies of the broadest circles of the population in capitalist countries, and by this means helped to lessen to a certain extent the danger of war".[31]

While discussions of disarmament languished, the international scene in the autumn of 1928 was enlivened by the signature of the Briand–Kellogg Pact, by which the nations of the world bound themselves to renounce war as an instrument of national policy. The proposal had emerged almost casually at the end of 1927 from correspondence between the French and United States

[27] *Documents of the Preparatory Commission for the Disarmament Conference,* Series VI (Geneva, 1928), pp. 230–276; the Turkish Government appears to have been invited to be represented in the commission at the suggestion of the Soviet Government (*League of Nations: Official Journal,* No. 4, April 1928, p. 583).

[28] *Documents of the Preparatory Commission for the Disarmament Conference,* Series VI (Geneva, 1928), pp. 289, 295–296.

[29] *Ibid.* pp. 312–313.

[30] *3 Sessiya Tsentral'nogo Ispolnitel'nogo Komiteta Soyuza SSR 4 Sozyva* (1928), pp. 772–794; *id. Postanovleniya* (1928).

[31] *SSSR: God Raboty Pravitel'stva (1927/28)* (1929), p. 3.

Governments, and had begun to take shape by the spring of 1928. At an early stage in the discussion a leading article in *Izvestiya* had marked Soviet interest in it:

> The greatest paradox of our time ... is the fact that some foreign policy aims of the two classic antipodes of the contemporary world coincide in certain respects. They consist of a tendency to postpone inevitable military clashes, of attempts to create, even temporarily, normal conditions for international trade. Realistic politicians should know how to draw *practical conclusions* from paradoxical situations.[32]

Litvinov, in his concluding speech at the fifth session of the preparatory commission on March 19, 1928, remarked bitingly that "the sincerity of this proposal could not be more convincingly tested than by confronting its authors with the Soviet project of a convention for total disarmament, which pursues the aim not of moral prohibition, but of annihilation of the possibilities of wars";[33] and a month later at the session of TsIK he made a point of the incompatibility of armaments with a ban on war.[34] An ironical article in *Izvestiya* recalled Kellogg's pronouncement that the Monroe Doctrine obliged the United States to take military action against "any Power in the world" that infringed it.[35] But the Soviet Government was not in principle opposed to pacific gestures, even if they had no more than a propaganda value; and the sourness of the Soviet reaction was dictated in part by the fact that the USSR was not among the fifteen select countries invited to become original signatories of the pact. The most utopian projects might have political significance. When Coudenhove-Kalergi launched his vision of a United States of Europe in Vienna in October 1926, its supporters were divided between those who desired to draw the Soviet Union into membership, and those who sought to organize Europe against the Bolshevik menace.[36] The intentions of the authors of the new pact

[32] *Izvestiya*, January 7, 1928.

[33] For this speech see p. 109, note 27 above.

[34] *3 Sessiya Tsentral'nogo Ispolnitel'nogo Komiteta Soyuza SSR 4 Sozyva* (1928), p. 790.

[35] *Izvestiya*, June 29, 1928.

[36] For an article on this subject see *Communist International* (Engl. ed.), November 15, 1926, pp. 21–23; it did appear in the Russian edition. The same ambiguity prevailed when Briand submitted his scheme for a united Europe to the League of Nations in September 1929.

in regard to the Soviet Union seemed equally undecided. During the summer of 1928 it became clear that Soviet diplomacy was working hard to bring about Soviet participation.

The controversies and diversions of opinion which evidently lay behind this decision are not on record. Litvinov was its most obvious champion. He had shown dramatically at Geneva how the international stage could be used to show up the hypocrisies of the capitalist Powers in their quest for peace. According to a well-informed plausible account, Chicherin opposed Soviet adherence to the pact, but "Litvinov advocated it, and with Bukharin's help won".[37] This was the moment when Litvinov effectively supplanted Chicherin in Narkomindel; and he could always count on Stalin's personal support against Chicherin.[38] Bukharin's rôle is more speculative. It is a remarkable fact that, though the pact was signed with considerable publicity in the Soviet as well as in the world press, and the decision of the Soviet Government to accede to it was announced, while the sixth congress of Comintern was in session, the pact was not mentioned either in the lengthy theses submitted by Bukharin on the international situation, or the still longer theses on the struggle against imperialist wars.[39] The latter did contain a single derogatory allusion to it. A condemnation of "official pacifism, by which capitalist governments mask their manoeuvres in relation to one another and in relation to the Soviet Union", was followed by an illustrative enumeration: "League of Nations, Locarno, disarmament conference, 'prohibition of war' etc."[40] This reticence, which extended to the numerous speeches delivered by Bukharin and other Soviet delegates at the congress, might be explained on the hypothesis that the theses were drafted at a time before the relevant decision had been taken, or that Bukharin, personally committed, did not wish to risk a clash with a predominantly hostile opinion on the floor of the congress.

The conspiracy of silence which pervaded the theses and the speeches of Soviet delegates was not observed in the foreign delegations. Before the congress the journal of the KPD had published a scathing article on the pact entitled "The Outlawry-

[37] L. Fischer, *The Soviets in World Affairs* (2nd edn. 1951), p. xiii.

[38] See p. 32 above.

[39] For these theses see pp. 203–204, 211–213 below.

[40] *Kommunisticheskii Internatsional v Dokumentakh* (1933), p. 799.

of-War Pact of Dollar Imperialism";[41] and a German delegate at the congress called it "an attempt to exploit contradictions in Europe in order to strengthen the international position of the USA".[42] Sémard of the French delegation described it as a mask for American imperialism, which might "sow pacifist illusions in the broad masses"; and Murphy of the British delegation called it "a preparation for war". An American delegate referred to "the Kellogg peace offensive" as "a smoke-screen to conceal preparations for war", designed to "nullify the struggle of the USSR for peace and disarmament".[43] In Paris, where the pact was signed, the PCF kept up an active campaign against it. *Humanité* came out with a series of articles denouncing it as "a pact for war" and a "pacifist trap", and labelling its promoters as "Les Tartuffes de la Paix".[44] A special issue on the day of signature, August 27, 1928, called for demonstrations against the pact in the name of "a united front of all workers against the imperialist murderers".[45] It is inconceivable that Comintern, if it had received a firm directive, could not have curbed this chorus of hostility. A remark later attributed to Chicherin that "the Soviet Government joined the Kellogg pact, and Comintern opposed the Kellogg pact",[46] does not carry conviction in these crude terms. But it may point to a moment when Comintern had not yet received instructions to conform to the latest turn in Soviet policy. If Bukharin, by prudence or by conviction, was a known supporter of accession, his enemies in Comintern may well have used the licence accorded by an indeterminate situation to connive at counter-demonstrations by foreign delegates at the congress.

It was Borah who claimed to have been the first American politician to raise the issue of Soviet participation.[47] Kellogg, when questioned about the inclusion of the Soviet Union in the pact, would only reply that the way was open for all nations; and Litvinov, as a result of a conversation with Stresemann in Berlin,

[41] *Die Internationale*, xi, No. 11, June 1, 1928, pp. 324–331.

[42] *Stenograficheskii Otchet VI Kongressa Kominterna* (1929), ii, 47.

[43] *Ibid.* 107, 140, 259; Bell also poured scorn on the League of Nations with its "fine words" on disarmament and "the outlawry of war" as "a screen for war preparations" (*ibid.* ii, 23).

[44] *Humanité*, August 17, 20, 24, 25, 26, 1928.

[45] This was reported without comment in *Izvestiya*, August 29, 1928.

[46] L. Fischer, *Men and Politics* (1941), p. 141.

[47] *Dokumenty Vneshnei Politiki SSSR*, xi (1966), 408.

came to the conclusion that "it would be an error to suppose that the Great Powers are in any way interested in our adhesion to the pact".[48] On August 5, 1928, when the signature was imminent, an interview with Chicherin appeared in *Izvestiya.* Describing it as "profoundly abnormal that these negotiations are proceeding without its [the Soviet Government's] participation", Chicherin observed that "it is still not too late", and repeated emphatically that "the possibility of participation by our government in the signature of the Kellogg pact is not excluded".[49] A cool pronouncement from the State Department in Washington indicated that, while countries other than the original signatories could accede to the pact as soon as it was signed, acceptance of a Soviet accession would not imply diplomatic recognition of the Soviet Government.[50] The signature of the pact by fifteen countries took place in Paris on August 27, 1928; and on the same day Herbette handed to Litvinov an official invitation (such as was apparently being sent to all other countries) to accede to the pact.[51] No hesitation was shown over the decision. On August 29, 1928, the presidium of TsIK recorded a formal resolution to accede;[52] and on the following day Litvinov, in an argumentative note which rehearsed at length Soviet criticism of the substantial deficiencies of the pact, communicated the favourable decision to Herbette.[53] The formal act of accession bore the date September 6, 1928.[54]

No sooner had the pact been signed than a certain division and jealousy sprang up between the original signatories and those who had merely been invited to adhere. Of the neighbours of the Soviet Union only Poland had been a signatory; and, while Lithuania, anxious not to compromise herself in the eyes of the western Powers by showing less devotion than Poland to the cause of peace, hastened to adhere, the other eastern European countries temporized. Nor, in the four months that followed the signature of the pact, had any of the original signatories ratified it. These conditions inspired in Moscow the idea of proposing to the European neighbours of the Soviet Union to conclude a separate pact

[48] *Ibid.* xi, 449, 454–455.
[49] *Ibid.* xi, 463–467.
[50] *Izvestiya,* August 23, 1928.
[51] *Dokumenty Vneshnei Politiki SSSR,* xi (1966), 487–489.
[52] *Sobranie Zakonov, 1928,* No. 60, art. 541.
[53] *Dokumenty Vneshnei Politiki SSSR,* xi (1966), 493–498.
[54] *Ibid.* xi, 503–506.

or pacts bringing the provisions of the Kellogg pact into immediate force between themselves.[55] On December 29, 1928, the Soviet Government made this proposal to the Polish and Lithuanian Governments, intimated that a similar proposal would be made to the Latvian, Estonian and Finnish Governments, once they had decided to adhere to the pact, and informed the French Government, which had served as intermediary for the Soviet accession, of what it had done.[56] The Lithuanian Government welcomed the proposal, and on January 4, 1929, addressed notes to the Latvian, Estonian and Finnish Governments expressing the hope that they would join in signing the pact.[57] The Polish Government, though with far greater reservations, approached the same governments, as well as the Rumanian Government which had not been included in the Soviet proposal, and which cautiously replied that it would welcome a Polish–Soviet pact, provided it too was invited to sign.[58] On January 10, 1929, the Polish Government somewhat grudgingly accepted the proposal in principle, but declared that the inclusion of Lithuania in the invitation, and the exclusion of Rumania, "makes the Polish position difficult". On the following day, Litvinov replied in a lengthy note, which continued past recriminations on the Polish–Lithuanian dispute, but made no objection to the inclusion of Rumania; and on January 19, 1929, the Polish Government declared its willingness to discuss procedure for signature, while repeating its desire to bring in the Baltic countries as signatories.[59]

From this point it became clear that the ambition of Poland

[55] The origin of the proposal appears to have been fortuitous. Pressed by the Soviet Government to take concrete steps to ease the Polish–Lithuanian tension (see *ibid.* xi, 551–552), Voldemaras, at a meeting with Zaleski in Königsberg in November 1928, suggested the conclusion of a pact similar to the Kellogg pact between all the countries of eastern Europe (*ibid.* xi, 755, note 221); the Soviet Government, informed of this *démarche*, eagerly took up the idea in a modified form.

[56] *Ibid.* xi, 639–649; owing to the existence of the Soviet treaty with Lithuania of September 28, 1926, the terms of the note were inappropriate, and the proposal was made orally to the Lithuanian Government.

[57] The Lithuanian *démarche* is known from the Latvian and Estonian replies, which were published in *Izvestiya*, February 1, 1929.

[58] *Ibid.* January 6, 1929.

[59] For these notes see *Dokumenty Vneshnei Politiki SSSR*, xii (1967), 20–28; the annoyance of the German Government at these proceedings was expressed in a telegram of January 18, 1929, from Stresemann to the German minister in Warsaw (*Auswärtiges Amt*, 2945/573824–5).

was to appear as the leader and sponsor of the non-Soviet signatories. In conversations on January 28 and 31 the Polish Ambassador informed Litvinov that Latvia, Estonia and Rumania (but not Finland) were ready to sign, and that the Polish Government raised no objection to the desire of Lithuania to accede separately.[60] No further difficulties arose. On February 9, 1929, the pact accepting the obligations of the Kellogg pact as valid between themselves was signed in Moscow by the Soviet Union, Poland, Latvia, Estonia and Rumania. The ceremony was filmed — the first intrusion of the cinema into Soviet, or perhaps into any, diplomacy.[61] Ratification by TsIK followed four days later.[62] Lithuania adhered separately, and Turkey and Persia also adhered later.[63]

These proceedings afforded a temporary but welcome distraction from the problem of disarmament. Only the Soviet Government — and, for different reasons, the German Government — was determined not to let it go by default. On August 20, 1928, Litvinov wrote to the president of the preparatory commission to enquire when the commission would reassemble to consider the Soviet draft of the previous March, and received a temporizing reply;[64] and, during the Assembly of the League of Nations in the following month, Cushenden was reported as engaged in attempts to postpone the session indefinitely.[65] At the session of TsIK in December 1928 Litvinov again denounced the delaying tactics of the majority of the commission.[66] In the same month, he sent another long protest to Geneva and received

60 *Dokumenty Vneshnei Politiki SSSR*, xii (1967), 55–58.

61 *Ibid.* xii, 68–70; *Izvestiya*, February 10, 1929.

62 *Ibid.* February 16, 1929.

63 *Dokumenty Vneshnei Politiki SSSR*, xii (1967), 68–70, 95–96, 135. The Soviet Government had shown from the outset a desire to associate the eastern countries with it in its adhesion to the pact; on August 28, 1928, it notified the Turkish, Persian and Afghan Governments of its intention to adhere on September 4 (the actual date of its adhesion was September 6), and suggested that they should adhere on the same date by way of demonstrating their solidarity with Moscow (*ibid.* xi (1966), 491).

64 *Ibid.* xi, 476–479.

65 *Izvestiya*, September 28, 1928.

66 *4 Sessiya Tsentral'nogo Ispolnitel'nogo Komiteta Soyuza SSR 4 Sozyva* (1928), No. 19, pp. 4–9.

another evasive answer. This time, however, the resources of procrastination had been exhausted. A definite, though still remote, date—April 15, 1929—was fixed for the sixth session of the commission.[67]

The commission met on the date named. Litvinov at once made his presence felt with a lengthy speech protesting against the long delays and the methods adopted by the commission.[68] On April 17, 1929, the Soviet delegation submitted yet another draft convention based, as Litvinov explained, on the three principles of a substantial reduction of existing armaments, of proportional reduction, and of the fixing of proportional coefficients; the draft cleverly copied some of the restrictions imposed on Germany under the Versailles treaty, in particular, the total prohibition of certain types of armament, including military aviation, and the limitation of the size of warships. In the course of a desultory discussion extending over three meetings, in which Litvinov constantly intervened, only the German, Italian and Turkish delegates manifested a polite interest in the Soviet proposals, and announced that they would abstain in any vote taken on them.[69] The bureau of the commission put forward a resolution proposing to proceed on the lines laid down at the previous session—a virtual shelving of the Soviet draft; only the Soviet and Chinese delegates objected, and the resolution passed without a vote, Litvinov recording a written protest.[70] Much time was spent on the chapter banning chemical warfare, which was virtually a recapitulation of the provisions of the protocol signed in 1925. Litvinov urged that signatories of the protocol who had not yet ratified it should be pressed to do so; and this was approved.[71]

The rest of the proceedings repeated the experience of previous sessions. Almost every other proposal for the limitation of any form of armaments encountered fatal objections from some quarter. The commission once more confined itself to the question what categories of armaments should be restricted, and discussed

[67] *Dokumenty Vneshnei Politiki SSSR*, xi (1966), 599–602.

[68] *Documents of the Preparatory Commission for the Disarmament Conference*, Series VIII (Geneva, 1929), pp. 12–15.

[69] *Ibid.* pp. 19–37.

[70] *Ibid.* pp. 37–41, 208–210.

[71] *Ibid.* pp. 49–55, 62–82; the Soviet Government had acceded to the protocol on December 2, 1927, during the fourth session of the preparatory commission, and ratified it on March 9, 1928 (*Dokumenty Vneshnei Politiki SSSR*, x (1965), 524–526).

no figures of coefficients of reduction. A noteworthy feature of the session was the increasingly marked concord between Soviet and German delegations. As early as December 1926 Stresemann had tried to interest Chicherin in the disarmament negotiations in Geneva on the plea that the Polish Government would invoke Soviet armaments as an excuse for refusing to disarm.[72] Shortly afterwards, Stresemann instructed Brockdorff–Rantzau that "Russian participation in the disarmament conference ... is urgently and much to be desired"; and Unshlikht was reported to have asked a German military representative to be kept informed on questions relating to disarmament, in view of their intention "to work together in common in this field".[73] When the Soviet delegation first appeared at Geneva in November 1927, the German delegation showed no great alacrity to support its proposal for total disarmament. But the production of the Soviet draft in March 1928 provoked a sufficient change of attitude to inspire a cynical comment in the Soviet press that, though the German Government cared as little as other western governments for disarmament, it was ready to utilize the Soviet initiative in order to convict the Allied Powers of their failure to comply with the obligation, implicit in art. 8 of the League Covenant, to reduce their armaments.[74] It was not, however, till April 1929 that coordination of their policies at Geneva almost automatically established itself.[75] The German delegation regularly proposed to write into the disarmament convention all the limitations and prohibitions imposed on Germany by the Versailles treaty, and was consistently supported by the Soviet delegation. The German delegation rather more hesitantly supported the numerous Soviet proposals and protests. The Italian and Turkish delegations generally tried not to take sides. Finally, on May 4, 1929, when everyone had become impatient to wind up an unfruitful session, the American and French delegations put forward a resolution rejecting any direct limitation, or even any obligatory limitation of expenditure on armaments, but approving "limitation and re-

[72] *Ibid.* ix (1964), 563–564.

[73] *Akten zur Deutschen Auswärtigen Politik,* Series B, v (1972), 226, 367.

[74] *Izvestiya,* March 27, 1928.

[75] It was suggested in Moscow that the German delegation has been moved by anger at the support now given by the United States delegation to the French case (*Dokumenty Vneshnei Politiki SSSR,* xii (1967), 251); but this explanation seems scarcely necessary.

duction of material ... by means of publicity of expenditure". This resolution secured twenty-two votes. The Soviet and Chinese delegations voted against it; Germany abstained, but Italy and Turkey voted with the majority.[76] Litvinov in his concluding speech on May 6, 1929, noted that the exclusion from the draft convention of every limitation to which exception was taken had resulted in a "refusal to adopt the principle of the reduction of any elements of armed forces whatever"; the commission had ceased to serve any purpose and should hand over the task to a disarmament conference, "the speediest convocation of which I now propose".[77] The commission dodged the issue by declaring only the "first part" of the session closed, and failing to set a date for the second part.

A leading article in *Izvestiya* celebrated Litvinov's victory:

> The Soviet delegation was able to reveal to the whole world from the Geneva tribune the hypocritical tactics of bourgeois democracy, to unmask the plans of the imperialist governments, to expose with complete clarity the aims pursued by the governments represented in the Geneva commission.[78]

The tactics of establishing the Soviet presence at Geneva, brilliantly executed by Litvinov, had begun to yield results. At a time when the Soviet appeal to the organized workers in western Europe was sagging, an effective channel of approach had been found to influential radical and progressive groups which, though themselves bourgeois in ways of life and thought, were frequently critical of their national governments and sympathetic to the international policies of the Soviet Government. In Moscow, this also contributed to the gradual "normalization" of Soviet foreign policy and Soviet diplomacy.

[76] *Documents of the Preparatory Commission for the Disarmament Conference*, Series VIII (Geneva, 1929), pp. 179–181; the defection of the Turkish delegate, who on his first appearance in 1928 had shown some sympathy for the Soviet proposals (see p. 109 above), did not pass unnoticed in Moscow (*Protokoll: 10. Plenum des Exekutivkomittees der Kommunistischen International* (n.d.), p. 490).

[77] *Documents of the Preparatory Commission for the Disarmament Conference*, Series VIII (Geneva, 1929), pp. 191–193.

[78] *Izvestiya*, May 9, 1929.

B: *Comintern and the Capitalist World*

*

CHAPTER 66

COMINTERN AND SOVIET FOREIGN POLICY

THE intrusion of diplomacy into the practice of a régime whose ambitions were international, and whose programme excluded the pursuit of purely national interest, followed almost automatically on its assumption of power, when imminent attack by hostile states imposed on it the necessity of manoeuvring between them as the sole means of salvation. The revolutionary government at once found itself precariously balanced between Germany and the Allies. Lenin, a few weeks after the Brest–Litovsk treaty had been signed and ratified, insisted that "our sole guarantee of a real peace, not a paper peace, is the rift between the imperialist Powers";[1] and in May 1918 he telegraphed to Shaumian, the Bolshevik commissar in the Caucasus:

> What saves us for the moment are simply the conflicts and the struggle between the imperialists. Have the skill to exploit these conflicts; for the moment we have to learn diplomacy.[2]

The diplomatic exploitation of such rifts was, however, not incompatible with a single-minded pursuit of the international revolutionary goal. As Lenin explained in theses which justified acceptance of the "shameful" Brest–Litovsk peace:

> We must decide questions not from the point of view of the preferability of this or the other imperialism, but exclusively from the point of view of the best conditions for the development and reinforcement of the socialist revolution which has already begun.[3]

It was indeed this incipient revolution which saved the régime in the ordeal of the civil war: "internal disintegration in the Entente states" had gone so far that "the Entente could not make war on us with its own armies".[4]

Lenin's optimistic view of the time-table of world revolution

[1] Lenin, *Polnoe Sobranie Sochinenii*, xxxvi, 168.
[2] *Ibid.* l, 73–74. [3] *Ibid.* xxxv, 247. [4] *Ibid.* xlii, 21.

made it easy to accept these temporary expedients to meet the emergency. But the difficulties confronting the régime did not evaporate even with the end of the civil war. Policies of diplomatic manoeuvre remained no less necessary. Lenin, looking forward to the Genoa conference in his report to the eleventh party congress in March 1922, explained the tactics to be followed:

> It is not indifferent to us whether we have to deal with those representatives of the bourgeois camp who tend towards a military solution of the question or with those who tend towards pacifism.[5]

In draft instructions to the Soviet delegation for the conference, Lenin defined the "chief political task" of the delegation as being to separate the "petty bourgeois, pacifist and semi-pacifist" wing from "the crudely bourgeois, aggressively bourgeois, reactionary bourgeois camp"; the aim would be "to improve a little its chances at the elections", and "to drive the wedge between the bourgeois countries united against us at Genoa". The function of the delegation was "in no way the development of communist views".[6] The procedures inaugurated in 1918 were still in order. But, with the change in the revolutionary time-table, the context in which they were applied had also changed. The function of diplomacy was no longer to further a socialist revolution that had already begun, but, for the more or less prolonged interval before that revolution could be consummated, to build up the economic well-being and power of an independent Soviet state. In Lenin's thinking, however, these measures retained their temporary character, being designed to enable the régime to "hold out" till the international revolution could come to its aid. In the very last of his writings, early in 1923, Lenin's chief anxiety was whether it could "hold out till the moment of the socialist revolution in the most advanced countries, ... till the day when the capitalist countries of western Europe have completed their evolution into socialism".[7]

So long as Lenin lived, the unique and distinguishing characteristic of Soviet foreign policy could hardly be denied. It had its built-in revolutionary component. World revolution was the postulate on which the policy, and indeed the very existence, of

[5] *Ibid.* xlv, 70. [6] *Ibid.* xliv, 407–408. [7] *Ibid.* xlv, 402.

the Soviet republic rested. The expedients accepted and commended by Lenin were designed to bridge the interval — longer, no doubt, than had been initially expected, but still of limited duration — till that consummation should be achieved. But, even before Lenin died, the ambiguities and embarrassments of this interpretation of Soviet foreign policy had begun to appear. With the formation of communist parties in the principal countries, and the foundation of the Communist International, other communists could challenge the right of the Soviet leaders to a monopoly of judgment on what would best serve the interests of world revolution. In 1920, in Persia and still more dramatically in Turkey, the exigencies of Soviet policy called for the support of a régime which was actively engaged in persecuting and killing native communists — a line which was later referred to, somewhat shamefacedly, as "the Kemalist path".[8] The secret military agreements with Germany, the beginnings of which went back to 1921, aimed at the rearming of the Reichswehr, which incidentally led to arming it for its other function, the suppression of German communist risings.[9] Moreover, the lapse of time, and the absence of any victories for the revolution outside the Soviet Union, made it more and more difficult to regard such policies as temporary expedients to tide over a crisis. It was at the fourth congress of Comintern in November 1922 that Bukharin explicitly defended the right of the Soviet republic to conclude an alliance with a bourgeois state, and to count on communists in the country concerned to support such an alliance; and his justification of this right struck a realistic, not to say cynical, note:

[8] For these episodes see *The Bolshevik Revolution, 1917–1923*, Vol. 3, pp. 292–294, 298–301; Martov, at the Halle congress of the USPD in October 1920, already accused the Bolsheviks of using the eastern peoples "as pieces on the chess-board of the diplomatic war against the Entente" (*USPD: Protokoll über die Verhandlungen des Ausserordentlichen Parteitags zu Halle* (n.d.), p. 214).

[9] One of the few explicit attempts to defend the delivery of Soviet war material to Germany by invoking the Kemalist precedent was made by the KPD leader, Ewert, in 1927: "War material was also delivered by Soviet Russia to the Turkish Government; that is a firm and uncontestable fact. But this same Turkish Government simultaneously persecuted communists in Turkey in the harshest manner; that is also an incontestable fact. Our party in Turkey worked under the most arduous conditions; yet the struggle of the national Turkish Government against the advance troops of western imperialism was supported by Soviet Russia. This must be made clear to the workers" (*Hamburger Volkszeitung*, March 1, 1927); but such frankness was rare. For the secret agreements see pp. 38–46 above.

> It was said in the Communist Manifesto that the proletariat will conquer the whole world. Well, that cannot be done with one finger, that must be done with bayonets and rifles.[10]

Only the Soviet Union possessed the bayonets and rifles. And a resolution of the congress asserted the duty of workers throughout the world to "proclaim their moral, political and economic solidarity with Soviet Russia".[11]

The decisive act which consecrated this development, and provided its theoretical under-pinning, was Stalin's promulgation of the doctrine of socialism in one country. The order of priority had been reversed. The dependence of the Russian revolution on world revolution, persistently asserted by Lenin, was repudiated; and the dependence of world revolution on the building of socialism in the Soviet Union automatically took its place. World revolution became a secondary factor in the formulation of Soviet policy. The gradual change of premiss and shift in emphasis was veiled by the constant repetition of what were textually identical formulas. When the fifth congress of Comintern in 1924, proclaiming the slogan of "Bolshevization", set in motion the cumulative process of the loyal submission of the member parties of Comintern to the central direction of Moscow,[12] the declared aim of the process was still to forge an effective instrument of international revolution. Two years later, at the fifteenth Russian party conference of October 1926, Stalin offered a further explanation:

> We regard the victory of socialism in our country, not as an end in itself, not as something self-sufficient, but as a support, as a means, as a way to the victory of the proletarian revolution in other countries.

And, taking up the argument formerly used by Lenin, he went on to claim that "the capitalists are not in a position to mobilize 'their' workers to fight against our republic", and that "the international situation of the republic is now based on this sympathy".[13] At the seventh IKKI a month later, Kolarov exhorted

[10] *Protokoll des Vierten Kongresses der Kommunistischen Internationale* (1923), p. 421; for this speech see *The Bolshevik Revolution, 1917–1923*, Vol. 3, p. 447.

[11] See *ibid.* Vol. 3, p. 446.

[12] See *Socialism in One Country, 1924–1926*, Vol. 3, pp. 92–94.

[13] Stalin, *Sochineniya*, viii, 263–264.

foreign communist parties to "repel any assault directed at the USSR";[14] and Stalin laboured the point at the same session:

> The interests and tasks of the proletariat of the USSR are intertwined and inseparably linked with the interests and tasks of the revolutionary movement in all countries, and *vice versa* the tasks of the revolutionary proletariat of all countries are inseparably linked with the tasks and achievements of the proletariat of the USSR on the front of socialist reconstruction.

Any attempts to oppose the "national" to the "international" tasks of the proletariat would be "a profound political error".[15] The resolution of the session "On the 'Russian' Question", while claiming that the party was "in all its work oriented to international revolution", which alone would guarantee the security of the Soviet Union, declared that the Soviet Union "is the chief organizing centre of international revolution".[16] Diplomats were more keenly alive to the implications of the changed climate, or less inhibited in announcing them. The British chargé d'affaires in Moscow reported in July 1926 that Stalin's rise to power would "impel the Soviet Government in the direction of becoming more of a Russian government and less of an international conspiracy organization". Six months later he put the matter in a nutshell to Litvinov: "Let Russia confine herself to building up her socialist state, and all will be well"; and Litvinov assented.[17]

An episode of the first months of 1927, though it received little publicity, showed that the incongruity of the two faces presented by the USSR to the world was still a source of embarrassment. Bukharin in a speech to the Moscow provincial party conference on January 8, 1927, designed to distract attention from the revelations of the secret Soviet–German military agreements, accused Germany of the sin of imperialism: "Germany has now been drawn into the defence of a general imperialist policy, not as an *object* of that policy, but already in a considerable degree as a *subject*, i.e. as one of the actively engaged forces on the imperialist political market". In particular he accused the German Govern-

[14] *Puti Mirovoi Revolyutsii* (1927), i, 16.

[15] Stalin, *Sochineniya*, ix, 28.

[16] *Kommunisticheskii Internatsional v Dokumentakh* (1933), p. 680; for this resolution directed mainly against the opposition see p. 139 below.

[17] *Documents on British Foreign Policy*, Series I A, *ii* (1968), 197–198, iii (1970), 24.

ment of working hand-in-glove with the other imperialist Powers in Lithuania.[18] This provocation could not be left unanswered. Schubert in a despatch to Brockdorff-Rantzau of January 15, 1927, expressed great indignation at Bukharin's attacks on Germany, and instructed him to protest to Litvinov. Brockdorff-Rantzau replied that he had already done so; and in a further conversation Litvinov hinted that steps had been taken to curb Bukharin's indiscretions.[19] About the same time Litvinov in conversation with the British chargé d'affairs professed to deprecate talk about world revolution by Bukharin and others.[20] The attacks on Germany were also sharply criticized by Chicherin in a letter to Stalin and Rykov of February 18, 1927, as damaging to Soviet–German relations.[21]

The emergence of Asia from 1925 onwards as a major preoccupation of Soviet international policy was another complicating factor. Hitherto the dilemma of reconciling encouragement of revolutionary movements and communist parties with support for national governments engaged in a struggle against western imperialism had arisen only in countries such as Turkey and Persia, where communist parties were still embryonic, and could be sacrificed without much compunction to the exigencies of Soviet foreign relations. In India and Indonesia the revolutionary ferment was at work, and derived much of its impetus from the October revolution. But no means had yet been found in Moscow of exercising any significant influence over it. What happened in China, however, introduced a new dimension. If in Europe the increasing remoteness of the revolutionary prospect made it relatively plausible to describe the defence of the sole revolutionary base in the Soviet Union as the primary immediate concern of the revolutionary movement, in China the revolutionary movement was an active force to be reckoned with, and a major threat to the imperialist Powers. The Chinese national revolution was pursuing a course which seemed to conform both to the Bolshevik revolutionary tradition and to the interests of Soviet diplomacy.

[18] For the speech see p. 47 above; for the passage about Lithuania see p. 81 above.

[19] *Akten zur Deutschen Auswärtigen Politik*, Series B, iv (1970) 65–67, 138–139.

[20] *Documents on British Foreign Policy*, Series I A, iii (1970), 23–25.

[21] See p. 47 above.

Here the Russian party, Comintern and the Soviet Government were engaged together in promoting a revolution in which national and social aims were intertwined, and whose victory would be a victory for the Chinese people, for the international proletariat and for the Soviet Union. It was only in 1927, when the national and social aims of the Chinese revolution diverged, that a dichotomy of purpose declared itself, and it became impossible to evade the question whether the directives from Moscow were designed to serve the cause of Chinese communism, now exposed to savage repression at the hands of Chinese nationalists, or of Soviet policy, which not implausibly regarded the promotion of national revolution in the colonial and semi-colonial countries as its most effective weapon both of offence and of defence against the capitalist world. The Chinese dilemma played a persistent part in the controversies between the party hierarchy and the opposition which raged in Moscow during that troubled year.

When the eighth IKKI met in Moscow in May, 1927, the Chinese disaster and the rupture of relations with Great Britain had produced a sharp change of mood. World revolution was now a remote and unreal prospect, the fear of war an overriding obsession.[22] The old phrases about the solidarity of the international proletariat with the proletariat of the Soviet Union acquired a new urgency in a new context. The primary task of communist parties was now to rally round the Soviet Union and defend it as the unique citadel of revolution against the assaults of the imperialists. Humbert-Droz wrote to Togliatti in February 1927 that "the interests of the USSR at the present hour, when England threatens a rupture, are certainly above everything else"; and in a further letter of April 8, 1927, he deplored "the passivity of our parties in regard to China and the connected danger of war against Russia".[23] The concluding section of the lengthy resolution of the eighth IKKI on the danger of war, headed "Tasks of Communist Parties", announced that "the central slogans of the present anti-war campaign should be defence of the Chinese and Russian revolutions", and that the masses should be

[22] See pp. 8–10 above.

[23] *Il Contrasto tra l'Internazionale e il PCI* (1969), pp. 239, 246 (Humbert-Droz archives, 0077, 0081).

mobilized for the defence of the Soviet Union "under the slogan 'the international proletariat defends its proletarian fatherland' ".[24] The party central committee on August 1, 1927, was the occasion of a still more pointed pronouncement by Stalin:

> There is one question which acts as a watershed between all possible groups, tendencies and parties, and is the test of their revolutionary or counter-revolutionary character. This question is now the question of the defence of the USSR.... An *internationalist* is one who without reservations, unconditionally, openly, honestly, is ready to defend and protect the USSR, because the USSR is the base of the revolutionary movement.[25]

It seemed a startlingly exclusive claim. But, when Stalin at the fifteenth party congress in December 1927 offered in two separate lists a schematic enumeration of the "tasks of the party" on the revolutionary and diplomatic fronts, he presented these activities as two facets of the same policy;[26] and, whatever embarrassments may have awaited those charged with the implementation of these instructions, it may be assumed that neither Stalin nor a majority of his hearers at the congress detected any incompatibility between the items on the two lists of desiderata.

The identification of the interests of the international revolutionary movement with those of Soviet diplomacy, which had begun to ring hollow in the ears of many foreign communists, was now contested in Moscow only by a battered and persecuted opposition in process of being expelled from the party. Trotsky at the eighth IKKI in May 1927 had concentrated his fire on the maintenance of the alliance with Kuomintang and of the Anglo-Russian trade union committee — two outstanding examples of the subordination of revolutionary principle to the exigencies of Soviet state policy.[27] Rakovsky, in his much interrupted speech at the fifteenth party congress in December 1927, challenged the myth of "a constant growth of the sympathies of the working class [in foreign countries] for the Soviet Union". He quoted an observation of the bourgeois *Kölnische Zeitung* that the Soviet Union, on the tenth anniversary of the revolution, could be treated

[24] *Kommunisticheskii Internatsional v Dokumentakh* (1933), pp. 715–716; for the resolution see pp. 144–145 below.

[25] Stalin, *Sochineniya*, x, 50–51.

[26] *Ibid.* x, 290–291.

[27] The alliance with Kuomintang will be discussed in a later section of this volume; for the Anglo-Russian committee see pp. 348–349 below.

not as "ideological danger", but "like any other state".[28] Trotsky continued to find the root of the evil in the doctrine of socialism in one country, which he described in 1928 as "a social-patriotic concept".[29] The miscalculations and failure of Comintern from 1923 to 1927, he wrote later, "killed the faith of the Soviet masses in world revolution". Comintern became an empty shell; Stalin regarded it as "a necessary evil to be used as far as possible for purposes of foreign policy".[30]

The expulsion of the opposition from the party and from Comintern removed the last restraints on the open and avowed pursuit of this course. In the defiant and uncompromising atmosphere of the ninth IKKI in February 1928, which adumbrated the turn to the Left in Comintern, Bukharin enunciated the approved policy with unusual bluntness:

> *Either the Soviet state is a proletarian state, and Comintern must stand on the side of the Soviet Union in the principal questions of the policy of the Soviet Union, as well as in the question of the danger of war, or it is not.* The Communist International has here to choose: Either—or! There is no third position.[31]

When the programme of Comintern adopted by the sixth congress six months later announced that "the victory of socialism is possible in the first place in a few capitalist countries, or even in one, taken separately", it also pointed to the deduction to be drawn by communists elsewhere:

> The development of socialism in the USSR and the growth of its international influence ... evoke the greatest sympathy towards it on the part of the broad toiling masses of the whole world, and a readiness of the oppressed classes of all countries to fight by every means for the country of the proletarian dictatorship in the event of an imperialist attack.

And "the defence of the USSR by all means" was inscribed among the "fundamental slogans" of Comintern.[32] Behind the scenes less ceremony was observed. What purported to be an

[28] *Pyatnadtsatyi S"ezd VKP(B)*, i (1961), 210–211; for this speech see Vol. 2, pp. 47–48.

[29] L. Trotsky, *The Third International After Lenin* (N.Y., 1936), p. 70.

[30] L. Trotsky, *The Revolution Betrayed* (Engl. transl., 1937), pp. 90, 97.

[31] *Internationale Presse-Korrespondenz*, No. 18, February 23, 1928, p. 373.

[32] *Kommunisticheskii Internatsional v Dokumentakh* (1933), pp. 17, 35, 45.

address delivered by Voroshilov on April 16, 1928, to a group of Comintern officials stressed the need, in the interests of the Red Army, of "correct relations" with some bourgeois states; the speaker instanced the dependence of the Red Army on the technical expertise of the military–chemical industry in the United States.[33] What had once seemed a paradox or a temporary expedient was now taken as a matter of course.

The unconditional priority now accorded to Soviet national interest had its implications in the field of organization. Comintern had been conceived as a unified organization of which the member parties were "sections". What set the Russian party apart from all the others was that it had made a revolution and taken over the government of a powerful state; it was for the other parties to learn from its experience and emulate its performance. As Kuusinen put it at the seventh IKKI in November 1926:

> A new international experience of the highest revolutionary importance has been presented to the workers of capitalist countries in recent years through the instructive spectacle of the Russian revolution.[34]

Lozovsky hammered home the same theme for the benefit of the CPGB in the foreword to an English report on the proceedings of the fourth congress of Profintern in 1928:

> There is no sense in creating an international organization if it is not to intervene, if it will not take up the essential problems, and will not endeavour to utilize the international experience for the purpose of straightening out the line of the labour movement of this or that country.[35]

The original conception of Comintern as a single disciplined organization was realized in a Soviet mould; this was the essence of the Bolshevization of the parties already proclaimed by the fifth congress in 1924.[36] A unitary policy centred on the defence of the Soviet Union could be planned and executed only under a supreme command and a general staff operating from Moscow;

[33] The document, found in the German archives (*Auswärtiges Amt*, 284/098508), was presumably supplied by a German agent; its authenticity is uncertain, but not improbable.

[34] *Puti Mirovoi Revolyutsii* (1927), i, 117; for a previous expression of this idea see *Socialism in One Country, 1924–1926*, Vol. 3, p. 70, note 3.

[35] *Report of the Fourth Congress of the RILU* (1928), p. 3.

[36] See *Socialism in One Country, 1924–1926*, Vol. 3, pp. 92–94.

and, though the command and the staff were in form international, nobody in the middle nineteen-twenties could doubt that they already represented a monopoly of power exercised by the Russian party. The delicate manoeuvres of the united front, involving the constant risk of falling into Right or ultra-Left deviations, were to be executed under the direction of IKKI and of the Comintern secretariat, reflecting the changing appraisals of the international situation by the Russian party and the Soviet Government. When Murphy at the ninth congress of the CPGB in October 1927 rejected with scorn the idea that IKKI was "not an international body at all, but some little organ of the VKP(B)", or that "four or five comrades from the Russian party are sitting down and issuing orders", and claimed that Comintern and the Soviet Government "are obviously two different institutions",[37] the formal correctness of his rebuttals was less impressive than the substantial truth that underlay the allegations. Humbert-Droz related that an article written by him just before the sixth congress of Comintern in July 1928, claiming that the Russian party was a section of Comintern like any other, and subject to its discipline, made Stalin furious.[38]

The corollary of this development was that Comintern directives were uniformly applicable to all parties. The diversity of revolutionary initiative was replaced by bureaucratic conformity. For a party to plead exceptional conditions which excused it from compliance with a general directive became a mark of heresy. As Togliatti, well schooled in Comintern theory and practice, wrote in an Italian party journal in 1929:

> Our party would have committed a most serious error if it had maintained that the Italian situation is an exceptional one, in which one does not find the same alignments portrayed by the organs of Comintern as characteristic for the period throughout the world.[39]

And Stalin a few months later, addressing the American party, enunciated the same principle:

> The foundation of the activities of every communist party . . . must be the general characteristics of capitalism, which are

[37] *The Ninth Congress of the CPGB* (1927), pp. 65–66.
[38] J. Humbert-Droz, *De Lénine à Staline* (Neuchatel, 1971), p. 321.
[39] P. Spriano, *Storia del Partito Communista Italiano*, ii (1969), 229.

the same for all countries, and not its specific characteristics in any given country.[40]

Parties soon lost the degree of flexibility necessary for the conduct of their affairs with due regard to the interests and opinions of their members; and leaders were promoted or dismissed on the strength, not of the confidence enjoyed by them in their own party, but of their unconditional loyalty to the behests of Moscow. In the scarcely exaggerated words of Trotsky's indictment:

> With the wedge of the Russian disputes, driven in by hammer blows of the state apparatus, the leaderships being formed at the moment in the communist parties of the west were disorganized over and over again. All this went on under the banner of struggle against factionalism.[41]

Even in details of organization pressure was brought to bear on foreign parties to adopt Soviet models. When Bukharin was finally removed from participation in Comintern early in 1929, he complained that "shouting plus compulsion" had replaced persuasion in its relations with the parties.[42] The assumption that an identity of interest between the state policies of the Soviet Union and the aims of foreign communist parties could be indefinitely preserved without sacrificing the international and revolutionary aura of Comintern had broken down. The semblance of it could be maintained only by rigid measures of discipline, constantly preached from Comintern platforms and harshly enforced by a Comintern bureaucracy.

[40] I. Stalin, *O Pravykh Fraktsionerakh v Amerikanskoi Kompartii* (1930), p. 3; for the crisis in the United States party see pp. 609–612 below.

[41] L. Trotsky, *The Third International After Lenin* (N.Y., 1936), p. 156.

[42] Quoted by Molotov in *Protokoll: 10. Plenum des Exekutivkomitees der Kommunistischen Internationale* (n.d.), p. 423.

CHAPTER 67

UNSTABLE STABILIZATION

In the first three months of 1926 governments and parties in Europe were in process of regrouping themselves after the Locarno treaties; and in the Soviet Union the internal crisis following the condemnation of Zinoviev by the fourteenth party congress in December 1925 had not been resolved. Both these uncertainties contributed to a slowing down in the work of Comintern. When the sixth IKKI met in February 1926, Zinoviev still functioned as president, and directed the debates. But he studiously remained on non-controversial ground; and the policies of Comintern, in Germany and elsewhere, were still directed primarily against the ultra-Left.[1] The personal situation was, however, plainly untenable in the long run. The presidency of Comintern was a lever of power in the ruling party; and it was quixotic to suppose that Zinoviev would not use it to further his own ends. The first instance of this use occurred in January 1926 with the proposed despatch of Gertrud Gessler on a mission to foreign capitals on behalf of the opposition.[2] The second compromising episode was the discovery that Belenky, another Comintern official, had been prominently engaged in organizing the "meeting in the forest" addressed by Lashevich in June 1926, and in other underground opposition activities.[3] These incidents provided a basis or pretext for the resolution of the party central committee of July 1926 censuring Zinoviev and expelling him from the Politburo.[4] It was not till October 1926 that the central committee, ostensibly at the request of ten foreign communist

[1] See *Socialism in One Country, 1924–1926*, Vol. 3, p. 496.

[2] See Vol. 2, pp. 8–9; it was about the same time that Zinoviev made abortive overtures to Ruth Fischer (see *Socialism in One Country, 1924–1926*, Vol. 3, pp. 337–338).

[3] See Vol. 2, pp. 4–5, 8.

[4] See *ibid.* p. 9. Trotsky in the course of the session made a strong attack on the Anglo-Russian trade union committee (see p. 328 below), and Zinoviev is said to have compared the opportunist tactics of Comintern with those of the Second International; Togliatti and Remmele defended the official line (*Voprosy Istorii KPSS*, No. 6, 1959, p. 34).

parties, withdrew Zinoviev from his post as president of IKKI and excluded him from further work in Comintern.[5] This was a necessary prelude to the seventh enlarged IKKI, which met eight months after the sixth on November 22, 1926. It mustered 100 voting delegates, of whom 38 were members of IKKI, and 91 non-voting delegates.[6] Bukharin took over the presidential chair from Zinoviev, whose letter of withdrawal was read at the first sitting.[7]

The new leader sounded a paean of triumph in his opening speech:

> The party of the Soviet Union has during the year won very many successes. It is marching on the road to socialism. It has easily overcome the so-called crisis about which so much was written.

But he also struck the appropriate international note: "We are children of the world revolutionary movement."[8] Bukharin's main report on the international situation, much shorter than usual, but supplemented by a printed report circulated to the delegates, revolved round the theme of the "stabilization of capitalism". The diagnosis of an "offensive of capital", already implicit in the recognition by the third congress of Comintern in 1921 that the advance of revolution had been slowed down by a recovery of capitalist forces, was repeated at the fourth and fifth congresses,[9] entered the current vocabulary of Comintern in 1925, and was a major theme of the fifth IKKI in March of that year.[10] It was sometimes qualified by such adjectives as "partial", "temporary" or "relative"; and this qualification became explicit at the sixth IKKI in February 1926.[11] The British general strike had seemed at first to justify a belief in the disintegration rather than the stabilization of capitalism; this conclusion had been drawn by Zinoviev in

[5] See Vol. 2, p. 17.

[6] *Puti Mirovoi Revolyutsii* (1927), i, 278.

[7] See Vol. 2, p. 19. A resolution was passed to abolish the post of president, but the proposal was referred to the next congress, since an amendment of the statute was required (*Puti Mirovoi Revolyutsii* (1927), ii, 468; the revised statute adopted by the sixth congress (see p. 220 below) omitted the provisions for the appointment of a president.

[8] *Ibid.* i, 7; for the optimistic atmosphere of the period see Vol. 1, pp. 11–13, 287–289.

[9] See *Socialism in One Country, 1924–1926*, Vol. 3, pp. 75–76.

[10] See *ibid.* Vol. 3, pp. 286–293.

[11] See *ibid.* Vol. 3, p. 494.

an article in *Pravda* of June 4, 1926. But Zinoviev was no longer an orthodox or authorized interpreter. An article in the party journal more cautiously described it as a "rhetorical simplification" to say that the strike meant "a *collapse* of stabilization"; it had merely thrown "a glaring light on the shape of the existing stabilization".[12] When Bukharin spoke at length at the fifteenth party conference in October 1926 on the current stabilization of capitalism, and named Great Britain and China as responsible for two "enormous breaches" made in it, he pronounced a nicely balanced verdict. To deny that capitalism in western Europe had in some degree recovered from the shocks of the post-war years and established a measure of stabilization was an ultra-Left illusion, which he attributed to Zinoviev and to Korsch. On the other hand, to pretend that the recovery could be lasting, and could lead to a stage of super-imperialism under American predominance, was a heresy of the Right.[13]

In his written report to the seventh IKKI Bukharin repeated this analysis. He called the United States "a country which expresses most sharply the upward curve of the capitalist economy", and included Japan and the British dominions as falling "partially" within this category. Sounding a note which was constantly reiterated in the next few years, he attacked the social-democrats for supporting capitalism, as represented by the United States, against socialism, as represented by the Soviet Union. But some more positive touches could be added to the picture. Having established the fact of stabilization, Bukharin turned to the three main forces which were undermining it: socialist construction in the USSR, the decline of British capitalism and of the British Empire, and the revolution in China. The "inescapable difficulties of the capitalist governments" were accompanied by "a sharpening of the class struggle". The duty of Comintern was to "support the most important centres of the international revolutionary movement, i.e. the British workers, the Chinese revolution and the USSR". "The unmasking of social-democracy" was "on the agenda", side by side with the struggle against Fascism and the white terror. But a section of the report on work in the trade

[12] *Bol'shevik*, No. 12, June 30, 1926, p. 4.

[13] *XV Konferentsiya Vseoyuznoi Kommunisticheskoi Partii(B)* (1927), pp. 3–21, 41, 44; the resolution of the conference accused the opposition of " 'ultra-Left' self-deception and 'revolutionary' adventurism" through its denial of partial capitalist stabilization (*KPSS v Rezolyutsiyakh* (1954), ii, 334).

unions did not suggest any alteration in the tactics of the united front. It called, with special reference to Germany, for "the most vigorous work in the trade unions and the energetic continuation of united front tactics", and referred to the "ever increasing radicalization" of social-democratic and non-party workers.[14] Bukharin in his briefer spoken report adopted a more demagogic tone. Stimulated perhaps by Stalin's denunciation of the opposition at the fifteenth party conference a few weeks earlier as "a social-democratic deviation", he directed much of his fire at the social-democrats, whom he accused of supporting the stabilization of capitalism, of preparing the way for new wars and of supporting the United States against the Soviet Union. He thus set a pattern which became increasingly familiar in Comintern invective in the next few years. He also broached another theme which had an important controversial future, dividing the post-war development of Europe into three stages: the initial period of tumult, of an "immediate revolutionary situation", when the social-democrats came out openly against the communists; the period of capitalist stabilization when the communists "conducted a small retreat"—the heyday of the united front; and the third period, just beginning, when the stabilization of capitalism "reveals in ever sharper form its inner contradictions", and "the movement of the working class to the Left" could be seen as "the clear expression of this process". But no precise conclusions were drawn, and the report ended with commonplaces.[15]

The debate on these large issues was colourless. Zetkin maintained that the stabilization of capitalism was merely a synonym for the class rule of the bourgeoisie.[16] Roy observed that "nowhere is the expression 'stabilization' less applicable than in England", and diagnosed the irrevocable decay of British imperialism:

> The imperialism which found its strength in capital export from the motherland is dead. England today can export no capital.

The British bourgeoisie was now attempting "to mobilize the auxiliary resources of the empire in order to overcome the present difficulties of British capitalism". In the more advanced parts of the empire, such as India, "the new British policy seeks to open

[14] *Puti Mirovoi Revolyutsii* (1927), i, 30–112.
[15] *Ibid.* i, 19–30. [16] *Ibid.* i, 294.

up domestic sources of capital".[17] This thesis, which was later to become the starting-point of an acute controversy, attracted no immediate attention. The only critic of any but minor points of Bukharin's draft theses was Treint, who repeated his view, already rejected by the French party congress in July 1926,[18] that the principal current antagonism in the capitalist world was a struggle between the United States of America and a Europe united in "an Anglo-European alliance against the United States". Belief in a fundamental Anglo-American antagonism had long been preached by Trotsky, whose slogan of a "United States of Socialist Europe" had recently been revived by the sixth IKKI.[19] The care which Treint took to disclaim any agreement with Trotsky did not save him from a sharp rebuttal of his opinions.[20]

The other speakers did little more than paraphrase Bukharin's views. Kuusinen denounced "the counter-revolutionary rôle of social-democracy", and balanced carefully the two potential deviations — the Left deviation which valued only "revolutionary propaganda for the ultimate goal", and renounced "practical revolutionary work among the broad masses of the workers", and the "Right opportunist deviation", which believed that, in a situation which was not immediately revolutionary, only "parliamentary and reformist work of all kinds" was practicable. He firmly commended continued participation in "non-party organizations and united front organs".[21] Thälmann, in his peroration, while purporting to agree with Bukharin, appeared to strike a slightly more aggressive note:

> What comrade Bukharin has said for the communist world-party we can repeat for the German communist party: we are

[17] *Ibid.* i, 328; he also qualified Bukharin's view of American capitalism by describing it as "just at the zenith of its power" (*ibid.* i, 328–329).

[18] See p. 469 below.

[19] See *Socialism in One Country, 1924–1926*, Vol. 3, pp. 506–507.

[20] *Puti Mirovoi Revolyutsii* (1927), i, 137–164; the version in the German record of the proceedings (*Protokoll: Erweiterte Exekutive der Kommunistischen Internationale* (n.d.), pp. 158–160) is no more than a skeleton outline. The speech drew replies from two official spokesmen, Pepper and Kurella (*Puti Mirovoi Revolyutsii* (1927) i, 164–170, 212–217, also abbreviated in the German version), and almost half of Bukharin's reply to the debate was devoted to it (*ibid.* i, 374–380). Pepper's shift in allegiance from Zinoviev to Bukharin on the eve of the seventh IKKI is graphically described in T. Draper, *American Communism and Soviet Russia* (1960), pp. 238–239.

[21] *Puti Mirovoi Revolyutsii* (1927), i, 116, 124.

> and remain the party of the revolution, of the overthrow, of the proletarian dictatorship. In this sense, and only in this sense, we are the party of the proletarian united front, of mass work, of day-to-day struggles against the bourgeoisie.[22]

But nobody wished to press this thorny issue. Bukharin's theses were not challenged, and were unanimously adopted. "*The fact of capitalist stabilization* (the growth of world production, the growth of international trade, the regularization of the currency, etc.)" was unconditionally recognized. But the qualification that this was "*a partial, unstable stabilization*" was no less emphatic. Anglo-American rivalry played the largest rôle in the growing confrontations between imperialist Powers. The USSR, the British workers and the Chinese revolution were named as "the most important focuses of the international revolutionary movement". The struggle against the threat of a new imperialist war involved "the unsparing exposure of 'pacifist', 'pan-European' and other social-democratic and bourgeois utopias". Encouraging symptoms were noted: "in a majority of countries there is observed a process of the radicalization of the masses of workers". The necessity of work in the trade unions as "the broadest organizations of the working class" was particularly stressed; so also was the struggle against the social-democrats who "finally and everywhere now stand on the side of bourgeois governments".[23] Many ideas and phrases which were shortly to find their place in the armoury of Comintern were ventilated at the seventh IKKI. But neither Bukharin's report nor the theses carried any hint of a radical change of front.

References to the trade unions in the debate were perfunctory, and were pitched in a minor key. Bukharin in his written report had confessed that "the masses think that the communists are good leaders in direct political clashes, but are unsuited to small day-to-day work, and understand neither the strategy nor the tactics of economic disputes". Kuusinen put in a *caveat* against the "politicization" of the trade unions. A line should be drawn between the party and the unions; the introduction of party slogans into the unions confused non-party workers.[24] But a trade

[22] *Ibid.* i, 270.

[23] *Kommunisticheskii Internatsional v Dokumentakh* (1933), pp. 626–643; "radicalization" was the accepted translation in western languages of the Russian *polevenie*.

[24] *Puti Mirovoi Revolyutsii* (1927), i, 99, 120.

union commission was also set up, and Lozovsky reported on its behalf. In the preceding debate on the British general strike, he had commented bitterly on the growing strength of "the united front established between social-democrats and Amsterdam trade union leaders on the one hand and the employers on the other".[25] His report on the trade union question opened with a long attack on the social-democrats, whom he accused of supporting trust-building, capitalist rationalization and, with particular reference to Germany, the acquisition of colonies. "The will among the workers for the united front" was said to be everywhere growing. But a new meaning seemed to be injected into the concept:

> To a significant extent the striving of the workers for the united front, for unity, for joint actions, for joint demonstrations, has recently strengthened; the social-democratic workers, against the will of their leaders, are for agreement with the communists, thus expressing a protest against the line of their own organizations....
>
> If we take into account all these processes going on at present within the workers' movement, we can say that the regrouping of forces, the shift within the working class occurs continuously from Right to Left, and not *vice versa.*

Lozovsky praised the successes of the united front, especially in Great Britain but also in France: "the best result of the united front is when we succeed in creating a single organ to direct workers' actions". But "waverings" could be detected among communists from two sides: "metaphysicians of unity" who wanted unity everywhere and in everything, and those who thought it "enough to chatter about unity" and did nothing to realize it in practice.[26] No debate took place on Lozovsky's report, perhaps

[25] *Ibid.* i, 498; for this debate see pp. 338–339 below.

[26] *Ibid.* i, 540, 546. The official record of Lozovsky's speeches at the seventh IKKI is puzzling. The Russians version of his report on the trade union question (*ibid.* i, 528–557) is almost twice as long as the German version (*Protokoll: Erweiterte Exekutive der Kommunistischen Internationale* (n.d.), pp. 646–479); the substance is similar, and some phrases and quotations occur in both, but the text rarely corresponds, so that the impression remains not of two versions of one speech, but of two speeches delivered by the same speaker on the same subject. The German may be an abbreviated and much revised version of the original speech; or alternatively the German may represent the speech as delivered, and the Russian a more elaborate write-up by Lozovsky for publication. Lozovsky probably spoke in German; but this is not decisive, since, in whatever language speeches were delivered, the official record was kept in Russian. The German version of Lozovsky's other speech

because Lozovsky was due to deliver a report on the same topic a few days later to the seventh congress of Soviet trade unions.[27] The resolution adopted at the end of the session noted that the growing concentration and rationalization of production, as well as technological development ("*the Americanization of production*"), strengthened resistance to workers' demands. It accused IFTU and the General Council of the British TUC of breaking trade union unity, but hopefully added that "*the consolidation of the Amsterdam International at the top runs parallel with a widening rift between top and bottom layers*". The united front was declared to be "a powerful instrument in the hands of the working class in all defensive and offensive battles". But a warning was issued both against "a formal and agitational approach to the united front" and against "tactics of 'unity at any cost' ". The admission that "we have hitherto not won a majority of the working class" sounded a note of uneasiness. The work of Profintern was to be strengthened. But the lengthy resolution carried no indication of a change of policy.[28]

The two major international events since the sixth enlarged IKKI deliberated in the previous March — the British general strike and miners' strike, and the victorious advance of the Chinese nationalist revolution — were the theme of important separate debates and resolutions on the British and Chinese questions.[29] It may have been the growing importance of the agrarian problem in China which prompted the appointment of a large and representative agrarian commission.[30] But the discussion of agrarian policy,

at the session (see pp. 338–339 below) is only half as long as the Russian, but appears to be a genuine abbreviation; subject to extensive omissions, it corresponds closely to the Russian text and presents none of the wide divergences of the report on the trade union question. For the drastic abbreviation of Treint's speech in the German version see p. 135, note 20 above; these problems do not arise on any other main speeches delivered at the seventh IKKI.

[27] For this report, which followed closely the lines of the IKKI trade union resolution, see *Sed'moi S"ezd Professional'nykh Soyuzov SSSR* (1927), pp. 249–275; Lozovsky's views at this time were expressed rather more boldly in an article in *Krasnyi Internatsional Profsoyuzov*, No. 12, 1926, pp. 535–549, in which he described the current stabilization as "insecure, relative and only temporarily stable".

[28] *Kommunisticheskii Internatsional v Dokumentakh* (1933), pp. 643–655.

[29] For the British resolution see p. 339 below; Chinese affairs will be discussed in a later section of this volume.

[30] *Protokoll: Erweiterte Exekutive der Kommunistischen Internationale, November–Dezember, 1926* (n.d.), p. 13; the Russian edition does not record the appointment or membership of commissions.

both in plenary session and in the agrarian commission, related mainly to the European peasant. The Russian delegates who spoke on the subject, Meshcheryakov and Dubrovsky, diagnosed rising peasant discontent, but argued that an agrarian movement could succeed only as part of a revolution led by the proletariat.[31] Dombal started from agrarian movements in the colonial and semi-colonial countries, went on to denounce international bourgeois peasant movements, and concluded hopefully that "the international revolutionary peasant movement is growing and expanding"; and Boškovič deprecated "the formation of separate centralized peasant parties", which might encourage the illusion that the peasants could act independently of the proletariat.[32] When Dengel, the president of the agrarian commission, reported on the last day of the session, he admitted—with a frankness rare in Comintern records—that it had not been possible to agree on a conclusion; and from his confused remarks it was apparent that the rift was similar to that which had so long bedevilled trade union policy—the difficulty of working within non-communist peasant organizations while also preaching revolutionary action to overthrow them. The resolution proposed, and adopted by the plenary session, took note of a draft submitted by Dombal and Dubrovsky as "material" for a resolution to be worked out by the presidium in time for the next session of IKKI.[33] Nobody during the proceedings seems to have mentioned Krestintern or its International Peasant Council.[34]

It was, however, the struggle against the opposition which still absorbed the attention of the Soviet leaders; and the debate on "the 'Russian' Question" launched by Stalin, though postponed till the second half of the session, was its major event, occupying ten sittings spread over a week. Zinoviev, Trotsky and Kamenev all exercised their right to speak, and were refuted in chorus by a galaxy of orators from the Russian party and from every other major member party of Comintern.[35] The conformity was significant. A feature of the debate was the discrediting of Radek, who

[31] *Puti Mirovoi Revolyutsii* (1927), i, 178–188.

[32] *Ibid.* i, 192–202.

[33] *Ibid.* ii, 348–352; the draft was not published, and nothing more was heard of the resolution.

[34] See p. 281 below

[35] See Vol. 2, pp. 19–20; a major item in the indictment against the opposition was that they had attempted to "carry the struggle into other communist parties, creating a platform for all opposition elements in the Communist International" (*Kommunisticheskii Internatsional v Dokumentakh* (1933), p. 681).

had been president of the Sun Yat-sen university since its foundation in 1925.[36] Stalin in his speech at the fifteenth party conference in October 1926 had reacted angrily to a witty lampoon by Radek in the Communist Academy a few weeks earlier on the doctrine of socialism in one country.[37] In his speeches at the seventh IKKI Stalin ignored Radek, and concentrated on more important targets.[38] But the ever-ready Neumann heaped fresh indignation on Radek's indiscretion. Katayama made the barbed remark that the instruction of young members of Kuomintang in the Sun Yat-sen university ought not to be left to "comrade Radek and his adherents". Kuusinen even more damagingly reported that Ruth Fischer and the other dissidents in the KPD had "complained to comrade Radek" about their treatment.[39] But the impression of a fundamental harmony, marred only by a handful of fractious dissidents of the Russian opposition and their counterparts in other parties, was maintained throughout the session.

The hegemony of Moscow was no longer exposed to a challenge of the kind offered by Bordiga at the previous session.[40] While "the Bolshevization and strengthening of the parties" was still proclaimed by Bukharin as the "main task", the essence of the situation was exposed by Togliatti with exemplary clarity and frankness:

> Of course, we have the statutes of the International which guarantee certain rights to certain comrades; but there is something which is not in these statutes, that is the position of the Russian party in the International, its function of leadership. That goes beyond the statutes.[41]

Nobody could doubt any longer that Soviet example and Soviet guidance were paramount. Opposition in the German and French parties was firmly and faithfully dealt with.[42] In May 1926, the

[36] See *Socialism in One Country, 1924–1926*, Vol. 3, p. 725.

[37] Stalin, *Sochineniya*, viii, 278–279; for Radek's remarks, perhaps toned down for the record, see *Vestnik Kommunisticheskoi Akademii*, xvii (1926), 245–249.

[38] For these speeches see Vol. 2, pp. 19–20.

[39] *Puti Mirovoi Revolyutsii* (1927), ii, 171–172, 288, 373; Radek was pointedly excluded from the amnesty accorded at the seventh IKKI to Brandler and Thalheimer (see pp. 415–416 below).

[40] See *Socialism in One Country, 1924–1926*, Vol. 3, pp. 500–502.

[41] *Puti Mirovoi Revolyutsii* (1927), i, 392, ii, 145.

[42] See pp. 414, 477–478 below; for the resolution against the Russian opposition see Vol. 2, p. 20.

Dutch party, not without prompting from Moscow, had expelled from its ranks two notable dissidents, Wijnkoop and Ravesteyn. The seventh IKKI appointed a commission to review the Dutch question; and Pepper presented its report. Wijnkoop was said from the first to have stood for an "outspokenly western leadership" in Comintern, and to have wished to treat the social-democrats as a "brother party". But both also exhibited an ultra-Left sectarianism. Since their expulsion they had formed a dissident so-called communist group, and attacked Comintern in the press. IKKI unanimously endorsed their expulsion, and addressed a manifesto to the Dutch party denouncing the renegades.[43]

A significant move was made to strengthen the central apparatus of IKKI. Togliatti, who submitted a resolution on the subject, explained that the aim was to replace the president by a "collective organization", and "to draw into the actual leadership of Comintern in an ever higher degree non-Russian, western European comrades". A political secretariat "consisting of new comrades from different parties" was to be set up. Members of IKKI were to be required to attend meetings in Moscow three times a year; and IKKI was to elect a presidium of eighteen members with seven candidate members, who were to reside in Moscow. The existing Orgburo of Comintern was to be abolished.[44] These reforms doubtless improved the efficiency of the central organization. The "national secretariats" set up by the sixth IKKI were subordinated to the new political secretariat.[45] The provisions for

[43] *Puti Mirovoi Revolyutsii* (1927), ii, 381–384; *Internationale Presse-Korrespondenz*, No. 16, February 5, 1927, p. 342.

[44] *Puti Mirovoi Revolyutsii* (1927), ii, 345–348; the published resolution merely provided for the abolition of the presidency, subject to necessary confirmation by the next congress (see p. 132, note 7 above), and instructed IKKI to make the necessary arrangements for the establishment of the political secretariat and other consequent changes (*Internationale Presse-Korrespondenz*, No. 16, February 5, 1927, p. 346).

[45] For these secretariats see *Socialism in One Country, 1924–1926*, Vol. 3, p. 909; Humbert-Droz in a letter to a correspondent many years later gave an account of their functions: "You seem to suppose that the territorial secretariats were well organized and worked with a standing personnel. This was not the case. In general, a member of the political secretariat or of the presidium was put at the head with a deputy or political collaborator at his side ... to these were added permanent or temporary representatives of the parties dependent on the secretariat, if they happened to be passing through Moscow ... The organization was therefore very flexible. The point was to

more frequent sessions of IKKI and for a large international presidium resident in Moscow were never fully carried out. But they enabled the Russian leaders of Comintern to select, recruit and reward individual members of important foreign parties whose fidelity was assured. Meanwhile the practice, pursued since the early nineteen-twenties, of attaching members of the Comintern secretariat to the principal foreign parties, for special occasions or for longer periods, had been standardized; and the stereotyped usages and vocabulary of Comintern were adopted in all parties. As an American Communist observed:

> Comintern representatives began to exist everywhere, and even Comintern lingo — Rusian lingo — words like nuclei and politburo — and we even had a plenum in the American party.[46]

These arrangements gave institutional form to the monopoly of leadership which was implicit in the much vaunted process of the Bolshevization of the parties and, ultimately, in the doctrine of socialism in one country.[47] Each successive session of IKKI helped to make the monopoly more effective and more secure.

After the seventh IKKI, and the departure of important Comintern and Profintern delegations for China,[48] a void occurred in Comintern activities. Togliatti went to Paris to organize the new base for the PCI in exile.[49] In the Comintern secretariat in Moscow he was replaced as head of the Agitprop section by Petrovsky (who worked in the CPGB under the name of Bennett), and as president of the trade union commission by Humbert-Droz.[50] Events did not, however, stand still. Early in 1927 a German party commentator, looking back on the seventh IKKI, discerned "a

collect as much information as possible and discuss the problems. The territorial secretariats could take no decisions." (B. Goldenberg, *Der Kommunismus in Lateinamerika* (1971), p. 550, note 32).

46 *Survey*, lv (1965), 122–123.

47 For earlier stages of the process see *Socialism in One Country, 1924–1926*, Vol. 3, pp. 522–524.

48 These will be discussed in a later section of this volume.

49 See p. 540, note 23 below.

50 These changes were recorded by Humbert-Droz (for whose activities in the trade union commission see p. 167 below) in a letter to Togliatti of February 26, 1927 (J. Humbert-Droz, *Il Contrasto tra l'Internazionale e il PCI* (1969), pp. 238–239 (Humbert-Droz archives, 0077)).

certain shift in the whole international development", illustrated by the progress of the Chinese revolution, by "the rapid growth of a revolutionary situation in England", and by the sharpening of contradictions between the USSR and the capitalist world.[51] Before the eighth IKKI met in May 1927, the elements of optimism had faded from the picture, and the international situation had turned sharply against the Soviet Union. The British Left had proved a broken reed, and the hostility of the British Government was inexorable. The mailed fist of British diplomacy was discerned behind the blows which fell on Soviet interests throughout the world. In April 1927 a raid on the Soviet Embassy in Peking, with the connivance of the diplomatic corps, was followed by Chiang Kai-shek's *coup* in Shanghai, which shattered the foundations of the policy pursued by the Chinese Communist Party and by its Soviet and Comintern mentors.[52] A month later, the Arcos raid in London repeated the pattern of the Peking raid; and, while the eighth IKKI was in session, news arrived that the British Government had broken off relations with the Soviet Union.[53] The embarrassments of the international situation inspired a recrudescence of opposition activity in the Russian party. The "declaration of the 83" was forwarded to the Politburo on the very day of the severance of Anglo-Soviet relations.[54] On every front the leaders of Comintern were on the defensive, and found themselves vulnerable to the imputation of a false optimism which had failed to foresee the dangers ahead.

The atmosphere of alarm and tension which so notably differentiated the eighth IKKI in May 1927 from its predecessor six months earlier was reflected in its organization. It was one-third as large as the seventh IKKI, mustering only seventy-one delegates, thirty-three with voting rights, from twenty-five countries.[55] It enjoyed none of the usual blaze of publicity; and neither

[51] *Die Internationale*, x, No. 2–3, February 1, 1927, p. 45; a further article in the same journal three months later protested that "the preparation of the imperialist war goes on in all capitalist countries hand in hand with the civil war against 'the enemy within' " (*ibid.* x, No. 9, May 1, 1927, p. 257).

[52] These events will be discussed in a later section of this volume.

[53] See pp. 25–26 above.

[54] See Vol. 2, pp. 25–26.

[55] *Kommunisticheskii Internatsional v Dokumentakh* (1933), p. 699. From this time sessions of IKKI were no longer described as "enlarged"; the sixth congress in 1928 removed from the statute of Comintern the provisions for "enlarged" sessions, which had resembled miniature congresses, and which

its proceedings nor those of the ninth IKKI in the following year were ever published in full.[56] After Bukharin had delivered the opening speech, Kuusinen, Bell of the CPGB and Bernard of the PCF acted as joint *rapporteurs* on the main theme of the session, the imminent threat of war, and introduced a long and detailed resolution on "The Tasks of the Communist International in the Struggle against War and the Danger of War"—the first ever devoted by Comintern to the subject.[57] A striking feature of the resolution, in contrast to its predecessors, was the disappearance of any reference to the stabilization of capitalism. It pointed out that the "relative equilibrium" established in the last few years in international affairs had been replaced by "open military conflicts" on a minor scale and by "an accumulation of combustible material ready to flare up at the dropping of the first spark". Premising that "international capital has already begun a war against the toiling masses of China", it spoke of the "epoch of great wars" inaugurated in 1914, and of capitalist contradictions as the cause of war. But this was not enough:

> All the contradictions of capitalist states among themselves fall into the background in face of the basic watershed which divides the whole world into two camps: in one stand the USSR and revolutionary China, in the other the whole capitalist world.

Great Britain stood "at the head of world reaction". China and the USSR were "key-points" in the danger of war and the main targets of imperialist aggression. Denunciation of the social-democrats, already familiar in Comintern pronouncements, acquired a fresh dimension when the Second International and IFTU were accused of complicity in the ideological preparations for an imperialist war:

> The whole treacherous campaign was meant to justify an attitude of "neutrality" in the event of a war of the capitalist countries against the USSR.

were to be replaced by regular meetings of permanent members of IKKI "as the organ elected by the congress" (*Stenograficheskii Otchet VI Kongressa Kominterna* (1929), v, 110).

[56] The partial and belated publication of the debate on China will be discussed in a later section of this volume.

[57] For reports of the session see *Pravda*, May 31, June 1, 1927; *Internationale Presse-Korrespondenz*, No. 54, May 24, 1927, p. 1167, No. 57, June 3, 1927, pp. 1225–1226.

And this, in turn, dictated a more cautious and sceptical application of the tactics of the united front. For, while these tactics were still essential (the need to work in non-party organizations was again emphasized at the end of the resolution), it could not be forgotten that "the so-called 'Left' democratic leaders ... are the most dangerous enemies of communism in the workers' movement"; Maxton and Purcell were among those named. Wars were classified in three categories: (*a*) "wars between imperialist states", (*b*) "national-revolutionary wars against imperialism", (*c*) "wars of capitalist counter-revolution against a proletarian revolution or a régime engaged in building socialism". The duty of communist parties in the two last categories was clear. The first category was covered by Lenin's formula of "the conversion of imperialist war into civil war". The detailed injunctions were vague. But what was required before and during the war was "work among the masses, in the factory, in trade unions, in the countryside, in the army"; and Lenin was quoted as stressing the need for a party to supplement its legal activities with an underground organization and illegal work. Slogans like a "people's army" or a "national militia" were outdated, and could only mislead. In the final analysis, the only correct slogan for communist parties was "Defence of the Chinese and Russian Revolutions", and the resolution ended with a catalogue of instructions to the parties for the conduct of the campaign against war.[58] The resolution was supplemented by a popular manifesto, apparently drafted under the immediate impact of the rupture of relations by Great Britain, which embroidered the theme of an imperialist war against the workers and peasants of the world:

> World imperialism and, first and foremost, British imperialism can no longer tolerate the existence of the only workers' and peasants' republic.... The reactionary Baldwin government is preparing war against the Soviet Union.... The war against the Soviet Union is a class war, a war against the proletariat. The great imperialist states know that the world proletariat watches over the Russian revolution.... The imperialists prepare war in order to strangle the revolution.

And the manifesto ended with the appeal: "Against the threatening war, for the revolutionary struggle."[59]

[58] *Kommunisticheskii Internatsional v Dokumentakh* (1933), pp. 699–717.
[59] *Pravda*, May 31, 1927.

The same themes dominated the separate resolutions debated and adopted at the eighth IKKI on the two countries directly involved in the threat of war, the one as prime mover, the other as victim: Great Britain and China. In both countries, the representatives of the non-communist Left had betrayed the hopes reposed in them, and turned against their communist partners; in both, the united front had been shaken to its foundations. The other main topic of debate was the struggle against the opposition in the Russian party, which by now openly challenged the leaders' policies in the international forum. Zinoviev, debarred from further participation in Comintern affairs, was not present. But Trotsky, though no longer a member of IKKI since the fifth congress,[60] was admitted as a non-voting delegate and delivered two fierce indictments of Stalin's policy in China, his sole supporter being Vujovič, the Yugoslav delegate and former worker in KIM, the only active supporter of the opposition with voting rights. While the condemnation of the opposition was a foregone conclusion, the drafting of the resolution gave rise to an embarrassing episode. It was proposed specifically to condemn a communication addressed by Trotsky to the Politburo attacking the Chinese policy of the party. The Italian delegation, represented by Togliatti and Silone, declined to condemn a document which they had not seen; Stalin refused to divulge to IKKI a document touching on the policy of the Soviet Government in China. After Kolarov had tried vainly to mediate, and Treint and Humbert-Droz had supported the Italian objection, Stalin angrily withdrew the proposal.[61] The text as finally presented by Togliatti in the name of the Italian, German, French, British, Czechoslovak and American delegations,[62]

[60] See *Socialism in One Country, 1924–1926*, Vol. 3, p. 91.

[61] J. Humbert-Droz, *De Lénine à Staline* (Neuchatel 1971), p. 283; I. Silone, *Uscità di Sicurezza* (1965), pp. 89–99, related the story, according to Humbert-Droz, "in a somewhat fictionized form", but "the substance of the story is correct". This item was originally published in the journal *Comunità* in 1949. The English version which appeared in the composite volume, *The God that Failed*, ed. R. Crossman (1950), pp. 83–119, was substantially rewritten; an accurate English translation appeared in I. Silone, *Emergency Exit* (1969), pp. 41–99. If Silone is right in saying that the withheld document was published in L. Trotsky, *Problems of the Chinese Revolution* (1932), it must have been Trotsky's counter-theses of May 17, 1927; it seems more probable that it was his letter to the Politburo of March 31, 1927 (these documents will be discussed in a later section of this volume).

[62] Togliatti's speech is in *Kommunisticheskii Internatsional*, No. 27 (101), 1927, pp. 6–14. Togliatti's offence was not, however, forgotten; Kuusinen at

launched into a general denunciation of the opposition, including both Zinoviev and Radek in its censure. Its only novelty was the first item in the indictment: "nullifying and discrediting the struggle of the Communist International against the danger of war". The specific charge against Trotsky and Vujovič was that they had attempted to disrupt the work of IKKI "by constantly distributing fractional material hostile to the party".[63] Trotsky aggravated his offence by circulating, in the name of Vujovič and himself, a reply to the resolution in which he claimed that "the defeats of the German proletariat in 1923, the defeats in Bulgaria and Estonia, and finally the defeat of the Chinese proletariat, have not only strengthened social-democracy at the expense of the communist party, but within the communist party have strengthened the Right wing at the expense of the Left".[64]

Bukharin, in making to the Moscow party organization a few days later the customary report on the proceedings of the session, spoke of "the central slogan" of the danger of war, and declared that in *proletarian republics* "defence of the fatherland ... is the first duty of communist parties". He cited the famous Stuttgart resolution of the Second International on the need to utilize the political and economic crisis of war to bring about the downfall of capitalism, and recalled that Lenin during the war of 1914 had rejected the simple slogan of peace (his differences with Trotsky were noted), and called for the transformation of imperialist war into civil war. At the present time, Bukharin observed, war had not begun, and "the Soviet Union, on whose banner *the slogan of peace* is inscribed, is an extraordinarily big political factor". The only correct slogan, he repeated, was "defence of the Russian and Chinese revolutions". Turning on the opposition, he roundly denied Trotsky's charge "that we *are at present weaker than before*". But he continued to insist on the reality of the temporary stabilization of European, and especially central European, capitalism:

> The regrouping of forces in the direction of the stabilization of capitalism, and the consolidation and reinforcement of its

the tenth IKKI more than two years later reminded him of his tenderness to Trotsky (*Protokoll: 10. Plenum des Exekutivkomitees der Kommunistischen Internationale* (n.d.), p. 624).

[63] *Kommunisticheskii Internatsional v Dokumentakh* (1933), pp. 741–745; for these proceedings see Vol. 2, pp. 24–25.

[64] For this declaration see Vol. 2, p. 25, note 2.

> political positions in Central Europe, are beyond doubt. Equally beyond doubt is Zinoviev's error when he recently said that the stabilization had already disappeared.[65]

With this long report Bukharin closed the account of the eighth IKKI. It had been an embarrassing occasion, and the party leaders had been more concerned to defend themselves against damaging attacks than to strike out a new line.

[65] *Pravda*, June 18, 1927; *Internationale Presse-Korrespondenz*, No. 65, June 24, 1927, pp. 1361–1373.

CHAPTER 68

PRESSURES FROM THE LEFT

THE eighth IKKI in May 1927 had been dominated by catastrophic events occurring shortly before, or during, its deliberations — the disaster in China, the final break with Great Britain and the fear of war. These events drove Comintern, automatically and almost unwillingly, into more uncompromising and more revolutionary postures. The hollowness of the united front as hitherto conceived, the futility of relying on the support of parties of the moderate Left, had been shown up. Premonitory symptoms of this development could indeed be traced back to an earlier period. The crisis in the Polish party in May 1926, when an initial inclination to temporize with Pilsudski and the PPS was vigorously denounced from Moscow,[1] might have seemed to foreshadow the new course. But Poland's proximity to the Soviet Union made this a special case. Illegal parties were always of necessity revolutionary and extremist, since no other option was open to them. "Fascism has destroyed *bourgeois*-democratic illusions", wrote the Italian party journal in June 1926; "the workers must therefore choose Soviet democracy".[2] Mistrust of the united front, hostility to social-democrats, contempt for the procedures of bourgeois democracy, demand for more direct revolutionary action by the masses — all these notes had been sounded at the eighth IKKI. But they were drowned by the persistent clamour of the threat of imperialist war, and no coherent policy or directive emerged. It was many months before the new line in Comintern was emphatically proclaimed at the ninth IKKI and the sixth congress in the following year. But the way was prepared by much that happened between the eighth IKKI in May 1927 and the ninth in February 1928.

The first dramatic event was a sudden insurrectionary outbreak in Vienna on July 15, 1927. Indignation had been felt at the indulgence shown by the Austrian authorities to para-military

[1] See pp. 564–566 below.

[2] Quoted in P. Spriano, *Storia del Partito Comunista Italiano*, ii (1969), 36.

organizations of the Right, which broke up workers' demonstrations and terrorized and sometimes killed workers. On February 6, 1927, the Austrian Communist Party published a programme calling for action "against the Fascist-monarchist danger", against the rehabilitation of Austrian finances through the agency of the League of Nations, which was part of "the economic offensive of the Austrian bourgeoisie against the workers", and against the attempt of the government "to integrate Austria into the front of international imperialism, into the imperialist war policy". While it ended with an appeal for "a united mass struggle", its tone was almost entirely defensive.[3] The party does not seem to have been responsible for a mass demonstration of workers which, on July 15, 1927, converged on the law courts, the parliament building and the university, regarded as the main citadels of reaction. The demonstration became a riot, the law courts were set ablaze and the police fired, killing about 100 of the insurgents. The communist party responded by proclaiming a general strike. But the trade unions, under predominantly social-democratic leadership, ignored the summons and called off a railway strike which had begun.[4] Three days later, when all was over, IKKI issued a flaming proclamation which hailed the heroic struggle of the Austrian workers and denounced "the treachery of Austrian social-democracy". It ended with a series of slogans:

> Down with social-democratic treachery! Life-and-death struggle against Fascist reaction! Arm the workers! Form workers' councils in Austria! Long live the victory of Red Vienna.

Izvestiya saw in the rising "*a clash of two different views of the world, of two different conceptions of justice, of social and state institutions*", and a vindication of the "*class principle*".[5] *Pravda* devoted the greater part of a leading article on the insurrection to "the treacherous role of social-democracy" and of "Left" social-democrats who were now "the *most dangerous* enemies of com-

[3] *Kommunisticheskii Internatsional*, No. 32 (106), 1927, pp. 21–24; it had originally appeared in *Die Rote Fahne*, February 6, 1927.

[4] For a description of these events by a member of the Austrian Communist Party see *Internationale Presse-Korrespondenz*, No. 73, July 19, 1927, pp. 1561–1562.

[5] *Izvestiya*, July 19, 1927; *Internationale Presse-Korrespondenz*, No. 74, July 22, 1927, pp. 1578–1579.

munism".[6] The Austrian Communist Party in a resolution of July 24, 1927, declared that a heavy blow had been struck at "the democratic illusion" of Austro-Marxism, "the theory of a peaceful democratic seizure of power", but confessed that its own organization had revealed "serious defects". The struggle must go on for a "workers' and peasants' government", and the party must develop into "the mass party of the Austrian proletariat".[7] Stalin, speaking in the party central committee, admitted that the Austrian party was weak, but defended it against criticism by Zinoviev on the plea that "to shatter social-democracy at a single blow is impossible".[8] An article in the Comintern journal described the event as "a turning-point", which "cuts the ground from under the feet of the Austro-Marxist swindle"; the disillusionment of the workers with the "treacherous leaders" would now "proceed relatively more quickly in Austria than in other countries".[9] Finally, on September 16, 1927, IKKI in a long resolution once more stressed "the tottering, insecure, transient character of capitalist stabilization", the treachery of social-democrats and the need for the communist party to rally the masses for the struggle".[10]

The Vienna rising coincided with the declared bankruptcy of Comintern policies in China and the final break with the Kuomintang Left. In Europe it coincided with a marked sharpening of the hostility of the British and French Governments to communism and to the Soviet Union. In Great Britain the passing of the Trade Disputes Act in July 1927 was widely regarded as the

[6] *Pravda*, July 22, 1927.

[7] *Internationale Presse-Korrespondenz*, No. 76, July 29, 1927, pp. 1629–1630.

[8] Stalin, *Sochineniya*, x, 5.

[9] *Kommunisticheskii Internatsional*, No. 35 (109), 1927, pp. 33–38.

[10] *Internationale Presse-Korrespondenz*, No. 100, October 14, 1927, pp. 2155–2158. At the sixth congress of Comintern in July 1928, where much criticism was heard of the ineffectiveness of the Austrian party (*Stenograficheskii Otchet VI Kongressa Kominterna* (1929), i, 92, 353, 609–610), it escaped formal censure; the spokesmen of a divided party did little to relieve current pessimism about its prospects (*ibid.* i, 134–136, 552–554, 566–568). Bukharin in the debate on the programme named the Vienna rising, together with the German fiasco of 1923 and the British general strike, as occasions which had revealed the nullity of the "so-called Left wing of reformism" (*ibid.* iii, 30). Criticism of the Austrian party continued a year later at the tenth IKKI (*Protokoll: 10. Plenum des Exekutivkomitees der Kommunistischen Internationale* (n.d.), pp. 69, 200–204).

celebration of the government's victory over the general strike and miners' strike of 1926, and it was followed by the collapse of the ill-fated Anglo-Russian committee.[11] On the other hand, straws in the wind seemed to give some encouragement. The execution of Sacco and Vanzetti in the United States in August 1927 provoked a wave of protests throughout western Europe, in which workers' and other Left parties participated jointly with communists.[12] Stalin, in an interview with foreign workers' delegations on November 5, 1927, deduced from these demonstrations that "the ground under the feet of capitalism is getting continually hotter and hotter", and that "conditions are ripening for new revolutionary events".[13] In the Soviet Union, the eighth IKKI of May 1927 left the opposition censured and defeated, but still fighting. During the rest of the year the struggle was further embittered by the charge, inspired rather by astute calculation than by plausible belief, that the opposition was lending aid and comfort to the external enemy.[14] On September 27, 1927, the exclusion of Trotsky, Vujovič and Rakovsky from IKKI was voted by its presidium.[15] Throughout the autumn the opposition was mercilessly and persistently harried by the party leaders. Any dissentient voice in Moscow or in the foreign parties was drowned in a chorus of indignant protests. The process culminated in the expulsion of the opposition at the fifteenth party congress in December 1927.[16]

The party congress, decisive in compassing the rout of the opposition, gave an uncertain lead on the issues of policy which were perplexing Comintern. Stalin's main report did not avoid a measure of ambiguity. He opened with an admission that production in the capitalist countries had risen above its pre-war level, followed by a passionate denial that this "stabilization" could be lasting: "out of stabilization is born the growing crisis of capitalism". He observed that "*the stabilization of capitalism is becoming more and more rotten and unstable*", and that, where-

[11] See pp. 346, 355–356 below.

[12] See p. 277 below.

[13] Stalin, *Sochineniya,* x, 215–216; Stalin again quoted this symptom of the "revolutionary energy" of the working class at the fifteenth party congress a month later (*ibid.* x, 284).

[14] See Vol. 2, pp. 29–31.

[15] See Vol. 2, p. 36.

[16] See Vol. 2, pp. 37–50.

as two years ago it had been possible to speak of "an ebb in the wave of revolution", there was now reason to believe that "*Europe is now plainly entering the phase of a new revolutionary upsurge*". But, when he came to discuss issues of policy, he had only words of commendation for the united front, and accused the opposition, through its attacks on the Anglo-Russian committee, of "rejecting out-and-out the idea of the tactics of a united front".[17] Bukharin, in the opening words of his report on the work of IKKI, referred to "the rising of the working class in Vienna", together with the British general strike and the strike movement in Germany (later he also cited the Sacco–Vanzetti demonstrations) as examples of "the sharpening of the class struggle". The change of emphasis was marked by repeated insistence on "the internal contradictions of capitalism".[18] Broaching "the question of the struggle for the united front", Bukharin asked whether any change was required in electoral tactics:

> The idea might easily arise that, in view of the complexity of the international situation of the USSR we must proceed *more mildly* in relation to social-democratic parties. It results, however, from the whole analysis which I have given in my exposition, that our electoral campaign should be used precisely in order to try to demonstrate to the workers that the communist party is the *only* revolutionary party of the working class.

Bukharin declared with emphasis that "the *peculiarity* of the tactics of the united front at the *present* time is a decisive application of the united front *from below*". He foresaw "embittered struggles with social-democrats for the soul of the working class"; and at the end of the "European" section of his speech he once more defined the task ahead:

> To shift the centre of gravity, in applying the tactics of the united front, to the *lower strata*, to sharpen the struggle against social-democracy and, in particular, against the so-called "Left" social-democratic leaders.

[17] Stalin, *Sochineniya*, 271–276, 285–286, 344–346.

[18] *Pyatnadtsatyi S"ezd VKP(B)*, i (1961), 624, 653, 692; this did not prevent Uglanov from accusing him of taking too favourable a view of capitalist development in Germany and omitting to stress "the other side" — a charge which Bukharin vigorously rebutted (*ibid.* i, 798, 822–828).

But in his peroration he ventured no more than the cautious hope that "the working class, having recovered a little from the defeats which it has suffered over a number of years, is beginning to rally its ranks, to raise its banner higher, to turn to the Left, to revolutionize itself"; and he seemed to pin his expectations for the immediate future on "the *colonial* struggle".[19] The speech did not succeed in dissipating an impression of lukewarmness in Bukharin's support for the adoption of more intransigent policies in Comintern; and the impending turn to the Left was associated with an already discernible decline in his authority.

The debate went some way to reinforce this impression. Both Lominadze, who spoke on China, and more emphatically Shatskin, hinted at Bukharin's neglect of a Right danger in Comintern.[20] Manuilsky, in an elusive speech, cunningly hedged his bets. He sharply criticized Lominadze and Shatskin, and thought it wrong to say that "the Right danger has increased in the last years". On the other hand, he agreed that "fire should be concentrated on the Right", and that social-democracy was now "our only enemy". In the most significant passage of the speech, he took the view that "our parties underestimate the tendency in the European workers' movement to move to the Left", and praised Bukharin's and Stalin's reports on the ground that "they mark a fresh breakthrough". He suggested that the parties "do not yet draw bold enough conclusions from their successes".[21] Bukharin, in a somewhat embarrassed reply, admitted that "there has been, and is, a Right danger", but not that it had "*grown* recently in the leading circles" of the parties; in so far as it had grown, it had "grown in the form of *Trotskyite* groupings, former ultra-Lefts being transformed into Mensheviks".[22] On this enigmatic note, the debate ended. The resolution of the congress detected "a sharpening of the chief contradictions both within the capitalist system and between the capitalist world and the USSR", and admitted only "a partial stabilization", which had in fact contributed to this result.[23] A circular addressed to the parties after the congress by the Agit-

[19] *Pyatnadtsatyi S"ezd VKP(B)*, i (1961), 653–658, 692; for instructions sent by Comintern in October 1927 to the British and French parties on electoral tactics see pp. 359, 498 below.

[20] For these speeches see Vol. 2, pp. 56–57.

[21] *Pyatnadtsatyi S"ezd VKP(B)*, i (1961), 742–759.

[22] *Ibid.* i, 839.

[23] *KPSS v Rezolyutsiyakh* (1954), ii, 447.

prop section of IKKI made the point that "the opposition 'episode' was by no means 'national' or 'Russian'", but had lessons for the workers everywhere. It had been encouraged by the apparent stabilization of capitalism, by the set-back in China and by the imperialist pressure on the Soviet Union. The defeat of the opposition coincided — the wish seemed father to the thought — with "the unmistakable beginning of a swing to the Left, the revolutionizing of the working class of western Europe, its corollary being a sharper struggle between social-democracy and communism".[24] The fifteenth party congress stood on a watershed between the period when the chief danger had come from the Left and a period when the chief danger would be seen on the Right.

The first months of 1928 were a fateful period in Soviet history. The "extraordinary" grain collections were accompanied by increasing pressure for rapid industrialization, by the exaltation of the rôle of the party and by the campaign against non-party specialists and experts in industry, in Narkomfin and in Gosplan. It remained for the ninth IKKI, falling within this critical period, to propound a concrete policy for Comintern. It cannot have helped that, at this moment, the Soviet leaders were intensely preoccupied by the menacing grain collection crisis,[25] and that only Bukharin was available to take charge of the proceedings. The session opened on February 9, 1928, with ninety-two delegates (forty-four with voting rights) from twenty-seven countries.[26] The leading article in *Pravda* on the eve of the session pointed to "the sharpening of the contradictions of capitalism, above all of the contradictions between the working class and the bourgeoisie", and defined the main task as "*the strengthening of the struggle against international social-democracy*".[27]

On the issues of principle confronting the ninth IKKI, the formulas of compromise hitherto accepted had been worn thin by constant usage and by the pressure of events. The most conspicuous crux was the formula of the united front. Initially in-

[24] *Internationale Presse-Korrespondenz*, No. 9, January 27, 1928, pp. 165–168.

[25] See Vol. 1, pp. 50–53.

[26] *Kommunisticheskii Internatsional v Dokumentakh* (1933), p. 746.

[27] *Pravda*, February 7, 1928.

spired by failure to recruit mass communist parties,[28] it was a logical concomitant of the NEP period and of the cult of the fellow-traveller. Designed to rally the workers, communist and non-communist, for resistance to the malign power of capitalism, it gradually passed from the defensive to the offensive, and was invoked to serve other more specific purposes sponsored by Comintern. Cooperation for these purposes with non-communist parties and their leaders ("the united front from above") was by no means excluded. But, as tensions grew, and these leaders came to resent communist infiltration into what they regarded as their domain, the united front became more and more a device to appeal to non-communist workers in the name of communism against their existing leaders and parties ("the united front from below").[29] Attempts to redefine or reinterpret the formula were, however, discouraged. The seventh IKKI in November 1926 slipped into its trade union resolution a commendation of "the struggle for unity from below", and deprecated "the tactics of 'unity at all costs' ".[30] Neither the seventh nor the eighth IKKI made any formal pronouncement on the question. But Bukharin at the fifteenth party congress in December 1927 commended "the united front from below";[31] and the resolution of the congress coupled "the energetic development of the tactics of the united front and the struggle for the removal from their posts of the social-imperialist leaders of the reformist bureaucracy".[32] The merit of the united front formula was its total flexibility. Slogans like "To the masses" and "Class against Class", originally coined to support the broader interpretation, became the hallmark of the revolutionary appeal for the united front from below. The change was perhaps less substantial than it appeared, since both the united front from above and the united front from below were designed to serve the same purpose: to encourage the resistance of the workers in capitalist countries to policies directed against the Soviet Union.

The practical question involved in all controversies about the united front was the attitude to be adopted to other parties of the

[28] See *The Bolshevik Revolution, 1917–1923*, Vol. 3, pp. 391–392, 406–407.
[29] See *Socialism in One Country, 1924–1926*, Vol. 3, pp. 74–75.
[30] *Kommunisticheskii Internatsional v Dokumentakh* (1933), pp. 651, 654.
[31] See p. 138 above.
[32] *KPSS v Rezolyutsiyakh* (1954), ii, 448.

Left, notably to the social-democrats. Ever since August 4, 1914, vituperation of social-democrats as renegades and traitors had been a familiar part of the ideological armoury of Bolshevism. At the founding congress of the German Communist Party in the last days of December 1918, Rosa Luxemburg called the social-democratic party and trade union leaders "the most infamous and greatest scoundrels the world has ever seen", and referred to the existing socialist government as "a government of bourgeois counter-revolution".[33] The Scheidemanns and the Kautskys, wrote Lenin, were "contemptible traitors to socialism"; the Scheidemanns were "direct", the Kautskys "covert", servants of the bourgeoisie; Bauer and Adler were "common traitors".[34] The Third International was conceived, not as a rival to the Second International, but as the heir of a defunct institution, as the Second had been of the First. "The International died in 1914", wrote Lenin in June 1918[35] — a theme frequently reiterated in his writings of the period. The foundation of the Communist International in March 1919 was a direct challenge to efforts at the Berne conference in January 1919 to revive the old social-democratic International; and it followed logically on the change in the name of the Russian party in March 1918 from "social-democratic" to "communist".[36] The second congress of Comintern in the following year completed the ostracism of the social-democrats by the adoption of the twenty-one conditions, leading directly to splits in the French and Italian socialist parties; and war was declared on the International Federation of Trade Unions (the "Amsterdam International") by the foundation of Mezhsovprof, the precursor of Profintern.[37]

While, however, ideological warfare against the social-democrats was never suspended, Lenin the practical politician was prepared to recognize a certain ambiguity and flexibility in relations with them, which he qualified by reference to the stage reached in the revolutionary process. Bolshevism "permitted an alliance with them as a necessary evil in an evidently non-revolutionary situation, but considered a breach and a split with

[33] *Bericht über den Gründungsparteitag der Kommunistichen Partei Deutschlands* (n.d. [1919]), pp. 24, 29.

[34] Lenin, *Polnoe Sobranie Sochinenii*, xxxix, 217, 255; xl, 136.

[35] *Ibid.* xxxvi, 460.

[36] See *The Bolshevik Revolution, 1917–1923*, Vol. 1, pp. 189–190.

[37] See *ibid.* Vol. 3, pp. 191–196, 203–207.

them inevitable on any serious sharpening of the struggle, and most of all at the beginning of a revolution".[38] It was therefore logical that, when the first flush of revolutionary optimism had faded, the introduction of NEP, the trade treaty with Great Britain and the third congress of Comintern in 1921 should have been followed by the proclamation of the policy of the united front.[39] Any "alliance" with social-democracy retained, however, its character as a temporary expedient and a "necessary evil". Disillusioned by the fiasco of the united front in Germany in 1923, and by the feebleness of the newly installed Labour government in Great Britain, the fifth congress of Comintern in June 1924 recalled once more the betrayal of August 1914, and observed that social-democracy everywhere "supports the imperialists of 'its own' fatherland". Social-democracy had become "the 'third' party of the bourgeoisie". The united front, concluded the resolution, could not be "a political coalition with counter-revolutionary social-democracy".[40] Trotsky, in the pamphlet *Where is Britain Going?* published in 1925, preached "an irreconcilable antagonism [of the British working class] to the conservative bureaucracy in the trade unions and in the Labour Party". He described the Fabians as more dangerous than the Conservatives, who were easily identifiable enemies:

> The Fabians, the ILPers, the conservative bureaucrats of the trade unions represent at the moment the most counter-revolutionary force in Great Britain.[41]

Yet united front tactics remained in force throughout 1925 and the first months of 1926, especially in Germany. At the sixth IKKI in March 1926 Thälmann called for a common struggle of the Roter Frontkämpferbund with "the comrades of the Reichsbanner" against Fascism; and Lozovsky made fun of the behaviour of some KPD organizations which forbade their members to talk to members of the SPD.[42]

[38] Lenin, *Polnoe Sobranie Sochinenii*, xxxix, 145.

[39] See *The Bolshevik Revolution, 1917–1923*, Vol. 3, pp. 406–407.

[40] *Kommunisticheskii Internatsional v Dokumentakh* (1933), pp. 399–401, 407.

[41] For this pamphlet see *Socialism in One Country, 1924–1926*, Vol. 3, p. 346.

[42] *Shestoi Rasshirennyi Plenum Ispolkoma Kommunisticheskogo Internatsionala* (1927), p. 174; for Lozovsky's remarks see pp. 400–401 below. United

The proclamation of the general strike in Great Britain in May 1926 by the General Council of the TUC, and the victorious advance in the autumn of the same year of the national revolutionary armies in China, seemed each in turn to provide a vindication of the fruitfulness of united front policies. In Great Britain disillusionment followed within a few days. In China it was delayed for some months, but proved all the more shattering when it came. Both experiments ended in humiliation and bitterness of defeat, and in fierce denunciation of the treachery of the non-communist Left; and when, even before the Chinese *débâcle*, the resolution of the fifteenth Russian party conference in October 1926, following massive broadsides from Stalin and Bukharin, asserted, however paradoxically, that the views of Trotsky and his supporters were "a direct approximation to the views of social-democracy", and pronounced the anathema on "a social-democratic deviation in our party",[43] a new dimension had been added to the campaign. During 1927 — a year of crisis and tumult in Comintern — cooperation with social-democrats was still intermittently practised and preached, notably at the anti-imperialist congress at Brussels in February and on the occasion of the Moscow celebrations of the tenth anniversary of the revolution. But what was described as "a plan of campaign" issued by Comintern for the anniversary contrasted the records of Bolshevism and of social-democracy over the past ten years, concluding that the function of social-democracy had been "*to serve the bourgeoisie and by its exertions to stabilize the régime*", and that in some countries (Germany, Bulgaria, Poland and Finland) it had collaborated with the bourgeoisie "in the work of repressions and of terror".[44] Identification of social-democrats with the Russian Mensheviks became a familiar theme.[45] After the expulsion of the

front policies had a stronger appeal to communists in Germany and Great Britain where an overwhelming majority of the working class belonged to "reformist" trade unions than in France and Italy, where the unions were both weak and divided.

[43] *KPSS v Rezolyutsiyakh* (1954), ii, 154–161; for this conference see Vol. 2, pp. 17–19.

[44] *Internationale Presse-Korrespondenz*, No. 101, October 15, 1927, pp. 2168–2169.

[45] Stalin, *Sochineniya*, x, 208–209; this was developed at length by Bukharin in a speech on the programme at the sixth Comintern Congress in July 1928 (*Stenograficheskii Otchet VI Kongressa Kominterna* (1929), iii, 122–129).

opposition at the fifteenth party congress in December 1927, all inhibitions were removed, and unbridled denunciation of social-democrats became part of the obligatory vocabulary of Comintern.

The unqualified condemnation of social-democratic parties and their leaders, and the gradual conversion of the united front into an appeal against those leaders to the masses of non-communist workers, implied the assumption that the social-democratic rank and file was more radical and revolutionary than its leaders. The slogan "To the Masses", originally proclaimed by the third congress of Comintern in 1921, was reiterated by the fifth congress in 1924.[46] The cautious lessons drawn from the failure of the revolutionary rising in Germany in 1923, and in Estonia in 1924, were forgotten, or were relegated to the past. Bukharin in his report to the seventh IKKI in November 1926 associated his "third period" with a "shift of the working class to the Left";[47] and Lozovsky boldly asserted that "the shift within the working class occurs continuously from Right to Left, and not *vice versa*". The main resolution of the session recorded "a radicalization of the masses in many countries".[48] During the following year the struggle within the party gave a fresh impetus to this diagnosis. If the opposition treated such episodes as the Pilsudski *coup* in Poland, the failure of the British strikes or the fiasco in China, as defeats which strengthened the stability of capitalist régimes, and for the time being postponed the prospects of revolution, the Comintern leaders, uncomfortably conscious of their own vulnerability, hailed these events as symptoms of the increasing instability of capitalism, and as evidence that the masses were becoming progressively more revolutionary.

The crumbling of capitalist stabilization, the unmasking of the social-democratic leaders as the allies and instruments of the bourgeoisie, and even of Fascism, and the consequent "turn to the Left" or "radicalization" of the disillusioned workers, inspired all the proceedings of the ninth IKKI. The same idea inspired the British resolution of the eighth IKKI in May 1927, which diagnosed "a sharpening of the class struggle" and "a speeding up of the tempo of differentiation in the workers' movement"; under

46 *Kommunisticheskii Internatsional v Dokumentakh* (1933), p. 401.
47 *Puti Mirovoi Revolyutsii* (1927), i, 29.
48 See p. 136 above.

this impetus, while "the leaders of the Labour Party and of the trade unions openly take the road of *rapprochement* with the ruling class, the working masses display a marked pull to the Left".[49] Later in the year the fifteenth congress of the Russian party, in its resolution on the work of IKKI, discerned a "radicalization of the worker masses", proceeding *pari passu* with "a sharp turn to the Right" on the part of the leaders of the Second International and of IFTU.[50] It was perhaps the only way in which consolation could be found for the disappointment of the British strikes in 1926, and the Chinese disasters of 1927.[51] Belief in the revolutionary potential of the proletariat, an essential postulate of Marxism, was transformed, without much examination of the evidence, into a prospect for the immediate future. As Trotsky afterwards put it, "the 'radicalization' of the masses became in Comintern not the description of a process, but a mere symbol of fate".[52] And this assumption that the masses were moving to the Left was closely associated, partly as cause, partly as effect, with the persistent assertion that the main danger in Comintern and in communist parties, including the Russian, now came from the Right — a prelude to the campaign against Bukharin himself.

The radicalization of the masses was associated with another popular slogan of the period "Class against Class". This was apparently inspired by the British general strike, when, for the first time in English history, "class stood against class". The phrase was frequently used in this context during the second half of 1926.[53] It then fell out of use, but reappeared somewhat mysteriously in discussions in the French commission set up by IKKI early in 1927, where it was introduced by Humbert-Droz into the field of electoral tactics. Under the French electoral system, parties of the Left — including the PCF, the socialists and Left bourgeois parties — whose candidates had been un-

49 *Kommunisticheskii Internatsional v Dokumentakh* (1933), p. 731.

50 *KPSS v Rezolyutsiyakh* (1954), ii, 448.

51 Trotsky pointed to the anomaly that the cry of "radicalization" had been raised (or rather revived) at a time when the workers after severe defeats were in retreat (L. Trotsky, *The Third International After Lenin* (N.Y., 1936), pp. 258–259); but even he believed, in the summer of 1928, on the strength of the recent German and French elections, that a process of radicalization had begun, though only in its "initial stages" (*ibid.* pp. 165, 259–260).

52 *Byulleten' Oppozitsii,* No. 8, January 1930, p. 2.

53 See pp. 318–319 below.

successful in the first ballot, commonly entered into bargains to support one another at the second ballot in order to vote down candidates of the Right. This blurred the dividing line of class between proletarian and non-proletarian parties; and the PCF was exhorted, in the name of "Class against Class", to abandon the practice. Humbert-Droz, who in his memoirs rashly claimed "exclusive paternity" for the phrase, explained the logic of the proposal:

> It was in no way intended to attack the Socialist Party, but to detach it from its electoral alliances with the bourgeoisie grouped in the radical party, in order to create a worker–peasant bloc comprising the Socialist Party, the Communist Party, CGT, the CGTU, and the organizations of small peasants. It meant then to confront the Socialist Party with a dilemma: either a united front of the workers or a bloc of the Left which enabled the bourgeoisie to draw away a part of the working class.[54]

This proposal appeared to reject electoral bargains against candidates of the Right in favour of bourgeois candidates of the Left, but to permit such bargains if made in favour of social-democratic or socialist candidates. But the distinction was irrelevant in terms of current French electoral practice, and Humbert-Droz's initiative was unpopular with a large majority of the PCF. For the moment a compromise formula was found.[55] It was only later, when Comintern began to put pressure on the French and British parties not to vote for socialist or Labour candidates, even where abstention was likely to lead to the election of candidates of the Right, and when it had become fashionable to treat socialist and Labour parties as in all repects equivalent to bourgeois parties, that the slogan "Class against Class" came into current use, being directed indiscriminately against all other parties of the Left. Thälmann afterwards claimed that "Class against Class" tactics had been "worked out by the ninth plenum for France and England".[56] But the phrase did not in fact figure in any resolution of the session, and did not become popular in the CPGB till some months later.

[54] J. Humbert-Droz, *De Lénine à Staline* (Neuchatel, 1971), p. 281.

[55] For these discussions see pp. 481–483 below.

[56] *Protokoll: 10. Plenum des Exekutivkomitees der Kommunistischen Internationale* (n.d.), p. 649.

The ninth IKKI differed from its predecessors in one formal respect: the main report and resolution related, not to the general situation, but specifically to "the opposition in the VKP(B) and in Comintern". This enabled Bukharin to deal with major issues in the form of a polemic against Trotsky, and heightened the tone of the debate. A passing mention of "great *difficulties*" coupled with a boast of the "*great economic successes*" was the only hint that the Soviet Union was in the throes of an appalling grain crisis. Abroad, capitalist rationalization had progressed; but so had "the radicalization of the working class". The opposition was at work in and outside the party and Comintern. It was necessary to "*sharpen* the offensive against the social-democratic enemy", since "the so-called Trotskyite opposition" was "objectively nothing else but the 'Left' wing of the social-democratic party". Bukharin's review of the situation in the principal communist parties ended with the diagnosis of "*a more or less firm international bloc with an avowed hegemony of the Right* (which appears especially clearly in *France*) *and with recognition of the ideological leadership of Trotskyism*". A two-day debate followed in which Thälmann, Doriot and delegates of the other principal parties echoed, and played variations on, Bukharin's themes without attempting to probe the deeper issues. Only two speakers, while carefully asserting their total agreement, seemed not wholly satisfied. Schüller, the representative of KIM, stressed a factor to which Bukharin had "pointed" in his report, "namely, the true social-democratic and Rightist nature of the opposition — Right in the worst sense of the word". Thorez, apologizing for a second intervention from the French delegation, dwelt on the problems which Bukharin had "thrown up" of "the necessity of a stronger Left orientation", and demanded "an energetic struggle against Trotskyism and against the other Right deviations in our party and in Comintern".

Whether in response to these hints or to other promptings, Bukharin in his reply to the debate just perceptibly shifted his ground. Trotskyism was still the chief danger, but must not be thought of as "any kind of 'Left' deviation". Almost everywhere (Germany was an admitted exception) "the axis of the Trotskyite opposition is to be found in the Right deviations". In conclusion, Bukharin stressed the necessity of "a struggle against

Right deviations within the communist parties" and of self-criticism to correct shortcomings and mistakes.[57] The resolution submitted with the report does not appear to have undergone any amendment, and was unanimously adopted. It greeted "the radicalization of the worker masses, expressed in the growth of the strike campaign, the heightening of the political activity of the working class, in the growth of the sympathy of the international proletariat for the USSR, in the expansion of elements of a new revolutionary upsurge in Europe". The remainder of the resolution was devoted to denunciation of the Trotskyite opposition, whose "evolution towards social-democracy" and "openly anti-Soviet position" rendered membership of it incompatible with membership of Comintern.[58] No specific mention was made of Right deviations or of the Right danger.

The only other general subjects on the agenda of the ninth IKKI were the trade union questions, the debate on which reflected the same limitations and ambiguities as the debate on Bukharin's report. Controversial debates were held, and resolutions adopted, on the British, French and Chinese parties; all these were variations on the theme of the radicalization of the masses and proclaimed uncompromising hostility to social-democrats and their counterparts.[59] A leading article in *Pravda* at the end of the session drew attention to the "international significance" of the British and French resolutions, and once more branded supporters of the opposition in foreign communist parties as "agents of social-democracy" in their ranks.[60] A decision to set up a Western European Bureau "for the establishment of a close link between IKKI and the western European sections of the Communist International"[61] was doubtless in-

[57] Bukharin's report and the debate were fairly fully reproduced in *Internationale Presse-Korrespondenz*, No. 18 (a special number), February 23, 1928, pp. 369–390; Bukharin's reply in a much truncated form, *ibid.* No. 26, March 10, 1928, p. 502. *Pravda*, February 17, 18, 1928, printed short summaries of the report and debate, but omitted Bukharin's reply.

[58] *Kommunisticheskii Internatsional v Dokumentakh* (1933), pp. 746–749.

[59] For the British and French debates see pp. 363–366, 504–506 below; a resolution on the KPZU was also adopted at the session (see p. 590 below).

[60] *Pravda*, February 28, 1928.

[61] *Internationale Presse-Korrespondenz*, No. 28, March 13, 1928, p. 547. Pyatnitsky at the sixth congress of Comintern a few weeks later commented that "it was absolutely impossible for IKKI to exercise leadership directly from Moscow, and it was therefore decided . . . to organize a Western Euro-

spired by determination to ensure the correct application of the policies of Moscow and the elimination from foreign parties of the influence of the opposition. Many speakers at the sixth congress of Comintern five months later hailed the ninth IKKI as a turning-point in the Comintern line. Heckert called it the beginning of "an energetic struggle with reformism", and connected it with the campaign against Right tendencies in Comintern; Lozovsky said that in the trade union question it gave the directions which the fourth congress of Profintern carried out.[62] Attention was drawn to its importance for the British, French and American parties.[63] But the ninth IKKI, though it indulged in gestures of defiance and intransigence, had done little to define in terms of policy the implications of the rift with social-democracy and the radicalization of the masses. The fourth congress of Profintern, which met a month later under Lozovsky's belligerent leadership, was concerned to work out their meaning for the trade unions.

pean Bureau abroad" (*Stenograficheskii Otchet VI Kongressa Kominterna* (1929), v, 105; this passage was omitted from the report of the speech in *Internationale Presse-Korrespondenz*, No. 114, October 8, 1928, p. 2242).

[62] *Stenograficheskii Otchet VI Kongressa Kominterna* (1929), i, 203, 207, 404.

[63] *Ibid.* i, 333, 491.

CHAPTER 69

PROFINTERN AND THE TRADE UNIONS

THE fiasco of the British general strike and the slow agony of the miners' strike were a landmark in relations between Moscow and the trade union movement in western Europe. Though premonitory signs had not been wanting, it came as a shock to discover how deep-seated was the antipathy of the western trade union leaders to revolutionary aims and policies, and the mistrust inspired by the procedures of Profintern, Comintern and the Soviet Government. These hostile attitudes found institutional shape in the British TUC and in the Amsterdam International. Earlier visions in Profintern of persuading or forcing IFTU into some form of cooperation faded. The figment of the Anglo-Russian committee was threadbare. The united front had become a transparent tactical device. What was not so easily recognized was the extent of the loyalty which "reformist" and counter-revolutionary leaders still commanded in the rank and file of the trade unions—in Great Britain, and scarcely less in Germany. Even in France and Czechoslovakia, where the movement had been split and Red trade unions created in the early nineteen-twenties, no further progress was made towards capturing the reformist strongholds. In Italy and Poland, Fascist or semi-Fascist régimes crushed the trade unions. In south-eastern Europe they scarcely existed. Only in Asia, where industrialization and a nascent proletariat were the creation of foreign imperialism, could trade unions be seen as a potentially revolutionary force; and these were very different institutions from the traditional trade unions of western Europe.

After the meeting of the central council in March 1926,[1] no significant session of Profintern was held for two years. The cautious and indecisive trade union resolution of the seventh IKKI in November 1926[2] was followed, according to a perhaps one-sided account by Humbert-Droz, by an embittered struggle.

[1] See *Socialism in One Country, 1924–1926*, Vol. 3, pp. 594–596.
[2] See p. 138 above.

Lozovsky fought with great tenacity to advance the cause of Profintern and the revolutionary trade unions affiliated to it. Tomsky continued to stand for united front policies and maintained a stubbornly sceptical attitude towards the revolutionary unions. Humbert-Droz, who had replaced Togliatti as president of the trade union commission of IKKI, strove to moderate between them, but was concerned mainly to block the ambitious plans of Lozovsky, who found himself isolated in the commission, and whose projects were constantly vetoed by the political secretariat or the presidium of IKKI.[3] The tension was doubtless relieved when Lozovsky left Moscow early in March 1927, on a mission to China.[4] The eighth IKKI in May 1927 condemned the Amsterdam International and the leaders of the trade unions affiliated to it, side by side with the Second International, in the context of the struggle against the danger of war, but in Lozovsky's absence made no specific pronouncement on the trade union question. The deepening crisis of the latter part of 1927, however, left no contentious issue unaffected. Bukharin at the fifteenth party congress in December 1927 proclaimed the growing rift with the social-democrats and the sharpening of the class struggle.[5] Having touched lightly on the problems of the organization of unorganized workers, and of trade union unity, he observed that "we must imperatively strengthen the work of *Profintern*, and regularize relations between the central council of trade unions and Profintern".[6] Lozovsky, fresh from his Far Eastern experience, devoted a major part of his speech to the problems of the Pacific. But in Europe he noted a turn in the trade union leader-

[3] The main source for this dispute is a letter from Humbert-Droz to Togliatti of April 8, 1927 (J. Humbert-Droz, *Il Contrasto tra l'Internazionale e il PCI, 1922–1928* (1969), p. 246 (Humbert-Droz archives, 0081)); Humbert-Droz in his memoirs describes his functions as "to defend trade union unity against Lozovsky's splitting aspirations" (J. Humbert-Droz, *De Lénine à Staline* (Neuchatel, 1971), p. 277).

[4] This will be discussed in a later section of this volume.

[5] See p. 153 above.

[6] *Pyatnadtsatyi S"ezd VKP(B)*, i (1961), 656; the only speaker who took up this question was Melnichansky, who, having denied the imputation of "unfriendly mutual relations between the two organizations", managed in a confused speech to reveal several points of friction (*ibid.* i, 787–789). The resolution of the congress on Bukharin's report recorded the need "to strengthen by all means Profintern and the minority movement", and to establish "a closer and more active link between Profintern and the central council of trade unions" (*KPSS v Rezolyutsiyakh* (1954), ii, 448).

ship to the Right—"what I call the statization of the summit of social-democracy in the reformist unions"—combined with a movement of the masses to the Left; and he deplored the failure of successive strikes, beginning with "the giant strike of the English miners", to crystallize into any serious result.[7]

Lozovsky evidently felt that the time had come to reassert the role of Profintern. In an article apparently written a few days after his speech, he looked forward to the fourth congress of Profintern, due to be held early in 1928. He hopefully contrasted "the coalescence of the reformist trade unions with the bourgeois state" with the radicalization of the masses and their growing sympathy for the working class of the Soviet Union. Referring to the Anglo-Russian committee as "one of the most important experiments in united front from above tactics", he claimed the collapse of the committee as proof that "the period of the united front from above is obviously finished".[8] In January 1928, with the ninth IKKI impending, preliminary discussions took place on the problems of the United States trade unions.[9] According to Lozovsky's subsequent account, however, they went beyond this narrow framework, and provoked "keen disputes", which opened up most of the controversial issues of the next two years—strike tactics, the rôle of communists in social-democratic and other "reactionary" trade unions, the formation of new revolutionary unions and the organization of hitherto unorganized workers. It was the first time that "new tactics, new methods of struggle" had been ventilated.[10]

The new tactics of which Lozovsky wished to make Profintern the standard-bearer turned mainly on two points. The first was a new emphasis placed on the strike weapon. Strikes had not hitherto played any conspicuous or distinctive rôle in Bolshevik theory. The strike as a practical weapon in bargaining with the employer had been developed by the British working class. The French syndicalists produced the first theory of strikes as a

[7] *Pyatnadtsatyi S"ezd VKP(B)*, i (1961), 697–699.

[8] A. Lozovsky, *Na Novom Etape* (1928), pp. 3–16. The article is dated December 15, 1927; the date and place of its original publication have not been traced.

[9] See pp. 598–599 below.

[10] *Kommunisticheskii Internatsional*, No. 23–24 (201–202), 1929, pp. 111–112; this speech, delivered a year later, is the only source for these discussions.

characteristic form of revolutionary action, which was non-political in the sense that it was independent of political parties and professed no specific political objectives. In Russia strikes were regarded both by the Tsarist authorities and by the early Bolsheviks alike as basically indistinguishable from other forms of insurgency. Lenin, in an article of June 1912 headed "A Revolutionary Uprising", hailed "the grandiose May strike of the all-Russian proletariat" in protest against the shooting down of workers in the Lena gold-mines in April of that year; and in January 1917, addressing a Zürich audience on the 1905 revolution, he had spoken of "the interweaving of economic and political strikes".[11] But he regarded the British trade unions with mistrust, the French syndicalists with hostility and the feeble Russian trade unions, since the days of his controversy with the Economists, with a certain veiled jealousy as potential rivals of the party and later of the Soviets.[12] After the revolution the party became seriously concerned both in the capture of the Russian trade unions and, once this was achieved, in their relations with the European trade union movement. But none of the argument turned on the question of strikes. The third congress of Profintern in July 1924 was the first to debate strike tactics. Lozovsky made a pugnacious speech in which he described the strike, like war, as "a continuation of the same policy, but by different means", and as "an organic and subordinate part of the general proletarian class strategy".[13] The main resolution of the congress included a brief section on "strike strategy", which opened with the bold assertion that "the economic struggle is, as never before, bound up with the political struggle". But the cautious conclusion was merely to call for "the greatest attention" to this question, since "an army marching to battle without a plan, without centralized leadership, without the subordination of separate units to a single directing will, is doomed to defeat".[14] As late as March 1926 the sixth IKKI adopted theses on "The Immediate

[11] Lenin, *Polnoe Sobranie Sochinenii*, xxi, 339, xxx, 313; these passages were quoted by Thälmann in his speech at the tenth IKKI in July 1929 (*Protokoll: 10. Plenum des Exekutivkomittees der Kommunistischen Internationale* (n.d.), pp. 672–674).

[12] See *The Bolshevik Revolution, 1917–1923*, Vol. 2, pp. 62–63, 100–103; for the Economists see *ibid.* Vol. 1, pp. 10–12.

[13] *Protokoll über den Dritten Kongress der Roten Gewerkschaftsinternationale* (n.d.), pp. 223–230.

[14] *Desyat' Let Profinterna v Rezolyutsiyakh* (1930), pp. 135–136.

Tasks of Communists in the Trade Union Movement", comprising seventeen chapters, and concluding with seventeen slogans, which did not refer to strikes at all.[15]

The British general strike of May 1926, and the protracted miners' strike, broke in on this atmosphere of indifference. The moral that its failure was due to unwillingness to carry it from the economic to the political plane, and that no valid distinction could be made between an economic and a political strike, was frequently drawn, not least by Lozovsky himself.[16] But nobody was in a hurry to generalize this lesson. Lozovsky at the seventh IKKI in November 1926 lamented that Comintern and Profintern were "not strong enough to defeat the strike-breaking of the Amsterdamers".[17] Yet the resolution on the trade union question adopted at the session, though it asserted that the general strike had changed the situation, and condemned the treachery of the Amsterdam International,[18] placed the whole emphasis on the united front and the need for trade union unity, and contained no call for strike action.

Throughout 1927, Lozovsky being absent for the greater part of the year in China, the issue was not reopened in Moscow, where attention was absorbed by the fear of imminent war. But in the autumn of 1927, a series of major strikes broke out in Germany, and were the occasion of acute friction between communists and social-democrats;[19] and this episode, if any special impetus was required, may have inspired Lozovsky's determination to evolve a more active strike policy for Profintern. An article dated January 13, 1928, on "Questions of Strike Strategy", provided a systematic review of the whole problem. Lozovsky bitterly attacked the support given by the reformists to the campaign for "industrial peace"; this meant a united front with the capitalists. On the political and economic content of strikes, he conceded that strikers might aim at short-term bargains with employers on wages and conditions. But long-term wage agreements were "in contradiction with our fundamental task of increasing the fighting

[15] For this "programme of action" see *Socialism in One Country, 1924–1926*, Vol. 3, p. 594.

[16] See pp. 317–318 below.

[17] *Puti Mirovoi Revolyutsii* (1927), i, 495.

[18] *Kommunisticheskii Internatsional v Dokumentakh* (1933), pp. 648, 650–651; for this resolution see p. 138 above.

[19] See p. 434 below.

capacity of the proletarian army". Compulsory arbitration was to be decisively rejected as a tool of the capitalists. The article ended with the maxim: "Strike strategy is part of our general class strategy."[20] About the same time when Lozovsky was canvassing the question in Moscow, Merker, a leader of the revolutionary trade union movement in Germany, wrote an article in the KPD journal entitled "More Clarity in the Struggle against Reformism". Many German communists, he declared, had followed in the wake of social-democratic trade union leaders, who toyed with partial demands, but "*ruthlessly stand in the way of political mass struggles*, or economic struggles with decisive political consequences".[21]

The other item in the new trade union tactics assiduously preached by Lozovsky in the first months of 1928 was the recruitment of hitherto unorganized workers. The principle that all workers should be organized in trade unions had always been maintained. But some vagueness surrounded the question into what unions those hitherto outside any union should be recruited. The third congress of Profintern in 1924 specifically concluded that "it would be in the highest degree unsuitable to form special organizations for the unorganized, since this would mean, even under some other name, to create parallel organizations in an unpropitious environment".[22] In the eclectic trade union resolution of the seventh IKKI in November 1926 it was laid down that, "in countries having a low percentage of organized workers, special attention must be paid to drawing unorganized workers into revolutionary unions".[23] But the context showed that this referred primarily to France and Czechoslovakia, where the movement was already split between reformist and revolutionary unions. When Lozovsky in January 1928 pressed the question of the organization of unorganized workers in the United States, where the percentage of organized workers was low, where the tightly integrated unions did nothing to encourage the admission of unskilled,

[20] *Krasnyi Internatsional Profsoyuzov*, No. 1, 1928, pp. 3–16; it was reprinted in A. Lozovsky, *Na Novom Etape* (1928), pp. 17–32, and a translation appeared in *Communist International* (Engl. edn.), March 1, 1928, pp. 111–118. For the campaign for industrial peace in Great Britain see pp. 368–369 below.

[21] *Die Internationale*, xi, No. 4, February 15, 1928, pp. 103–108.

[22] *Desyat' Let Profinterna v Rezolyutsiyakh* (1930), p. 134.

[23] *Kommunisticheskii Internatsional v Dokumentakh* (1933), p. 652; for this resolution see p. 138 above.

mainly Negro, labour, and where the prejudice against so-called "dual unionism" was exceedingly strong, he stirred a hornet's nest by revealing how closely the question of organizing unorganized workers was linked with the question of founding new revolutionary unions, and thus splitting the movement in countries where it had not hitherto been divided.[24] It was not only in the United States that traditional resistance to a divided trade union movement was powerful. In Great Britain Horner, an unimpeachable communist, "never believed in 'forming new unions' ", and later sought to dissolve the break-away revolutionary United Mineworkers of Scotland.[25] Lozovsky himself had always been sensitive to charges of "splitting" the movement, and had sought to place the responsibility for it on Amsterdam. But he was now prepared to admit that the new line involved "dualism, i.e. dual leadership within a single trade union organization", and argued that this must not be approached "from a formal standpoint".[26]

Nor did it help that the unorganized workers to whom communist parties would make their appeal, and who would form the nucleus of the new revolutionary unions, belonged mainly to the least privileged strata of workers — Negroes in the United States, immigrants in France, and the unemployed in Great Britain and Germany.[27] The powerful trade unions of the capitalist countries had grown up as organizations of skilled workers, whose interests and outlook they still represented. The Soviet trade unions were not immune from this tradition, and had shown a stubborn resistance to the admission of the unemployed to their ranks.[28] Lozovsky had become acquainted in China in 1927 with trade unions of a very different kind — unions based not on individual, but on collective, enrolment, and depending for their funds on levies from employers, not on workers' contributions.[29] When Melni-

[24] For the American aspects of the question see pp. 598–600 below.

[25] A. Horner, *Incorrigible Rebel* (1960), p. 107; for this episode see pp. 393, 397 below.

[26] A. Lozovsky, *Na Novom Etape* (1928), p. 37.

[27] In Great Britain, an influx of unemployed miners accounted for the temporary rise in membership of the CPGB in 1926 (see p. 336 below); for the high percentage of unemployed workers in the KPD see p. 402, note 13 below.

[28] See *Socialism in One Country, 1924–1926*, Vol. 1, pp. 366–367; for their attitude to wage differentials between skilled and unskilled labour see *ibid.* Vol. 1, pp. 376–377.

[29] The Chinese unions will be discussed in a later section of this volume.

chansky replied to Lozovsky at the fifteenth Russian party congress in December 1927, his curiously emphatic insistence that trade unions adhering to Profintern would be successful only if they accepted the principle "that each individual member of the trade union must participate independently in its organization, and must pay members' dues",[30] seemed to betray a fear that Lozovsky might seek to introduce in Europe, under the auspices of Profintern, this new type of trade union. The fear was groundless. But it was nevertheless true that the mission of Profintern, as now conceived by Lozovsky, to awaken the latent class-consciousness of masses of unorganized workers, responded to the appearance even in some capitalist countries of a pool of unskilled and unemployed workers imperfectly catered for by the existing trade unions, and that this situation had some analogies with the situation in the Soviet Union, where the trade unions were increasingly faced with the task of incorporating in the proletariat and in their own membership a large army of peasants recruited into industry under the five-year plan.[31] These needs were difficult to reconcile with established trade union traditions as understood in the west; and opposition spokesmen denounced "demagogic romanticism about unorganized workers" as a relapse into childishness.[32] But the problem was real enough, and lent powerful support to the challenge presented to these traditions by Lozovsky on behalf of Profintern.

Lozovsky's aggressive and uncompromising views did not yet command widespread assent. When the ninth IKKI met, a trade union commission was set up, and was the scene of a sharp debate on February 12, 1928. As usual, the proceedings of commissions were not published; and exactly what Lozovsky said is not known. But its substance can be gleaned from an article by him on "Results and Prospects of the United Front and of Unity", written on February 2, 1928, and published shortly afterwards in the Comintern journal. The united front and unity, declared Lozovsky, "do not have as their purpose to gloss over existing disagreements or to find a middle line between reformism and communism", but to establish "the independence of the working

[30] *Pyatnadtsatyi S"ezd VKP(B)*, i (1961), 790; for this debate see p. 167, note 6 above.

[31] See Vol. 1, pp. 546–547, 560–561.

[32] Tasca quoted in *Protokoll: 10. Plenum des Exekutivkomittees der Kommunistischen Internationale* (n.d.), p. 83.

class from the bourgeoisie"—in Marxist terms, its conversion into "a class for itself". He tentatively approached the strike issue with examples from the British miners' strike of 1926 and the recent strikes in Germany. When the trade union leaders betrayed the interests of the workers, could one assume that workers "had not the right to come out and strike" against the will of the leaders? This was "a clash between formal right and the interests of the workers". The fiction of legality must be discarded:

> *The struggle for leadership in the trade unions is a question of force, not of trade union law.* This means that we should entertain no illusions about the possibility of winning over the trade union leaders ... The reformist trade union leadership has linked its fate with the bourgeois state, and can be overthrown only with it.

Lozovsky demanded "an end to metaphysical talk on the theme of the united front and unity, and a decisive end to the tactics of *unity for the sake of unity*". Whatever the method, the aim was "the conquest of the masses".[33] These views did not go unchallenged in the commission. Togliatti delivered a scathing attack on Lozovsky's ambitious projects, which Lozovsky more than once tried unsuccessfully to interrupt. Togliatti agreed with the move to the Left; but "we must take this step with the masses". He was against Lozovsky's "strike strategy", and against tactics leading to the expulsion of communists from reformist unions. The creation everywhere of new unions meant splitting the movement: the slogan "organize the unorganized" must not be applied in a way incompatible with the struggle for unity. Profintern should work for "the solidarity of the masses", direct the economic struggles of the working class, organize new unions on a factory basis and continue the struggle for unity. Humbert-Droz, known as a faithful lieutenant of Bukharin, was more restrained, but made plain his opposition to a policy which would pit Red trade unions everywhere against reformist unions, and thus split and weaken the movement.[34] Thälmann made some show of modera-

[33] *Kommunisticheskii Internatsional*, No. 6–7 (132–133), 1928, pp. 61–72; the article which had the sub-title "Before the Fourth Congress of Profintern", was reprinted in A. Lozovsky, *Na Novom Etape* (1928), pp. 33–48, and there dated February 2, 1928.

[34] Excerpts from the speeches of Togliatti and Humbert-Droz were published from the Tasca archives in *Annali, 1966* (Milan, 1966), pp. 440–444; it is not clear whether the archives contain a full record of the proceedings.

tion, and was careful to express agreement with Bukharin. But he rejoiced that "great progress" had been made since the trade union resolutions of the sixth and seventh IKKIs; and he devoted the greater part of his speech to "Right deviations" in the KPD.[35]

In the plenary session Lozovsky remained in the background — a sure sign that his views had not received official endorsement; and the presentation of a report on the trade unions was entrusted to the cautious and uncommitted Humbert-Droz. The report was a model of tact and ambiguity; the official response to Lozovsky's call for more aggressive tactics was still uncertain. Humbert-Droz detected "a radicalization of the masses and increasing sympathy for communists in the trade union movement". Revolutionary phrase-making and opportunist tactics "borrowed from the reformists" were both deprecated. Splitting tactics were condemned; "it would be not only an error, but a crime, to call on revolutionary elements to leave reformist organizations and found independent revolutionary organizations". Yet — here came some concessions to Lozovsky — the collapse of the Anglo-Russian committee was a symbol of change in the situation in the past two years; the reformist leaders were now fighting on the side of the bourgeoisie against the Soviet Union. Mass expulsion of communists from reformist unions could not be met by mere passivity, or by turning one's back on the whole trade union movement. On the other hand, "over-hastily to found a new trade union organization" was also undesirable. To organize the unorganized workers was an essential task for communists; but they should do it "as fighters for the unity of the trade union movement". Finally, the organization of strikes was important. But strikes for day-to-day demands should not in principle be rejected in favour of the general strike.[36]

The resolution, much briefer and more incisive than Humbert-Droz's report, showed more marks of Lozovsky's masterful hand, and was probably the product of hard bargaining behind the scenes. It plunged straight into the strike question by affirming that, with the growing concentration of capital, "the strike tends rapidly to take on a political character, so that the forces of the

[35] Thälmann's speech, but none of the other speeches in the commission, was published in *Internationale Presse-Korrespondenz*, No. 26, March 10, 1928, pp. 492–494; for the parts of the speech relating to the KPD, see pp. 432–433 below.

[36] *Internationale Presse-Korrespondenz*, No. 26, pp. 487–491.

proletariat clash with the forces of the bourgeois state". This meant "the mobilization of the masses". Meanwhile "the shift of social-democratic politicians and trade union leaders to the Right" threw into relief the rôle of strikes as a form of "the broad mobilization of the masses", directed "*against* compulsory arbitration, *against* social-democratic fidelity to wage agreements, and as a general rule in favour of short-term wage agreements". Every strike should be "*an arena of the struggle for leadership between communists and reformists*" — a significant battle-cry in the new philosophy of strikes; the goal was "the conquest of the masses". On the other hand, communists were not "to be always, in all conditions, for an immediate strike", and a warning was issued against "misuses of the slogan of a general strike". Elsewhere the resolution showed a new sharpness of tone. The problem of expulsions was met in the same ambiguous terms as in Humbert-Droz's report. But a note of warning was added:

> The attempt to remain within the ranks of the trade union organization must *never* among communists lead to renunciation of active revolutionary political work in the trade unions.

The former emphasis on the united front and on work in reformist unions had disappeared. But no specific change of line was proclaimed. New emphasis was laid on the need to organize both unemployed and hitherto unorganized workers; but the forms of organization to be adopted were left discreetly vague. Only in the United States, where "the overwhelming majority of the workers" were not organized, were communists instructed to "organize trade unions on their own initiative in branches of production in which the workers are entirely, or almost entirely, unorganized". The concluding demand for "great flexibility in the application of revolutionary tactics" covered almost any contingency.[37] When the executive bureau of Profintern prepared its report for the forthcoming congress of Profintern to meet a month later, it adopted a more cautious, even pessimistic tone. Reflecting on experiences in Great Britain and in China, it confessed that since the third congress of 1924 "the power of the bourgeoisie has significantly strengthened" — a rare admission in official pronounce-

[37] *Kommunisticheskii Internatsional v Dokumentakh* (1933), pp. 750–755; for the American section of the resolution see pp. 598–599 below. For the trade union resolution of the seventh IKKI see p. 138 above.

ments at this time — but consoled itself with the reflexion that "the temporary stoppage of struggles is in the overwhelming majority of cases only a state of armed truce".[38]

The fourth congress of Profintern sat from March 17 to April 3, 1928. No less than 421 delegates from 47 countries attended, as against 311 delegates from 39 countries at the third congress in 1924; Asia, Africa and Latin America were more numerously represented than ever before.[39] The struggle between "Rightists", who clung with varying degrees of tenacity to the tradition of a united front for immediate goals with other Left parties, especially in the trade union movement, and radical "Leftists", who saw social-democrats as their most dangerous enemies, was reflected covertly but insistently in the debates of the congress. Humbert-Droz, bringing to the congress the greetings of IKKI, leaned cautiously to the conservative side:

> *The defence of the day-to-day interests of the proletariat is no reformist deviation*, it is on the contrary the way, the right way.[40]

Tomsky, in a long speech of welcome, reverted to the differences between rationalization in capitalist countries and in the Soviet Union, and declared that threats to the Soviet Union, including "blockade and semi-blockade", must be repelled "with the support of all class-conscious workers of western Europe and with the undoubted sympathy of millions and millions of the oppressed of the east". He hinted lightly in a single sentence at the bone of contention:

> Economic struggles without political struggles will not suffice to bring the working class to power; but economic struggles are a necessary way to conquer the masses.

But he did not raise the issue of the united front; and he loudly protested the loyalty of the Soviet trade unions to Profintern.[41]

[38] *Desyat' Let Profinterna v Rezolyutsiyakh* (1930), pp. 157–158.

[39] *Protokoll über den Vierten Kongress der Roten Gewerkschaftsinternationale* (n.d), pp. 474–475.

[40] *Ibid.* p. 16.

[41] *Ibid.* pp. 16–26; according to Lozovsky, the speech "was cited for several months by all the Rightists as a model speech" (*Protokoll: 10. Plenum*

Lozovsky then delivered the main report on the "Results and Tasks of the International Trade Union Movement".[42] He showed no eagerness to force controversial issues. He repeated the analysis of the stabilization of capitalism which had been familiar for the past two years, and dwelt on the renewed offensive of capital against the working class and against the trade unions—in Great Britain and the United States as well as in Fascist countries—and on the radicalization of the workers' movement which this must produce. He was eloquent on the well-worn theme of the rôle of social-democrats and reformists as allies of the bourgeoisie. He then moved uneasily into a discussion of the united front, explaining, sagely but unhelpfully, that "some comrades" made a fetich of the united front without understanding it; it was, "on the one hand, a method of conquering the masses, on the other, one of the most important methods of struggle against reformism". On the question of "unity" with the Amsterdam International, which was convicted of "megalomania" for claiming "a monopoly of the whole international trade union movement" and described as "a tool of the capitalists", Lozovsky rehearsed the tortuous arguments which had done duty four years earlier.[43] Stress was repeatedly laid on the need to mobilize the growing revolutionary fervour of the masses against the existing leaders. The speech ended with the melodramatic appeal:

> Into the factories! Into the workshops! To the masses!

Lozovsky expressed himself with studied caution, but left the impression that he had written off as hopeless further cooperation with reformist unions and that his optimism had led him to underestimate the continuing hold of these unions on the workers.[44]

Throughout the congress the basic conflict centred mainly round the German and British delegations, representing two major countries where the trade union movement had not been

des Exekutivkomitees der Kommunistischen Internationale (n.d.), p. 727). For the argument about rationalization see Vol. 1, pp. 341–343; for the attitude of the Soviet trade unions to Profintern see *Socialism in One Country, 1924–1926,* Vol. 3, p. 565.

[42] *Protokoll über den Vierten Kongress der Roten Gewerkschaftsinternationale* (n.d.), pp. 33–90.

[43] See *Socialism in One Country, 1924–1926,* Vol. 3, pp. 564–567.

[44] These were the impressions which he tried to dissipate when he replied to the debate (*Protokoll über den Vierten Kongress der Roten Gewerkschaftsinternationale* (n.d.), pp. 265–267).

split, and where a broad interpretation had been given to united front policies. Both Horner of the British delegation and Heckert of the German delegation, under cover of polite acceptance in principle of Lozovsky's views, continued to believe in the hold of the reformist unions over a majority of the workers, refused to treat them as simply tools in the hands of capitalists and stressed the importance of working in and with them.[45] On the other hand, Monmousseau, the French delegate, thought that the period in which the CGTU could usefully appeal to the CGT to form a united front was over. He admitted that "our chief weakness is lack of contact with the masses", and recognized the danger of "passivity and discouragement".[46] The Norwegian trade union federation was unique in having avoided a split by refusing to affiliate either to Amsterdam or to Profintern. But this rugged independence gave little satisfaction in Moscow.[47] Brandler, making his last appearance on an official communist platform, endeavoured unsuccessfully to dissociate himself both from the leadership of the KPD and from the Right.[48]

The debate took a more sensational turn with a speech from Nin, the Spanish member of the executive bureau of Profintern. Nin occupied a position well to the Left of any other speaker at the congress, and anticipated much that, a year later, became the official line. His views were perhaps not uncongenial to Lozovsky, though Lozovsky himself could not have expressed them at this time. He admitted that "in the front-rank capitalist countries"— Germany, Czechoslovakia and France—"we have not only achieved no great progress, but have even receded". But he did not draw the same conclusion as Heckert and others, who wished "to let things take their course". On the contrary, Lozovsky's theses represented "an important change in our tactics, ... a turn to the Left, a clear quite decisive turn". He denounced any at-

[45] For Horner's and Heckert's speeches see pp. 367–368, 436 below.

[46] *Protokoll über den Vierten Kongress der Roten Gewerkschaftsinternationale* (n.d.), pp. 33–90.

[47] *Ibid.* pp. 213, 232–233. The Finnish trade unions were in the same situation, and Lozovsky in February 1928 had looked forward to the formation of a Soviet–Norwegian–Finnish trade union federation, which would be more effective than the defunct Anglo-Russian committee (A. Lozovsky, *Na Novom Etape* (1928), pp. 40–41); the failure of these efforts was lamented by Tomsky in his report to the eighth Soviet trade union congress in December 1928 (*Vos'moi S"ezd Professional'nykh Soyuzov SSSR* (1929), pp. 52–53).

[48] For Brandler's speech see p. 436 below.

tempt "to damp down our criticism of the Amsterdam Left", or to regard the revolutionary trade unions as an obstacle to some kind of abstract "unity in capital letters". It was not enough to victimize Walcher for what was "a decisive, definite, clear trend towards the liquidation of Profintern". The same trend had been apparent in Czechoslovakia and in France, as well as in the Soviet Union, where "many leaders of the trade union central council were decisive supporters of the liquidation of Profintern and the entry of the Russian unions into the Amsterdam International". He added, when challenged, that they had been "sly enough to record this in no resolution", but that he was "very well informed about the private proceedings". This led up to a general attack on the Soviet trade unions. The workers were "completely excluded from the control of production". The unions were "completely isolated from the mass of workers", and faced a danger of "the breakdown of trade union democracy and the exclusion of the masses of workers from the task of socialist construction". He ended by reaffirming that Lozovsky's theses "show us the way we have to go".[49] Significantly, Nin was the only speaker at the congress to bring up the Shakhty scandal, which had been divulged a few days earlier,[50] and was the signal for a tightening of the screw in almost every field of policy.

Kozelev, president of the Soviet metal workers' union, reacted sharply. Nin, he retorted, had "carried out the directives of Trotsky and other oppositionists to the best of his will and knowledge"; the charge of seeking to liquidate Profintern was "a lie borrowed from the same arsenal of the Trotskyite opposition". But the clash forced to the surface rifts hitherto discreetly veiled. In sharp contrast to Nin, he declared that Lozovsky's theses "discover no new America and mark no 'new course' in the trade union movement". He then returned to the speech which he had perhaps intended to make, and rounded on Heckert, who was alleged to have breathed a "sigh of relief" that the Soviet delegates had introduced an amendment to the theses stressing "the task of conquering the masses within the reformist unions". This too, Kozelev explained, did not represent "a sharp turn-

[49] *Protokoll über den Vierten Kongress der Roten Gewerkschaftsinternationale* (n.d.), pp. 179–183; for Walcher see pp. 434–436 below.

[50] See Vol. 1, p. 584; Yaglom reproached Nin later in the debate for using this incident to justify his oppositional standpoint (*Protokoll über den Vierten Kongress der Roten Gewerkschaftsinternationale* (1928), p. 229).

about, a new era, a new course in Profintern". He spent much time exposing deviations in the trade union policies of the KPD, and justifying the long-drawn and abortive negotiations of the Russian metal workers' union with the Metal Workers' International in Berne. Finally, he noted "the backward mentality of the masses of workers" and the strength of "traditions", especially in Germany and Great Britain. He accused Horner of paying tribute to trade union tradition and saying that British Communists wanted to conquer the unions "on the basis of the statutes". Horner at once rebutted these charges.[51] Kozelev had clearly been at pains to show that Profintern was steering a safe middle course, that nothing had changed, and above all that no turn to the Left was contemplated.

After this exchange, acrimony could not be eliminated from the debates. Yaglom, an important Soviet trade union leader and editor of *Trud*, launched an impassioned attack on Nin, whom, like Kozelev, he branded as a supporter of the opposition. He safeguarded himself by also criticizing the "Right deviation", and Walcher and Brandler by name. But he went out of his way to eulogize Tomsky; and the general tenour of his speech ranged him with the Right on issues of collaboration with reformist unions.[52] Lozovsky's summing-up was a masterly exercise in smoothing over cracks that had appeared during the debate. He defended himself against the charge of neglecting work in the reformist unions or of giving encouragement to splitting tactics. He evaded the question whether his theses represented an innovation in policy; every congress had to find new ways of coping with new problems. He was ironical about Brandler's "programme of action" — Brandler was a safe target — and condemned his slogan of workers' control of production. He mildly reproached Nin, who had worked in the Soviet Union for six years and ought to have known better, for his sweeping attack on the Soviet trade unions. He did not respond directly to Yaglom's appeal to make it clear that the negotiations of the Soviet trade unions with Amsterdam had been undertaken "*in agreement with Profintern and in accordance with its decisions*". But he quoted the letter

[51] *Ibid.* pp. 183–192; the text of the Soviet amendment has not been available.

[52] *Ibid.* pp. 228–234; significantly Horner was the only other delegate who so much as mentioned Tomsky (*ibid.* p. 101).

of the party central committee of January 13, 1926, which energetically denied "*counter-revolutionary* slanders about a proposed entry of the Soviet trade unions into the Amsterdam International".[53]

When the theses emerged from the drafting commission, Lozovsky named among the sections that had been strengthened those relating to "the *rapprochement* between the reformist trade unions, on the one hand, and the bourgeois state and *entrepreneurs*' organizations, on the other"; to "the work of adherents of Profintern in reformist trade unions" (this presumably in response to the Soviet amendment); and to "the strengthening of revolutionary unions" in countries where the movement was split.[54] The hint of a necessary change of front since the third congress in 1924 was conveyed by the assertion in the theses that "in recent years" the leaders of the reformist unions had taken a stand against the workers and been transformed into "direct tools of capitalist organizations"; the Amsterdam International had become "the tool of the capitalists". Where the third congress had condemned "sectarian attempts to organize the united front solely 'from below' ", the fourth congress proclaimed that "the fundamental slogan must be the united front from below". The theme of the "radicalization of the masses" was taken over from the ninth IKKI. While the leaders had turned to the Right, the masses had moved to the Left; this struck a revolutionary note. The specific injunctions were, however, cautious. The unorganized workers must be drawn into revolutionary unions, and independent revolutionary unions must be strengthened. But, in countries where the trade union movement was not already split, "the central task" was "the conquest of the reformist unions". What was required was "a united front of all workers of all tendencies, unity in action, in the struggle against capital". This did not mean, however, as it had sometimes been interpreted to mean in France, Czechoslovakia and Germany, "unity at all costs"; it meant "the united front from below, directly in the factories, in the lower links of the reformist trade unions". A concluding "programme of action" was a tactful blend

[53] *Ibid.* pp. 265–278. For Yaglom's appeal see *ibid.* p. 250; for the letter of January 13, 1926, see *Socialism in One Country, 1924–1926*, Vol. 3, p. 588.

[54] *Protokoll über den Vierten Kongress der Roten Gewerkschaftsinternationale* (n.d.), pp. 476–477.

of day-to-day and revolutionary demands, with the former predominating.[55] No less than twelve commissions were set up to deal with the affairs of individual countries;[56] and, apart from the general theses, the congress adopted resolutions on the trade union movements in Great Britain, Germany, the Netherlands, India, Ireland, the United States, France and Czechoslovakia.[57]

Following the directives in the resolution of the ninth IKKI, strike policy received a good deal of attention at the congress. Lozovsky in his main report noted that, owing to the concentration of capital, the modern strike was becoming "more than ever a real war"; the miners' strike was a more important event than Sadowa or Tsushima. Strikes could no longer be treated merely as economic struggles:

> One must study the power relations of the working class and the bourgeoisie, as well as power relations within the working class.

Every strike must be considered separately. Latin countries in particular were warned against the light-hearted proclamation of a general strike for which the workers were not prepared. Such "deviations on the French pattern" were attributed to "anarcho-syndicalist survivals". Contrary "deviations on the German pattern", which consisted in waiting to act till the apparatus had been won over, were ascribed to "fetichism and social-democratic survivals".[58] During the debate a French delegate rebutted the imputation evidently aimed at the CGTU of rushing into ill-prepared strikes.[59] The section on strikes in the main resolution, which was strengthened in the drafting commission,[60] reiterated "that the strike is exactly the same as a war, and that in war the greatest deployment of *all* forces and clarity about aims is desirable". Supporters of Profintern were specifically enjoined "to lead

55 *Desyat' Let Profinterna v Rezolyutsiyakh* (1930), pp. 174–188; for the resolution of the third congress see *Socialism in One Country, 1924–1926*, Vol. 3, pp. 550–556.

56 *Protokoll über den Vierten Kongress der Roten Gewerkschaftsinternationale* (n.d.), p. 267.

57 *Ibid.* pp. 589–634.

58 *Ibid.* pp. 57–58, 64–65.

59 *Ibid.* pp. 238–240.

60 *Ibid.* p. 476.

strikes without the approval and against the will of the reformist leaders"; this gave effect to the cardinal injunction of the ninth IKKI to make the strike "*an arena of struggle ... between communists and reformists*". But warnings against rash action were again issued, and the section ended with a two-pronged exhortation:

> Adherents of Profintern should constantly remember that ... a systematic and obstinate struggle must be conducted to conquer a majority of the workers united in the reformist unions, and to reinforce the independent revolutionary organizations.[61]

Lozovsky attacked the reformists for supporting compulsory arbitration in industrial disputes; this was an attempt "to make the class movement of the proletariat subject to bourgeois courts". He detected waverings on this question in the ranks of the KPD.[62] The congress passed a special resolution denouncing compulsory arbitration as a device of *entrepreneurs* and capitalist governments, with the collusion of reformist leaders, to counter the sharpening of the class struggle, and comparable to Fascist attacks on the rights of the workers.[63]

A British delegate drew attention to the plight of the "trade Internationals" or "international trade secretariats". Lozovsky in a report of November 1926 maintained that the Internationals "play an altogether inconspicuous part", and were no more than "information bureaus", but admitted that most of them were hostile to Profintern.[64] Of the thirty-two trade Internationals only the Food Workers' International and the International of Educational Workers were affiliated to Profintern;[65] the rest had

[61] *Desyat' Let Profinterna v Rezolyutsiyakh* (1930), p. 179.

[62] *Protokoll über den Vierten Kongress der Roten Gewerkschaftsinternationale* (1928), pp. 41, 59; the KPD journal called arbitration a "trip-wire" used by the reformists to nullify strike policy, and to renounce the right to strike (*Die Internationale*, xi, No. 9, May 1, 1928, p. 258; see also an article by Merker, *ibid.* xi, No. 14, July 15, 1928, pp. 485–495).

[63] *Desyat' Let Profinterna v Rezolyutsiyakh* (1930), p. 215.

[64] *Krasnyi Internatsional Profsoyuzov*, No. 12, 1926, pp. 543–544; the Mineworkers' International was said to have behaved particularly badly in 1926, having voted in advance to call an international strike in support of the British miners, and then declining to take any action (*Sed'moi S"ezd Professional'nykh Soyuzov SSSR* (1927), p. 268).

[65] *Mezhdunarodnoe Profdvizhenie za 1924–27 gg.* (1928), pp. 149–153; for these two Internationals see *Socialism in One Country, 1924–1926*, Vol. 3, pp. 543–544.

become impregnable citadels of the influence of IFTU, which at its conference in Paris in August 1927 had modified the statutes in such a way as to preclude the admission to them of Red trade unions even where a majority in such unions desired it.[66] Prompted by this unpromising situation, the fourth congress of Profintern reviewed the rôle of the International Propaganda Committees (IPCs), of which seventeen were enumerated in the report of the executive bureau of Profintern to the congress, though it was admited that not all these had been formally constituted, and that most of them only functioned in a few countries.[67] At the congress an attempt was made to harness them to the general drive for more aggressive attitudes. The *rapporteur* recalled that their full official title was "International Propaganda and Action Committees", and thought that they should be "converted chiefly into action committees". The transport and miners' IPCs were singled out for praise, and were evidently the most vigorous; the textile committee had done little.[68] A paragraph on the IPCs was hastily inserted in the main resolution, proposing that they should be transformed into "organizing and directing organs of the economic struggle of the workers in their respective branches of production";[69] and a special resolution on the IPCs was also adopted by the congress. This was apparently not published; but the greater part of it, consisting of injunctions for more forceful action, was incorporated as a chapter in the resolution on organization.[70] The unpublished resolution included, however, one item omitted from that chapter: a call for especially intensive propaganda against "the war plans of imperialism" by the transport, metal-workers' and miners' IPCs.[71]

66 *Protokoll über den Vierten Kongress der Roten Gewerkschaftsinternationale* (1928), p. 194.

67 *Mezhdunarodnoe Profdvizhenie za 1924–27 gg.* (1928), pp. 82–148; for these committees see *Socialism in One Country, 1924–1926*, Vol. 3, pp. 531–532, 540–544, 563–564, 595.

68 *Protokoll über den Vierten Kongress der Roten Gewerkschaftsinternationale* (n.d.), pp. 354–357.

69 *Ibid.* pp. 477–478.

70 *Ibid.* pp. 486–487; *Desyat' Let Profinterna v Rezolyutsiyakh* (1930), pp. 197–199. For the paragraph in the main resolution see *ibid.* p. 186.

71 See the detailed summary of the unpublished resolution in *Internationale Presse-Korrespondenz*, No. 34, April 3, 1928, p. 630; it is an odd example of haphazard procedure that this item, obviously omitted for reasons of discretion from the published resolution, should have appeared in this summary in a widely circulated news-sheet.

The congress devoted the greater part of two sittings to the question of juvenile workers, hearing reports from German and French delegates, and a handful of other speeches. Neglect of the subject in the past was admitted; it was only in May 1927 that Profintern had set up a commission to deal with it.[72] The seventh IKKIM a month later had devoted a long resolution to capitalist rationalization and its oppressive consequences for the young worker;[73] and in the following year it reverted to the question with renewed emphasis. Capitalist rationalization was said to have given an "enhanced rôle" to juvenile workers; and the participation of juvenile workers and trainees in strikes was "of crucial importance". Youth leagues were exhorted to support trade union commissions on juvenile labour in countries where they existed, and to call for their formation where they did not.[74] The main bone of contention at the congress was the participation of young workers in strikes. Some old-fashioned trade unions opposed this — allegedly on the ground that they did not wish to encourage competing claims from juveniles. The Polish delegate pointed out that children began to work in Polish textile factories at the age of ten; the Chinese delegate put the age in Shanghai at seven or eight.[75] The resolution strongly supported strikes by young workers in support of their claims, which were said to be on the increase; it noted that a large part of the proletariat in Asian countries consisted of juveniles and children, and endorsed the resolution of the pan-Pacific trade union conference of June 1927; and it insisted that every trade union affiliated to Profintern should have its youth section, and every national trade union federation, as well as the executive bureau of Profintern in Moscow, have its youth secretariat.[76] It is significant that no mention was made of KIM, or of the resolution of IKKIM of June 1927,

[72] For the reports see *Protokoll über den Vierten Kongress der Roten Gewerkschaftsinternationale* (n.d.), pp. 278–289; for the reply to the debates see *ibid.* pp. 303–304.

[73] *Internationale Presse-Korrespondenz*, No. 81, August 12, 1927, pp. 1761–1764.

[74] R. Schüller *et al., Geschichte der Kommunistischen Jugendinternationale*, iii (1930), 221–226.

[75] *Protokoll über den Vierten Kongress der Roten Gewerkschaftsinternationale* (n.d.), pp. 297, 303.

[76] *Desyat' Let Profinterna v Rezolyutsiyakh* (1930), pp. 222–225; the pan-Pacific conference will be discussed in a later section of this volume.

throughout these proceedings.[77] Nobody at the congress showed much interest in work among peasants. But a commission was set up to deal with it. Antselovich, president of the Soviet agricultural workers' trade union, was given ten minutes to report on it in the plenary session. He stressed the growing importance of the hired worker in the countryside whose position (everywhere outside the Soviet Union) had deteriorated; and he submitted a resolution which was adopted without discussion. It laid down a programme of action in quite unrealistic detail, and instructed the executive bureau of Profintern to act in conjunction with Krestintern and with the agricultural workers' IPC (a body of which no other record seems to exist).[78] It remained a dead letter.[79]

One sitting was devoted to a debate on Fascism, introduced by the French delegate, Monmousseau. The keynote of his speech was that Fascism could no longer be regarded as a specifically Italian phenomenon, but as an instrument of the temporary stabilization of capitalism, and of the offensive against the working class. He appeared to hesitate between two discordant views. Since reformist leaders worked in alliance with the bourgeoisie, they might be identified with Fascists. Others, however, believed that the reformist leaders were not committed to promoting the turn of the bourgeoisie towards Fascism, and could not be regarded as Fascists. Monmousseau pointed out that, unlike the Fascist unions, the social-democratic unions were mass organizations; and he drew the old distinction between masses and reformist leaders.[80] A Polish delegate attempted a more profound analysis. Fascism had come to power in Poland, "not in a direct

[77] At the sixth congress of Comintern three months later the official delegates of KIM demanded "the drawing of young workers into the economic struggle" (*Stenograficheskii Otchet VI Kongressa Kominterna* (1929), i, 67); but opinion in KIM appears to have been divided. An article on the session of IKKIM in December 1928 explained that this was the *one* question on which the Right opposition challenged the leaders, proposing to instruct young workers only to refrain from acting as strike-breakers (*Internationale Presse-Korrespondenz*, No. 6, January 8, 1929, p. 113); presumably the opposition was silenced, or voted down.

[78] *Protokoll über den Vierten Kongress der Roten Gewerkschaftsinternationale* (n.d.), pp. 491–493, 581–589.

[79] A year later an article remarked that the directives of the fourth congress on agricultural workers "are being realised only slowly" (*Internationale Presse-Korrespondenz*, No. 37, April 30, 1929, p. 898).

[80] *Protokoll über den Vierten Kongress der Roten Gewerkschaftsinternationale* (n.d.), pp. 359–366.

struggle against the revolutionary working class, but under the banner of a struggle against reaction". This had made it possible to win the support of the petty bourgeoisie; even democratic parliamentary forms had been preserved. The social basis of Polish Fascism consisted of the bourgeoisie, the landowners, the large well-to-do middle peasants and "the upper strata of the urban petty bourgeoisie". The conclusion was radical. Under the guise of Fascism, "monopoly capitalism strives to defeat the workers' movement by capturing the trade unions and expelling revolutionary elements from them". Dimitrov, the Bulgarian delegate, who since his exclusion from Bulgaria in 1923 had worked in Comintern and Profintern, described Fascism as "the last phase of the class-rule of the bourgeoisie", and explained that in the countries of south-eastern Europe, where no real bourgeois-democratic revolution had taken place, and where the bourgeoisie was still weak, Fascism had been imposed from above by the power of the state.[81] A long analytical resolution on Fascism, said to have been "agreed with the Italian, Polish and Bulgarian delegations, and with the representatives of other countries ruled by a Fascist dictatorship",[82] listed Bulgaria, Spain, Portugal and Lithuania, as well as Italy and Poland, as countries under Fascist rule, and alleged that Fascist methods were used against the revolutionary workers' movement in most other European countries. The League of Nations and the ILO were denounced as allies of Fascism. Where "Fascist trade unions have succeeded ... in grouping workers in their ranks", supporters of Profintern were urged to work in these unions in order to rally the workers against the leaders; a separate section devoted to Italy suggested doubts whether these tactics could be applied in that country.[83]

Separate resolutions were adopted on the Minority Movement in Great Britain, on the special problems of the German trade union movement and on the tasks of CGTU in France.[84] Heller reported on well-worn lines on the trade union movement in colonial and semi-colonial countries. Imperialism was described as a struggle for markets, for raw materials and for capital invest-

[81] *Ibid.* pp. 366–368, 371–373.

[82] *Ibid.* pp. 506–508.

[83] *Desyat' Let Profinterna v Rezolyutsiyakh* (1930), pp. 225–231.

[84] *Protokoll über den Vierten Kongress der Roten Gewerkschaftsinternationale* (n.d.), pp. 589–594, 594–603, 623–629; for these resolutions see pp. 368, 436, 509 below.

ment. The recent falling off in foreign investments in China and India was attributed to "various causes", including the growth of capital investment in Africa; the controversy on decolonization which raged at the sixth congress of Comintern four months later had not yet broken out. A comprehensive survey of Asia and the Middle East ended with the slogan: "Proletarians of the west and oppressed peoples of the east, proletarians of the west and proletarians of the east, unite!"[85] The resolution followed the report, but contained an additional section on Latin America.[86] The Irish question forced itself on the attention of a somewhat impatient congress. The revolutionary Workers' League of Ireland, headed by Larkin, was affiliated to Profintern. It had been recognized by the seventh IKKI in November 1926 as the only section of Comintern in Ireland, and instructed to transform itself as soon as possible into a communist party;[87] and Larkin himself had visited Moscow on several occasions. Rivalry, however, occurred between the league and the much larger and older Irish Labour Union affiliated to the British trade union movement. This organization had no defined political commitment, and included a Left wing comparable to the Minority Movement; but, unlike the Workers' League, it maintained relations with the Irish Free State government. Bitter recriminations broke out between Larkin and Hardy, the representative of the British Minority Movement, at a session of the executive bureau of Profintern in 1926, and continued in the press. Carney, who led the Irish delegation at the fourth congress, was in a fighting mood. He issued a statement which was apparently tantamount to a declaration of the withdrawal of the Workers' League from Profintern, and made a speech at the congress in which he rounded sharply on Horner and Hardy of the British delegation and on Lozovsky. Hardy replied in a slightly more restrained statement on behalf of

[85] *Protokoll über den Vierten Kongress der Roten Gewerkschaftsinternationale* (n.d.), pp. 388–405; for decolonization see p. 214 below.

[86] *Desyat' Let Profinterna v Rezolyutsiyakh* (1930), pp. 202–204; Latin American affairs will be discussed in a later section of this volume.

[87] *Stenograficheskii Otchet VI Kongressa Kominterna* (1929), v, 137; no such decision has been traced in the published records of the seventh IKKI. Larkin, according to Stewart, who worked with him in Ireland in 1924, was unwilling to cooperate in founding a communist party (R. Stewart, *Breaking the Fetters* (1967), pp. 147–152); he told the ninth congress of the CPGB in 1927 that the league "really represents the revolutionary aspirations of Comintern in Ireland" (*Internationale Presse-Korrespondenz*, No. 99, October 11, 1927, p. 2128).

the British delegation.[88] After this the Irish delegation was mollified, and informed the congress that reports of an impending withdrawal of the Workers' League from Profintern rested on a misunderstanding.[89] A commission under the tactful presidency of Ryan, an Australian delegate, struggled for a week to draft an agreed resolution. This recognized the Workers' League of Ireland as "the first Irish union which had joined Profintern", but instructed it to carry out a campaign in other unions for the formation of "revolutionary groups" which would maintain direct relations with the Minority Movement in Great Britain. The basis of cooperation between the Workers' League and these groups was to be established at an "unofficial conference". The crux was an instruction to the Workers' League to engage in united front tactics, on the approved Profintern model of a campaign demanding unity with the official trade union organization in Dublin. The majority of the Irish delegation opposed the clause in the commission; and in the final version of the resolution the point was left open for further discussion.[90] The Irish question continued to smoulder at the sixth congress of Comintern in July 1928. Further complaints of neglect were heard, and Carney made another angry speech, but without producing any visible reaction.[91]

The mutual, and unresolved, conflict between the leaders of the Soviet trade unions and Profintern imparted an air of uncertainty and hesitation to the results of the fourth congress. The call for more aggressive action was recorded in Lozovsky's speeches and in the resolutions of the congress. But it was balanced and attenuated by emphasis on more modest desiderata propounded by other delegations or other members of the Soviet delegation; and the far-reaching theses seemed to meet all objections and to cater for all tastes. The price of their unanimous acceptance was an uneasy and ambiguous compromise. While, however, no formal decision had been taken and no new line of

[88] *Protokoll über den Vierten Kongress der Roten Gewerkschaftsinternationale* (n.d.), pp. 169–173, 240–242.

[89] *Ibid.* pp. 304–305.

[90] *Ibid.* pp. 493–496. For the final version see *ibid.* pp. 608–611; whether this was ever submitted to the congress is not clear.

[91] *Stenograficheskii Otchet VI Kongressa Kominterna* (1929), i, 142, iv, 135–136, 218–220.

action prescribed, the general tenour of the proceedings left little doubt that the congress had weakened the resistance of the Right, and set the course for more aggressive policies, which would deepen the rift between revolutionaries and reformists, between communists in the international trade union movement and its social-democratic leaders. Later Lozovsky described how "we were feeling our way towards new tactics, new methods of work", how "at the fourth congress of Profintern we gave shape to the directives of the ninth IKKI to seize with all our might the leadership of the economic struggle without or against the reformist unions", and how the sixth congress of Comintern "confirmed our decisions".[92] It was a one-sided, but not unfair, picture of the course of events. Tomsky's fortunes were declining. According to one account, he ventured on an open challenge to Lozovsky in Profintern and was defeated in the Politburo.[93] But it was not till a year later, at the tenth IKKI in July 1929, that Lozovsky boldly claimed that the fourth congress of Profintern and the sixth congress of Comintern had executed a "sharp turn", which was "ideologically unacceptable" to Yaglom and Tomsky.[94]

A report issued at the time of the fourth congress offered a comprehensive enumeration of adherents, actual and potential, of Profintern in three categories. The first category of trade union organizations directly affiliated to Profintern accounted for 13,862,000 members. Of these the largest were the Soviet and Chinese trade unions (10,248,800 and 2,800,000 respectively). Next in size came the French CGTU (525,000); and this category also included the Czechoslovak Red trade union federation MOS (196,000), as well as such organizations as the Workers' League of Ireland (18,000) and the Belgian Chevaliers du Travail (8000). The second category consisted of "revolutionary minorities" which, though forming part of trade union organizations not affiliated to Profintern, themselves maintained relations with Profintern. The total of 2,874,000 members in this category included minorities in Germany (1,000,000 — clearly an estimate,

[92] *Kommunisticheskii Internatsional*, No. 23–24 (201–202), 1929, p. 111.

[93] Letter from Trotsky in Alma-Ata to his supporters, based on information from Moscow (Trotsky archives, T 1588).

[94] *Protokoll: 10. Plenum des Exekutivkomitees der Kommunistischen Internationale* (n.d.), p. 727.

since no regular minority organization existed), Great Britain (800,000 — the membership of the NMM), Japan (600,000), the United States (250,000), Australia (130,000), Poland (100,000), Czechoslovakia (70,000) and France (60,000). The third category of sympathizing organizations unable owing to police repression to maintain formal relations with Profintern numbered 368,230 members; the countries concerned included Japan (the 39,000 members of the Hyogikai), Italy (10,000), Bulgaria (8000) and Poland (8000). The totals in all three categories were swollen by the inclusion of figures for Latin American trade unions whose status was dubious and sometimes fictitious; and a high proportion of the other figures quoted rested on little more than guess-work.[95] In some important countries (notably France and Czechoslovakia) the rift between communists and non-communists in the trade unions had been carried to the point of forming rival organizations, which were more or less directly sponsored by Profintern and owed allegiance to it. In other countries (notably Great Britain, Germany and the United States) the communists never formed more than an insignificant minority in the trade union movement, or were anything more than a thorn in the side of the official leadership. In countries where trade unions were officially banned and persecuted, Profintern promoted and subsidized illegal unions, though it rarely achieved any substantial success. Finally, in China, in the Middle East and in several Latin American countries, trade unions created by various agencies, communist or other, received the blessing of Profintern. But these embryonic organizations had little resemblance to the trade unions of western capitalist countries. To tabulate all these diverse and frequently unstable situations under the rubric of the relation of the organizations concerned to Profintern was a quixotic enterprise; and Profintern statistics presented a blurred amalgam of fact and fantasy.

[95] *Desyat' Let Profinterna v Rezolyutsiyakh* (1930), pp. 171–174; the situation in Latin America, which especially preoccupied Lozovsky at this time, will be discussed in a later section of this volume.

CHAPTER 70

THE SIXTH CONGRESS

THE sixth congress of Comintern exceeded its predecessors both in length and in the number of delegates. It held forty-six sittings from July 17 to September 1, 1928. Of these, sixteen were occupied by the preliminaries and by Bukharin's main report on "The International Situation and the Tasks of Comintern"; seven by a debate on the threat of imperialist wars; five by the programme of Comintern; twelve by the colonial question; and six by the situation in the Russian party, by organizational questions and by the concluding proceedings. The number of delegates was recorded as 532, of whom 381 had voting rights.[1] The session was transferred from the traditional meeting place of previous congresses in the Kremlin to the pillar hall of the trade union headquarters, the largest hall in Moscow.[2] The proceedings were perhaps more polyglot than those of earlier congresses. But the main speeches, including those of Bukharin, were still delivered in German, though complete records were kept in Russian.[3]

The forthcoming congress had been one of the items on the agenda of the party central committee at its session of July 4–12, 1928, when, notwithstanding insistence on the Right danger, it was decided to leave Bukharin in sole charge of the proceedings.[4] Much of the discussion in the committee appears to have turned on the draft Comintern programme.[5] The main items which were to occupy the congress were announced in a statement of IKKI

[1] *Stenograficheskii Otchet VI Kongressa Kominterna* (1929), v, 159; the German version (*Protokoll: Sechster Kongress der Kommunistischen Internationale* (n.d.)) was planned in four volumes, of which the second, covering the debate on the programme (sittings 24–28), never appeared.

[2] J. Humbert-Droz, *De Lénine à Staline* (Neuchatel, 1971), p. 310.

[3] Bukharin's speeches which appeared in *Internationale Presse-Korrespondenz*, No. 72, July 25, 1928, pp. 1297–131, No. 81, August 8, 1928, pp. 1469–1483, No. 91, August 28, 1928, pp. 1707–1726, were all described as "re-translated from Russian".

[4] See Vol. 2, p. 64.

[5] See p. 226 below.

on the eve of its opening. They were (1) the hollowness of the alleged "stabilization" of capitalism and the transition of the member parties of Comintern to offensive tactics (2) the programme of Comintern (3) the danger of war (4) the national and colonial question, and (5) socialist construction in the USSR.[6] A leading article in *Pravda* embroidered the five themes of the congress, and laid particular stress, as a vital element of the first, on "a sharpening of the struggle against social democracy".[7] Bukharin's opening report was devoted to the first theme, which in a sense dominated the rest. But all the issues were intertwined, and constantly recurred throughout the proceedings of the congress. The second, third and fourth items were the subjects of separate reports and debates; discussion of the affairs of the Soviet Union was limited to reports by Varga and Manuilsky, and denunciations of the opposition by a succession of foreign delegates.

Though much controversy occurred on points of detail, the main lines which the congress was to follow were clearly laid down. The expulsion of the opposition had removed any danger of dissent within the Russian party; the numerous communications addressed to the congress by exiled members of the opposition were unknown to the mass of delegates.[8] No foreign party threatened serious opposition on any major issue. Nevertheless, the congress met in an uneasy atmosphere. Bukharin had for some weeks been conspicuous by his frequent absences from the offices of Comintern; and, though his preoccupation with the programme and other preparations for the congress served as an excuse, it might be felt that he was withdrawing himself from work over which he no longer had full control.[9] While his secret visit to Kamenev may not yet have come to Stalin's knowledge, he had

[6] *Internationale Presse-Korrespondenz*, No. 67, July 17, 1928, pp. 1209–1210.

[7] *Pravda*, July 17, 1928. The IKKI statement, which may have been drafted by Bukharin, observed not very conspicuously that "our enemy on a world scale is now social-reformism"; the *Pravda* leader was designed to ensure that this item did not lack precision or emphasis.

[8] They included at least three communications from Trotsky, one from Preobrazhensky, and a joint memorandum from Radek and Smilga (see Vol. 2, pp. 67–68); copies of Trotsky's critique of the draft programme were apparently distributed to members of the programme commission with a strict injunction to return them at the end of the session (statement by Cannon in L. Trotsky, *The Third International After Lenin* (N.Y., 1936), p. 356).

[9] J. Humbert-Droz, *Il Contrasto tra l'Internazionale e il PCI* (1969), p. 253 (Humbert-Droz archives, 0084).

shown his hand at the session of the party central committee immediately before the congress; and Stalin retaliated, in a way which openly discredited Bukharin's authority, by insisting on the extensive amendment of the draft theses which Bukharin had prepared and circulated to the delegations.[10] The situation was under control. Stalin could safely depart on his usual holiday in the south, leaving Molotov to contain and restrain Bukharin. Before the end of the congress, the principal foreign delegates were well aware that Bukharin had forfeited the confidence of the party majority, and was only in name the spokesman of the party line. The hollowness of Bukharin's position and the uncertainty of the outcome infected all the proceedings of the congress.[11] Togliatti was said to have called the congress "a dull, sad parade of loyalty", at which "one cannot speak the truth about the most important and essential current issues"; even the Russians "give us the feeling that the congress was for them a heavy burden of which they cannot rid themselves". Thorez complained of Bukharin's devotion to socialism in one country, and spoke of uneasiness and lack of information among foreign delegates.[12]

The principal aim of the party leaders was to confirm and complete the swing to the left in Comintern adumbrated five months earlier at the ninth IKKI. This involved some revision of the official view of the condition and prospects of contemporary capitalism. Initial optimistic estimates of the prospects of European or world revolution had long ago been replaced by sober recognition of a partial and temporary recovery of the capitalist system.[13] Even after the ninth IKKI in February 1928 a disciple of Bukharin could write in the party journal that it was "radically wrong, tactically harmful, and crudely mistaken theoretically" to suppose that western capitalism was on the verge of a breakdown.[14] But, with the opposition eliminated, and Comintern moving towards the Left, this temporizing view of the prospects of capital-

[10] See Vol. 2, p. 69; for the points on which the draft was amended see p. 196 below.

[11] For the intrigues against Bukharin behind the scenes see Vol. 2, p. 69; these nullified the official denial of disagreements in the Politburo (*ibid.* p. 64).

[12] This anonymous report is in the Trotsky archives, T 2447.

[13] See pp. 132–133 above.

[14] *Bol'shevik*, No. 5, March 15, 1928, p. 35.

ism could no longer be tolerated; and Stalin, reviewing the international scene on the eve of the sixth congress, named "the contradictions which have ripened ... in the camp of the imperialists" as the most conspicuous development since the previous congress in 1924.[15] Remmele, in a pre-congress article in the Comintern journal, entitled "Under the Banner of Sharp Class Antagonisms", used the wave of strikes, as well as recent election figures (notably those of May 1928 in Germany), to demonstrate the growing power of communist parties in Europe.[16] A leading article in *Pravda* on the day the congress opened listed the workers' risings which had occurred since the previous congress in 1924, and concluded by recording "*a sharpening of the struggle against social-democracy*".[17]

When the congress met, Bukharin's theses on the international situation had been amended to meet Stalin's criticisms.[18] On four points in particular Bukharin's cautious and now conservative outlook had led him to deviate from the requirements of the party line. He had made it appear that capitalist stabilization was still holding its ground; in speaking of the struggle against social-democracy, he had not made it clear that the struggle also extended to so-called Left social-democracy; in denouncing the Right deviation in communist parties, he had ignored the necessity of fighting against the manoeuvres of the "conciliators"; and he had neglected the need for "iron discipline in communist parties".[19] The speech in which Bukharin introduced the amended theses extended over two sittings, and the debate lasted for a fortnight. Bukharin did his best, as he had done at the party congress six months earlier,[20] to conform to the requirements of the

[15] Stalin, *Sochineniya*, xi, 197–198.

[16] *Kommunisticheskii Internatsional*, No. 25–26 (151–152), 1928, pp. 7–17; for the German elections see pp. 437–438 below.

[17] *Pravda*, July 17, 1928.

[18] See p. 195 above. Neither the original nor the amended version was published; for the final text see pp. 202–204 below.

[19] Stalin, *Sochineniya*, xii, 19–23. As regards the second point, Lenz in an article in the KPD journal in June 1928 (see p. 641 below) had complained that not enough emphasis was laid in Bukharin's draft programme on the Left as "the most harmful fraction in social-democratic parties"; this must have preceded Stalin's objection and perhaps directly or indirectly inspired it. Thälmann at the congress declared that the question "had great importance as a principle", and that the German delegation would present an amendment to Bukharin's theses on this point (see p. 198 below).

[20] See pp. 153–154 above.

new line. He postulated "three periods of post-war development": a first period of "*acute revolutionary crisis*" from 1917 to 1921; a second period of "*restoration of the productive forces of capitalism*" since 1921; and a third period, just beginning, of "*capitalist reconstruction*", coinciding with "*a growth of forces opposed to capitalism and an exceedingly rapid development of its internal contradictions*". He laboured heavily over the capitalist contradictions of the third period. It was the very success of capitalism (improved technology, rationalization, etc.) which had aggravated its contradictions. Bukharin repeated the assertion that "*the British–American antagonism forms at present the axis of all the contradictions between the imperialist states*". If capitalist stabilization "*provides an economic backing for social-democracy*", it was also true that "*the contradictions of stabilization create a foundation for the development of communist parties*".[21] The tactical line required to carry out the new policy was "an orientation totally antagonistic to the social-democrats". This was to be applied at every level, as Bukharin put it, "from the factory cell to the League of Nations". It was "a course set for the destruction of bourgeois state power, a course set for revolution". As at the fifth congress, any intention to abandon the tactics of the united front was disclaimed; but the united front was to be pursued "in a majority of cases ... *from below*". Taking Comintern as a whole, "the central danger" now came from "the Right deviation".[22]

The debate was more remarkable for an abundance of hints and innuendos than for plain speaking. Open attacks on Bukharin were barred. But a little mild sniping was evidently in order. Murphy, who held an eccentric position in the British delegation, criticized Bukharin's emphasis on "stabilization" in the second and third periods as one-sided and unreal.[23] The American delegation was split on the present condition and prospects of American capitalism, and took sides for or against Bukharin.[24] Hannington, a British delegate, reproached Bukharin with having failed to speak of unemployment (it received only one passing

[21] *Stenograficheskii Otchet VI Kongressa Kominterna* (1929), i, 26–40.

[22] *Ibid.* i, 51–58; for the united front at the fifth congress see *Socialism in One Country, 1924–1926*, Vol. 3, pp. 74–75.

[23] *Stenograficheskii Otchet VI Kongressa Kominterna* (1929), pp. 137–138; for Murphy p. 373 below.

[24] See pp. 603–605 below.

mention in the theses), and devoted his whole speech to this issue, describing the neglect of work among the unemployed as "a very serious omission on the part of Comintern".[25] Varga, in his annual report to Comintern on the economic situation in 1927, had described that year as "the best year for the capitalists since the end of the war".[26] He now qualified this favourable verdict by embarking on a theoretical analysis of the "technological revolution" resulting from technical progress, rationalization and the increase of fixed capital at the expense of labour; this had created "*for the capitalists*" a temporary condition of "brilliant prosperity in face of huge mass unemployment". He thought that Bukharin had diagnosed the situation without deducing the consequences: the neglect of unemployment in the theses should be corrected.[27] Thälmann announced that the German delegation was "in complete agreement with the basic line" of Bukharin's theses as approved by the Russian party delegation, but would introduce in the political commission some amendments designed to "sharpen the general assessment of the situation" and to draw attention to "the rôle of the Left wing of social-democracy". Events in the four years since the last congress of Comintern — the British general strike, the Chinese revolution, the wave of strikes, the Vienna rising, the Sacco–Vanzetti campaign — demonstrated "the growth of the contradictions of capitalism in the period of relative stabilization". Much of Thälmann's long speech was occupied by oblique or direct references to the notorious divisions in the KPD. But he returned in his peroration, received with rapturous applause, to proclaim that "capitalist stabilization is rotting away" and that "a new period of revolutionary upsurge is ripening".[28] Lominadze reasserted "the sharpening and development of the contradictions of capitalist stabilization". After de-

[25] *Stenograficheskii Otchet VI Kongressa Kominterna* (1929), pp. 186–192.

[26] *Internationale Presse-Korrespondenz*, No. 15, February 15, 1928, p. 293; for Varga's views at the fifth congress of Comintern in 1924 see *Socialism in One Country, 1924–1926*, Vol. 3, pp. 75–76.

[27] *Stenograficheskii Otchet VI Kongressa Kominterna* (1929), i, 221–228; Varga reverted to the theme in the debate on the programme (*ibid.* iii, 52–63).

[28] *Ibid.* i, 333–346; for the divisions in the KPD see pp. 438–442 below. The subsequent observation in J. Humbert-Droz, *De Lénine à Staline* (Neuchatel, 1971), p. 331, that Bukharin's and Thälmann's views at the sixth congress, especially on stabilization, were "plainly contradictory", owed something to hindsight, but was not unfounded.

nouncing his other enemies on the Right, he proceeded, with the help of quotations from Marx, to refute Varga's view of the relation of unemployment to the rise in fixed capital; he rather condescendingly acquitted Bukharin on the ground that Bukharin had spoken exclusively of the United States.[29] Petrovsky, speaking as a member of the British delegation under the name of Bennett, accused Varga of painting too rosy a picture of British economic prospects.[30] Denunciation of social-democrats was an easy and popular theme. Vasiliev, a member of the Comintern secretariat, found a source of weakness in "an insufficiently active struggle against the social-democratic past of the communist parties".[31] Nobody at the congress openly dissented from these views. But Münzenberg, though he too called for "an implacable struggle against social-democrats", was alarmed that work in auxiliary organizations not exclusively or ostensibly communist, like MOPR and MRP, might be treated as "a semi-Menshevik deviation", and protested uneasily that such work had "nothing in common with 'an opportunist policy' or a 'Right' deviation".[32] Others of those present, especially British and German delegates active in trade union work, evidently viewed with apprehension a policy designed to treat the non-communist radical Left as irreconcilable enemies.

The trade union question was not on the agenda of the congress; and Bukharin in his main report, unsure of his ground, offered some strangely inconclusive reflexions on it. The "political authority" of party workers in the trade unions was growing; on the other hand, "their specific authority as trade union workers, as good leaders of a strike movement", was small. Communist workers failed to establish "correct relations" with non-communists because they relied too much on command, not on persuasion. These were conservative criticisms. On the other hand, some communists in trade unions "became so at home with social-democratic methods that they did not carry out party directives", and lacked initiative instead of taking "*a leading rôle* in the strike movement".[33] Nobody else spoke out in the debate

[29] *Stenograficheskii Otchet VI Kongressa Kominterna* (1929), i, 460, 470–472.
[30] *Ibid.* i, 510.
[31] *Ibid.* i, 123.
[32] *Ibid.* i, 101–102.
[33] *Ibid.* i, 52–53.

except Lozovsky, who gave his own version of what took place at the fourth congress of Profintern. He brought into the open the radical changes in policy which had been discreetly veiled in the ambiguous formulas of that congress. He admitted, indeed boasted, that its decisions contradicted those of the third congress in 1924; times had changed. Among the new lines adopted by the congress he named the following: a sharpening of the struggle against reformist trade unions and the Amsterdam International; the united front "chiefly from below"; leadership in the economic struggle (i.e. in strikes) against the official trade union bureaucracy, and insistence on its political character; encouragement of Red trade unions in countries where the movement was already split, and intensified protest against the exclusion of communists from reformist unions. He stressed again the importance of independent strike action led by communists in the trade unions. The slogan "Zwingt die Bonzen", said to have been put forward by some German communists (which meant pressure on reformist trade union leaders), was condemned as "a slogan of passive waiting, and not of the active mobilization of the masses". Failure to carry out the decisions of the fourth congress of Profintern meant support for "Right liquidationist tendencies, which exist—it is true, to a small extent—in our ranks".[34] In a more aggressive speech in the later debate on the programme, Lozovsky called the reformist unions "*schools of capitalism*" and "*an extension of the bourgeois state apparatus within the working class*".[35]

The question of Fascism hovered uneasily in the background of the congress. A declaration denouncing Italian Fascism was approved, on the proposal of a British delegate, at the first sitting: this alleged that "the Fascist régime is making feverish preparations for war".[36] Bukharin made a passing reference, in the report introducing his theses, to Poland as a "Fascist state".[37] But Fascism

[34] *Ibid.* i, 401–418. Lozovsky admitted continued opposition to these decisions in the German and American parties (see pp. 435–437, 598–600 below).

[35] *Stenograficheskii Otchet VI Kongressa Kominterna* (1929), iii, 84.

[36] *Ibid.* i, 22–23. More than a year earlier the secretariat of Comintern had written to Münzenberg to propose a campaign against Fascism, and set up a committee with Maggi as chairman to organise it (J. Humbert-Droz, *Il Contrasto tra L'Internazionale e il PCI* (1969), p. 239 (Humbert-Droz archives, 0077)); but nothing is known to have come of this.

[37] *Stenograficheskii Otchet VI Kongressa Kominterna* (1929), i, 42.

in its broader application received scant attention in the ensuing debate. Thälmann bracketed reformism with Fascism as "two methods of holding down the working class", and spoke of "the development of reformism into social-Fascism".[38] Togliatti, who alone could not evade the issue, handled it with embarrassed ingenuity. On the eve of the congress he had published in *Pravda* a long analysis of the situation;[39] this he now repeated in muted form. In Italy the economic crisis had "come somewhat to a stop in its development"; the régime had obtained foreign capital, had put pressure on the workers and had "helped the bourgeoisie to recognize more clearly its interests". Fascism was "the most consistent and perfected form of reaction". But it was not the only form. While paying lip-service to the view that social-democracy was the most dangerous enemy, Togliatti refused to equate social-democrats with Fascists. Ideological links existed between Fascism and social-democracy, which sometimes employed Fascist methods. Yet "profound differences" existed between them; Fascism was "a movement of the petty and middle bourgeoisie, dominated by the big bourgeoisie and the landowners", while social-democracy had its roots in the "broad working masses". Togliatti contrived to conclude that "*the fundamental task*" of communist parties was "*the most implacable struggle* against social-democracy". But he found the application of this principle in the French and German, rather than in the Italian, parties.[40] In Italy and Poland it was increasingly unreal to ask communists to regard social-democrats as their major enemies.

Togliatti then moved on to the still more treacherous ground of party discipline. This had been little discussed in the debate, though Murphy, eager at this time to curry favour with the authorities, had remarked that "real leadership in the world revolution is still not sufficiently concentrated in Comintern", and that the need was urgent to transform Comintern into "an international communist party".[41] Togliatti laid down the principle

[38] *Ibid.* i, 336.

[39] *Pravda,* July 17, 1928; it also appeared in *Internationale Presse-Korrespondenz,* No. 71, July 24, 1928, p. 1291, No. 73, July 27, 1928, p. 1324.

[40] *Stenograficheskii Otchet VI Kongressa Kominterna* (1929), i, 499–505; for the discussion of Fascism in the programme commission of the congress see pp. 231–233 below.

[41] *Stenograficheskii Otchet VI Kongressa Kominterna* (1929), i, 143.

that a communist party, in forming its leadership, "should follow a definite political line and proceed by way of an open political struggle when this is necessary", and went on:

> We have to recognize that in some cases this rule has not been followed, and has been replaced by an unprincipled struggle and by compromises between groups.

Then, having invoked the words of the dying Goethe "More light!", he concluded:

> The vanguard of the proletariat cannot fight in darkness. The central core of the revolution cannot be formed in an unprincipled fractional struggle.

Finally he pleaded for caution before carrying the inner-party political struggle "into the sphere of organizational measures", i.e. expulsions.[42] Togliatti made it plain that his remarks, though couched in general terms, were prompted by the current crisis in the KPD;[43] and they were not pursued by other speakers. But they sufficed to make it clear that Togliatti at this time was, like Bukharin, a less than enthusiastic champion of the turn to the Left in Comintern.

Bukharin, in his reply to the debate, did little more than reiterate his conclusions with rather more emphasis on the contradictions and revolutionary potentialities of the third period. He discerned "*different types* of unemployment" in different countries, e.g. in Great Britain and the United States. But all these forms were expressions of the contradictions of capitalism, and could be used "for the purpose of *intensifying the class struggle*". Bukharin ended his speech with a stirring appeal to Comintern to "close its ranks for revolution, for civil war, for the victory of

[42] *Ibid.* i, 508–509; the two passages quoted above *in extenso* are omitted from this text, but appear in the original text in *Annali, 1966* (Milan, 1966), p. 505. The corrections were made by agreement between Tasca, the then Italian delegate to Comintern, and the official of the secretariat charged with preparing the stenographic record for publication (*ibid.* p. 522); according to P. Spriano, *Storia del Partito Comunista Italiano*, ii (1969), 178, the omitted passages appeared in Italian and French versions of the speech in *Lo Stato Operaio* and *Correspondance Internationale*. Nothing in the records confirms Togliatti's statement in *Rinascità*, July 11, 1964, that he was prevented from finishing his speech by lack of time.

[43] See p. 441, note 104 below.

the dictatorship of the proletariat".[44] The theses adopted at the end of the congress opened with the theme of the three periods. The third period was marked by the simultaneous growth of the economy of capitalism and of the economy of the USSR beyond the pre-war level, and pointed the way to a catastrophic conclusion:

> This third period ... makes inevitable a new phase of imperialist wars between the imperialist powers, wars by them against the USSR, wars of national liberation against imperialism and the interventions of the imperialists, gigantic class struggles.... This period inevitably leads through the further development of the contradictions of capitalist stabilization to a further shattering of capitalist stabilization, and to an acute aggravation of the crisis of capitalism.

The social-democrats were firmly identified as the most dangerous enemies of the communists: social-democracy appeared "in the rôle of the last reserve of the bourgeoisie, as the bourgeois 'workers'' party". A passage relating to trade unions dwelt on "provocation on the part of the reformists", who in many countries "are forcing the exclusion of communists (and of Leftists in general) from trade union organizations". Failing energetic action, this might lead to the isolation of communists "from the whole mass of proletarians organized in trade unions"; it was imperative "to conduct a resolute struggle against the splitting policy of the Amsterdam International and of its national sections". The resolution also called for "special attention to the *careful preparation* of strikes" as well as "*boldness in conducting them*". It proclaimed that "*every strike must be an arena for the struggle for leadership between Communists and reformists*", and that strikes should be organized, where appropriate, "against the will of the trade union bureaucracy". Without mentioning the formation of new unions, it raised the slogan of "the organization of the unorganized". In a short section on Fascism, the resolution reverted to the theme of the fifth congress, and explained that "the ideology of class collaboration, this official ideology of social-democracy, has many points of contact with the ideology of Fascism"; it also noted the threat to peace from "the Fascist dic-

[44] *Stenograficheskii Otchet VI Kongressa Kominterna* (1929), i, 604–606, 615.

tatorship in Poland and Italy". After dealing at length with the affairs of individual parties, it appealed for "a strengthening of proletarian discipline", necessary to enable the proletariat to confront "all the forces mobilized by imperialism", and, having proclaimed the need for "greater inner democracy", concluded:

> This does not exclude, but presupposes, the universal strengthening of our inner-party discipline, the unconditional submission of minority to majority, the unconditional subordination of lower organs, as well as of other party organizations, to the directing party centres, and of all sections of Comintern to its executive committee.[45]

The second place on the agenda was filled by that other main Soviet preoccupation of these years—the danger of war, now indissolubly linked with the third period. The main resolution of the congress referred to "the problem of the struggle against the threatening imperialist war" as one of "the chief international tasks of the communist movement at this moment";[46] and a lengthy and discursive debate was staged on measures to be adopted by communist parties. Since the eighth IKKI had pronounced on the war danger in May 1927,[47] the international prospect had changed. The threat of war had not been lifted. The inevitability of war under capitalism remained an item of the Bolshevik creed; the imminent danger of war had become a postulate of Soviet policy, and a theme of propaganda designed to inculcate vigour and vigilance in dealing with potential enemies at home and abroad. Bukharin repeated at the fifteenth Russian party congress of December 1927 the "central slogan" launched at the eighth IKKI of "the defence of the Russian and Chinese revolutions".[48] Stalin on the eve of the sixth congress of Comintern in July 1928 could still speak of "the danger of fresh imperialist wars and interventions" as the "fundamental con-

[45] *Kommunisticheskii Internatsional v Dokumentakh* (1933), pp. 769–793; a few months later Stalin reminded the leaders of the KPD of the concluding passage, being careful to assign its authorship to Bukharin (Stalin, *Sochineniya*, xi, 303).

[46] *Kommunisticheskii Internatsional v Dokumentakh* (1933), p. 708.

[47] See pp. 144–145 above.

[48] *Pyatnadtsatyi S"ezd VKP(B)*, i (1961), 652.

temporary question".[49] Humbert-Droz at a meeting in the Latin secretariat during the congress tried to convince the PCF that "the axis of the work of the party, as of the struggle of the whole Comintern, is the question of the danger of war";[50] and, while the congress was in session, *Izvestiya* celebrated the anniversary of the outbreak of war in August 1914 with an article "Between Two Wars", which sought to remind its readers "not so much of the past as of the future war".[51] But in China the crushing of workers and peasants by the nationalist forces made it difficult to treat imperialist intervention as the sole or principal danger; and in Europe the failure of other Powers to follow Great Britain in breaking off relations with the Soviet Union made the threat of joint military action seem less plausible. The threat presented by the smaller countries on the western frontiers of the Soviet Union, egged on by France and Great Britain, was not neglected. But the attention of the world was still riveted on the sharp dispute between Great Britain and the United States on naval disarmament which had broken out at the three-Power conference in Geneva of June–August 1927; and the disagreements between the imperialist Powers were more apparent than the prospect of united action by them against the Soviet Union.

Bell, who acted as *rapporteur* on the question at the congress, had no difficulty in finding "symptoms of the approach of war" in the antagonisms and rivalries between the capitalist Powers — the Anglo-American rivalry ("the fundamental contradiction in the imperialist camp"), the rivalries between Great Britain, France and Italy, between France, Italy and Yugoslavia, between Great Britain, France and Germany, and between the United States, Japan and Great Britain in the Pacific.[52] He was followed by no less than four co-*rapporteurs* — Grieco, Schneller, Lovestone and Barbé. But, after the arduous controversies of the debate on Bukharin's theses, the debate on the danger of war, which dragged on for four days, was left to second-rank delegates and proved something of an anti-climax. The subject was stale. Lozovsky, some months earlier in an outburst of frankness, had written that "fairly broad strata of workers do not believe in the possibility of

49 Stalin, *Sochineniya*, xi, 200.
50 *Classe contre Classe* (1929), p. 236; for this meeting see pp. 514–517 below.
51 *Izvestiya*, August 4, 1928.
52 *Stenograficheskii Otchet VI Kongressa Kominterna* (1929), ii, 8–35.

war in the immediate future", and that the resolution of the eighth IKKI of May 1927 on the danger of war was "scarcely known to broad circles of trade union workers".[53] On the eve of the congress, an article in the KPD journal admitted that the campaign against war "does not have a convincing effect on the masses, and must be felt by them as exaggeration, nervousness and hysteria". Intensive propaganda had been conducted after the eighth IKKI, "but later fell off, as if one realized that the danger of war had at first been exaggerated".[54] Togliatti, in the debate on Bukharin's report, had noted an impression that "all this is done to pay tribute to theses which have been adopted rather than in virtue of any real consciousness of the inevitability of war".[55] In the debate in the commission Vasiliev, speaking as delegate of IKKI, complained that little had been done to give effect to the resolution of the eighth IKKI on the danger of war. He alleged that German workers were content to believe that "the League of Nations had enough influence and power to avert the danger of war", and that "in all parties the special apparatus for work in the army is very weak".[56] Bell had some reason to complain in his concluding speech that most orators had "repeated a series of commonplaces" or dealt with secondary questions.[57] The debate came to life only when, at the very end, Yaroslavsky intervened to raise the vexed question of the work of parties in the armed forces of the capitalist Powers.

The question had a long history. Lenin in September 1917, in an article on "Marxism and Insurrection", which was designed to distinguish Marxism from Blanquism, dwelt primarily on the necessity that the people should be ripe for revolution:

> To be crowned with success, the insurrection must rely not on a conspiracy, not on a party, but on an advanced class.... The insurrection must be based on the revolutionary impetus of the people.

But, he added, moving to a more practical plane, since the Kornilov affair the Petrograd and Moscow Soviets "command a

[53] A. Lozovsky, *Na Novom Etape* (1928), p. 18; the article was dated December 15, 1927.

[54] *Die Internationale*, xi, No. 14, July 15, 1928, pp. 493–494.

[55] *Stenograficheskii Otchet VI Kongressa Kominterna* (1929), i, 500.

[56] *Ibid.* ii, 132–134.

[57] *Ibid.* ii, 194–195.

majority among the workers and soldiers of the capitals".[58] The breakdown of discipline and the sapping of the loyalty of the troops, first at the front, and later in the capitals, was a major factor in the victory of the revolution. Bolshevik participation in this process was, for obvious reasons, not much publicized at the time. While it was widely celebrated after the event, and became a familiar item in party history, the example failed to inspire young and struggling communist parties in western Europe, and the Soviet leaders seem to have been chary of raising the question. One of Lenin's few recorded mentions of it was in a note to the Politburo of February 1922, provoked by the vote of a German trade union in favour of a "strike against war":

> Only a revolutionary party, tested and prepared in advance, with a good illegal apparatus, can successfully conduct the campaign against war; the method of the struggle is not the strike against war, but the organization of revolutionary cells in the belligerent armies and their preparedness to make the revolution.[59]

The twenty-one conditions of 1920 imposed on parties adhering to Comintern "the special necessity of persistent systematic propaganda in armies", and added that, "where this agitation is prohibited by exceptional laws, it must be conducted illegally". A further clause required parties "to carry on systematic agitation in their armies against all oppression of colonial peoples".[60] According to Trotsky, the Military-Scientific Society in 1924 sponsored a study on the art of civil war, which was, however, terminated owing to opposition from Comintern — apparently on the ground of its association with Trotsky.[61]

Such records as exist of the abortive communist risings in

[58] Lenin, *Polnoe Sobranie Sochinenii*, xxxiv, 242–247.

[59] *Ibid.* xliv, 379; this item was first published in *Pravda*, January 20, 1929, when Comintern had become interested in the question. An account of Bolshevik activities in the Russian armies from 1915 to 1917 by a "worker-correspondent of *Pravda*" appeared in the KPD journal in 1929 (*Die Internationale*, xii, No. 14, July 15, 1929, pp. 443–449), probably translated from a Russian source which has not been identified.

[60] *Kommunisticheskii Internatsional v Dokumentakh* (1933), pp. 100–104; for the twenty-one conditions see *The Bolshevik Revolution, 1917–1923*, Vol. 3, pp. 193–195.

[61] L. Trotsky, *The Third International After Lenin* (N.Y., 1936), p. 146.

Bulgaria and Germany in 1923 and in Estonia in 1924[62] do not suggest that the infiltration of the national armies had played any part in their planning and preparation. The question does not seem to have been raised in Comintern documents of the period; and in Great Britain acute embarrassment, with threats of prosecution, resulted from the appearance in the communist *Workers' Weekly* of an appeal to soldiers not to "turn your guns on your fellow-workers".[63] It was the non-communist Lansbury who, two months before the British general strike, but when a major strike of miners seemed inevitable, called on British troops not to fire on British workers.[64] The general strike collapsed through inner weakness, and the miners' strike never acquired a revolutionary dimension. The attitude of the troops was not in question; and one of the rare allusions to it in the voluminous Comintern literature on the strike was a wistful comment, some months later, in a resolution of the eighth congress of the CPGB:

> The capitalist state derives a vast amount of its strength from the fact that the workers who are members of the fighting forces are still loyal to it. It must be part of the functions of the Labour movement to carry the workers' message to the forces and to enlighten them as to their duty to the working class.[65]

The issue was raised in more concrete form by the decision of the British Government at the end of the year to meet the threat of the advance of the Chinese nationalist armies by reinforcing the British garrison in Shanghai. IKKI issued a manifesto on January 28, 1927, denouncing imperialist designs on China, but did not go beyond an appeal to mobilize "all organizations which can hinder the sending of armed forces against the Chinese

[62] See *The Interregnum, 1923–1924*, pp. 194–195, 219–223; *Socialism in One Country, 1924–1926*, Vol. 3, pp. 284–285. An article in the Russian party journal quoted the experience in Estonia in 1924, as well as in China in 1927, as proof of the need for work in the armed forces as a prelude to a successful revolution (*Bol'shevik*, No. 25–26, December 31, 1928, pp. 75–76).

[63] See *Socialism in One Country, 1924–1926*, Vol. 3, p. 28.

[64] *Workers' Weekly*, March 12, 1926.

[65] *The Eighth Congress of the CPGB* (1926), p. 70; the use of the word "Labour", rather than "communist", is significant. The NMM had set up a committee during the miners' strike "to maintain friendly relations with the forces", the duty of which was "to prevent antagonism between the strikers and miners and the workers in the army, navy and air force" (*NMM: Report of the Third Annual Conference* (1926), p. 30).

people".[66] The general resolution of the eighth IKKI in May, 1927, and the special resolution on China, both contained, inconspicuously included in long lists of desiderata for the campaign against war, appeals for work in armies and navies.[67]

Throughout this time, though reluctance was shown to air the question in official publications and pronouncements of Comintern,[68] increasing hopes rested on the activity of young communists. The executive committee of the Communist Youth International (IKKIM), meeting in June 1927 in Moscow, heard a report from a French delegate, and passed a resolution, on "the practical tasks and methods of work in the army".[69] Shatskin at the fifteenth Russian party congress in December 1927 asserted that one-half, if not three-quarters, of all "anti-militarist work" done in imperialist armies was to be credited to the youth leagues.[70] The eighth IKKIM two months later claimed for the youth leagues "great success in their struggle against the danger of war and in their work in armies and navies".[71] At the seventh congress of the Soviet Komsomol in May 1928 Shatskin explained that infiltration was especially important in the armed forces of France, Great Britain, Germany and the United States, and that young communists should not shrink from enlisting even in voluntary armies:

> We should enter the voluntary armies not only individually, but by sending large groups into the armies to work for their demoralization, for the revolutionizing of the young workers in them.[72]

[66] *Internationale Presse-Korrespondenz*, No. 13, February 1, 1927, pp. 241–242.

[67] *Kommunisticheskii Internatsional v Dokumentakh* (1933), pp. 717, 729. For the general resolution see pp. 144–145 above; the Chinese resolution will be discussed in a later section of this volume.

[68] The journal of Comintern in the summer of 1927, in quoting a speech of Zetkin of 1922, ostentatiously preferred, "owing to 'freedom of speech' as interpreted under the capitalist dictatorship of Great Britain", to omit passages on propaganda in the armed forces (*Kommunisticheskii Internatsional*, No. 28 (102), 1927, p. 6); the reference was to the Campbell prosecution of 1924 (see *Socialism in One Country, 1924–1926*, Vol. 3, p. 28).

[69] *Internationale Presse-Korrespondenz*, No. 65, June 24, 1927, p. 1361.

[70] *Pyatnadtsatyi S"ezd VKP(B)*, i (1961), 729.

[71] For this resolution see p. 265, note 23 above. For claims of successful action in the French army and navy by the PCF and the Communist Youth League see pp. 496–497 below.

[72] *VIII Vsesoyuznyi S"ezd VLKSM* (1928), p. 284.

No evidence, however, exists of any substantial success enjoyed by these tactics.

Bold spirits demanded stronger action by the party. As a writer remarked in the KPD journal:

> Communist parties work everywhere where there are workers, in workers' quarters, in factories and villages. They have no reason to make an exception in regard to the barracks and warships in which workers and peasants in uniform live in extremely arduous conditions.[73]

The issue was, however, neglected at the fourth congress of Profintern in March 1928, except for a vague appeal in a subsidiary resolution for action by transport workers, metal workers and miners to resist "the war plans of imperialism";[74] and it seemed likely to suffer the same fate at the sixth congress of Comintern till Yaroslavsky bluntly reopened the question at the very end of the perfunctory debate on the danger of imperialist war, in which he was the sole spokesman of the Russian party. The draft theses commended the slogan of "soldiers' Soviets", but apparently only for use in an immediately revolutionary situation, and added that "it will be impossible in a majority of cases to apply the slogan of soldiers' Soviets to paid armies"; the exception as applied to "the voluntary British army" provoked a protest from a British delegate.[75] Yaroslavsky, in what was probably a prepared speech, did not comment on this explosive issue. But he complained that "Bolshevik work in the army and navy" from 1902–1903 onwards, and its eventual contribution to the victorious revolution, had been "not sufficiently studied". The moral most directly drawn was, rather surprisingly, for Germany. The KPD had its Roter Frontkämpferbund; but what was required was a serious study of "work in the *existing* German *state* army". In general, what was needed was not only propaganda, but to "create an organized force in the army which could at the right moment attract the workers to its side".[76] This, though still lacking in precision, was plainer and franker speaking than had

[73] *Die Internationale*, xi, No. 14, July 15, 1928, p. 496.

[74] See p. 185 above.

[75] *Stenograficheskii Otchet VI Kongressa Kominterna* (1929), ii, 104; for this intervention see pp. 372–373 below. This is the only authority for the original text of the draft theses, which was not published.

[76] *Stenograficheskii Otchet VI Kongressa Kominterna* (1929), ii, 191–194.

yet been heard from a Comintern platform. Bell, in winding up the debate, did not mention Yaroslavsky's intervention except on a minor point about propaganda among coloured troops.[77]

The draft theses were now submitted for examination to a large and representative commission.[78] When Bell eventually presented them for adoption by the plenary session of the congress, he explained that they had been abbreviated to avoid repetition and revised in some particulars.[79] The final text combined the two views of the impending imperialist war. They emphasized "the contradictions between the imperialist Powers in the struggle for markets", while continuing to insist that "the chief political front of all the imperialist Powers is more and more openly directed against the Soviet Union and the Chinese revolution". The theses followed those of the eighth IKKI in distinguishing between three different kinds of war, each making its distinctive demand on the proletariat: wars between imperialist Powers, national-revolutionary wars waged by oppressed nations and war waged against a proletarian revolution or a proletarian state. In the two last categories, the duty of the proletariat and of communist parties was plain. In wars between imperialist Powers, their rôle was summed up in Lenin's famous injunction to turn the imperialist war into a civil war.

> Communists [declared the theses] do not separate the struggle against war from the class struggle, regarding it as part of the general class struggle of the proletariat directed to the overthrow of the bourgeoisie.

The moral was, however, not quite clear. If capitalism made war inevitable, and if proletarian revolution would be hastened by war between imperialist Powers, it was difficult to explain why the prospect of such a war should be feared or resisted. Yet the charge that communists "encourage imperialist wars in order to hasten the revolution" was dismissed in the theses as "senseless slander"; and nobody in the debate welcomed this prospect, ex-

[77] *Ibid.* ii, 196.

[78] *Ibid.* ii, 199–200; the proceedings of the commission were, as usual, not published, but were reflected in an article by Schneller, one of the co-*rapporteurs* in *Die Internationale*, xii, No. 1–2, January 15, 1929, pp. 21–26.

[79] *Stenograficheskii Otchet VI Kongressa Kommunisticheskogo Internatsionala* (1929), v, 113–119; for the theses see *Kommunisticheskii Internatsional v Dokumentakh* (1933), pp. 793–831.

cept—by implication—the Italian delegate Tasca, who, in the debate on the programme, ventured on the hope that "the present period between two great world wars will also be the period between two great revolutions, the one which in 1917 was victorious over one-sixth of the globe, and the one which will free the rest of the globe from the bloody disintegration of capitalism".[80] The theses did not endorse any such prophecy. The illusions of pacifism and disarmament as propagated by the League of Nations were firmly exposed, and laid at the door of the social-democrats; communists could not be against war as such. Some ingenuity was displayed in distinguishing the Soviet proposals at Geneva for total disarmament from the hypocritical propaganda of the imperialist Powers. Much attention was devoted to the differences in the attitude to be adopted by the proletariat to the army in imperialist and in proletarian countries. A somewhat confused passage, which must have been added or revised in the commission, recommended propaganda about grievances "not only within the army, but outside it—in parliaments, in mass meetings etc." This called for "detailed acquaintance with the army, with the conditions of service", and for "an assessment of the moral condition of the army, and the political situation in the country at the given moment".[81] The conclusion on "soldiers' Soviets" was obviously the product of cautious and careful drafting:

> Revolutionary work in the army must be bound up with the general revolutionary movement of the masses of the proletariat and poor peasantry. In the presence of an immediately revolutionary situation, when the factory proletariat moves to the formation of Soviets, the slogan of soldiers' Soviets becomes actual, and assists the link between the mass of soldiers and the proletariat and poor peasantry in the struggle for power.
>
> Even in paid armies, communists will, when conditions per-

[80] *Stenograficheskii Otchet VI Kongressa Kominterna* (1929), iii, 105.

[81] *Kommunisticheskii Internatsional v Dokumentakh* (1933), p. 818; the resolution of the congress on colonial countries was more explicit: "In order to secure the immediate withdrawal of the armed forces of imperialism from the oppressed countries, communist parties should work unceasingly to organize mass actions to resist the transfer of armies and ammunition to the colonies. Systematic agitational and organizational work in the armies for fraternization with the insurgent masses in the colonies should prepare the armies of occupation to go over to the side of the worker–peasant revolution and of its armed forces" (*ibid.* p. 869).

mit, organise the mass of soldiers under the slogan of soldiers' Soviets, and mobilise it for the struggle against the generals and the bourgeoisie.[82]

It may be doubted whether the theses provided much practical guidance to communist parties. But every part of them was clearly designed to widen the scope of the class struggle and the unbridgeable gulf between communists and imperialists. The theses were accompanied by a short resolution exhorting the central committees of all communist parties to prepare for an "international day" as part of the campaign "against imperialist wars and for the defence of the Soviet Union".[83]

After five sittings devoted to a discussion of the programme of Comintern,[84] the congress turned to its fourth scheduled topic — the debate on the colonial question. The congress was now nearly a month old, and in a crowded week no less than twelve sittings were held. Bukharin, absorbed in work on the programme, did not appear. Kuusinen was in charge, and presented lengthy theses "On the Revolutionary Movement in Colonial and Semi-Colonial Countries". "Co-reports" were delivered by Togliatti (on the rôle of communist parties in metropolitan capitalist countries), by the delegates of Indonesia, India and China (on their respective countries), and by Humbert-Droz (on Latin America). These elaborate arrangements contrasted with the perfunctory treatment of the theme at the fifth congress four years earlier.[85] On the other hand, the preoccupation at that time with nationalism in Europe had faded. Contrary to the precedent set at previous congresses, the colonial question was isolated from the question of national minorities in European countries, which figured only in the debates on the programme.[86] Kuusinen's theses, as their title indicated, were concerned exclusively with the non-European world.

The debate on the theses was the liveliest, and most incon-

[82] *Ibid.* p. 818.
[83] *Stenograficheskii Otchet VI Kongressa Kominterna* (1929), vi, 176; *Kommunisticheskii Internatsional v Dokumentakh* (1933), pp. 831–832.
[84] See pp. 226–227 below.
[85] See *Socialism in One Country, 1924–1926*, Vol. 3, pp. 87–90, 617–620.
[86] See pp. 228–229 below.

clusive, of the congress. Kuusinen was a competent official of no great intellectual stature or strong personal convictions. He spoke to an ill-defined brief at a time when the party line had not yet been firmly drawn, or the notorious disputes between leaders finally resolved. Differences in the situations and revolutionary potentialities of different colonial countries admittedly existed. Yet it was incumbent on the congress to promulgate directives of principle applicable to all. Before the congress, the view that the revolution in colonial and semi-colonial countries was still in its bourgeois-democratic stage, and that the immediate task of communist parties in these countries was to support the national bourgeoisie in its struggle against imperialist domination, still held the field in Comintern. In China the treacherous abandonment of the revolutionary cause by Chiang Kai-shek and a large part of the national bourgeoisie caused acute embarrassment, and led to some adjustments of doctrine. But the bourgeois-democratic character of the Chinese revolution was still asserted; nor could the Chinese experience be regarded as typical. When Kuusinen presented his theses to the congress, he evaded altogether the theoretical problems of the bourgeois-democratic revolution in the colonies. He brushed aside China on the plea that a great deal had already been said about it, and devoted more than half his speech to India, the classic home of imperialism, where "a profound revolutionary crisis" might be expected in the not too distant future.[87] The Indian question proved to be the most contentious of the whole congress. In the opinion of most Indian and British communists, the growth of native capitalist industry in India — the process labelled "decolonization" — was creating a bond of common interest between Indian and British capitalists and leading the former to desert the revolutionary camp. This was substantially Roy's argument against Lenin in the famous debate at the second congress of Comintern in 1920; and it pointed to a close parallel between the Chinese and Indian situations. But this view encountered strong opposition in Comintern; nor would a decision to write off the alliance with the national bourgeoisie have made much sense in the less advanced Asian, or in the Latin American, countries, where a bourgeois national movement

[87] *Stenograficheskii Otchet VI Kongressa Kominterna* (1929), iv, 7; the Chinese and Indian questions will be discussed in a later section of this volume.

offered better revolutionary prospects than a proletarian rising. In these conditions, the presentation of a coherent and uniform policy offered formidable difficulties. As Ch'u Ch'in-pai, the Chinese delegate, pragmatically observed, the only point of the discussion was to define the degree of revolutionary spirit or of venality displayed by the national bourgeoisie.[88] The theses drafted by Kuusinen raised few issues of principle, and revealed no desire for political innovation. Nothing said in them supported the view that the Chinese precedent justified a reconsideration of policy elsewhere. In India, they predicted that "the reformist bourgeoisie, or a part of it, will, in an acute revolutionary situation, at first rally to the national-revolutionary camp, and will thus play for some time an objectively revolutionary rôle". It would therefore be "an ultra-Left error" to equate the "national-reformists" (this was apparently a new term) in India, or in Egypt, with "the ruling counter-revolutionary bloc of imperialists and feudalists". In spite of isolated incidents, the Swarajists in India, unlike Kuomintang, "have not yet betrayed the struggle for national liberation":

> Communists must at the present stage concentrate their chief fire, not against them, not against the national bourgeoisie, but against our present immediate chief enemy, against the imperial ruling feudal bloc.[89]

Most speakers in the long debate followed the example of the co-*rapporteurs* in confining their observations to the problems of their own country. Some powerful voices were, however, also raised in criticism of the general line of the theses. Among the conspicuous advocates of a more radical course were Schüller, the representative of KIM, who suggested that to rely on "the objectively revolutionary rôle" of the national bourgeoisie was to repeat the error of the Chinese Communist Party, and Lominadze, who at this period missed no opportunity of appearing as the enemy of the national bourgeoisie, and argued that cooperation with it was now "a past phase of development".[90] But the speaker to plunge most deeply into these turbulent waters was Lozovsky,

[88] *Ibid.* iv, 476.
[89] Quoted *ibid.* iv, 216, 374; both these passages were eliminated from the final text.
[90] *Ibid.* iv, 216–218, 447–450.

who transferred to the eastern scene his commitment to independent communist penetration of the trade unions, and his rejection of any alliance with the reformists. While denouncing the theory of "*decolonization of colonies*", he fully recognized the process of industrialization in China and India and the growth of "*capitalist relations*", dismissed the attempt to treat these countries as "agricultural hinterlands", and declared that "political slogans" such as the dictatorship of the proletariat and the peasantry were not applicable to them. He admitted that conditions varied from one colonial country to another and that the cases of China and India were not parallel. But he strongly criticized the passage in the theses defending the Swarajists and warning Indian communists not to concentrate their fire on the national bourgeoisie, and argued that the main task was the creation of "*independent workers*' organizations".[91] Lozovsky was one of the few delegates at the congress who appeared to be consciously and deliberately driving Comintern policy towards the Left; and his efforts led to substantial revisions of the draft theses. The passage which he had particularly criticized was dropped in favour of a longer and more sophisticated formulation. The revolution in the colonial countries was characterized in the new version as a bourgeois-democratic revolution "organically linked with the struggle for national liberation from imperialist enslavement", but a revolution which also marked "the preparation of the preconditions for a proletarian dictatorship and a socialist revolution". Such parties as the Swarajists in India or the Wafid in Egypt represented "an opposition of reformists and conciliators". Nevertheless they had a certain importance:

> The national bourgeoisie does not have the significance of a force struggling against imperialism. But this bourgeois-reformist opposition has its real, special significance—both negative and positive—in the development of the revolutionary movement in so far as, in general, it enjoys mass influence.

It could retard this development by restraining the masses from revolutionary action; on the other hand, it could accelerate "the process of the political awakening of the broad toiling masses".[92] Considered as an instruction to the unschooled communist parties

[91] *Ibid.* iv, 368–379.

[92] *Kommunisticheskii Internatsional v Dokumentakh* (1933), pp. 845, 850.

of colonial countries, this cryptic pronouncement left much to be desired.

The ambiguous position of the nationalist bourgeoisie was more readily explained by splitting it into two sectors — the big capitalist bourgeoisie and the petty bourgeoisie of peasants, traders, artisans and intellectuals. The elements of this division were present in the doctrine of a revolutionary bloc of workers and peasants under the leadership of the proletariat; in countries having a predominantly peasant population and a minute proletariat, some such conception was required in order to make sense of revolutionary policy and ideology. It was inherent in Stalin's call of 1925 for such a bloc in India against "the conciliationist part of the bourgeoisie".[93] In China the original bloc with the national bourgeoise as a whole, expressed in the alliance with Kuomintang, gave way after the proclamation by the seventh IKKI in November 1926 of the slogan of agrarian revolution, and after Chiang Kai-shek's desertion of the revolutionary cause in April 1927, to the bloc with the petty bourgeoisie in the form of the abortive alliance with the Left Kuomintang. This example also demonstrated, however, the danger of putting any trust in the revolutionary propensities of the petty bourgeoisie. The Indian prospect seemed less unpromising. The report submitted by IKKI to the sixth congress, in its section on India, was unexpectedly sympathetic to "the petty bourgeoisie and the intelligentsia", which showed signs of emancipating itself from the leadership of the national bourgeoisie and forming a genuine "Left wing";[94] and though Kuusinen in his speech ignored the issue of the petty bourgeoisie, his theses contained a surprisingly decisive pronouncement on the question:

> In general, in the first stage of the bourgeois-democratic revolution in these countries we can count on the whole petty bourgeoisie, as a class, as a motive force of the revolution, side by side with the proletariat.[95]

The debate revealed considerable bewilderment. The dissentient Indian delegate Tagore argued strongly that "petty

[93] Stalin, *Sochineniya*, vii, 147–148.
[94] *Die Komintern vor dem 6. Weltkongress* (1928), pp. 529–530.
[95] *Stenograficheskii Otchet VI Kongressa Kominterna* (1929), iv, 448.

bourgeois elements in the country which have been proletarianized are sometimes more revolutionary than the proletariat itself", and that "the petty bourgeois intelligentsia, the urban petty bourgeoisie, will play a definite rôle in the revolutionary movement in the colonies" and in the formation of an anti-imperialist front.[96] Lominadze, on the other hand, complained that Kuusinen had lumped together "the whole petty bourgeoisie *en bloc*" as a revolutionary force, and vehemently denied this rôle to the urban petty bourgeoisie.[97] The theme of agrarian revolution was not pursued very far. But Schüller alleged that the CCP had "missed the turning-point of the revolution by not developing the agrarian revolution in time"; and the lone Persian delegate expressed the inconvenient opinion that the agrarian revolution would be betrayed by the petty bourgeoisie as well as by the big bourgeoisie when the moment came.[98] The weight of opinion behind the scenes leaned, however, to a liberal interpretation of the united front; and the final text of the theses included a sympathetic discussion of the rôle of the petty bourgeoisie which had been absent from the original draft. It was now explained that the national bourgeoisie was not uniform: a distinction must be drawn between those who had gone over to the imperialists ("the so-called *compradore* bourgeoisie"), and the "national-reformists" who held an intermediate position. "*The petty bourgeoisie* in these colonial and semi colonial countries"—the artisans, "the petty bourgeois intelligentsia (students etc.)", and the urban poor—"plays a very important rôle". Meanwhile, "the peasantry, side by side with the proletariat and as its ally, is a driving force of the revolution". But a later passage conveyed a sharp warning against "an incorrect estimate of the character and rôle of *petty bourgeois parties*", which were "linked with the national bourgeoisie". In particular, "the petty bourgeois intelligentsia, which stands at the head of these parties" was "the representative of the *capitalist development* of its country". Once questions of the agrarian revolution and the dictatorship of proletariat and peasantry were raised, the revolutionary character of these parties disappeared. On this topic, as on others, the immensely long resolution was a compromise which blurred rather than clarified theoretical and practical issues. After a not very frank exposition by Kuusinen of the changes introduced in the drafting com-

[96] *Ibid.* iv, 294–295. [97] *Ibid.* iv, 448–449. [98] *Ibid.* iv, 218, 252.

mission, it was unanimously adopted on the last day of the congress.[99]

Surprisingly little attention was paid at the congress to relations between the parties of metropolitan countries and those of colonial and semi-colonial territories. Katayama read a brief homily on their unsatisfactory character, censuring the "criminal neglect" by the CPGB of Ireland and India, and the similar failure of the Netherlands and American parties in Indonesia and the Philippines.[100] An Algerian delegate spoke of the problems of creating an independent Algerian party under native leadership, which had been solved in the past year, thanks to the "close collaboration" of the PCF.[101] But this seems to have been an isolated instance. Tagore, the Indian delegate, protested in the debate on the programme against a passage in the draft asserting that "the colonial movement of the proletariat" should be placed "under the leadership of the revolutionary proletarian movement in the corresponding imperialist countries".[102] The long resolution of the congress on colonial questions briefly noted that the relations of metropolitan communist parties and trade unions with revolutionary organizations in the colonies were, "with the exception of a few cases, ... not satisfactory", but offered only the conventional exhortation to establish "close, regular and constant relations with the revolutionary movement in the colonies".[103] No other cognizance was taken of the question at the congress except in a clause added to the statutes of Comintern requiring that "member sections of Comintern, sections in metropolitan countries and in their colonies, and sections in neighbouring countries, should maintain with one another close links of organization and information".[104]

After the major debates on the international tasks of Comintern, on the danger of war, on the programme and on the colonial

[99] *Ibid.* v, 132–135. The final text is in *Kommunisticheskii Internatsional v Dokumentakh* (1933), pp. 832–870; for the passage quoted see *ibid.* pp. 846–849, 852.

[100] *Stenograficheskii Otchet VI Kongressa Kominterna* (1929), i, 303.

[101] *Ibid.* iv, 252–255.

[102] *Ibid.* iii, 119.

[103] *Kommunisticheskii Internatsional v Dokumentakh* (1933), pp. 867–868.

[104] For the amendments to the statute see p. 220 below.

question, one further task awaited the congress: to endorse the policies of the Russian party and to condemn the expelled opposition. On August 22, 1928, Varga and Manuilsky delivered economic and political reports on the state of the USSR; and on the following day a succession of orators from foreign parties denounced the opposition in uniform and unqualified terms.[105] The congress then adjourned for several days, no doubt in order to put the finishing touches on the resolutions. These were duly approved at two final sittings on August 29 and September 1, 1928. Apart from the main resolutions, the congress in its last stages adopted a resolution on MOPR,[106] resolutions on the exclusion of heretics from the German and French parties[107]—pendents to the resolution on the Russian opposition—and a resolution confirming the admission to Comintern of communist parties of Korea, Cuba and Ireland, and admitting parties of New Zealand, Paraguay, Colombia and Ecuador.[108] It also approved a number of amendments to the statute of Comintern adopted by the fifth congress in 1924, many of them designed to register decisions previously taken or practices already adopted. They set forth the obligation to form party fractions in international non-party organizations such as Profintern, MOPR and MRP; abolished the office of the president of Comintern; provided for the establishment of bureaus of Comintern in foreign countries and required parties to submit to their decisions; transferred the administrative functions of IKKI, which was no longer expected to meet more than twice a year, to its presidium, and abolished the institution of the "enlarged IKKI"; and finally called for closer relations between parties, and especially between parties in colonial countries and the respective metropolitan countries.[109] The congress also approved the new programme of Comintern.[110]

[105] See Vol. 2, p. 70.

[106] See p. 279 below.

[107] See pp. 442, 518–519 below; the congress also deposed a dissident group from the leadership of the Netherlands CP, and called for a reconstitution of the party (*Kommunisticheskii Internatsional v Dokumentakh* (1933), pp. 874–875).

[108] *Stenograficheskii Otchet VI Kongressa Kominterna* (1929), v, 136–138, vi, 174–175.

[109] *Ibid.* v, 107–112. For the final text of the statutes see *Kommunisticheskii Internatsional v Dokumentakh* (1933), pp. 46–51; for the statute of 1924 see *Socialism in One Country, 1924–1926,* Vol. 3, pp. 893–900.

[110] See p. 234 below.

Bukharin in his final speech spoke of the varied work and unusual duration of the congress, which he referred to as "the 'long parliament' of revolutionary communism". He must have been conscious of his own diminished status; and he avoided all controversial questions. By way of peroration, he read to the congress a manifesto to be issued in its name "To All Workers of the World, to All Toiling Peasants, to the Oppressed Peoples of Colonies, to Soldiers and Sailors of Capitalist Armies". The manifesto, in its roll call of imperialist Powers, for the first time gave pride of place to the United States, "at whose sea-gates stands the statue of Liberty". It dwelt eloquently on the social-democratic betrayal of "*the class* interests of the proletariat"; and its concluding slogans marked, more clearly than the long and argumentative resolutions, the new orientation of Comintern policy:

> Against social-democratic unity with the bourgeoisie—for the class unity of proletarians! Against reformism and Fascism—for the proletarian revolution![111]

It was Bukharin's last appearance on a Comintern platform and as the authorized spokesman of the Russian party in Comintern.

The congress over, Bukharin made the customary report on September 5, 1928, to the Moscow party organization, and Molotov two days later to the Leningrad organization. Bukharin gave rather more prominence to his special preoccupation, the programme; but the speeches did not differ substantially in content or tone. Bukharin, whatever his initial hesitations, now subscribed wholeheartedly to the new line. He noted "changes in the character of the general crisis of capitalism" since the fifth congress in 1924, and quoted at length the congress resolution on the "third period". He spoke of the danger of war, and the need for "an intensified struggle against social-democracy", concluding that "the central, most important and decisive danger in Comintern is the *Right* danger"; and he ended with a routine denunciation of the Trotskyite opposition and of the foreign groups which supported it.[112] The extended theses on the results

[111] *Stenograficheskii Otchet VI Kongressa Kominterna* (1929), v, 140–145, vi, 181–186.

[112] *Pravda*, September 12, 1928 (Bukharin), September 13, 1928 (Molotov); both speeches appeared in *Internationale Presse-Korrespondenz*, No. 108, September 28, 1928, pp. 2059–2078.

of the congress circulated by IKKI hailed it as "the dawn of a new period", characterized by a sharpening of all the current contradictions — between the imperialist Powers themselves, between them and the USSR, between capital and labour, and between the imperialist Powers and the colonial and semi-colonial countries. The swing to the Left, the campaign to eradicate the Right deviation from foreign parties, and above all the exposure of social-democracy as the sworn enemy of communism and the ally and instrument of reaction, were essential ingredients of the new policy; social-democratic parties were "an Agitprop for imperialism and participants in the preparation of war against the Soviet Union".[113] So long as the struggle against the Right deviation in the Russian party continued to preoccupy the Soviet leaders, any departure from this line seemed unthinkable. But it was none the less true that the sixth congress powerfully confirmed the determination to impose on the member parties of Comintern a uniform policy and uniform tactics, and that this determination, which rode roughshod over the variety of local demands, prejudices and traditions, had the effect of creating parties whose strict loyalty to Moscow militated against their appeal to the workers in their own countries. The policy of Bolshevization announced at the fifth congress in 1924 was carried to its logical conclusion.

[113] *Internationale Presse-Korrespondenz*, No. 125, November 9, 1928, pp. 2489–2494; a note explained that publication had been delayed "on technical grounds".

CHAPTER 71

THE COMINTERN PROGRAMME

THE fifth congress of Comintern in 1924 had bequeathed a draft programme to its successor; and the sixth IKKI in 1926 had created a standing commission to promote its further discussion in advance of the sixth congress.[1] The draft programme of 1924 was in four chapters. The first was devoted to a Marxist analysis of the growing contradictions of capitalism, the concentration of capital and the capitalist exploitation of colonies. It was noted that the victory of socialism in the USSR had been followed by defeats in Finland, Bavaria and Hungary (the 1923 fiasco in Germany was not mentioned); but no theoretical conclusions were drawn from this delay in the realization of world revolution. Social-democracy, pacifism and Fascism were all named as tools of the bourgeoisie. The second very brief chapter described the ultimate goals of a communist society. The third chapter was devoted to the struggle for the overthrow of the bourgeoisie and to the transitional period; the problem of war communism, NEP and the co-existence of different economic systems; the rôle of workers, peasants and petty bourgeoisie; the struggle against religion; and the proclamation of national self-determination for subject peoples. The last chapter, headed "The Road to the Dictatorship", dealt with party strategy and tactics. The united front and the slogan of a worker–peasant government were declared to be "an important constituent part in the tactics of communist parties for the whole pre-revolutionary period". Support of the Soviet Union was "the strongest instrument of organization in the hands of the international working class", and communist parties were called on to submit to "the international class discipline" of the Communist International.[2]

Owing to the long delay in convening the sixth congress, the commission appointed by the sixth IKKI was still-born. By 1928 the 1924 draft programme had come to seem altogether too

[1] See *Socialism in One Country, 1924–1926,* Vol. 3, pp. 1007–1008.

[2] For this draft see *ibid.* Vol. 3, pp. 1007–1008.

simple and theoretical, taking little account of current political realities and controversies. The turn in international relations in Europe had exposed the Soviet Union to fresh dangers; the Chinese revolution had revealed the immense potentialities of revolt in the colonial and semi-colonial countries; mounting tensions within the Soviet Union demanded the adoption by Comintern of more vigorous and more aggressive policies. On May 9, 1928, with the congress now impending, IKKI set up a fresh commission, which on May 25 approved a revised draft programme to supersede the draft of 1924.[3] The revised draft bore only an intermittent resemblance to the earlier version. The previous first chapter was now split into two. The first reshaped the analysis of the contradictions of capitalism, especially emphasizing imperialism, "the highest phase in the development of capitalism", as the decisive factor. The second, diagnosing "the general crisis of capitalism", attacked "international social-democracy of all shades", including the Second and Amsterdam Internationals, and Fascism which "makes its appearance side by side with social-democracy". While the contradictions of capitalism range "*the camp of the imperialist states*" and "*the dictatorship of the proletariat*" against one another, contradictions also arise within the capitalist sector, notably between American and European (especially British) capitalism, and between the metropolitan and colonial or semi-colonial countries. The third chapter on the ultimate goal of communism reproduced with few variations (this was the point of closest correspondence between the two drafts) the second chapter of the earlier version, but added a paragraph explaining that the attainment of communism presupposed the temporary existence of the "lower phase" of socialism, which still admitted distribution according to work and not to needs, as well as the divisions between intellectual and physical work and between town and country.

The remainder of the revised draft diverged widely from its predecessor. Its fourth and fifth chapters replaced the third chapter of the 1924 draft on the transitional period. The principal social and economic measures of the Soviet régime were rehearsed,

[3] *Stenograficheskii Otchet VI Kongressa Kominterna* (1929), iii, 6, 156. The proceedings of the commission were not published, but it may be assumed that the draft was mainly the work of Bukharin; a note from the commission explained that the draft had been modified in the light of changed conditions (*Internationale Presse-Korrespondenz*, No. 53, June 2, 1928, p. 955).

and commended as an example for other dictatorships of the proletariat yet to be established. Some variations were foreseen. In countries with high capitalist development ("the United States, Germany, Great Britain etc."), the dictatorship of the proletariat and expropriation of large-scale means of production could be proclaimed as an immediate goal. In countries with a moderate level of capitalism and "survivals of semi-feudal relations in agriculture" ("Russia before 1917, Poland etc."), an interweaving of proletarian revolution with bourgeois-democratic demands must be envisaged; agrarian revolution here played a substantial rôle, and account must be taken of small producers. In colonial and semi-colonial countries ("China, India etc."), where "feudal-mediaeval relations" still predominated, and industrial development had not proceeded far enough for "independent socialist construction", the transition to the dictatorship of the proletariat would have to pass through a number of stages, represented by the establishment of "a democratic dictatorship of the proletariat and the peasantry". The fifth chapter analysed the significance of the USSR for the international socialist revolution — a theme broached in the earlier version, but now more extensively elaborated. The sixth and last chapter on "the strategy and tactics of the Communist International" was entirely changed. It opened with a criticism of all other professed workers' movements, such as anarchism, syndicalism, Fabianism and guild socialism, which "coincide *with social-democracy*, that chief enemy of the proletarian revolution"; Sun-Yat-sen-ism in China and Gandhism in India played the same part. Where the revolutionary wave was rising, the parties should lead the proletariat "to a direct attack on the bourgeois state". Where this condition was absent, the party must rally the workers and poor peasants behind partial demands; in this situation, the tactics of the united front (in a phrase borrowed from the earlier draft) became "an important constituent part in the tactics of communist parties for the whole pre-revolutionary period". The draft programme ended by drawing attention to the danger of imperialist wars, and by calling on communist parties for concerted measures to avert it.

The draft received unusually wide publicity[4] and was widely

[4] It was published in *Pravda*, May 27, 1928, in *Kommunisticheskii Internatsional*, No. 22 (148), 1928, pp. 48–79, and in *Internationale Presse-Korrespondenz*, No. 53, June 2, 1928, pp. 955–970; it is also in *Stenograficheskii Otchet VI Kongressa Kominterna* (1929), iii, 156–192.

discussed. Between June 14 and July 3, 1928, five "discussion sheets" of a single page each appeared in *Pravda* containing comments, many from members of foreign parties, on various points of the programme. Varga attempted to revive the old argument about war communism and NEP, arguing that the former was normal, and NEP an exceptional expedient, and was answered by Kuzmin who defended NEP as a necessary condition of the link with the peasantry.[5] Madyar, a Hungarian member of the secretariat, who had worked in China, complained that the draft paid insufficient attention to the national question, especially outside Europe.[6] The last discussion sheet carried a broadside by Zetkin, criticizing the identification of social-democracy with Fascism and, by implication, the virtual abandonment of the united front.[7] At the session of the party central committee on July 5, 1928, Stalin rejected all major criticisms of the form or content of the draft, suggesting only that minor improvements of style or formulation might be made in the programme commission of the congress [8] The committee approved the draft programme in principle, but encouraged members of the committee to put forward "proposals for textual changes" at the congress.[9]

When the congress met, on July 17, 1928, it appointed a large programme commission, on which nearly every delegation was represented, to prepare a final draft.[10] The commission met for the first time on July 31, 1928, and held thirteen sittings extending over the month of August.[11] It was interrupted by a discussion of

[5] *Pravda*, June 14, 17, 1928. [6] *Ibid.* June 24, 1928.

[7] *Ibid.* July 3, 1928; Zetkin's article also appeared in *Internationale Presse-Korrespondenz,* No. 64, July 6, 1928, pp. 1172–1173, No. 65, July 10, 1928, pp. 1189–1190. Thalheimer submitted a memorandum to the commission in which he criticized the attitude to "partial demands" (*Stenograficheskii Otchet VI Kongressa Kominterna* (1929), iii, 48–49).

[8] Stalin, *Sochineniya*, xi, 141–156.

[9] *Pravda,* July 13, 1928; for this session see p. 193 above. Bukharin, in his conversation with Kamenev on July 11, 1928 (see Vol. 2, pp. 65–66), is reported as complaining that Stalin had "spoiled" the programme in many places and wanted himself to act as *rapporteur* on it at the congress. This story is unconfirmed, and seems inconsistent with Stalin's mild speech on the draft programme (see note 8 above); either Bukharin in speaking, or Kamenev in recording the conversation, may have inadvertently transferred to the programme Stalin's interference with Bukharin's theses for the congress (see p. 195 above).

[10] *Stenograficheskii Otchet Kongressa Kominterna* (1929), i, 99–100.

[11] *Ibid.* iii, 6; no record was published of any proceedings of the commission, except part of a speech of Bukharin (*Kommunisticheskii Inter-*

the programme in a series of five plenary sittings of the congress on August 9–14, 1928, opened and closed by major speeches from Bukharin, who had ample opportunity to demonstrate his expertise. No other figure even of second rank in the Soviet hierarchy, except Lozovsky, took part in this discussion. The programme was referred back to the commission, which finally appointed a small drafting commission consisting of Bukharin, Molotov (no doubt, as Stalin's watch-dog), Skrypnik, and a representative of the KPD, together with Humbert-Droz as secretary, to hammer out a final text.[12] This was presented by Bukharin to the last plenary sitting of the congress on September 1, 1928, and was adopted without further discussion to the accompaniment of the singing of the Internationale.[13]

The programme in its final form was a mixture of old and new. A sharp argument occurred on the old crux of the significance of "war communism" and its relation to NEP. The draft programme of May 25, 1928, by-passing former controversies, dismissed war communism as "an organization of rational consumption for purposes of defence at a time when the productive forces of the country are declining"; while it had given valuable help in crushing the resistance of hostile strata, "it cannot be considered as a system of 'normal' economic policy of the dictatorship of the proletariat". Varga in the programme commission contested this view, maintaining that war communism was an important and normal element in the establishment of the dictatorship; and Bukharin tartly retorted that this attitude lay at the root of the errors of the Hungarian régime of 1919, which had suffered shipwreck owing to failure to meet the demands of the peasantry and the urban petty bourgeoisie. Bukharin and Varga both re-

natsional, No. 31–32 (157–158) (1928), pp. 32–40), which anticipated some sections of his speech of August 9, 1928, in the plenary session of the congress. It was originally intended to publish the records of the commission in abbreviated form in Vol. 2 of the German edition of the congress proceedings (*Die Internationale*, xi, No. 19, October 1, 1928, p. 657; J. Humbert-Droz, *De Lénine à Staline* (Neuchatel, 1971), p. 314); this volume never appeared (see p. 193, note 1 above). The Russian edition stated that the proceedings of the commission would be published separately (this was not done), and contained only a somewhat abbreviated record of the debates on the programme in plenary session (*Stenograficheskii Otchet VI Kongressa Kominterna* (1929), iii, 6).

[12] J. Humbert-Droz, *De Lénine à Staline* (Neuchatel, 1971), p. 313.

[13] *Stenograficheskii Otchet VI Kongressa Kominterna* (1929), v, 128–132.

stated their case in the plenary sittings of the congress; and Bela Kun made a brief statement expressing agreement with Bukharin.[14] The passage remained unchanged in the final text of the programme. Bukharin, arguing for the universal applicability of the expedient of NEP, concluded that "a certain maintenance of market relations will be indispensable in all other countries".[15]

Dominant and obsessive themes of the programme were the "partial, temporary, rotten" character of the stabilization of capitalism and the radicalization of the masses; and it diagnosed "an absolute deterioration in the position of the working class, even in a number of developed capitalist countries". It expatiated both on imperialism as the current phase of a decaying capitalism and on the revolutionary rôle of colonial and semi-colonial countries; "the revolutionary process in the colonies" was "an expression of the profound general crisis of the capitalist system". The category of "colonial and semi-colonial countries (China, India etc.)" in the draft of May 25, 1928, was extended in the final version to include "dependent countries (Argentina, Brazil etc.)"; and a fresh category was postulated of "still more backward countries (e.g. some parts of Africa)". Here there were hardly any hired workers, tribal ways of life predominated, and imperial rule took in the main the form of military occupation; national independence and a national rising were the only goals that could be proclaimed. The revolutionary significance of the building of socialism in the USSR, its international obligations to the revolution, and the obligation of the international proletariat to the USSR, were elaborated in a special chapter (ch. V); and this theme, coupled with insistence on the danger of an attack by the imperialist Powers, recurred at several points in the programme.

The relegation to the debate on the programme of the question of national minorities in Europe[16] led to a sharp and significant clash between two Czechoslovak delegates, Reiman and Harus. The former complained of neglect of the national question, which

[14] *Stenograficheskii Otchet VI Kongressa Kominterna* (1929), iii, 29–30, 63–68, 150–152, 155; the final text is in *Kommunisticheskii Internatsional v Dokumentakh* (1933), pp. 24–25. For Varga's article in *Pravda*, June 14, 1928, see p. 226 above; for the origins of the dispute see *The Bolshevik Revolution, 1917–1923*, Vol. 2, p. 169, note 3.

[15] *Stenograficheskii Otchet VI Kongressa Kominterna* (1929), iii, 154.

[16] See p. 213 above.

"plays an extraordinarily important rôle ... in the territory of capitalist countries". The latter, conscious of the dangers which this issue might present to his own country, launched an attack on Skrypnik, whom he accused of justifying "armed struggle for national self-determination" by national minorities; it was impossible to ask Polish communists to "place themselves at the head of an armed struggle for the self-determination of Ukrainians and White Russians oppressed by the Poles". He claimed Lenin's authority for the view that a proletarian party "strives to create the strongest possible state", and that "*the proletariat of the oppressed nations must strive for union with the proletariat of the oppressing nation*"; and he wished to see these principles inscribed in the programme. This view, though buttressed by an allusion to the nationalities in the Soviet Union, was fiercely denounced by Skrypnik.[17] Bukharin avoided the issue, at any rate in public discussion. But a brief new section was inserted in the programme on "The National and Colonial Questions", which called both for "full self-determination, i.e. self-determination to the point of political separation", and for "the voluntary union and centralization of the military and economic resources of all peoples liberated from capitalism for the struggle against imperialism and for the building of a socialist economy".[18]

The agrarian section of the programme provoked sharp controversy on the issue of land nationalization. Lenin, in the theses on the agrarian question adopted by the second congress of Comintern in 1920, referring to the position of the small and middle peasant proprietor, bluntly declared that "in the majority of capitalist countries there can be no question of the immediate complete abolition of private property by the proletarian government".[19] Bukharin, in the draft programme of May 1928, repeated this reservation in regard to "the most advanced capitalist countries, where the principle of private property has struck roots among the broadest strata of the peasantry".[20] Much had, however, happened since 1920. In China the slogan of agrarian revolution had been proclaimed by the seventh IKKI in November 1926; and "nationalization of all land" figured without challenge

[17] *Stenograficheskii Otchet VI Kongressa Kominterna* (1929), iii, 36, 72–73, 116–117.

[18] *Kommunisticheskii Internatsional v Dokumentakh* (1933), p. 22.

[19] *Ibid.* p. 135.

[20] *Stenograficheskii Otchet VI Kongressa Kominterna* (1929), iii, 175.

in the section of the draft programme relating to colonial and semi-colonial countries.[21] Moreover, more radical views of Soviet agrarian policy were now gaining ground in Moscow. On the eve of the congress, Karpinsky, a leader of the kolkhoz movement, and known as an advocate of collective agriculture, published an article in the Comintern journal, severely criticizing the agrarian section of the draft programme, and observing caustically that in most advanced capitalist countries "*no, or practically no, peasantry*" existed. He argued that "*Comintern has no ground for renouncing the complete and immediate nationalization of all land*". Large estates with all buildings and inventory should be confiscated, and converted into state Sovkhozy; small holdings cultivated by small and middle peasant households should be exempt from confiscation and should receive assistance, and in case of need additional land, from the state fund. Apart from such aid, the proletarian dictatorship should give "*especial support and encouragement to cooperative, collective farms*".[22]

The discussions in the programme commission of the congress remained unpublished. But Renaud Jean, a French delegate, proposed to tone down the passages relating to land nationalization and the hegemony of the proletariat over the peasantry, and to guarantee in stronger terms the small peasant's right to ownership of his land; he was severely criticized in plenary session by Sémard.[23] On the other hand, Dengel came out for complete nationalization, and argued that, since buying and selling of land was to be prohibited, to recognize property in land was illusory.[24] Bukharin admitted that "many members of the programme commission" agreed with Renaud Jean — perhaps a hint of his own predilections. But, balanced between two extremes, he evaded criticisms from both.[25] The draft text was maintained with minor verbal changes. The conservative note of caution was somewhat strengthened by the admission that "small individual holdings" could be drawn only gradually into a "socialist organization of production and distribution", and that "any forced break-up of

[21] *Ibid.* iii, 181.

[22] *Kommunisticheskii Internatsional*, No. 25–26 (151–152), 1928, pp. 52–57; for Karpinsky see Vol. 1, pp. 171–172. Similar views were expressed by a German writer in *Die Internationale*, xii, No. 13, July 1, 1928, pp. 469–475.

[23] *Stenograficheskii Otchet Kongressa Kominterna* (1929), iii, 94–95.

[24] *Ibid.* iii, 46.

[25] *Ibid.* iii, 146–149.

their economic way of life or their compulsory collectivization would lead only to negative results".[26] The relation of the peasantry to the proletariat, and the rôle of both in the coming revolution, also provided embarrassing problems for the programme-makers. Sémard recalled that the fifth congress in 1924 had approved the slogan of a "worker–peasant government" as a synonym for the dictatorship of the proletariat, and wished to introduce it into the programme.[27] Skrypnik quoted Lenin's definition of the dictatorship of the proletariat as "a special form of class alliance" between the proletariat and "the numerous non-proletarian strata of toilers, petty bourgeoisie, small property-owners, peasantry, intelligentsia etc.", and proposed to embody this in the programme.[28] Both these pleas were silently rejected.

The vexed question of Fascism, and of the relation of social-democracy to it, lightly touched on in the debates on Bukharin's theses, was treated more thoroughly in the debates on the programme. The draft programme, in the course of a denunciation of social-democracy, bracketed it with Fascism as twin agents of the bourgeoisie.[29] What was said in the programme commission of the congress is not known, but some hints can be gleaned from the debate on the programme in plenary session. Bukharin noted that "very detailed and ... very interesting discussions" had taken place in the commission on the link between social-democracy and Fascism, and reserved his comments for his final speech.[30] Dengel, the KPD spokesman, determined to keep the question to the fore, complained that the draft programme did not show up "the rôle of Fascism in the development of monopoly capitalism", diagnosed in Germany and in Great Britain "a transition to social-Fascist methods", and declared that "the ideological *rapprochement* of social-democracy with Fascism has long ago been realized".[31] Several delegates — notably those of Poland, the

[26] *Kommunisticheskii Internatsional v Dokumentakh* (1933), pp. 20–21, 23.

[27] *Stenograficheskii Otchet VI Kongressa Kominterna* (1929), iii, 92, 97; for the identification in 1924 see *Socialism in One Country, 1924–1926*, Vol. 3, pp. 74–75.

[28] *Stenograficheskii Otchet VI Kongressa Kominterna* (1929), iii, 110–111; the reference given by Skrypnik is incorrect, and the quotation, if authentic, has not been identified.

[29] *Ibid.* iii, 165; for the final text of this passage see p. 233 below.

[30] *Stenograficheskii Otchet VI Kongressa Kominterna* (1929), iii, 30–31.

[31] *Ibid.* iii, 44–45.

United States and Great Britain—contested the view that Fascism was a specific phenomenon of not fully developed capitalist countries (especially those which had no colonies), which used Fascist methods as an alternative to the method, open only to more highly developed countries, of seducing social-democracy into a coalition with the bourgeoisie. The British delegate rejected the claim of the Labour Party that no ground existed in Great Britain for the rise of Fascism.[32] What appeared to be the prevalent opinion treated Fascism as a phenomenon common to all developed countries, where all measures of repression exercised by the dictatorship of the bourgeoisie, ranging from the parliamentary system to the open use of violence, had a Fascist character. But Sémard noted that Fascism was not the only form of reaction; it should not be identified with "every kind of reactionary situation and every kind of reactionary phenomenon".[33]

Bukharin summed up cautiously. He firmly rejected the view which confined Fascism to undeveloped or backward economies, but otherwise tried to give satisfaction to all trends of opinion. In an ingenious theoretical argument he maintained that reformism, like the earlier German "revisionism", was the specific outcrop of a working class which had "crystallized out of a reservoir of proletarianized peasantry, of a proletarianized urban middle stratum", and therefore retained "*petty bourgeois* traits". Bukharin suggested that the true criterion which determined the application of Fascist methods was not the degree of development in the country concerned, but the extent to which capitalist stability had already been shaken. Fascist tendencies were inherent in social-democracy. Bukharin even used, with substantial reservations, the contentious term "social-Fascist":

> In the first place, without any doubt social-democracy has *social-Fascist tendencies*. Secondly, these are *tendencies* and not a finished process.

The conclusion was that it would not be reasonable to "put social-democracy into one heap with Fascism": communists might appeal to social-democratic workers or lower social-

[32] *Ibid.* iii, 34, 74, 98–100.

[33] *Ibid.* p. 93; nobody repeated the crude distinction enunciated a few months earlier in an article by Lozovsky: "Fascism directs coercion [*nasilie*] against the workers, Bolshevism against the bourgeoisie" (A. Lozovsky, *Na Novom Etape* (1928), p. 14).

democratic organizations, but not to Fascist organizations. This was what Togliatti had said at an earlier sitting of the congress. But Bukharin had provided arguments which would soon be used to blur the distinction.[34] Only minor changes were made in the draft programme as a result of this discussion. The final text firmly maintained the parallel between Fascism and social-democracy:

> Side by side with social democracy, with whose help the bourgeoisie crushes the workers and lulls their class vigilance, comes *Fascism*.

It was noted that Fascism used such weapons as "anti-Semitism, frequent attacks on usurious capital and indignation with parliamentary 'chatter' ", and that "a combination of social demagogy, corruption and active white terror, together with extreme imperialist aggressiveness in the sphere of foreign policy, are characteristic traits of Fascism". At the same time:

> Adapting itself to changes in the political scene, the bourgeoisie uses both the methods of Fascism and the methods of coalition with social-democracy, while social-democracy itself at the most critical moments for capitalism often plays a Fascist rôle.[35]

Finally, the concluding section of the programme on measures to be taken to counter the threat of imperialist war against the Soviet Union, which in the draft had been confined to the proclamation of appropriate slogans and to a coy mention of an "obligatory combination of legal and illegal methods of work", was strengthened by the inclusion — doubtless as the result of Yaroslavsky's intervention — of a specific demand for "organized work in army and fleet". The programme, which in its introduction had described Comintern as "the one centralized international party of the proletariat", ended with an appeal for "international class discipline, of which the most important pre-condition is the strictest international discipline in communist ranks", involving

[34] *Stenograficheskii Otchet VI Kongressa Kominterna* (1929), iii, 138–139, 143–145; for Togliatti's speech see p. 201 above. For "social-Fascism" see Note C, pp. 638–643 below.

[35] *Kommunisticheskii Internatsional v Dokumentakh* (1933), pp. 11–12; for the original draft of this passage see *Stenograficheskii Otchet VI Kongressa Kominterna* (1929), iii, 165–166.

"the unconditional execution by all communists of the decisions of the leading organs of Comintern".[36]

The programme was adopted at the final meeting of the congress on September 1, 1928.[37] The chief emotion registered was perhaps relief that the long period of gestation was over at last. The programme was too verbose, too much addicted to compromise formulas on crucial issues, and above all too much involved in current political controversies, to make a very impressive document. Trotsky, who had submitted to the congress a long critique of the draft programme, rejected the final version as "contradictory and eclectic, and, chiefly, because it adopts the principle, hostile to internationalism, of socialism in one country".[38] An enthusiastic German delegate praised it in contrast with the draft of 1924 as a call for action, and proposed to call it a "programme–manifesto".[39] It indubitably devoted more attention to current issues which vexed and sometimes divided communist parties. But it did not notably contribute to their elucidation. The duty of providing Comintern with a programme had been discharged. It was consigned to the archives, and rarely or never invoked either by the parties or by the central organs in Moscow.

[36] *Kommunisticheskii Internatsional v Dokumentakh* (1933), pp. 45–46. For Yaroslavsky's insistence on organized work in armies see p. 210 above; Sémard in the debate on the programme had also demanded the insertion of this phrase (*Stenograficheskii Otchet VI Kongressa Kominterna* (1929), iii, 97).

[37] *Ibid.* v, 132.

[38] The statement, written for the first issue of the French opposition journal *Vérité*, September 13, 1929, is in Trotsky archives, T 3925.

[39] *Stenograficheskii Otchet VI Kongressa Kominterna* (1929), iii, 109.

CHAPTER 72

THE NEW LINE HARDENS

DURING the winter of 1928–1929 the old tradition of a united front with radical movements in other countries, now contemptuously dubbed the united front "from above", was still fighting a rear-guard action against the new line of repeated and uncompromising onslaughts on social-democrats and other Leftists in political parties and in the trade unions. Events had in part justified, in part refuted, the pronouncements of the sixth congress of Comintern on the danger of imperialist war and the prospects of revolution. Symptoms of the coming world economic crisis could already be detected. Seeds of future wars were being sown in the Far East. But the short-term prospect of war, in particular of war against the Soviet Union and of war between Great Britain and the United States — the two prospects which haunted the Soviet imagination and inspired much Soviet propaganda — was visibly receding. The long-standing tension between the Soviet Union and Great Britain was being markedly relaxed.[1] This process was welcomed and encouraged by Soviet policy-makers, among other things, as a contribution to the success of the five-year plan, which began to dominate Soviet thinking at this time; the expected victory of the Labour Party in the approaching general election opened up prospects more favourable than anything achieved since 1924 under the Conservative government. The fifth Union Congress of Soviets in May 1929 was able to congratulate itself that "the aggressive designs of capitalist states ... have not been crowned with success", and that in Great Britain and the United States "a movement aiming at the development of economic links with the USSR has been strengthened". Yet, while tension between capitalist countries still brought the danger of war, and in view of their "incessant demonstrations of hostility against the Soviet Union", it was necessary to "strengthen the defence capacity" of

[1] See pp. 30–35 above.

the country.[2] A few weeks later, the formation of a British Labour government carried with it the assurance of a resumption of diplomatic relations with Great Britain. At the moment when the first five-year plan received formal approval, and on the eve of the world economic crisis and of the struggle to collectivize the Soviet peasant, a partial *détente* had been achieved in Soviet relations with the western countries.

These achievements might have provided a growing opportunity to win support through non-party Left organizations in western countries. In the event a massive anti-Fascist congress in Berlin in March 1929[3] proved to be the last successful effort of this kind sponsored by the authorities in Moscow. The autumn of 1928 which followed the sixth congress of Comintern was a tense and critical moment in Stalin's struggle against party opposition on two fronts.[4] It was marked by the voluntary or enforced withdrawal of Bukharin, who after his return from holiday early in November 1928 ceased to visit the offices of Comintern or to occupy himself with Comintern affairs.[5] He played no part in the succession of crises in the German, British and American parties, all of them arising more or less directly from the promulgation of the new line in Comintern, and all involving bitter feuds between national party leaders, the outcome of these crises being bound up with what happened in Moscow. In this turmoil, any movement towards cooperation or conciliation was quickly branded as a Right deviation, and was frustrated in practice by two campaigns which tended more and more to merge into one another: denunciation of western social-democrats and Leftists as agents of capitalism, and denunciation of the western Powers in general as imperialists engaged in the preparation of war against the Soviet Union.

The campaign against social-democracy was now centred on

[2] *S"ezdy Sovetov v Dokumentakh*, iii (1960), 150–151.

[3] See pp. 310–313 below.

[4] See Vol. 2, pp. 75–82.

[5] J. Humbert-Droz, *De Lénine à Staline* (Neuchatel, 1971), p. 340; the American communist Wolfe, arriving in Moscow early in January 1929 and asking to see Bukharin, was "told that Bukharin was too sick to be seen, that he was away on vacation, and similar evasions"; later he met Bukharin, who ironically informed him that, "by a vote of five to four, I am too ill to function as chairman of the Communist International" (T. Draper, *Soviet Russia and American Communism* (1960), pp. 392–393).

the trade unions, and derived fresh impetus from the party struggles in Moscow. The first overt blow struck at the Right deviation in the Russian party was the eviction of Tomsky and his supporters from the leadership of the Soviet trade unions during the eighth Soviet trade union congress in December 1928.[6] Tomsky had devoted a brief concluding section in his main report to the congress to international affairs, referring in conventional terms to the break-up of the Anglo-Russian committee, to the congress of Friends of the Soviet Union and to the League against Imperialism. He also boasted that the Soviet trade unions had collected a strike fund of 5 million rubles, and were ready to help strikers anywhere in the world.[7] Lozovsky's report on the work of Profintern was a far more flamboyant performance. He harped on the war danger, spoke of strikes all over the world which "mark the beginning of a new revolutionary wave", and detected the symptoms of a Right deviation even within Profintern.[8] Pollitt and Monmousseau spoke as British and French fraternal delegates; the former pronounced the situation in Great Britain to be "objectively revolutionary".[9] The resolution unanimously adopted on Lozovsky's report called for the formation of strike committees, the organization of unskilled workers, and the drawing of unorganized workers into the struggle against capitalism, and demanded "*no concessions to open or concealed reformist tendencies in the ranks of Profintern*".[10] But the main significance of the occasion was the removal from their posts of those leaders of the Soviet trade union movement, Tomsky's faithful followers, who had hitherto constituted within the movement the most powerful source of opposition to the aggressive international policies preached by Lozovsky at the fourth congress of Profintern and the sixth congress of Comintern.

Lozovsky set out to consolidate his victory. In the second half of January 1929 the executive bureau of Profintern convened a conference in Berlin for the express purpose of considering strike strategy and tactics; for some reason, the fiction was maintained

[6] See Vol. 1, pp. 556–560.

[7] *Vos'moi S"ezd Professional'nykh Soyuzov SSSR* (1929), pp. 52–54; for the League against Imperialism and the Friends of the Soviet Union see pp. 296–310 below.

[8] *Vos'moi S"ezd Professional'nykh Soyuzov SSSR* (1929), pp. 208–227.

[9] *Ibid.* pp. 227–234.

[10] *Ibid.* pp. 554–556.

that the conference was held in Strasbourg, though well-founded fear of the French police would probably have deterred Lozovsky and other Profintern officials from venturing on French soil.[11] The conference was attended by representatives of Germany, France, Great Britain, Belgium, Austria, Hungary and Poland. No detailed record of the proceedings was published. But a memorandum signed jointly by Tanner and Pollitt, and circulated within the NMM at the time of the conference, pleaded for recognition of "the need for a flexible strike policy without falling into the error of overlooking national circumstances and traditions", and argued that, if a strike occurred, "attempts should be made to split the bureaucracy by getting some or all the unions to make the strike official" — a policy of action through the reformist leaders which was poles apart from Lozovsky's belligerent approach.[12] It seems unlikely that the British delegation at the conference, led by Tanner, reconciled itself easily or wholeheartedly to the view of the majority which supported Lozovsky; and, while the long resolution of the conference appears to have been adopted unanimously, some dissent was evidently manifested in the course of the proceedings.[13] The resolution "On Questions of Strike Policy", adopted after reports by Heckert and an unnamed Polish delegate, propounded such slogans as "Do not trust the trade union bureaucrats — they will betray you", "Take your fate into your own hands", and "Prepare for a struggle — otherwise you will be

[11] The account of the conference by Lozovsky in *Krasnyi Internatsional Profsoyuzov*, No. 2, 1929, pp. 93–95, the brief summary in the English edition of the journal, the *Red International of Labour Unions*, No. 5, February 1929, p. 229, and the note preceding the text of the resolution in *Desyat' Let Profinterna v Rezolyutsiyakh* (1930), pp. 236–237, locate the conference in Strasbourg; *The Worker*, April 5, 1929, states that it was held "recently" in Berlin. The diary entry for January 19, 1929, of Tanner, the British delegate, preserved in the library of Nuffield College, Oxford, contains the single word "Berlin"; this seems conclusive.

[12] It was published in *The Worker*, April 12, 1929, but dated "January 1929".

[13] The reports in *Krasnyi Internatsional Profsoyuzov* and in *Desyat' Let Profinterna v Rezolyutsiyakh* contain no hint of dissent; but the *Red International of Labour Unions*, No. 5, February 1929, p. 229, cautiously records that "the great majority of those attending came to the firm conviction that the policy of the fourth RILU [i.e. Profintern] congress was perfectly sound", and that "the tentative instructions of the RILU executive bureau were adopted as the basis of the conference's decisions". The omission of the British from the list of delegations at the conference in *Desyat' Let Profinterna v Rezolyutsiyakh* (1930), p. 236, looks like a Freudian slip.

destroyed". It demanded the formation of independent democratically elected strike committees, and stressed the need for "units of self-defence". In advanced capitalist countries, where the bourgeoisie and the reformists aimed at "the replacement of strikes by compulsory arbitration", it must be recognized that "every strike acquires a political character". The injunction that one element in the strike campaign should be "to strengthen the campaign against the preparation of war with the USSR" was a reminder of a constant Soviet anxiety. While every clause of the resolution seemed to breathe hostility to the social-democratic unions, the conclusion recorded once again that "the question of work in the reformist trade unions remains in full force in accordance with the resolution of the ninth plenum of IKKI, of the fourth congress of Profintern and of the sixth congress of Comintern".[14]

Lozovsky's article on the conference in the Profintern journal emphasized the essential conclusion that "the reformist trade union apparatus has become part of the bourgeois state, with the special function of breaking strikes"; the conference had "approached the strike as a species of war", and indicated to the fighting proletarian army the defensive and offensive action calculated to ensure to it the maximum success in the struggle". But Lozovsky also recorded that the conference had taken no decision about unorganized workers, since "this question has still to be specially discussed in Profintern and Comintern". He went on:

> This is a new question, a complicated question, requiring fundamental discussion, and the conference therefore acted correctly in taking no decision on the question.[15]

An article by a Profintern official in the English edition of the Profintern journal which carried the report of the conference revealed, without mentioning the conference, the source of resistance to Lozovsky's persistent advocacy of the recruitment of the unorganized worker:

> Most of our British comrades consider that there are very few active workers outside the ranks of the trade union move-

[14] For the resolution see *ibid.* pp. 237–263; Lozovsky claimed later that "we worked out the resolution for the international strike conference" (*Kommunisticheskii Internatsional*, No. 23–24 (201–202), 1929, p. 126).

[15] *Krasnyi Internatsional Profsoyuzov*, No. 2, February 1929, p. 96.

> ment, and that it would be dangerous for the NMM to accept into its ranks all those workers who belong as yet to no trade union. The fallacy of this is proved by the case of France, Germany, Poland and Czechoslovakia.[16]

The British trade union movement, even more than the German or the French movement, had a momentum of its own which rendered it unamenable to Profintern or Comintern pressures for uniformity on a Soviet model.

Lozovsky was not the man to be deterred by a minor set-back. He continued the fight in a trade union commission set up to prepare for the tenth IKKI. The commission held two sessions in February and May 1929, and Lozovsky delivered polemical speeches in both. At the first his main target was Pyatnitsky, who tried to maintain that the congresses of Profintern and Comintern in 1928 had changed nothing, and continued to put forward the familiar injunctions to work in the existing unions: "build cells, win over the factory committees, win over the unions". What had changed the situation, declared Lozovsky, was the treachery of the social-democrats; and he exhorted the workers to "come out against the strike-breaking apparatus of the reformist trade unions". He devoted the greater part of his speech to the question of organizing unorganized workers, which he had broached at the fourth congress of Profintern a year earlier. It had now become urgent owing to rationalization, which increased the number of unskilled and women workers in industry, most of them unorganized, and to rising unemployment. Lozovsky quoted Rosa Luxemburg on the significant role of unorganized workers in strikes and on the need to mobilize them for action. In countries like France and Czechoslovakia, where revolutionary trade unions affiliated to Profintern already existed, these unions should recruit the unorganized workers; in countries where the trade union movement was not already split, the creation of new revolutionary unions might be required. In a rash outburst of rhetoric, Lozovsky exclaimed that "the part of the working class which is organized in reformist trade unions, and follows reformist leadership, is the most socially reactionary part of the working class"; and he defended himself a little uneasily against the charge that he was preaching an exodus from the existing trade unions. Unorganized

[16] *Red International of Labour Unions*, No. 5, February 1929, pp. 200–202, 205.

workers who did not join trade unions might be enrolled in organizations like MRP or the Roter Frontkämpferbund (Lozovsky was thinking primarily of Germany). *"The point is, under whatever label, under whatever name, to organize tens of thousands of unorganized workers."*[17] Bell, the British delegate, admitted that British workers suffered from "a certain craft union complex" and that trade unionists sometimes acted without regard to the interests of the unorganized workers. He cautiously supported Lozovsky against Pyatnitsky, but protested against Lozovsky's charge that social-democratic trade unions represented "the most backward and most reactionary sections of the working class".[18]

The debate was resumed at a further session in May 1929. On this occasion Lozovsky's major assailant was Gusev, who had argued that it was impermissible to turn the trade unions into "organs leading mass political and economic demonstrations", and that the overthrow of a bourgeois government was not their function. This Lozovsky fiercely denied. Gusev had objected to the creation of new unions. Lozovsky maintained that "to come out *against new unions in principle*" was contrary to the decisions of the ninth IKKI and the fourth congress of Profintern. The theses which the commission would submit to the tenth IKKI must formulate "the question whether or not the trade unions have as their task the overthrow of the power of the bourgeoisie".[19] The sharpness of the controversy suggested that Lozovsky still had powerful opponents in the party.

Whatever hesitations may have been prompted by Lozovsky's brash assault on the trade unions, the twin themes of the anathema on social-democrats and radicals of the Left and of the rising tide of revolution increasingly dominated the propaganda issuing from Moscow. Manuilsky in what was evidently an authoritative article of February 1929 denounced Rightists who wanted to cooperate with social-democrats on a basis of "growing into revolution",

[17] *Kommunisticheskii Internatsional*, No. 23–24 (201–202), 1929, pp. 110–118.

[18] *Communist Review*, No. 6, June 1929, pp. 362–370; this appears to have been the only speech other than Lozovsky's which was ever published.

[19] Lozovsky's speech was published in *Kommunisticheskii Internatsional*, No. 23–24 (201–202), pp. 118–127; this is the sole available source for the session of May 1929.

and endeavoured to extract revolutionary optimism from an unpromising situation:

> The "defeated" Chinese revolution and the "defeated" English general strike have in their total effect contributed ... in a far higher degree to the general disintegration of the capitalist system than the factor of the defeat of the proletariat could contribute to capitalist stabilization.[20]

On March 2, 1929, IKKI issued a proclamation on the forthcoming tenth anniversary of the foundation of Comintern, which rehearsed again the familiar revolutionary themes. The Russian workers had shown in 1917 how "the struggle against imperialist war" could be converted into civil war, and had overthrown the might of capital. They had set the example:

> In Europe and Asia, in America and Africa, the oppressed classes have everywhere risen against their oppressors, against the organizers of imperialist slaughter.

The "illusions of capitalist stability" had been destroyed. Social-democracy had been revealed as "a faithful prop" of the bourgeoisie; and the link between "reformism and Fascism" established by the sixth congress of Comintern was cautiously reasserted. "The oppressed of the whole world" were prepared for a new revolutionary wave directed "against capitalist exploitation, against the yoke of imperialism, against the dictatorship of the bourgeoisie" as well as "against reformism and Fascism".[21] Long and detailed theses issued on the same occasion by the Agitprop of IKKI recalled that the Communist International "grew and became strong in the struggle against social-democracy", and, in a denunciation of Fascism, referred to "its coalescence with social-democracy for the struggle against the revolutionary offensive".[22] A special number of *Pravda* for March 3, 1929, included greetings from the principal foreign parties, and articles by such Comintern celebrities as Bela Kun, Lozovsky, Gusev, Teodoro-

[20] *Internationale Presse-Korrespondenz,* No. 15, Feburary 15, 1929, pp. 285–290.

[21] *Pravda,* March 3, 1929; for the resolution of the sixth congress see p. 203 above.

[22] *Pravda,* February 28, 1929; *Internationale Presse-Korrespondenz,* No. 21, March 5, 1929, pp. 443–452.

vich, Cachin and Reinstein, a survivor of the first congress, as well as by Zinoviev on the historical antecedents of Comintern. On the following day Kuusinen appears to have been the principal speaker at a commemorative gathering.[23] What was striking in these proceedings was the absence of Bukharin or of any mention of his name.

The theme was vigorously pressed throughout the summer of 1929. The Agitprop of IKKI issued theses on the occasion of the May 1 celebrations which began by recalling the proclamation of May 1 by the Second International forty years earlier as an "international proletarian day". A long historical review ended by denouncing the "blood-bath" of May 1, 1928, in Warsaw carried out by "the Polish socialist police-butchers". Finally, the note of the offensive was struck. Communists must struggle "for the right to the streets, for the right to strike", and were assured that their fighting capacity had grown.[24] Within a few days of the issue of these appeals, the Berlin police, under the command of a social-democratic chief, fired on a May Day street demonstration of communist workers held in defiance of police prohibition, and twenty-five workers were killed. This tragedy caused *Pravda* to insist on "the necessity of decisively sharpening the struggle against social-democracy", and to invoke "the iron logic of the unfolding class struggle";[25] and MOPR issued an appeal on behalf of "the victims of the white terror and of Fascism".[26] On May 16, 1929, a conference of representatives of thirteen communist parties in western capitalist countries which met in Berlin to make preparations for the international day of protest against war planned for August 1, 1929, opened its proceedings with a protest against the May 1 massacre in Berlin, which it attributed to "the social-Fascist police armed to the teeth" and to "the imperialists and their social-Fascist accomplices", referring to "the bloody blow struck by the social-Fascists".[27] The term "social-Fascism" to stigmatize the cooperation of social-democrats with

[23] *Pravda*, March 12, 1929.

[24] *Internationale Presse-Korrespondenz*, No. 31, April 9, 1929, pp. 711–712, No. 32, April 12, 1929, pp. 735–736, No. 33, April 16, 1929, pp. 764–765, No. 34, April 19, 1929, pp. 802–804.

[25] *Pravda*, May 8, 1929; for the events in Berlin see p. 458 below.

[26] *Internationale Presse-Korrespondenz*, No. 42, May 14, 1929, p. 1027.

[27] *Ibid.* No. 44, May 22, 1929, pp. 1062–1063; for this conference see p. 246 below.

the "Fascist" bourgeoisie became henceforth a regular ingredient in Comintern's vocabulary of vituperation.[28]

The campaign against the social-democrats, and the struggle to wrest the leadership of the trade union movement from their hands, was, however, cunningly tempered in Comintern propaganda, and in part overshadowed, by the campaign against the imperialist war-mongers. The limitations of the attempt to combine the two campaigns were, however, revealed in a curious interlude at the beginning of 1929. In November 1928 the International Women's League for Peace and Freedom, a radical organization with strong pacifist leanings, announced that it intended to hold a conference in Frankfurt on January 5–6, 1929, to protest against the use of poison gas in war, to which Profintern, MRP, the League against Imperialism, and the International Anti-Militarist Union in the Netherlands were invited to send delegates. Lozovsky at the eighth Soviet trade union congress in Moscow in December 1928 cited the proposed conference as a symptom of growing fear of war among the bourgeoisie. He reported that the question of Soviet participation had not yet been decided, adding ironically: "Of course, we could suggest some conclusions, but we will not frighten them."[29] When the time came all the invited organizations were represented. It was a very stormy occasion, since it proved difficult to find common ground between communists and non-communists. Several speakers had mixed receptions; and a German communist woman delegate, who argued that "capitalist force must be destroyed by force", and that, since some states were already arming women, communist women must employ the same weapons, was shouted down. Chernyshova, the Soviet trade union delegate, speaking for five million women workers in the Soviet Union, explained that the delegation, having discovered only after its arrival in Frankfurt the true character of the conference, had decided not to participate in its debates, but to make a statement which would be handed to the press. She concluded that "a conference like the present one cannot save us from war", and that the danger of war could be removed from the world only "*when the working classes*

[28] See Note C, pp. 638–643 below.
[29] *Vos'moi S"ezd Professional'nykh Soyuzov SSSR* (1929), pp. 254–255.

take the road which the Russian workers and peasants have taken for the annihilation of imperialist war". The versatile Münzenberg also made a declaration, for which he obtained fourteen signatures, to the effect that the discussion of gas warfare was "no serious measure against the threatening war", but rather diverted attention from the machinations of the war-mongers. War could be averted not by "small, even if well intentioned, conferences", but only through "the revolutionary mass action of the working class".[30] The organizers of the conference can hardly have regarded the holders of such views as anything but a disturbing element, and are unlikely to have sought cooperation with them again. Another blow had been struck at the united front. The campaign against war had become another divisive force in relations between communists and other parties of the Left.

The incessant emphasis on the danger of imperialist war which dominated Comintern propaganda at this time had its own anomalies. The threat of war against the Soviet Union, which had appeared real and imminent in the summer of 1927, had already begun to fade, and was greeted with scepticism or indifference, when the sixth congress of Comintern assembled in July 1928.[31] A year later still, the danger presented itself only in local clashes in the Far East which seemed minor and remote to most people in the western world. Belief in the inevitability of war as the result of imperialism no longer implied, for most communists outside the Soviet Union, the prospect of the early and automatic fulfilment of the prophecy. As a delegate at the sixth congress of the PCF in April 1929 put it, "all the presuppositions for a world war are present", but "the watchword of its immediate advent may be treated simply as a symbol".[32] The symbol had, however, in Comintern circles become obsessional. As the danger receded into the future, and the propaganda lost its initial plausibility and immediacy, the tone grew more strident. The traditional May Day manifesto for 1929 was concerned exclusively with the war

[30] *Internationale Presse-Korrespondenz*, No. 2, January 8, 1928, pp. 36–38; a briefer report appeared in *Pravda*, January 8, 1929, according to which a majority of the conference refused to include any mention of the Soviet proposals in its resolution.

[31] See pp. 205–206 above.

[32] *Internationale Presse-Korrespondenz*, No. 33, April 16, 1929, p. 767; another French communist complained of "lack of understanding and scepticism in regard to the acute danger of war" (*ibid.* No. 27, March 22, 1929, p. 606).

danger; the international situation "reeks of the powder of fresh wars, as before 1914". Once more "*class stands against class*". The treason of the Second International in 1914 was recalled. Those whose lives had been sacrificed to this "deceit" had unhappily not saved coming generations from new wars: they had prepared the way for a war whose consequences would be still more frightful — "the war between Great Britain and the United States for world hegemony". The vision was conjured up of a future war in which "the Pacific Ocean will be transformed into a sea of blood".

> In the capitalist twilight of the gods of the next years [the manifesto went on], a catastrophe is impending before which the mass annihilations of the war of 1914 will pale. Through the weapons of the most modern technique of extermination, the gas war, even the cities of the hinterland will be turned into mass cemeteries, and the differences between front line and hinterland will disappear.

The manifesto concluded with an appeal to the masses for the "international day" against war proclaimed by the sixth congress and now planned for August 1, 1929.[33] The Agitprop theses for May 1 forged a link between the two well-worn themes:

> *The struggle against Fascism and social-democracy is an integral component part of the struggle against imperialist war, for the defence of the Soviet Union.*[34]

And the conference of May 16, 1929, to prepare for the "international day" of protest against war did not neglect the parallel campaign against the social-Fascists.[35]

The unpublicized, but widely known, disgrace of Bukharin, who had been severely censured in the resolutions of the Politburo of February 9, 1929, and of the party central committee of April 23, 1929,[36] added an air of unreality to the proceedings of Comin-

[33] *Pravda*, April 14, 1929; *Internationale Presse-Korrespondenz*, No. 33, April 16, 1929, pp. 747–751. For the resolution of the sixth congress see pp. 211–213 above.

[34] For these theses see p. 243 above.

[35] See p. 243 above.

[36] See Vol. 2, pp. 89, 91–92.

tern throughout this period. It was in this uncertain atmosphere that preparations were made for the tenth IKKI, convened for July 3, 1929. Manuilsky opened a long article on the forthcoming session with a criticism of the "political impressionism" which always expected to find "new features" and "new stages". He issued a warning against "attempts of the Rightist and conciliators" to whittle away the conclusions of the sixth congress on the so-called "stabilization of capitalism", and affirmed that "organized" capitalism was capitalism in decline. He hailed "the radicalization of the masses"; rejected interpretations of the united front of the kind accepted by the third congress of Comintern in 1921; denounced "Left" social-democracy as "the most dangerous, most noxious brand of reformism"; and demanded "the liquidation of fractional groups" in communist parties. In effect, he added nothing to the prescriptions of the sixth congress a year earlier, except perhaps a renewed emphasis on the struggle against "Rightists and conciliators" in all parties.[37] When the session opened, Bukharin's absence was not referred to; and the tactics of the party spokesmen became clear. By repeated insistence on the intensification of the class struggle between capital and labour, on imperialist oppression of the colonies, and on the threat of imperialist wars, they exposed the hollowness of policies of compromise, isolated the communists as the only true revolutionary party, and denounced the social-democrats as their worst enemies; and by this approach they cautiously paved the way for the condemnation of Bukharin. The two aims were interconnected. Bukharin had resisted, though weakly and inconsistently, the swing to the Left in Comintern, and the application of methods of monolithic discipline to foreign communist parties. Emphasis on the new policies coincided logically with his downfall.

With Bukharin withdrawn from the scene, IKKI seemed to lack central direction.[38] The main draft theses, circulated in advance, on the international situation and the tasks of Comintern, were presented in two major reports by Kuusinen and Manuilsky.

[37] *Pravda*, June 14, 15, 16, 18, 1929; *Internationale Presse-Korrespondenz*, No. 52, June 18, 1929, pp. 1253–1256, No. 53, June 21, 1929, pp. 1292–1295, No. 54, June 25, 1929, pp. 1319–1321.

[38] According to J. Humbert-Droz, *De Lénine à Staline* (Neuchatel, 1971), pp. 374–375, Molotov was still too inexperienced in Comintern affairs to function effectively, and real power was in the hands of Manuilsky for political questions and Pyatnitsky for organization.

Kuusinen deprecated the tendency to over-estimate the potentialities of technical development and rationalization under capitalism, and asserted, in opposition to Varga, that capitalist rationalization brought about "*an absolute deterioration in the position of the working class*". As the contradictions of the capitalist world increased, bourgeois class rule would take on more and more openly Fascist forms, supported by the social-democrats ("social-Fascism"); this would drive the workers further and further to the Left and create the conditions for a "*proletarian offensive*". He evoked the equation between social-democracy and Fascism, and the now popular catchword "Social-Fascism", which "develops out of reformism and social democracy":

> The aims of Fascism and social-democracy are the same, the difference consists in the slogans and to some extent in the methods.[39]

Manuilsky spoke of "the declining curve of capitalist stabilization", and reaffirmed that "organized" capitalism was capitalism in decay. He detected "a process of *radicalization* of the working class" even in the United States and Great Britain. The task of communist parties, he declared, was to win over the broad masses of the workers and prepare for the seizure of power. He buried the united front under the now customary definition of it as "neither a coalition with the social-democratic leaders nor a policy of coming to an understanding with their functionaries from below, but rather a *direct appeal* of the communist party to the mass of the workers, social-democratic and non-party, organized and unorganized". He ended with the now ritual denunciation of the social-democrats, and of Right-wing "opportunists" and "conciliators" in communist parties who supported them. He attacked Tasca (under his current pseudonym of Serra) with asperity as "the Zarathustra of conciliationism", but mentioned no other names.[40]

The speakers in the debate took their cue from the *rapporteurs*. Varga, whose authority, in spite of some criticism from the Left,

[39] *Protokoll: 10. Plenum des Exekutivkomitees der Kommunistischen Internationale* (n.d.), pp. 5–49.

[40] *Ibid.* pp. 50–85.

had still been recognized at the sixth congress,[41] had recently reported, though with some cautious reservations, "an improvement of the business situation in countries of high capitalism" in the first quarter of 1929.[42] This now rendered him suspect as a sympathizer with Bukharin; and he, Pepper, Humbert-Droz, Ewert, Lovestone and Tasca were named, with varying degrees of disapproval, as dissidents. The debate dragged on inconclusively for several days. Varga tried hard to reconcile his economic conscience with the party line, and was prepared to admit that the position of the workers had deteriorated relatively, though not absolutely — an explanation which stressed more heavily than ever the rising curve of capitalist production.[43] His compatriot Bela Kun devoted most of a long speech to an analysis of social-Fascism, which replaced reformism as an instrument for the salvation of capitalism in a period when the stabilization of capitalism was being shattered; and he reproached the conciliators for treating parliamentarianism and social-democracy, on the one hand, and Fascism and the corporative state, on the other, as "two systems different *in principle*". The ever-ready Martynov described social-Fascists as "the ideologues of the workers' aristocracy".[44] Varga defended himself against attacks by Bela Kun and Kolarov in a further speech which was repeatedly interrupted by Bela Kun, Neumann, Thälmann and Kuusinen. Varga was the first speaker to mention Bukharin, recalling an incident at the fourth congress of Comintern in 1922, when Bukharin objected to the inclusion in the party programme of "transitional" demands, and was overruled by Lenin and his colleagues;[45] and Ulbricht, in a savage speech, referred to "the Bukharin, Humbert-Droz, Ewert group" and "the comrades round Bukharin".[46] But most speakers contented themselves with vague strictures on the Right, or on minor figures in other parties.

On July 9, 1929, at the eleventh sitting, Molotov at last put in

[41] See pp. 198–199 above.

[42] *Internationale Presse-Korrespondenz*, No. 41, May 13, 1929, p. 984.

[43] *Protokoll: 10. Plenum des Exekutivkomitees der Kommunistischen Internationale* (n.d.), pp. 164–176.

[44] *Ibid.* pp. 182–192, 230.

[45] *Ibid.* pp. 332–344; for the incident see *Socialism in One Country, 1924–1926*, Vol. 3, p. 1002.

[46] *Protokoll: 10. Plenum des Exekutivkomitees der Kommunistischen Internationale* (n.d.), pp. 365–366.

an appearance to deliver an authoritative speech designed to focus the debate. On the eve of the session an editorial article in the party journal had struck an uncompromising note. It had pointed to "the wave of strikes" and "the growth of discontent and mass radicalization", both among workers and among the "oppressed peasants" of colonial countries, and had quoted Molotov as asserting that "we have entered with both feet on a phase of major revolutionary events of international importance".[47] Molotov in his speech now described "the *struggle against* the Right and the conciliators", which had an *international* character, as "the fundamental point in the development of the Communist International since the sixth congress". He named Humbert-Droz, Serra, Meyer and Ewert as offenders, and accused Varga of reaching "opportunist conclusions" and playing a "reactionary role". He reverted to the theme of the radicalization of the workers' movement already proclaimed by the sixth congress, and diagnosed "*a new revolutionary wave*", of which strikes in Germany, Poland, France, Czechoslovakia and India were evidence. The aim must be "*to win a majority* of the working class", with "the political mass strike" as the most effective weapon. This meant a struggle against social-democracy and social-Fascism. The motto must be: "Complete annihilation of the Right, complete annihilation of opportunism." In conclusion, he convicted "a number of prominent members of the VKP(B)" of failing to detect "a most obvious Right-opportunist deviation", quoting Bukharin's memorandum of January 30, 1929, to the Politburo, and the subsequent joint statement of Bukharin, Rykov and Tomsky. He criticized Bukharin's recent *Pravda* article, and spoke of "the line of comrade Bukharin's group" which "coincides with the Right deviation". For the first time, the deviation of Bukharin, Rykov and Tomsky, and their dissent in the Politburo, had been brought into the open and publicly pilloried.[48]

Delegates of smaller parties who followed Molotov in the debate hesitated to plunge into the cauldron of Russian party quarrels. Neumann and Thälmann had no such inhibitions.

[47] *Bol'shevik*, No. 12, June 30, 1929, pp. 3–10.

[48] *Protokoll: 10. Plenum des Exekutivkomitees der Kommunistischen Internationale* (n.d.), pp. 404–439; none of the speeches, however, appeared in the press. For the attack on Bukharin and the *Pravda* article see Vol. 2, pp. 95–96.

Neumann harshly dissected Bukharin's *Pravda* article, condemned Varga's economic views, and ended with a strident outburst: "We are marching forward from the defensive to the counter-attack, to the offensive and on to the armed assault, to the struggle for Soviet power." Thälmann followed in more pedestrian style. He attacked Bukharin, Rykov, Tomsky and Frumkin, and touched lightly on the Rightist dissidents in other parties, including the conciliators in the KPD, but reserved his main assault for the later debate on the trade unions.[49] Mif, now head of the eastern section of the IKKI secretariat, renewed the attack launched at the sixth congress on the theory of decolonization in India. The theory, he argued, led inevitably to the conclusion that the native bourgeoisie would become more independent and more powerful, and would clash with the foreign imperialists; the theory was thus the basis of the false tactics of an alliance with the native bourgeoisie. This reversal of the earlier argument ingeniously removed the embarrassment displayed by Kuusinen in reconciling rejection of the theory with the advocacy of an uncompromising Left policy.[50] Manuilsky and Kuusinen replied to the debate in a tone far sharper than that of their original speeches: both concentrated their fire heavily on Bukharin and on his real or alleged supporters and sympathizers. Manuilsky denounced the Right, the conciliators and those who kept silent, delivered a sermon on social-Fascism, and severely criticized the waverings of the CPGB. Kuusinen followed suit in slightly less belligerent vein. He attributed the slogan "Class against Class" to Marx, and declared that the new line was simply "revolutionary class war".[51]

The main resolution on Kuusinen's and Manuilsky's reports underlined and made more specific the pronouncements and prescriptions of the sixth congress a year earlier. Renewed emphasis was placed on the contradictions of capitalism.

> In spite of the rivalry and fierce struggle within the capitalist camp, the fundamental world-wide contradiction between the capitalist world and the USSR, as the two in principle opposite

[49] *Protokoll: 10. Plenum des Exekutivkomitees der Kommunistischen Internationale* (n.d.), pp. 467–477, 544–561.

[50] *Ibid.* pp. 481–482; the debate at the sixth congress will be discussed in a later section of this volume.

[51] *Ibid.* pp. 572–633; for Manuilsky's criticism of the CPGB see pp. 391–392 below.

economic and political systems, grows ever sharper. An attack of the imperialists on the USSR is the chief danger.

The new events of the past year were the coming into power of governments headed by the SPD in Germany and by the Labour Party in Great Britain. This provided a further opportunity to identify social-democracy as a main bulwark of the bourgeoisie and enemy of communism, and to brand it as "social-Fascism". It was confidently assumed that the masses of workers, disillusioned by these proceedings, were moving rapidly towards revolution, and would flow into the communist parties, if these gave a strong lead, through "the application of new forms of the united front from below". Following the denunciation of the Right, the resolution also noted that "conciliationism, appearing as cowardly opportunism and covering open liquidationism, ... has taken on the rôle of the Right within Comintern". The "conciliators", who were not named, were called on to separate themselves from "Right deviators" and to submit to Comintern decisions.[52]

In the atmosphere of heightened tension created by Molotov's speech, a debate on tactics in "the economic struggles" was introduced by extensive reports from Thälmann and Lozovsky. Thälmann saw 1928 as a year in which the proletariat had ceased to react passively to the capitalist offensive and had experienced "a revolutionary upsurge". He depicted communist and social-democratic trade unions as engaged in a battle for the hegemony of the working class. He hailed the new tactics inaugurated in the spring of 1928 at the ninth IKKI and the fourth congress of Profintern through the application of the "united front from below" and of the slogan "class against class", and quoted Lenin in support of "political revolutionary mass strikes". He dealt at length with deviations in the KPD, but for good measure also denounced "the Yaglom–Tomsky group" in the Soviet trade unions.[53] Lozovsky was mainly concerned to emphasize "*the rôle of economic struggles in the general picture of the class war*", enumerating four stages in the process: economic strike, political strike, insurrection and civil war. He analysed different types of

[52] *Kommunisticheskii Internatsional v Dokumentakh* (1933), pp. 876–888.

[53] *Protokoll: 10. Plenum des Exekutivkomitees der Kommunistischen Internationale* (n.d.), pp. 634–680; for the passages on the KPD see p. 462 below.

strike and attempted to lay down rules for their effective conduct and leadership. He detected in the current situation "*a heightened political sensitivity of the broad masses of workers*". Lashing out at Right deviators and conciliators in all parties, he came round to the basic issues of the organization of unorganized workers and, more cautiously, of the creation of new unions. The problem was not, as the Right supposed, to gain the leadership of existing unions, but to win over the masses by setting them against the reformist leaders. Room was found in a long report for a narrative of the defeat of Tomsky and his supporters at the eighth Soviet trade union congress in December 1928, as well as for denunciation of heretics in the trade union movements of other countries.[54] The debate was desultory. Campbell of the CPGB showed some disquiet over the practical issues of the organization of unorganized workers and the formation of new trade unions, and regarded Lozovsky's formulas as "too simple and too schematic".[55] Smolyansky, a worker in Profintern, had been attacked by Lozovsky for an article in the party journal on "Trade Union Problems in the Third Period", which attempted to distinguish between the process of conquering the trade union apparatus in Fascist and in bourgeois states; Lozovsky maintained that the trade union apparatus was quite as much part of the state apparatus in one as in the other. Smolyansky now defended himself by quoting the passage in the resolution of the fourth congress of Profintern which described "the conquest of the reformist trade unions" as "the central task of adherents of Profintern"—the only hint in the debate that opposition to Lozovsky was still alive in Profintern itself.[56] Togliatti cunningly accepted "the general line of the theses", but devoted most of a long speech to the difficulties of applying them in particular countries. He accused Lozovsky of having, "in his articles and even in his report", advocated the creation of new trade unions everywhere, and of appearing to prefer "a small kernel of active

[54] *Protokoll: 10. Plenum des Exekutivkomitees der Kommunistischen Internationale* (n.d.), pp. 681–741.

[55] *Ibid.* pp. 756–761; for the situation in the CPGB see pp. 387–389 below.

[56] *Protokoll: 10. Plenum des Exekutivkomitees der Kommunistischen Internationale* (n.d.), pp. 761–764; for Lozovsky's attack see *ibid.* p. 701, and reply *ibid.* pp. 857–858. Smolyansky's article appeared in *Bol'shevik*, No. 11, June 15, 1929, pp. 71–84. For the resolution of the fourth congress of Profintern see p. 182 above.

workers" to mass trade unions — a tendency which he branded as "pure anarcho-syndicalism".[57]

The resolution, the longest of the session, had been drafted in advance in the trade union commission of IKKI, and was subject to some amendment during the session.[58] Its starting-point was recognition of "the constant *growth* of class contradictions and the *extension* of the front in the class struggle". Its sharpest sallies were reserved for the "social-Fascist trade union bureaucracy" and for the slogan of "economic democracy", described as "the official slogan of the Amsterdam International" and as "an international programme of strike-breaking". It noted "the ever increasing activity of the *unorganized* workers", and demanded, in countries where no independent revolutionary trade union movement existed, "the increased *enrolment in trade unions, on the basis of the platform of the revolutionary opposition*, of new male and female unorganized workers". Communists could not be "*in principle against splitting the trade unions*". But this none too clear injunction was further obscured by an ambiguous section on the conditions which justified the formation of new trade unions. Such action was declared to be possible "only on a rising wave of strikes, only where the political struggle has acquired great asperity, where substantial masses of workers have already *understood* the social-Fascist character of the reformist trade union bureaucracy, and where these masses actively support the creation of a new union".[59] Hesitations within the Russian party, as well as opposition in important foreign parties, still inspired some cautious reservations, and inhibited the proclamation of an all-out offensive against the social-democratic trade unions. Lozovsky was not yet in a position to enforce the aggressive policies which he had sponsored since the beginning of 1928. But the tenth IKKI of July 1929 was a further landmark on the road.[60]

[57] *Protokoll: 10. Plenum des Exekutivkomitees der Kommunistischen Internationale* (n.d.), pp. 777–788; according to Lozovsky's angry rebuttal (*ibid.* p. 854), Togliatti formulated his charges in sharper and more precise terms than appeared in the official record of his speech.

[58] *Ibid.* p. 875; neither the original draft nor the amendments have been published.

[59] *Kommunisticheskii Internatsional v Dokumentakh* (1933), pp. 888–908.

[60] At the sixth session of the central council of Profintern in December 1929 Lozovsky continued to attack "reformist atavism" in foreign trade unions and "Right deviations" in Soviet trade unions; several speakers, including Lozovsky, detected a "loss of tempo", which was interpreted to

No other major debate was held during the session. But two sittings, immediately after Kuusinen's and Manuilsky's reports and before the main debate, were devoted to a report by Barbé on preparations for the "international day" on August 1. Nothing new was said. Barbé breathed defiance of the governments which would attempt to interfere with the demonstrations, but reproached the parties with the inadequacy of their preparations. Delegates of all the principal parties hailed the proposal in conventional terms, which did not always conceal a certain lack of enthusiasm. Pyatnitsky intervened with instructions and exhortations; and Barbé in his concluding speech criticized the absence of concrete preparations in many parties.[61] In the main debate a member of the organization section of the secretariat made an attack, undeterred by interruptions from Togliatti, on the central committee of the PCI, which had passed a resolution at the end of February 1929 to the effect that work in the army "can in view of the difficulties of this work only be developed to a restricted extent".[62] Manuilsky filled the last section of his reply to the debate with protests against the weak response of the parties to the appeal for the international day and the "defensive mood" which prevailed among them; and the manifesto issued at the end of the session significantly complained of the "passivity" of "opportunist elements" on this issue.[63] In the event, though the parties obeyed the behests of Comintern and issued manifestoes and appeals, they failed to arouse the enthusiasm of the workers, or even of their own members; and such demonstrations as were held made little impact. Trotsky argued in anticipation that "the disintegration of Comintern" and "the new upsurge of social-

mean a lagging of the organization behind the masses (*Protokoll der VI Session des Zentralrats der Roten Gewerkschaftsinternationale* (1930), pp. 4–28, 79, 123, 217–218, 255–256, 273).

[61] *Protokoll: 10. Plenum des Exekutivkomitees der Kommunistischen Internationale* (n.d.), pp. 86–163; for the international day against war see p. 213 above.

[62] *Ibid.* 459–461; for this session of the central committee see pp. 555–556 below. Some Italian communists objected to the anti-war demonstrations on the plea that war would help them in their struggle against the Fascist authorities — an argument which does not appear to have occurred to any other party (L. Secchia, *L'Azione Svolta dal Partito Comunista in Italia* (1970), p. 248).

[63] *Protokoll: 10. Plenum des Exekutivkomitees der Kommunistischen Internationale* (n.d.), pp. 598–601; *Kommunisticheskii Internatsional v Dokumentakh* (1933), pp. 908–911.

democracy" had weakened the possibilities of direct revolutionary action, and that the "Red day" of August 1 was doomed to failure.[64] The eleventh congress of the CPGB in November 1929 recorded that in Great Britain "the international Red day campaign revealed all the weaknesses of our party—our isolation from the broad masses, no roots in the factories, under-estimate of the war danger and pacifist illusions".[65]

The most novel and effective resolution of the tenth IKKI was, however, one condemning Bukharin on the basis of the unpublished resolution of the Russian party central committee of April 23, 1929, and of his *Pravda* article of June 30, 1929, excluding him from further work in Comintern, and terminating his membership of the presidium of IKKI. The resolution was not debated in open session, and was obviously the product of controversial discussion behind the scenes. Remmele presented it in a perfunctory speech at the final sitting for approval in principle, with the reservation that some passages in it still needed to be "worked over" in the political secretariat. It was not published till some weeks later.[66] Sentences of expulsion were also pronounced or confirmed on prominent dissidents in other parties. Humbert-Droz, having refused pressing invitations from Manuilsky and Kuusinen to speak in reply to the attacks made on him during the session, addressed a letter to IKKI on July 15, 1929, expressing loyalty and "absolute discipline" in regard to decisions of Comintern and its organs, even when they did not coincide with his "personal opinion". He was, however, dropped from the presidium and the political secretariat. Shortly afterwards, under threat of expulsion from the party, he signed a humble declaration confessing his errors and his "fractional attitude", and undertaking to comform to the party line, "not only by discipline, but being fundamentally convinced that it is the only possible, and therefore the only just, policy in the present situation".[67]

[64] *Byulleten' Oppozitsii* (Paris), No. 1–2, July 1929, pp. 32–36.

[65] *Resolutions of the 11th Congress of the CPGB* (n.d.), p. 13.

[66] *Protokoll: 10. Plenum der Exekutivkomitees der Kommunistischen Internationale* (n.d.), pp. 876–877; for the resolution and its publication see Vol. 2, pp. 95–96.

[67] J. Humbert-Droz, *De Lénine à Staline* (Neuchatel, 1971), pp. 398–401.

In Comintern, as in the Russian party, Bukharin's downfall and disgrace coincided with the adoption both of tougher and more uncompromising policies and of a more rigidly enforced standard of conformity; the changes, if not directly promoted by Stalin, matched the ruthless determination and narrow suspiciousness of his temperament. No fixed moment in time, no particular incident, marked the turning-point. The erosion of the comparative diversity of Lenin's Comintern had already set in when the fifth congress in 1924 proclaimed the "Bolshevization" of the parties.[68] The span of four years which elapsed before another congress of Comintern — in Lenin's days, an annual event — was convened, advertised the fact that major decisions were now taken on the responsibility of IKKI and its secretariat, which served, under a thin international veneer, as the foreign department of the Russian party. The process of welding a diversity of parties into a single unified and disciplined whole was progressive. It gained momentum from the fear in Moscow that successive oppositions in the Russian party would enlist sympathizers in foreign communist parties — a fear that could be allayed only by insisting that these parties should give unanimous and unconditional support to the Soviet leaders in their struggle against the opposition, and that any member refusing such allegiance should be expelled forthwith. The monolithic character bred in the Russian party by the struggle against the opposition was thus extended to Comintern and to its individual parties. The result of these pressures was to build up in all principal parties, by a dual process of encouragement and exclusion, a group of leaders bound to Moscow by ties of self-interest as well as of loyalty, since any revolt against the authority of Comintern would be also a revolt against their authority. From 1929 onwards discipline was on the whole maintained within the parties. Overt recourse to the central organs of Comintern was unnecessary, and publicity and scandal were avoided. The parties were no longer independent entities, but, what they had always been in name, "sections" of Comintern enjoying a strictly limited autonomy.

This solution provided, however, no escape from the dilemma which had confronted Comintern ever since 1920, when the "twenty-one conditions" of admission were discussed and im-

[68] See *Socialism in One Country, 1924–1926*, Vol. 3, pp. 92–94.

posed by its second congress.[69] The Bolshevik conception of revolution was international; its standard-bearer and chosen instrument must be an international organization. The bankruptcy of the Second International had resulted from its failure to make its decisions binding on its member parties and to ensure that they were carried out. No such blemish must mar the prospects of the Third International. When, however, as was inevitable in the conditions of the nineteen-twenties, the congresses and the central organs of Comintern were increasingly subjected to the predominant influence of the Russian party, or, as the struggle against the opposition became acute, of the Russian party leaders, the dilemma assumed a new and more insidious form. The decisions of Comintern could be, and were, imposed on the parties, but only at the cost of alienating a larger and larger number of workers in the countries concerned, who failed to respond to what seemed the wilful and sometimes plainly inappropriate dictates of a remote and alien authority. The British and American parties remained small sects, which had no mass following, and attracted a decreasing number of sympathizers. In Germany, France and Czechoslovakia, mass communist parties effectively split the workers' movement, but never succeeded in dominating it. At the end of the nineteen-twenties they still waged war against the social-democrats in increasingly unfavourable conditions. Everywhere the strengthening of the links that bound party leaders to Moscow weakened their hold on the rank and file of the workers.

[69] See *The Bolshevik Revolution, 1917–1923*, Vol. 3, pp. 193–195.

CHAPTER 73

AUXILIARY BODIES

THE auxiliary organizations sponsored or supported by Comintern, in which communists cooperated with non-communists for specific purposes, and which thus indirectly served the ultimate promotion of communist aims, reached their peak in the middle nineteen-twenties, when international relations were still in the period of relative *détente* inaugurated in 1921, and when united front policies interpreted in the broadest sense were still popular in Moscow. The climate of opinion changed gradually. The first symptoms appeared in different contexts at different dates. But by 1927, when both tensions in the party and international tensions were at their height, and when mistrust of social-democrats and other parties of the Left had become acute, the future of the auxiliary bodies was clouded. Mutual recriminations between communists and non-communists of the Left in Germany, Great Britain, France and other European countries, reached new levels of exasperation; and, though feelings between leaders were more embittered than in the rank and file of the parties, they were an effective bar to cooperation. Moreover, as the crisis sharpened, Comintern, through the formation within these organizations of communist fractions subject to party instructions,[1] increasingly sought to deprive their communist members of all freedom of action, insisting on their rigid adherence to changing directives from Moscow, so that, with the turn to the Left in Comintern, the auxiliary bodies became no longer organs of cooperation, but platforms from which communists enunciated their uncompromising doctrines and policies. For a short period it seemed as if *ad hoc* "front" organizations — the League against Imperialism

[1] New articles inserted in the statute of Comintern at the sixth congress in July 1928 made the formation of such fractions mandatory (*Kommunisticheskii Internatsional v Dokumentakh* (1933), p. 47); Pyatnitsky explained that, when the statute was last revised by the fifth congress in 1924, such fractions did not exist (*Stenograficheskii Otchet VI Kongressa Kominterna* (1929), v, 108).

being the most successful example—in which communists, though active behind the scenes, left the centre of the stage to other Left-wing groups or parties, might serve as a more effective substitute for permanent auxiliary bodies. But they too were soon subject to the same process of erosion. By the end of 1929 the practice of cooperation with non-communists in joint organizations had been virtually abandoned; and the auxiliary bodies originally formed to give effect to it dwindled into insignificance.

(*a*) *The Communist Youth International* (*KIM*)

The falling-off of the communist youth movement noted in the spring of 1926[2] was diagnosed in Moscow as the result of its neglect by communist parties. But to revitalize the youth leagues as an independent force at a time when the main object was to mobilize their support in the campaign against the opposition was an uphill task. In July 1926 the presidium of IKKI passed a resolution calling for more support from parties for the movement, and for the formation of groups and cells of youth leagues whereever party groups or cells existed; a noteworthy feature of the resolution was the omission of any reference to KIM.[3] The sixth session of the executive committee of KIM (IKKIM) opened on November 10, 1926, in advance of the seventh IKKI.[4] Shatskin's main report was concerned with the struggle against the opposition in the VKP(B) and its allies in foreign parties. The sole dissentient seems to have been the Czech delegate Michaleč, who defended the opposition declaration of October 16, 1926. He was denounced by a succession of speakers; and the official resolution began bravely by proclaiming that, after a period of temporary depression, the communist youth movement was "now undoubtedly again on the path of progress and consolidation". It anticipated many of the points made in the resolution of the seventh IKKI. It condemned Michaleč and Vujovič by name. It gave its blessing to united front tactics (especially to visits of non-party youth delegations to the Soviet Union), but admitted

[2] See *Socialism in One Country, 1924–1926*, Vol. 3, pp. 996–997. For the constitutional relation of KIM to Comintern see *ibid.* Vol. 3, p. 987 note 2; but, whatever its formal status, it had by 1926 lost the last vestiges of independence, and become in fact an auxiliary organization.

[3] *Internationale Presse-Korrespondenz*, No. 93, July 13, 1926, p. 1523.

[4] For the seventh IKKI see pp. 132–142 above.

that these tactics had sometimes led to "gross opportunist errors". It referred to "the growing danger of war" and proclaimed the slogan:

> Defence of the Soviet Union against attacks of the imperialists; the Soviet Union is the only fatherland of the workers of all countries.

It attacked "capitalist rationalization" and its consequences. Finally, it expressed regret that the July appeal of the presidium of IKKI had not met with an adequate response, and that relations between parties and leagues were still unsatisfactory. But it encountered some embarrassment in defining these relations:

> The enlarged IKKIM considers it obligatory for all sections of KIM to recognize leadership by the party and party discipline. Only in cases when the line of this or that party differs from the line or from the directives of the Communist International, or diverges from them, the Communist Youth League cannot and should not, in the struggle for the Bolshevik line, allow itself to be bound by party discipline (for example, in the May days in Poland), remembering that the discipline of the Communist International is more rigorously binding than the discipline of the party.[5]

A few days later, however, Kuusinen at the seventh IKKI spoke with little enthusiasm of the achievements of KIM, and complained that "our youth movement at present has too little attraction for non-party youth". Later in the proceedings, a spokesman of KIM, without challenging these criticisms, proclaimed the complete loyalty of the organization to Comintern and its rejection of the opposition, mentioning Vujovič and Michalec̆ as the only two dissenters: both of these had been condemned.[6]

After the lull in party affairs in the first months of 1927, KIM was quickly drawn into the crisis caused by the Chinese dis-

[5] R. Schüller *et al.*, *Geschichte der Kommunistischen Internationale*, iii (1930), 208–221; the proceedings were briefly reported in *Internationale Presse-Korrespondenz*, No. 141, November 19, 1926, pp. 2451–2455; *The Young Communist International: Between the Fourth and Fifth Congresses* (1928), pp. 129–130. Vujovič had already been excluded from work in KIM (see Vol. 2, p. 12), and presumably did not attend the session of IKKIM. For the declaration of October 16, 1926, see Vol. 2, p. 15; for the Polish "May error" see pp. 563–566 below.

[6] *Puti Mirovoi Revolyutsii* (1927), i, 123, ii, 257–262.

asters and the breach in Anglo-Soviet diplomatic relations in April and May. As early as December 1926 the British Young Communist League at its congress in Sheffield proclaimed its support for the Chinese revolution; it afterwards claimed to have distributed leaflets among soldiers and sailors destined for China, and sent propagandists to the ports where they were to embark.[7] The seventh IKKIM sat from June 18 to 27, 1927. After Shatskin had opened the session, Manuilsky delivered a two-day report on the results of the eighth IKKI in the previous month. At the end of what was reported as "a lively discussion", the committee unanimously passed a resolution endorsing the conclusions of IKKI on the international situation and its condemnation of Trotsky and Vujovič.[8] This was followed by a report of Schüller on the danger of imperialist war, and a further report on "the tasks and methods" of work in armies, leading up to a long resolution which was distinguished by some nuances, above all, by a sense of personal involvement, from the corresponding pronouncements of Comintern. It protested "*against the danger of imperialist war and against militarism*", as well as "*against the obligatory military training of the young*" as "part of the imperialist army system". Quoting an observation of Liebknecht that "he who has the young, has the army", it stressed the importance of "*practical and regular work in the army and navy*", but issued a warning against pacificism, which was said to have permeated the American youth league. It called on KIM for "a mighty and active campaign of solidarity with the Soviet Union and the Chinese revolution". United front tactics were to be applied in the struggle against the imperialist war and for the defence of the Russian and Chinese revolutions, but combined with exposure of the bankruptcy of the Socialist Youth International and of the treachery of its social-democratic leaders. This meant that joint youth committees might be formed locally and in factories for "broad masses of workers", but not centrally. Finally, it was important to build up strong organizations "in centres of the armaments industry and in ports", but—it was cryptically added—to resist attempts by the bourgeoisie "to drive KIM

[7] *The Young Communist International: Between the Fourth and Fifth Congresses* (1928), p. 135.

[8] *Internationale Presse-Korrespondenz*, No. 64, June 21, 1927, p. 1655, No. 74, July 22, 1927, p. 159; for the eighth IKKI see pp. 143–147 above.

altogether into illegality".[9] It seems to have been the most detailed public pronouncement on these questions up to this time. The seventh IKKIM adopted a resolution on the British youth league, whose central function, in the light of the breach in Anglo-Soviet diplomatic relations, consisted in "performing its rôle as leader of the young in the struggle against imperialist war".[10] It adopted resolutions on the trade union question, and on the education of the young. On the latter issue it rejected social-democratic demands for the extension of education to the age of sixteen on the ground that this was a device to "conceal" the problem of unemployment and stave off the competition of young workers. Education should be extended "to the age of 16 and further", but should be conducted in schools attached to places of production, and those in training should receive payment.[11]

While, however, IKKIM and the central machinery of KIM functioned with formal efficiency as a junior auxiliary of Comintern,[12] less success attended efforts to breathe fresh life into the communist youth leagues. The main work of KIM, apart from assistance rendered to Comintern in the defeat and elimination of the opposition, was to galvanize support among the youth leagues for campaigns initiated by Comintern, notably the campaign against imperialist war.[13] Visits of young workers' delegates to the Soviet Union were organized.[14] International Youth Day was celebrated with speeches and processions on the first Sunday of every September.[15] The activity of KIM was subordinated to that of Profintern in such issues as strikes, unemployment and rationalization in capitalist countries.[16] Attempts to promote participation by youth leagues in non-party mass organizations came to little, except perhaps in sport.[17] But Shatskin,

[9] *Internationale Presse-Korrespondenz,* No. 65, June 24, 1927, p. 1381; No. 75, July 26, 1927, pp. 1608–1611.

[10] *Ibid.* No. 77, August 2, 1927, pp. 1660–1662.

[11] *Internationale Presse-Korrespondenz,* No. 80, August 9, 1927, pp. 1742–1745; for the advocacy of factory schools by the Russian Komsomol see Vol. 1, pp. 479–480.

[12] For the status of KIM see p. 260, note 2 above.

[13] *The Young Communist International: Between the Fourth and Fifth Congresses* (1928), pp. 8–32.

[14] *Ibid.* pp. 43–48.

[15] *Ibid.* pp. 138–142.

[16] See pp. 186–187 above.

[17] The delegate of the British league to the sixth congress of Comintern in July 1928 dilated on relations between KIM and Sportintern (for which see

speaking on KIM at the fifteenth party congress in December 1927, admitted "difficulties", including a reduction in numbers in many organizations and the disappearance of some.[18] Youth leagues fell at this time into three categories. Leagues functioning legally in important countries numbered ten; sixteen leagues in smaller or remoter countries furnished only occasional information; seventeen leagues, including all those in Asia, led an illegal existence. Comprehensive totals of membership of all leagues other than the Soviet Komsomol were quoted: 117,621 for June 1927, 95,200 for December 1927 (the drop being explained by repressions against the Chinese, Italian, Yugoslav and Bulgarian leagues), and 127,232 for mid-1928.[19]

With the atmosphere of crisis and apprehension thickening in Moscow, the leaders of KIM clearly felt that more was required. As usual, they attributed failure to defects in organization; and in January 1928 an international organization conference of KIM was summoned in Berlin—the *venue* being a tribute to the importance of the German league. The conference found that stagnation in membership was a general phenomenon; only the Swedish league had significantly increased in numbers. Great fluctuations in membership were a feature of all leagues. Resolutions were passed on the improvement of methods of recruiting, on the need for periodical organization conferences, and on the principle of organization by cells.[20] The eighth IKKIM immediately followed the ninth IKKI in February 1928. Its main

Socialism in One Country, 1924–1926, Vol. 3, pp. 965–967), but aroused no response (*Stenograficheskii Otchet VI Kongressa Kominterna* (1929), i, 398–399).

[18] *Pyatnadtsatyi S"ezd VKP(B)*, i (1961), 729.

[19] *The Young Communist International: Between the Fourth and Fifth Congresses* (1928), pp. 143–144. The numbers in various youth leagues were returned in 1929 as follows: Germany 22,000, Sweden 14,000, Czechoslovakia 10,000 ("in reality only 5000 paying members"), France 8000, United States 3479, Great Britain 900 (*Protokoll: 10. Plenum des Exekutivkomitees der Kommunistischen Internationale* (n.d.), pp. 264–265). The German youth league was the largest, most active and most independent of the leagues; it spawned a para-military organization, the Roter Jungsturm, which stood to it in the same relation as the Roter Frontkämpferbund to the party, and with 25,000 members eclipsed the league itself in numbers, exciting some feelings of rivalry and jealousy (*Jugendinternationale*, No. 6, February 1927, p. 17).

[20] Information is derived from a brief account of the conference in *The Young Communist International: Between the Fourth and Fifth Congresses* (1928), pp. 134–137, and from resolutions of the eighth IKKIM a month later endorsing its results (see below).

resolution specifically declared its adhesion to the conclusions of the senior organ, which it proceeded with some variation of emphasis to endorse, trouncing the defeated opposition in the Russian party, hailing the intensified struggle against social-democracy "on an international scale", and calling for "a strengthened support of the Comintern line". It repeated previous pronouncements on the danger of imperialist war and work in the armies, dealt once more with the perennial trade union question, and announced the creation of a Western European Bureau of KIM.[21] Like IKKI, it passed separate resolutions and on the trade unions and the Chinese revolution.[22] A further resolution approved the work of the organization conference of the previous month in Berlin and the conclusions reached by that conference.[23] With the opposition now crushed, and the major congresses of Comintern and KIM impending in the summer, it seems to have been a routine occasion. Shatskin, at the eighth Komsomol congress in May 1928, complained that IKKI "takes very little interest in what goes on in KIM", and admitted that the Komsomol passed resolutions about it and failed to carry them out.[24]

When the sixth congress of Comintern assembled on July 17, 1928, a compliment was paid to KIM by allowing its chief delegate Schüller to make a long report immediately after Bukharin's opening report on the work of IKKI. The speech contained the usual blend of eulogy, criticism and exhortation, and broke no fresh ground.[25] In the ensuing debate, Vasiliev, a delegate of IKKI, drew attention to the poor membership record of the youth leagues and discounted their claim to be regarded as

[21] *Internationale Presse-Korrespondenz*, No. 34, April 3, 1928, pp. 634–636, No. 35, April 5, 1928, pp. 647–648; for the ninth IKKI see pp. 163–165, 175–176 above.

[22] Chinese affairs will be discussed in a later section of this volume.

[23] *Internationale Presse-Korrespondenz*, No. 39, April 20, 1928, pp. 707–710.

[24] *VIII Vsesoyuznyi S"ezd VLKSM* (1928), pp. 297–298; a spokesman of KIM at the tenth IKKI in July 1929 said that he could not remember a representative of Comintern ever visiting the offices of KIM during his four years of work there (*Protokoll: 10. Plenum des Exekutivkomitees der Kommunistischen Internationale* (n.d.), p. 277). Jealousy between the Komsomol and the Soviet trade unions may explain the absence of any reference to KIM in the debates of the fourth congress of Profintern in March 1928 on problems of juvenile labour (see pp. 186–187 above).

[25] *Stenograficheskii Otchet VI Kongressa Kominterna* (1928), i, 64–94.

mass organizations. Thälmann invoked "the anti-militarist traditions of proletarian youth and of the Komsomol in the struggle against imperialist war".[26] Khitarov formally announced the acceptance by the KIM delegation of Bukharin's theses, and declared that KIM "has always been one of the most faithful props of Comintern". But he vigorously rejected any "limitation of our political activity", and claimed for KIM "the right to speak on particular party questions, to state our opinion, and to instruct our leagues in the appropriate spirit".[27] While several representatives of youth leagues spoke, Schüller in his concluding speech complained that no party leader except Thälmann had displayed any interest in the youth movement, which he described, on the basis of quotations from Lenin, as "a mass school of communism".[28] The main resolution of the congress exhorted KIM to extend and improve its methods of work and recruitment, and cited participation in mass organizations, including trade unions, and "anti-militarist work" as its principal tasks, but significantly warned it "to avoid ... attempts to usurp the place of the party in the leadership of the working class (so-called avant-garde movements)".[29] KIM and the youth leagues, no less than the communist parties themselves, were subject to firm discipline from above.

The fifth congress of KIM was convened on August 20, 1928, before the Comintern congress had run its course. *Pravda* in a leading article expressed confidence that "the most important questions of the international revolutionary movement worked over by Comintern" would form the starting point of its labours.[30] After a formal opening, at which speeches were made by Khitarov, Bukharin and Thälmann,[31] the regular sittings began on August 28 and continued till September 18, 1928. The debates seem to have produced few novelties.[32] Bukharin reappeared on September 8, 1928, to make a report on the sixth congress of Comintern

[26] *Ibid.* i, 125–127, 346. [27] *Ibid.* i, 351–355. [28] *Ibid.* i, 575–587.

[29] *Kommunisticheskii Internatsional v Dokumentakh* (1933), pp. 783–784.

[30] *Pravda*, August 10, 1928.

[31] *Ibid.* August 21, 1928.

[32] They were summarized at some length in *Internationale Presse-Korrespondenz*, No. 94, August 1, 1928, p. 1751, No. 97, September 4, 1928, p. 1851, No. 98, September 7, 1928, pp. 1867–1869, No. 101, September 11, 1928, pp. 1915–1918, No. 103, September 14, 1928, pp. 1981–1982, No. 105, September 18, 1928, pp. 2025–2026, No. 106, September 21, 1928, pp. 2039–2042; for some of the major speeches see *ibid.* No. 121, October 30, 1928, pp. 2367–2402.

which had now ended; and a resolution was promptly passed that "the decisions of the Comintern congress will form the basis for the labours and the decisions of the fifth world congress of KIM and for the activity of all its sections in the time to come".[33] Apart from a long general resolution covering most of the issues raised at the congress,[34] an "anti-war" resolution, a colonial resolution, and resolutions on work in the trade unions and in sport were passed; and, following the precedent of Comintern, a new programme and statute were adopted. Khitarov wound up the proceedings with the assurance that "the young soldiers of communism will be the best campaigners against imperialist war and the best defenders of the Soviet Union and the colonial peoples".[35] The official history of KIM admitted that, in the four years which separated the fifth from the fourth congress, the youth leagues had proved unable "to mobilize around themselves the broad masses of young workers, ... and in this way to draw them into the struggle for the goals of the proletariat". The claim that the fifth congress "inspired all the sections of KIM with new energy, and directed their work to the field of true communist mass work among the young workers" rests on a doubtful foundation.[36]

Little was said at the Congress about relations between youth leagues and communist parties. The question whether the chain of command from IKKI to the youth leagues passed through IKKIM or through the parties was never formally resolved. It ceased to be significant when all spoke with a single voice. But the principle was enunciated in the statute of KIM in uncompromising terms:

> The political activity of a communist youth league is subordinate nationally to the communist party of the country concerned. In the event of differences, the communist youth league adheres to the decisions of the Communist International

[33] *Ibid.* No. 101, September 11, 1928, p. 1918.

[34] *Ibid.* No. 120, October 26, 1928, pp. 2362–2363, No. 122, October 30, 1928, pp. 2417–2418, No. 123, November 2, 1928, pp. 2449–2451; R. Schüller *et al.*, *Geschichte der Kommunistischen Jugendinternationale*, iii (1930), 227–238.

[35] *Internationale Presse-Korrespondenz*, No. 121, October 30, 1928, pp. 2400, 2402; for the text of the statute see *The Young Communist International: Between the Fourth and Fifth Congresses* (1928), pp. 233–238.

[36] R. Schüller *et al.*, *Geschichte der Kommunistischen Jugendinternationale*, iii (1930), 103, 132.

and the Communist Youth International, and places international discipline above national party discipline.

Fidelity to the decisions taken in Moscow was the key-note of the congress. It was noteworthy that, when Comintern sought to utilize the British and French youth leagues and their leaders in an effort to defeat a refractory so-called Right wing in the leadership of the British and French parties,[37] it dealt directly with the individuals, and organizations concerned, and that KIM was effectively by-passed in these transactions.

Fidelity to Comintern and to its policies continued to be the watch-word of KIM. Its customary manifesto for May 1, 1929, gave precedence to political slogans ("Against the imperialist war", "Defence of the Soviet Union", "Support of the oppressed colonial peoples", and "Down with social-democracy") over such questions as hours of work, paid holidays, and "equal pay for equal work".[38] But the realities were less reassuring. The struggle against the Right deviation in the Russian party, and the discrediting of Bukharin, had shaken many communist parties; and the effect on the youth leagues had been still more disastrous, even where their leaders had been recruited to support the official line. Even the Soviet Komsomol did not escape the shock.[39] The curtain was lifted on the embarrassments of the situation at the tenth IKKI in July 1929. Khitarov, speaking on behalf of the presidium of KIM, asserted his independence by some unusually sharp criticisms of Manuilsky, whom he accused of an insufficiently critical attitude to the Right. Then, turning to the affairs of KIM, he complained that previous speakers had referred to it "with a smile and with the wish to stick pins into us somewhere"; and he rejected the theory said to have been propounded by some Comintern leaders at the time of the sixth congress that the youth movement should be "depoliticized". He referred to the great waverings in the German youth league in the previous autumn, and added that "certain hesitations in regard to the party line" had persisted, though he appeared to assume that they had now been cured. He ended, however, with the damning admission that the development of the leagues "lags behind events", and that "their system of work

[37] See pp. 381, 393–394, 503, note 144 below.

[38] *Internationale Presse-Korrespondenz*, No. 35, April 23, 1929, p. 826.

[39] See Vol. 2, p. 177.

and leadership is a backward, and in large measure a social-democratic, one".[40] Pyatnitsky launched a sweeping attack on KIM and the youth leagues, alleging that nothing had been done to carry out the behests of the sixth congress, and that the numbers of all the principal leagues had declined since that date. He argued that, while recruitment for the youth league was "broader" than for a party, since young workers were admitted "without any conditions", the recruits were young and had no previous social-democratic traditions, so that KIM could "inoculate them more easily with communism". A delegate of KIM lamented "the absence of mass youth organizations".[41] A brief exhortation to the youth leagues to engage in more "work among the masses" figured in the resolution of the session.[42] But the troubles were not yet over. In September 1929 the whole leadership of the turbulent German communist youth league was replaced. Two months later, when IKKIM held its next session, the total membership of all leagues, other than the Komsomol, was less than 90,000, or, according to another estimate, 72,000.[43] The dilemma of many foreign communist parties confronted the youth leagues in an intensified form. Mass recruitment on a large scale encouraged dissentient opinions. Insistence on rigid conformity was an obstacle to recruiting. Few of the leagues possessed much vitality; and KIM was perforce more often concerned to restrain than to inspire.

(b) *International Workers' Aid (MRP)*

The British general strike and miners' strike proved to be a landmark in the operations of MRP. To dispense relief to those overtaken by great natural calamities like the Russian famine or the Japanese earthquake, or to striking workers, as in Germany in the winter of 1923–1924,[44] had been a main function of the

[40] *Protokoll: 10. Plenum des Exekutivkomitees der Kommunistischen Internationale* (n.d.), pp. 209–216. For the trouble in the German youth league see p. 448 below; for "de-politicization" as an issue in the Komsomol see Vol. 2, pp. 167–168.

[41] *Protokoll: 10. Plenum des Exekutivkomitees der Kommunistischen Internationale* (n.d.), pp. 264–268, 356.

[42] *Kommunisticheskii Internatsional v Dokumentakh* (1933), p. 888.

[43] *IX S"ezd VLKSM* (1931), pp. 221–226, 251. For the 1928 figures see p. 264, note 19 above.

[44] See *Socialism in One Country, 1924–1926*, Vol. 3, p. 945.

organization. Within a few hours of the proclamation of the general strike in Great Britain, the central committee of MRP in Berlin sent out an appeal to all its members to organize support of all kinds for the strikers, and, when the general strike collapsed, aid was continued for the now isolated miners.[45] On September 12, 1926, the fifth anniversary of the foundation of MRP, the central committee of the organization in Berlin announced that, of the 40 million gold marks (20 million rubles or £2 million) collected during the five years of its existence, 11 millions had been collected for the British miners.[46] In Czechoslovakia MRP collected for the miners one million korun, and in France 47 million francs.[47] A list of contributions from various German districts amounting in all to nearly 120,000 marks was published, with Berlin responsible for almost half.[48] The British section of MRP attempted to work in collaboration with humanitarian organizations such as the Friends' Relief and the Save the Children Fund, which provided relief in cash and in kind to unemployed workers and their families, and does not seem to have made independent collections. These events strengthened the already existing links of MRP with the trade unions.[49] British, South African, Chinese and Japanese, as well as Soviet, trade unions were named as having taken out collective membership of MRP. These arrangements enabled Münzenberg in the summer of 1926 to claim for MRP a total membership of 15 millions, with sections in all the countries of Europe and North America, as well as in Argentina, Australia, South Africa, India, China and Japan.[50]

[45] For several letters of appeal and of thanks for sums received see W. Münzenberg, *Solidarität* (1931), pp. 291–299.

[46] *Internationale Presse-Korrespondenz*, No. 113, September 10, 1926, pp. 1918–1919.

[47] W. Münzenberg, *Solidarität* (1931), pp. 396, 398.

[48] *Ibid.* p. 354.

[49] A letter signed by Korostelov as "president of the MRP section attached to the Russian trade union central committee", referred to the contributions sent to the British TUC on May 5 (250,000 rubles) and on May 7, 1926 (2 million rubles) as the product of "our collections carried out jointly with the Russian trade unions" (*ibid.* p. 291); for these contributions see p. 318 below. A report of the party control commission of 1925 noted that responsibility for "the political representation of MRP in the USSR" rested on the trade union central council (quoted from archives in S. Vygodsky, *Vneshnyaya Politika SSSR* (1963), p. 340).

[50] *Internationale Presse-Korrespondenz*, No. 113, September 10, 1926, pp. 1918–1919, No. 137, November 12, 1926, p. 2391. For the foundation of the Chinese section of MRP in 1925, a letter from its committee to the central

The year 1927 was the last in which joint action and joint demonstrations by communist and radical sympathizers could be conducted in an atmosphere of mutual confidence. Münzenberg was the prime mover in the foundation of the League against Imperialism at its congress at Brussels in February 1927, though MRP as an organization was only peripherally concerned.[51] MRP was extensively involved in the Sacco–Vanzetti campaign in August 1927, its particular function being to organize appeals by well-known intellectuals and artists in many countries pleading for clemency and protesting against the executions.[52] The international tensions of the year, however, and in particular the increasingly bitter rift between the communists and the reformist trade unions reacted disastrously on the kind of cooperation which MRP had set out to promote. Mutual vilification precluded partnership even for specific and limited purposes. The few Left-wing radicals who still tried to bridge the rift lost credit on both sides. Social-democratic parties and reformist trade unions rigorously enforced the ban on membership of MRP or MOPR; and Münzenberg in the summer of 1926 boasted that MRP was "one of the organizations best hated by social-democrats".[53] On the other hand, mistrust began to be felt in some circles in Moscow for an organization which, thanks to Münzenberg's enterprise and fund-raising capacities, retained an independence of party or Comintern control unknown in other auxiliary organizations. Kuusinen at the seventh IKKI in November 1926 had to defend

committee of MRP in Berlin, and a monster demonstration of 200,000 workers in Peking see W. Münzenberg, *Solidarität* (1931), pp. 458–462; the central committee of the CCP at its session in July 1926 passed a resolution that the work of MRP should remain under party direction "in terms of policy", but that the highest posts should be held by "non-party Leftist elements"; party members working in it should comprise not more than one-third of its staff, and should adopt a "grey", i.e. not specifically party, attitude in matters of propaganda (*Documents on Nationalism, Communism, and Soviet Advisers in China*, ed. Wilbur and Howe (1956), pp. 313–317).

[51] For this congress see pp. 296–301 below.

[52] W. Münzenberg, *Solidarität* (1931), pp. 337–340.

[53] *Internationale Presse-Korrespondenz*, No. 94, July 16, 1926, p. 1539. As early as 1924, the third congress of Profintern noted that the reformists "have started a furious campaign against MRP because it aids strikers" (*Desyat' Let Profinterna v Rezolyutsiyakh* (1931), pp. 139–140); and four years later the reformist trade union leaders "fought by every means" against MRP support for striking German metal workers (*Die Internationale*, xi, No. 5, March 1, 1928, p. 139).

it against unnamed comrades who might think it "superfluous".[54]

Immediately after the celebrations of the tenth anniversary of the revolution, on November 20–22, 1927, an international congress of MRP was held in Berlin, and opened, in Münzenberg's phrase, a new "chapter in the history" of the organization. Delegates of some twenty countries attended the congress, including a Negro railway worker from Sierra Leone and a representative of the Kuomintang Left. Three delegates of the Soviet trade unions were refused visas, and failed to arrive. Goldschmidt, the German professor who had figured at the Brussels congress of the League against Imperialism, presided; Ledebour appears to have been the only outstanding political personality. Münzenberg, reporting on six years of achievement, announced the main theme of the congress:

> Side by side with the old unalterable tasks of MRP is the new great and important task, the serious revolutionary work of MRP in the social-political field.

What this meant was revealed in a debate on relations with the World Relief Organization recently established by the League of Nations. It was pointed out that the statute of the organization contained a clause permitting it to intervene only with the approval of the League of Nations; this was held to prove that its supposed political neutrality was a sham. Successive speakers urged MRP to "break the monopoly" of bourgeois relief organizations, and stressed its political aims. These were defined in the resolution of the congress:

> In opposition to bourgeois welfare organizations, the Salvation Army and social-democratic workers' welfare, MRP is a proletarian relief organization, upheld by the broad masses of workers, with the one and only purpose of helping the workers in their great economic struggles and in times of mass need and mass misery.

The emphasis on aid to workers on strike was carried over into a resolution on relations with the trade unions. MRP was "no trade union, and no substitute for a trade union". But the failure of the trade unions to finance aid in long economic struggles, or to take

[54] *Puti Mirovoi Revolyutsii* (1927), i, 124.

account of the unorganized workers, showed that trade union action was not enough.

> In the correct recognition of this fact [continued the resolution] MRP has included in its programme the mobilization of the financial and moral resources of all workers far beyond the framework of trade union organization, of the peasants, the intellectuals and petty bourgeois strata, to support such economic mass struggles and gigantic strikes.

A report on the visit of an international MRP delegation to the Soviet Union for the anniversary celebrations kept the achievements of the revolution, and the challenge to emulate them, well in view.[55] Thälmann wrote an enthusiastic article in which he exhorted all communists to join MRP and "support with all their power this truly proletarian auxiliary organization for the class struggle".[56]

These belligerent gestures did not save MRP from attack at a time when the Comintern line was swerving strongly to the Left, and social-democrats were denounced as the worst enemies of communism. At the sixth congress of Comintern in July 1928 Münzenberg found himself for the first time on the defensive. Bukharin in his main report had referred in passing to "sympathizing organizations", but mentioned only Krestintern and the League against Imperialism, and admitted that the latter was vulnerable to criticism.[57] Münzenberg pleaded that Comintern had hitherto always advocated "work and agitation in auxiliary and mass organizations"—work which some comrades now regarded as "semi-Menshevik, or at best work of an inferior order", and described as "opportunist policy" or "a 'Right' deviation". MRP and MOPR, "non-communist organizations, but under our influence", were not in themselves mass organizations, like the trade unions or the cooperatives, but they created "points of contact". "We want," exclaimed Münzenberg, "to interest the millions of indifferent workers who live apathetically, who have never taken part in political events." In this respect, the cultural activities of MRP were also important: the film "Battle-

[55] W. Münzenberg, *Solidarität* (1931), pp. 183–187.

[56] *Internationale Presse-Korrespondenz*, No. 9, January 27, 1928, pp. 177–178.

[57] *Stenograficheskii Otchet VI Kongressa Kominterna* (1929), i, 55–56.

ship Potemkin" had been seen by 5 million workers.[58] MRP was included in the resolution on Bukharin's report with other auxiliary organizations, which communists were urged to join, support and assist. But, unlike MOPR, it was not honoured by a special resolution devoted to it.[59]

In the summer of 1928 the climate in Moscow was already unfavourable not only to loose interpretations of the united front, but to the kind of independence which Münzenberg's ingenuity and initiative had enabled him to establish for himself. Münzenberg, a communist by conviction, nevertheless moved most easily among fellow-travellers. This aptitude was no longer consonant with the moods and policies of the Comintern leaders, and Münzenberg's personal position was undermined. The headquarters of MRP remained in Berlin. But after the congress of November 1927 no further conferences of the organization were held there; and the Moscow office, directed by a faithful official of MRP and of Comintern, an Italian *émigré* and an old Bolshevik named Misiano, apparently became more important.[60] Münzenberg's talents were, however, not yet exhausted. The anti-Fascist congress in Berlin in February 1929,[61] though nominally organized by an independent committee, seems to have been his brain-child; and the congress in a resolution paid its tribute to the work of MRP:

> In the openly terrorist countries MRP with its many-sided contacts and its international position can render extraordinarily important services in supporting mass strikes and other

[58] *Ibid.* i, 101–106.

[59] *Kommunisticheskii Internatsional v Dokumentakh* (1933), p. 784; for the resolution on MOPR see p. 279 below.

[60] According to B. Gross, *Willi Münzenberg* (1967), p. 189, the office was run by Misiano, Shalito, the Latin American Jewish editor of its news-sheet, an Austrian office manager, and a Russian accountant; Misiano was apparently a faithful follower and disciple of Münzenberg. A photograph of the imposing Moscow premises of MRP (though not, significantly of the Berlin headquarters) appeared in W. Münzenberg, *Solidarität* (1931), facing p. 433; the same building presumably also housed the Soviet section of MRP. Both Misiano and Korostelev, head of the Soviet section of MRP, had been elected to the central committee at the Berlin congress of December 1927 (*Voprosy Istorii*, No. 11, 1968, p. 190). A. Tivel and M. Kheimo, *Desyat' Let Kominterna v Tsifrakh* (1929), p. 370, lists as organs of MRP a central committee (no place of meeting named), and an executive committee and general secretariat located in Berlin.

[61] See pp. 310–313 below.

mass movements, as well as the "legality campaigns" of trade union and other workers' organizations.[62]

The twelfth congress of the KPD in June 1929 heard a stout defence by Münzenberg of his position, which doubtless found many sympathizers in his audience:

> There are a few comrades who say: It is a contradiction that Willi Münzenberg is for the Left party line, and yet runs MRP and similar organizations which do not follow a very Left policy. These people are either very stupid or very superficial.... Such a united front manoeuvre can be carried out only if the party itself pursues a regular revolutionary line. The more we work in the trade unions, in the cooperatives, in MRP etc., the more firmly and unswervingly we follow the party line.[63]

Münzenberg did not attend the tenth IKKI in Moscow in July 1929, and nobody seems to have mentioned MRP throughout the proceedings. But Pyatnitsky's disparaging remarks about the non-party organizations evidently applied to it; and it was as true of MRP as of MOPR that Germany was the only country outside the Soviet Union where it could claim mass support.[64] In Germany, the organization penetrated every part of the country through eighteen provincial secretariats, and its cultural and propaganda activities continued.[65] In other countries it could at best arouse occasional interest for specific campaigns.[66] Its principal usefulness at this time, as seen in Moscow, was to support and encourage strikes, especially through its influence on workers not organized in trade unions; Lozovsky wished it to concentrate on recruiting unorganized workers, presumably in countries where Red unions were non-existent or ineffective.[67] But

[62] W. Münzenberg, *Solidarität* (1931), p. 342.

[63] *Protokoll des 12 Parteitags der KPD* (n.d. [1929]), p. 198.

[64] For these remarks see p. 280 below.

[65] For a description of the organization see W. Münzenberg, *Solidarität* (1931), pp. 350–386.

[66] MRP had six newspapers or journals in Germany (one an illustrated with a circulation of 400,000), and one each in France, Belgium, Czechoslovakia, the Netherlands and the USA (A. Tivel and M. Kheimo, *Desyat' Let Kominterna v Tsifrakh* (1929), p. 370).

[67] *Kommunisticheskii Internatsional*, No. 23–24 (201–202), 1929, p. 113; for support given by MRP to strikes in Germany and in Czechoslovakia see W. Münzenberg, *Solidarität* (1931), pp. 371–375, 393.

the unique success of MRP in its earlier days had been due largely to its ability to project itself as a non-party organization of sympathizers with the Soviet Union. When this endeavour was abandoned and attitudes towards the Soviet Union were sharply polarized between communists and social-democrats, MRP remained as a mere shell, emptied of the vigour and enthusiasm of its original conception.

(c) *International Red Aid (MOPR)*

The organization International Red Aid (MOPR) was important, like MPR, primarily as a means of attracting sympathizers from other parties for the proletarian and Soviet cause; its normal activities were confined to the organization of campaigns of protest against acts of oppression and brutality directed against workers, and the material support of the dependants of prisoners. Its second international conference, consisting of seventy-two delegates from forty-two countries, was held in Moscow from March 24 to April 5, 1927. The first sitting took place in the Meyerhold theatre, and was followed by a performance of Tretyakov's play, *Roar, China!* A total membership of 10 millions was claimed, of whom 6 millions were individual members. An executive committee of fifty-five was elected, with Zetkin as president, and Katayama, Marty and Stasova as her deputies.[68] Advantage was taken of a visit by Lansbury to Moscow in July 1926 to hold a meeting of the committee, at which Lansbury gave an account of the aid rendered by the British section (known as International Class War Prisoners' Aid) to British workers in prison or on strike and their families.[69]

A feature of 1927 was the attention devoted to China. Early in March 1927 MOPR issued a proclamation against the "mass terror" practised by the foreign imperialists in Shanghai; unfortunately confidence was still expressed at the moment in "the national-revolutionary armies of Canton" which were about to advance on the city.[70] The attack on the Soviet Embassy in Peking in April 1927 was marked by a protest of MOPR against "the

[68] *Internationale Presse-Korrespondenz*, No. 33, March 25, 1927, p. 720, No. 37, April 8, 1927, p. 805, No. 45, April 26, 1927, pp. 940–941.

[69] G. Lansbury, *The ICWPA* (1928).

[70] *Internationale Presse-Korrespondenz*, No. 29, March 11, 1927, pp. 626–627; events in China will be discussed in a later section of this volume.

barbaric murder of 25 Chinese communists".[71] In July 1927 the "white terror" in China provoked another appeal; at the end of the year MOPR once more protested against the "streams of blood" and "mass shootings" which had followed the Canton rising.[72] A meeting organized jointly by MOPR and the "Hands off China" society was held in Moscow on January 11, 1928, and was addressed by Lozovsky.[73] But international concern with the plight of the British miners, or the fate of the Chinese revolution, was eclipsed, as Pepper pointed out in an article in the Comintern journal,[74] by the immense wave of sympathy and indignation at the death sentence on the two young Italian–Americans, Sacco and Vanzetti. MOPR was at the centre of a massive campaign of protest against the sentence, issuing two appeals early in August 1927 to "the workers and intellectuals" of the world.[75] The indignation was not exclusively, perhaps not even predominantly, inspired by communists. But the party press, *Humanité* being especially conspicuous in the campaign, resounded with denunciations of American justice; and protests and demonstrations by other Left parties and groups in many countries were eagerly reported. Two vehement protests from MOPR followed the execution of the sentence on August 22, 1927.[76] The presidium of IKKIM declared that "American imperialism murdered Sacco and Vanzetti", and Gorky called the act "not judicial process, but class reprisal".[77] Stalin three months later recalled "the murder of two workers ... which aroused the working class of the whole world".[78]

The functions of protest and publicity continued to dominate

[71] *Internationale Presse-Korrespondenz*, No. 48, May 6, 1927, p. 1014.

[72] *Ibid.* No. 77, August 2, 1927, p. 1662, No. 126, December 28, 1927, p. 2937.

[73] *Ibid.* No. 4, January 13, 1928, p. 83.

[74] *Kommunisticheskii Internatsional*, No. 37(111), 1927, pp. 112–117.

[75] *Internationale Presse-Korrespondenz*, No. 80, August 9, 1927, p. 1727, No. 83, August 16, 1927, p. 1800; appeals were also issued by IKKI (*ibid.* No. 80, August 9, 1927, p. 1726), by the executive bureau of Profintern (*ibid.* No. 81, August 12, 1927, p. 1756, No. 84, August 19, 1927, p. 1827), and at the last moment by Krestintern (*ibid.* No. 85, August 23, 1927, p. 1846).

[76] *Ibid.* No. 85, August 23, 1927, p. 1846, No. 86, August 26, 1927, p. 1870; Münzenberg at the sixth congress of Comintern in July 1928 paid special tribute to the work of MOPR in the Sacco–Vanzetti compaign (*Stenograficheskii Otchet VI Kongressa Kominterna* (1929), i, 105).

[77] *Izvestiya*, August 27, 28, 1927.

[78] Stalin, *Sochineniya*, x, 215.

the activities of MOPR throughout 1928. March 18, the anniversary of the Paris commune, was celebrated as the fifth anniversary of MOPR, with a special issue of *Internationale Presse-Korrespondenz* devoted to it, and the opening on that day in Moscow of the second congress of its Soviet branch, attended by two veterans of the Paris commune.[79] The proceedings ended with the election of an executive committee of fifty with Stasova as its president.[80] As international tensions increased, it was Lozovsky who, more than anyone else, detected in MOPR a potential ally and support of his uncompromising trade union policies. The organization attracted a surprising amount of attention at the fourth congress of Profintern in March 1928. The *rapporteur* who introduced a resolution on MOPR claimed that "our Russian section is the only one in the whole world which has done much to help political prisoners", and noted that work in China, Italy and Bulgaria was especially urgent.[81] The resolution, couched in hyperbolic terms, declared that MOPR had won "the confidence of the broad million-strong masses of the proletariat without distinction of party", and constituted a "united front organization against bourgeois class justice, white terror and Fascism", as well as against "the suppression and persecution of revolutionary trade union organizations". It appealed to trade unionists to join MOPR, to participate in its campaigns, and to raise collections for its support.[82] The customary May 1 manifesto of MOPR in 1928 was a roll-call of victims, individual and collective, of imperialist oppression and terror in almost every country in the world.[83] Another proclamation of May 1928 denounced Polish and Italian Fascism and incipient Austrian Fascism, and a further proclamation a few weeks later called for "protest action"

[79] *Ibid.* No. 22, March 1, 1928, pp. 431–446, No. 30, March 20, 1928, p. 581; for the foundation of MOPR and its association with the Paris commune see *Socialism in One Country, 1924–1926*, Vol. 3, p. 950. Four veterans of the Commune settled in the nineteen-twenties in Moscow, where they lived under the protection of MOPR, and were to be seen on anniversaries of March 18 and other ceremonial occasions. For an account of them see *Voprosy Istorii*, No. 3, 1972, pp. 118–123; their photographs appeared in *Pravda*, March 18, 1928.

[80] *Internationale Presse-Korrespondenz*, No. 32, March 27, 1928, p. 610.

[81] *Protokoll über den Vierten Kongress der Roten Gewerkschaftinternationale* (n.d.), p. 484.

[82] *Ibid.* pp. 656–657.

[83] *Internationale Presse-Korrespondenz*, No. 42, May 1, 1928, pp. 753–754.

against "the bloody Fascist terror" in Italy.[84] A MOPR "international day", with a procession of workers, was announced for June 30–July 1, 1928, in Cologne.[85] The sixth congress of Comintern set up a commission to draft a resolution about MOPR, which was adopted without report or discussion in plenary session.[86] The only novelties in the resolution, which described MOPR as "a most important instrument for carrying out the tactics of the united front", were the emphasis placed on the struggle against Fascism (with which MRP was also associated) and on the recruitment of "social-democratic workers organized in the trade unions, and broad masses of working women".[87]

Since MOPR was less a standing institution than a framework for conducting periodical campaigns, and since the quality of the national sections varied widely, figures of membership were speculative and in part unreal. Some of the membership was individual, but much of it, especially in the Soviet Union and China, consisted of groups collectively enrolled. In 1928 the total membership was returned at 7,800,000, including 3,541,000 members in the Soviet Union; during the six years of its existence MOPR claimed to have raised more than 10 million rubles by collections, and spent more than 9 million on relief.[88] Stasova in an article on the organization of MOPR in the Soviet Union, claimed for it 3·5 million members, of whom 72·8 per cent were non-party, organized in 47,000 cells in factories, schools and other institutions, in the Red Army, and in the villages; but much of this network can have existed only on paper. A journal *Put' Mopra* was published, and large quantities of pamphlets and posters circulated.[89] Germany was the one other country where any extensive organization was set up. Since May 1926 a periodical had appeared under the title *MOPR: Zeitschrift für Kampf und Arbeit der Internationalen Roten Hilfe*. At the end of 1926 the German section was reported to have 165,000 members, rather more than half of them communists, and only 2000 social-

[84] *Ibid.* No. 51, May 29, 1928, p. 925, No. 56, June 12, 1928, p. 1014.

[85] *Ibid.* No. 60, June 26, 1928, p. 1086.

[86] *Stenograficheskii Otchet VI Kongressa Kominterna* (1929), v, 127.

[87] *Kommunisticheskii Internatsional v Dokumentakh* (1933), pp. 872–873.

[88] A. Tival and M. Kheimo, *Desyat' Let Kominterna v Tsifrakh* (1929), p. 369.

[89] *Internationale Presse-Korrespondenz*, No. 22, March 1, 1928, pp. 436–437; the international organization was said to have distributed in 1927 more than 3 million copies of 135 publications in fourteen languages (*ibid.* p. 439).

democrats; the hostility of the social-democratic leaders to MOPR was attributed to a "bad conscience".[90] A conference of the German branch in Berlin on March 25–26, 1929, reaffirmed its status as an organization "for the support of workers in economic mass struggles, lock-outs and strikes", and as "a non-party mass organization for the promotion of practical proletarian solidarity". The conference was also concerned to rebut "attacks of the SPD and of the Brandler faction", whom it accused of attempts "in certain localities to mobilize and misuse MOPR against particular parties, especially against the KPD".[91]

The diminished status of MOPR, as of other auxiliary organizations rooted in the conception of the united front, was visible at the tenth IKKI in July 1929, though it attracted more notice than any of the other auxiliary organizations. A spokesman of MOPR, intervening in the debate on preparations for the anti-war day on August 1, defined the three main tasks of MOPR as being to mobilize the "broad masses" for the campaign against war, to "demonstrate to the masses of workers and peasants the inner connexion between Fascism, the white terror and the danger of war", and to help and support those who were victimized for their opposition to war. He claimed that the organization published thirty-five journals in different countries, and planned to make a film. But he ended with the complaint that communist parties gave no space to MOPR in their press, and "absolutely under-estimated" its opportunities as "a non-party class organization" to appeal to strata which the parties failed to reach. It was not a very impressive performance, and Pyatnitsky brushed it roughly aside. Not all the mass organizations, he declared, yet had communist fractions; where such existed they worked badly, and provided "no proper leadership by the communist party". In Germany MOPR was "in part ... a mass organization", elsewhere not even that.[92] Like the other auxiliary organizations, MOPR continued to exist for several years longer. But it lacked a dynamic personality like that of Münzenberg to mask the neglect into which it had fallen.

[90] *Ibid.* No. 34, March 29, 1927, pp. 743–744.

[91] *Ibid.* No. 31, April 9, 1929, p. 710.

[92] *Protokoll: 10. Plenum des Exekutivkomitees der Kommunistischen Internationale* (n.d.), pp. 105–107, 268.

(*d*) *The Peasant International* (*Krestintern*)

The decline in the fortunes of Krestintern was apparent when its journal *Krest'yanskii Internatsional* stopped publication in the spring of 1926.[93] Dombal, the acting secretary-general of the institution, wrote an article on its third anniversary in October 1926, in which he announced the foundation of the International Agrarian Institute and a project for a new journal, the *Internationaler Bauern-Korrespondent*, to be published in German in Berlin, but found little else to celebrate.[94] Dombal attended the seventh enlarged IKKI in November–December 1926 as a delegate of the Polish party, and Boškovič as a Yugoslav delegate.[95] Both spoke on peasant affairs. Dombal noted with apprehension "the creation of the black-green International of *junkers* and large-scale peasants attached to the Agrarian Institute in Rome", which was "closely bound up with the League of Nations", and "the participation in its foundation of the Agrarian Bureau in Prague (the so-called Green International)", but looked to the growth of "peasant internationalism" as "a revolutionary factor".[96] Boškovič drew such satisfaction as was possible from communist activity among the peasants of many countries.[97] But neither they nor Dengel, who presided over the agrarian commission, mentioned Krestintern. During 1927, occasional pronouncements were issued in the name of Krestintern. But the institution never appeared as a framer or as an executor of policy. The session of IKKIM in the summer of 1927 held a debate on work among young peasants; and its presidium issued a long and confused resolution advocating both work in non-party peasant organizations and support for "revolutionary peasant organizations which belong to Krestintern".[98] But these exhor-

[93] See *Socialism in One Country, 1924–1926*, Vol. 3, pp. 955–956.

[94] *Internationale Presse-Korrespondenz*, No. 127, October 22, 1926, p. 2193. The first issue of the journal in German did not appear till the autumn of 1927; but an English edition, *Farmers' and Peasants' International Correspondent*, also published in Berlin, appeared regularly throughout 1927. For the International Agrarian Institute see *Socialism in One Country, 1924–1926*, Vol. 3, pp. 956–957.

[95] *Pravda*, November 26, 27, 1926; *Puti Mirovoi Revolyutsii* (1927), i, 8.

[96] *Ibid.* i, 196.

[97] *Ibid.* i, 198–202.

[98] *Internationale Presse-Korrespondenz*, No. 85, August 23, 1927, pp. 1860–1862.

tations had no practical meaning. A later session of IKKIM recorded that only in Poland, Rumania and Bulgaria (where activities were strictly illegal, and must have been negligible) was the work of youth leagues "on the land" taken seriously;[99] and a report of the following year admitted that the agrarian commission of KIM "did not achieve great results".[100]

The one sphere in which Krestintern might theoretically have played an important role was the colonial and semi-colonial world, where, as in pre-revolutionary Russia, peasants formed an overwhelmingly preponderant part of the population, and where, given the weakness of the bourgeoisie and of the working class, the national cause was bound up with the conception of peasant revolt.[101] When, however, Meshcheryakov, one of the few Russian workers in Krestintern, suggested at the fifth IKKI in March 1925 that Krestintern should be put in charge of all work among peasants in colonial countries,[102] the proposal received no encouragement. Some attempt was made to involve Krestintern in Soviet relations with Kuomintang. But the appointment of Hu Han-hin, during his visit to Moscow in 1926, as a member of the International Peasant Council was a gesture which ultimately brought ridicule on its sponsors; and the occasional manifestoes on Chinese affairs which Krestintern issued in 1926 and 1927 were empty words. Insistence at the seventh IKKI in November 1926 on the important rôle of the agrarian question in the Chinese revolutionary movement owed nothing to Krestintern; nor did Krestintern contribute to it in any way.[103]

A symptom, rather than a cause, of the weakness of Krestintern was its lack not only of any specific peasant programme in any country (a uniform peasant policy was scarcely conceivable), but of any organization outside the Soviet Union. Dombal, when he sketched his initial plan for a Peasant International, evidently envisaged a union of peasant parties under Communist leadership on the model of Comintern.[104] This ambition was scotched in an

99 *Ibid.* No. 35, April 5, 1928, p. 648.

100 *The Young Communist International: Between the Fourth and Fifth Congresses* (1928), pp. 122–123.

101 For Trotsky's remark that the League against Imperialism was "a translation of Krestintern into colonial language" see p. 297, note 10 below.

102 *Rasshirennyi Plenum Ispolkoma Kommunisticheskogo Internatsionala* (1925), pp. 342–343.

103 Chinese affairs will be discussed in a later section of this volume.

104 *Pravda*, June 19, 1923; see also *The Interregnum, 1923–1924*, p. 198.

article published in the Comintern journal in advance of the fifth congress of June 1924, which firmly explained the inadmissibility of peasant parties; only peasant unions and organizations not committed to party programmes or party discipline should be encouraged.[105] The same note was struck in the vague resolution of the fifth congress on relations between Comintern and the International Peasant Council.[106] Bukharin's report on the agrarian question at the fifth IKKI in March 1925, which ignored Krestintern, once more maintained that peasant organizations should have "not the form of a political party, but the form of a peasant union". He clearly envisaged something in the nature of a trade union, which communists would either take over or infiltrate. Varga argued that this analogy was false, and that a peasant union would in effect be a party, though not a communist party. Dombal too claimed that a union and a party were distinguished only in name, and, relying on the Polish precedent, that "political organizations of the peasantry are not harmful".[107] Bukharin firmly retorted that the difference between a party and a union was not that one was political and the other was not, but that parties must have "a definite programme, strict discipline etc."; and the ban on peasant parties was maintained in the theses adopted at the session.[108] There the matter remained for three years, during which party and Comintern leaders sedulously neglected Krestintern.

The twilight existence of Krestintern on the fringes of the network of Comintern organizations was illustrated at the celebrations of the tenth anniversary of the revolution in November 1927. The *Internationaler Bauern-Korrespondent* had at length made its appearance in Berlin to grace the anniversary. Its second issue in October 1927 contained an announcement that visits of foreign peasants' delegations to Moscow were being organized by the newly founded union of the Soviet agricultural cooperatives, and that applications to participate should be addressed to its

[105] *Kommunisticheskii Internatsional*, No. 3–4, May–June 1924, p. 178.

[106] See *Socialism in One Country, 1924–1926*, Vol. 3, p. 87.

[107] *Rasshirennyi Plenum Ispolkoma Kommunisticheskogo Internatsionala* (1925), pp. 327, 340–341, 353–354; for the Polish parties see pp. 570, note 30, 586–589 below.

[108] *Rasshirennyi Plenum Ispolkoma Kommunisticheskogo Internatsionala* (1925), pp. 356–358; for the debate and resolution see *Socialism in One Country, 1924–1926*, Vol. 3, pp. 309–310, 953–954.

president, Kaminsky. This was followed by an open letter from the "International Peasant Council (Peasant International)", signed by Dombal, urging peasant organizations of all countries to respond to the invitation.[109] Peasant delegates, to the number of forty-six, from nine countries — Germany, France, Italy, Austria, Czechoslovakia, Sweden, Norway, Finland and Mexico — came to Moscow for the occasion. Delegates from Far Eastern countries, as well as from Yugoslavia and Bulgaria, had failed to obtain exit permits.[110] A number of delegates asked to hear a report from the presidium of Krestintern on the peasant movement; and a one-day conference was held on November 15, 1927.[111] According to the Soviet delegate, Meshcheryakov, four points were placed on the agenda: confiscation of large estates and distribution of land to the peasantry; the right of national self-determination, including secession; the struggle against war; and the creation of workers' and peasants' governments.[112] But the official record shows no trace of political discussions. Dombal made a report, in which he upheld "the unalterable conclusion", drawn by Krestintern from the lesson of the Russian revolution, that an alliance between workers and peasants must be "the axis of day-to-day work among the peasants of all countries". Meshcheryakov expatiated on the benefits derived by the peasants from the revolution, and argued against the formation of separate peasant parties. The resolution rehearsed in conventional terms the ten-year achievements of the USSR and the tasks of the international peasant movement; it did not mention Krestintern at all.[113] After the conference, the delegates made tours of various

[109] *Internationaler Bauern-Korrespondent*, Special No. 2, October 1927, pp. 24–26; *Kommunisticheskii Internatsional*, No. 51 (125), December 23, 1927, pp. 27–28. For the union of agricultural cooperatives see Vol. 1, p. 148.

[110] *Internationale Presse-Korrespondenz*, No. 1, January 3, 1928, pp. 13–14; larger numbers were recorded — perhaps in anticipation — in *Internationaler Bauern-Korrespondent*, Special No. [3], November 1927, p. 45.

[111] *Internationale Bauernberatung: Stenogram und Beschlüsse* (1928), p. 8. This abbreviated record of the proceedings, with an introduction by Dombal, was issued by Krestintern; no Russian version has been traced. The conference was also reported in the *Internationaler Bauern-Korrespondent*, Special No. [4], December 1927, pp. 53–57.

[112] *Kommunisticheskii Internatsional*, No. 51 (125), December 23, 1927, pp. 27–28.

[113] *Internationale Bauernberatung: Stenogram und Beschlüsse* (1928), pp. 8–17, 25–27, 42–46.

parts of the Soviet countryside before returning home.[114] These achievements encouraged Dombal, in a speech at the fifteenth Russian party congress in the following month, to call Krestintern "a mass non-party organization uniting revolutionary and opposition peasant organizations of all countries". He did not pretend that "we have done very much". But his hopes of future support led him to hail it as "an ever strengthening revolutionary union of the working class with the peasantry".[115] The *Internationaler Bauern-Korrespondent* appeared at monthly or two-monthly intervals during 1928. Each issue carried an article by Dombal, and articles from peasant correspondents in a wide diversity of locations, not excluding Asia, Latin America and California. But Krestintern was rarely, if ever, mentioned in its columns; and that institution seemed to have relapsed into its normal quiescence. The fourth congress of Profintern in March 1928, in a long and ineffective resolution on work among the peasantry, instructed its executive bureau to deal with these questions in conjunction with Krestintern, but made no other reference to it.[116]

The sixth congress of Comintern in the summer of 1928 was the occasion of a brief and somewhat half-hearted attempt to resuscitate the lifeless remains of Krestintern. This was in part a response to the growing influence of the International Agrarian Bureau, which had had some success in bringing together disparate agrarian organizations throughout Europe; it held a conference in Prague in May 1928 under the presidency of Hodža, the Czechoslovak agrarian leader, to prepare the way for an international peasant congress which actually took place a year later.[117] This evidently demanded some counter-demonstration from Moscow. But a revival of Krestintern might also be seen as the logical consequence of the turn to the Left in Comintern policy, and of the abandonment of cooperation with other parties of the Left in favour of direct revolutionary action. It would, at first sight, make little sense to campare this feeble and derelict institution with the powerful and energetic leadership of Profintern.

[114] *Internationaler Bauern-Korrespondent*, Special No. [4], December 1927, was devoted to records of their impressions.

[115] *Pyatnadtsatyi S"ezd VKP* (B), i (1961), 793–798.

[116] See p. 187 above; Krestintern had sent a message of greeting to the congress (*Pravda*, March 22, 1928).

[117] For an account of these proceedings see G. Jackson, *Comintern and Peasant in East Europe* (1966), pp. 138–150.

Nevertheless, the dilemma confronting both was the same. Cooperation with mass non-communist organizations of workers and peasants implied acceptance of compromises with capitalist régimes; the adoption of such policies, not always openly avowed but followed from 1925 onwards, made the existence of Krestintern superfluous and sometimes embarrassing.[118] Rejection of cooperation and wholesale denunciation of non-communist parties and groups, combined with direct incitement to revolutionary action, carried the risk of isolating communists from the mass of workers and peasants. In the spring of 1928 this seemed, in regard to the peasant movement in eastern and central Europe, a reasonable risk to take. Only in Poland had the support of non-party peasant organizations yielded any results; and these were due to the reinforcement of peasant discontent by nationalist grievances.[119] If, however, revolution was once more on the agenda, Krestintern might yet prove a serviceable instrument. Even Trotsky in exile in his letter to the congress wrote that it was time to review "the long drawn out experiment" of a peasant International "from the standpoint of proletarian internationalism", and complained that Bukharin's draft programme ignored its very existence.[120]

At the sixth Comintern congress Bukharin, who had had no dealings with Krestintern for more than three years, spoke grudgingly in his main report of the need "to analyse separately the question of the peasant movement and of such an organization as, for example, *Krestintern*", and thought that the party would have "to help Krestintern to turn itself into a genuine live organization". Hitherto it had achieved little, in the four years of its existence, beyond "publication of miscellaneous materials".[121] Kolarov condemned the work of Krestintern as unsatisfactory, and wished it "to speak to the peasant masses" as an independent

118 For a campaign against Profintern on similar grounds, which failed to develop, see *Socialism in One Country, 1924–1926*, Vol. 3, pp. 585–586.

119 See pp. 586–589 below.

120 L. Trotsky, *The Third International After Lenin* (N.Y., 1936), p. 227; Trotsky held that "the peasantry can be attracted to internationalist politics only if it is torn away from the influence of the bourgeoisie by the proletariat, and if it recognizes in the proletariat not only its ally, but its leader", and that "attempts to organize the peasants of the various countries into any independent international organization, over the heads of the proletariat and without regard to the national communist parties, are doomed to failure" (*ibid.* p. 224).

121 *Stenograficheskii Otchet VI Kongressa Kominterna* (1929), i, 55–56.

organization "in the name of a worker–peasant alliance under the leadership of the proletariat", but gave no indication how this was to be achieved.[122] After Hungarian and Czechoslovak delegates had voiced their criticisms, Grieco, the Italian delegate, roundly declared that Krestintern had been paralysed by "the absence of a Comintern agrarian policy", that "the peasantry in Europe knows nothing of Krestintern", and that "the peasants will not come to us out of politeness for Krestintern".[123] Dombal expressed a confidence in the future not, perhaps, untinged with anxiety. He boldly declared that the liquidation of Krestintern would mean the liquidation of "the revolutionary peasant movement", and that "Krestintern must be a mass peasant non-party political organization, taking as its task, on the basis of an alliance of the working class with the peasantry, the organization of the peasant masses for the revolutionary struggle". On vexed questions of organization he was tactfully vague. Party workers in Krestintern should form the nucleus of the agrarian commission of IKKI, which should watch over "the execution of agrarian policy by the different sections of Comintern"; and he repudiated the proposal made by a Hungarian delegate to go back on the decision of the fifth IKKI not to form peasant parties.[124] Bukharin in his reply also once again denounced this proposal. Where peasant parties already existed, they must be won over; to create a new party would mean "competition with the communist party of the proletariat".[125] He said nothing more about Krestintern; and the only mention of Krestintern in the resolutions of the congress was a routine call "to take urgent measures to revitalize" its work.[126]

Any hopes that were entertained of kindling peasant revolutions under Comintern or Krestintern auspices quickly faded. In March 1928 A. P. Smirnov, who had been removed from his post as People's Commissar for Agriculture of the RSFSR, ceased to be titular secretary-general of Krestintern, and was succeeded by

[122] *Ibid.* i, 164–165.

[123] *Ibid.* i, 242, 288, 314–315; Grieco at the fifth IKKI in March 1925 had spoken, without special reference to Krestintern, in favour of an active radical peasant policy, directed primarily at the poor peasants (*Rasshirennyi Plenum Ispolkoma Kommunisticheskogo Internatsionala* (1925), pp. 345–349).

[124] *Ibid.* i, 438–448.

[125] *Ibid.* i, 607.

[126] *Kommunisticheskii Internatsional v Dokumentakh* (1933), p. 784; a section of the resolution on anti-militarist work among the peasantry (*ibid.* p. 802) did not mention Krestintern.

Teodorovich, his former deputy in Narkomzem, who had lost his post there at the same time.[127] But this arrangement proved temporary. Shorly after the sixth congress Kolarov, a faithful servant of Comintern, became secretary-general of Krestintern;[128] and Dombal, who had been the spokesman and factotum of the institution from the outset, was removed—also without any public announcement.[129]

Dombal's dismissal marked the real end of Krestintern. Teodorovich, in an article in the issue of *Pravda* celebrating Comintern's tenth anniversary, recalled the modest past achievements of Krestintern, but said nothing of its future rôle.[130] *Internationale Bauern-Nachrichten* continued to appear, devoting progressively less attention to specifically peasant problems and more to the current political questions which preoccupied Comintern. The name of Krestintern was still occasionally invoked in its pages for propaganda purposes. The issue for March 1929 carried greetings to the anti-Fascist congress from an anonymous "president of the Peasant International", and a reply from the president of the congress addressed to "the International Peasant Council".[131] The sinister rôle of Fascism in peasant countries, especially in Rumania and Poland, was repeatedly stressed. An article in the Comintern journal of June 1929 denounced non-communist peasant parties and organizations as "allies of the Fascists", and proclaimed it as the essential task of Comintern "to intensify the class struggle in the countryside" and to mobilize the peasants against the threat of war; Krestintern was not mentioned.[132] In the following month, at the tenth IKKI, Varga predicted an agrarian crisis due to the collapse of prices for agricultural products. Skrypnik, speaking of countries where oppressed national minorities consisted mainly of peasants, called on the proletariat of these countries "to lead and develop the revolution-

[127] *Malaya Sovetskaya Entsiklopediya*, viii (1930), 89; for the changes in Narkomzem see Vol. 1, p. 58.

[128] *Bol'shaya Sovetskaya Entsiklopediya* (2nd edn.), xxi (1953), 580.

[129] After the congress the name of the *Internationaler Bauern-Korrespondent* was changed to *Internationale Bauern-Nachrichten*. The first issue to appear under the new title carried an article by Dombal (pp. 82–85) on the death of Radič; thereafter Dombal's name disappeared from the pages of the journal.

[130] For this issue of *Pravda* see pp. 242–243 above; the article emphasized the status of Krestintern as a non-party organization.

[131] *Internationale Bauern-Nachrichten*, No. 3, 1929, pp. 38–39.

[132] *Kommunisticheskii Internatsional*, No. 23–24 (201–202), 1929, pp. 33–36.

ary peasant movement". Teodorovich hailed "the radicalization of the peasant masses", and recalled Engels's famous prophecy that the proletariat would "complete the proletarian revolution with a peasant war"; an Italian delegate, Di Vittorio, thought that the attitude of communist parties to the peasant question had improved somewhat since the sixth congress, but was still unsatisfactory.[133] Both Teodorovich and Di Vittorio were described as delegates of "the communist fraction of Krestintern", but neither referred to the work or functions of that institution.

The oddest part of these proceedings was that none of the speakers showed any knowledge of an initiative being undertaken at that very moment in Berlin. In May 1929 the Green International had held its first general assembly in Prague, at which seventeen countries had been represented.[134] As in the previous year, some counter-stroke was required; and a committee was set up in Berlin in the first days of July to prepare for a European peasant congress.[135] The congress met in November 1929 and further congresses were held in December 1930 and April 1932.[136] But the movement never gathered momentum, or attracted much publicity. From 1929 onwards, the very name of the Peasant International virtually disappeared from the records.

(e) *The International Women's Secretariat*

The fourth international conference on work among women met in Moscow from May 29 to June 10, 1926, under the shadow of the decision taken a month earlier to convert the autonomous

[133] *Protokoll: 10. Plenum des Exekutivkomitees der Kommunistischen Internationale* (n.d.), pp. 168, 180, 200, 450.

[134] For sources see G. Jackson, *Comintern and Peasant in East Europe* (1966), pp. 148–150; the Green International, together with other international agricultural organizations, was denounced in *Kommunisticheskii Internatsional*, No. 23–24 (201–202), 1929, p. 34, as an adjunct to the "Fascist war machines" of the bourgeoisie.

[135] A long report on the proceedings of the committee, which also passed a resolution denouncing imperialist preparations for a second world war, appeared in *Internationale Bauern-Nachrichten*, No. 6–8, 1929, pp. 81–90. This is the last issue of the journal that has been traced; it also contained (*ibid.* pp. 68–69) an appeal signed by "the presidium of the International Peasant Council" to support the anti-war day proclaimed for August 1, 1929 (see p. 255 above).

[136] *Shest' Let Bor'by za Krest'yanstvo* (1935), ed. V. Kolarov, pp. 18–34.

International Women's Secretariat into a department of IKKI.[137] The very title of the gathering reflected the change; the three previous conferences had been styled "conferences of communist women". Nor was the fourth conference a mass assembly like its predecessors. It was attended only by eighteen voting, and forty-seven non-voting, delegates. These formed "a small circle of leading comrades from the most important parties of west and east, together with some experienced women workers from the rank and file of the parties"; they included representatives of IKKI, of KIM, of MOPR and of Krestintern.[138] Two main impressions emerge from the record of what transpired: the firm hand kept on the proceedings by IKKI (Togliatti and Geschke, respectively, opened and closed the conference, and Fried, a member of the Orgburo of IKKI, made the report on organization), and the preponderant part played by women delegates of the USSR, who dominated the debates and confidently laid down the line for others to follow and imitate. Everything was done to show that the women's section was to be fully geared to the policies and organization of Comintern.

Zetkin, though in Moscow, was too infirm to attend the conference, and an eloquent letter from her was read at the opening. As throughout the previous period, controversy revolved round the two issues of the system of women delegates' meetings, and of participation in non-party women's organizations. Herthe Sturm, who made the principal report on the work of the women's secretariat, complained that women were a small minority in all western communist parties, and that the parties paid little attention to work among them; the conclusion was the need for more energetic action by the women's section to correct their shortcomings. Sturm retreated from her previous sceptical attitude to the institution of delegates' meetings,[139] and called for "a decisive and clear attitude to *the preparation and organization of women*

[137] See *Socialism in One Country, 1924–1926*, Vol. 3, p. 986.

[138] *Pravda*, June 1, 1926; *Tätigkeitsbericht der Exekutive der Kommunistischen Internationale, Februar bis November 1926* (1926), p. 32; *Internationale Presse-Korrespondenz*, No. 108, August 24, 1926, p. 1811. A full record of the proceedings, including a list of delegates, was published belatedly, *ibid.* No. 22, February 25, 1927, pp. 425–464, No. 28, March 11, 1927, pp. 561–619; the resolutions had already appeared *ibid.* No. 115, September 17, 1926, pp. 1939–1966.

[139] See *Socialism in One Country, 1924–1926*, Vol. 3, pp. 980, 982.

delegates' meetings". A general report by Artyukhina on work among women in the Soviet Union was followed by a number of detailed reports from districts and factories. The moral of a Soviet model held up for others to follow scarcely needed to be drawn. Artyukhina made a separate report on the delegates' meetings, and the topic was frequently raised in the debates on other reports. Few foreign representatives were persuaded of the usefulness in their own countries of a system designed to indoctrinate and recruit semi-literate women workers in the Soviet Union; no Soviet representative believed that a system which worked well in Soviet conditions could be inapplicable elsewhere. Nobody ventured to oppose the principle of delegates' meetings. But, in the course of much desultory discussion, a German representative stated that, though meetings for women workers had been held in Germany, nothing had been introduced that could be called "a real system of women delegates' meetings". A French delegate spoke of "conferences of women delegates ... on the basis of quite clear demands", e.g. on the question of the war in Morocco. A British delegate explained that the CPGB had abandoned its opposition to the idea of delegates' meetings only under pressure of the women's secretariat, that the meetings held had not been organized "in the same way as they are organized in Russia", and had been attended chiefly by housewives, since housewives and employees constituted a majority of the female membership of the party.[140] Togliatti wound up with the argument that this was no mere question of organization, which might be answered differently by different parties, but an integral part of the tactics of the united front.[141] The resolution adopted by the conference explained how the system worked in the Soviet Union, and how it might be adapted to western countries, and praised (perhaps a little hypocritically) the attempts to apply it to Germany, Great Britain and Finland.[142]

Further differences of opinion also occurred on the issue of participation in non-party women's organizations which had already troubled the sixth IKKI a few months earlier.[143] Sturm quoted the example of the German Roter Frauen- und Mädchen-

[140] *Internationale Presse-Korrespondenz*, No. 22, February 25, 1927, pp. 443–445, 458, No. 28, March 11, 1927, p. 568.

[141] *Ibid.* No. 28, March 11, 1927, pp. 577–578.

[142] *Ibid.* No. 115, September 17, 1926, pp. 1958–1959.

[143] See *Socialism in One Country, 1924–1926*, Vol. 3, pp. 985–986.

bund, which, though originally created by the party, now had a 70 per cent non-party membership and set itself in opposition to the women's section of the KPD.[144] An elaborate resolution provided for party control of such organizations, and stipulated that they could in no case be regarded as a substitute for delegates' meetings. An appendix to the resolution dealt with the formation of new non-party women's organizations under communist auspices. This was pronounced legitimate with several careful reservations:

> In countries of western Europe and America, the formation of new general organizations on the initiative of the communist party is not to be recommended. It is, however, perfectly permissible, depending on the economic and political conditions of the moment, to create proletarian women's organizations for *purposes of specific action*.... The decision on the creation of such organizations rests with the central committee of the party.[145]

A British delegate eulogized the rôle of women in the British general strike, and the conference issued an appeal to women all over the world to continue their support of the striking miners.[146] A report on organization by a member of the organization section of IKKI heavily stressed the importance of enrolling women party members in factory cells;[147] and appropriate resolutions were passed on this question, and on work among women in the east, work among peasant women, and questions of education and the press.[148] The resolutions received the formal approval of the Orgburo of IKKI on July 30, 1926;[149] the interval suggests that the final drafting may not have been completed at the conference itself. The function of the conference was clearly to establish the

144 *Internationale Presse-Korrespondenz*, No. 28, March 11, 1927, pp. 590–591.

145 *Ibid.* No. 115, September 17, 1926, pp. 1960–1963; according to the English edition, *International Press-Correspondence*, No. 69, October 26, 1929, pp. 1206–1209, the appendix was added to the resolution, on a motion of Kuusinen, only after it had been approved by the Orgburo on July 30, 1926 (see note 149 below).

146 *Internationale Presse-Korrespondenz*, No. 28, March 11, 1927, p. 579, No. 93, July 13, 1926, pp. 1521–1522.

147 *Ibid.* No. 22, February 25, 1927, pp. 458–461.

148 For the text of all the resolutions see *ibid.* No. 115, September 17, 1926, 1926 (see below).

149 *Ibid.* No. 108, August 24, 1926, pp. 1811–1812.

authority of IKKI and of its women's secretariat over the organization and activities of women members of foreign parties. On the level of organization, this was no longer contested. But Kuusinen, in his report to the seventh IKKI in November 1926, observed that, though many good resolutions had been passed about women workers, they had been weakly carried out. Sturm, speaking on behalf of the women's section, again praised the work of women party members in the British general strike, and the "outstanding successes" of the KPD in introducing meetings of women delegates, but could find nothing else to mitigate the general picture of neglect.[150]

Little evidence can be found of the vitality of a woman's communist movement outside the confines of the Soviet Union. An international women's day was celebrated on March 8, 1927, with a manifesto issued by Clara Zetkin.[151] First meetings of women's delegates were reported from seven German cities early in 1927,[152] but are not known to have had any sequel.[153] In May 1927 women members of the CPGB attended a women's conference in Huddersfield sponsored by a committee on which the trade unions, the Labour Party and the cooperatives were represented. The proceedings were stormy. Protests were made at the failure to invite a Russian delegation; and, in spite of the efforts of Margaret Bondfield, the principal Labour delegate, resolutions put forward from the platform were voted down.[154] A conference was held in Moscow as an adjunct to the congress of Friends of the Soviet Union on the occasion of the tenth anniversary of the revolution, with Zetkin presiding and Krupskaya and Kollontai being among the speakers.[155] But the women's movement attracted only intermittent notice on special occasions. At the fourth congress of Profintern in March 1928 a French woman delegate, Alice Brissot, referred to the growing importance of women in industry and the need to organize them; and a Soviet delegate

[150] *Puti Mirovoi Revolyutsii* (1927), i, 123, 318–325.

[151] *Internationale Presse-Korrespondenz*, No. 25, March 4, 1927, pp. 501–503.

[152] *Ibid.* No. 12, January 28, 1927, pp. 238–239.

[153] The blame for the breakdown was later placed on the "Rightists" (*Protokoll: 10. Plenum des Exekutivkomitees der Kommunistischen Internationale* (n.d.), p. 350).

[154] *Internationale Presse-Korrespondenz*, No. 65, June 24, 1927, pp. 1381–1382.

[155] *Ibid.* No. 122, December 13, 1927, pp. 2792–2793.

complained of neglect, by all parties except the Russian, of the women's movement.[156] A British delegate pointed out that in Great Britain only 20 per cent of women workers, and a negligible proportion elsewhere, were organized in trade unions.[157] Brissot submitted a long resolution dealing with every aspect of women's work in the trade unions, and a brief resolution proposing the creation of a women's committee attached to the executive bureau of Profintern.[158] At the sixth congress of Comintern in July 1928, a woman delegate from South Africa struck an unfamiliar note by asserting that the children of communist leaders rarely grew up good communists, and attributing this to the failure of husbands to share their interests with their wives; this she thought worthy of the attention of IKKI and its women's section. A German representative criticized the exploitation of women in industry and the failure to attract non-party women to the meetings of women delegates, which had an exclusively communist character.[159] Neither intervention ruffled the calm indifference of the congress to these problems.

A period of quiescence was broken by an outburst of publicity in celebration of the international women's day on March 7, 1929. Slogans from IKKI and an appeal by Zetkin were circulated in advance, both dwelling especially on the rôle of women in the campaign against war;[160] and IKKI issued a further manifesto on the day itself. After almost total neglect of the theme at three successive sessions of IKKI and at the sixth congress, the tenth IKKI in July 1929 was brought back to it by a long speech from a member of the women's section of IKKI. The speaker drew attention to the largely increased employment of women at low wages in industry, and argued that in Great Britain and the

[156] *Protokoll über den Vierten Kongress der Roten Gewerkschaftsinternationale* (n.d.), pp. 173–174, 206–208.

[157] *Ibid.* p. 218.

[158] *Ibid.* pp. 499–500; for the main resolution see *Desyat' Let Profinterna v Rezolyutsiyakh* (1930), pp. 218–222. After the congress, the central council voted to establish the women's committee, consisting of representatives of the principal European countries, and of the United States, Mexico and China (*ibid.* p. 234); its activities were reported on at the sixth session of the central council in December 1929 (*Protokoll der VI Session des Zentralrats der Roten Gewerkschaftsinternationale* (1930), p. 93).

[159] *Stenograficheskii Otchet VI Kongressa Kominterna* (1929), i, 237–239, 366–368.

[160] *Internationale Presse-Korrespondenz*, No. 19, February 28, 1929, pp. 385–386.

United States this increase had gone hand in hand with a reduction in the total labour force and was a contributory factor to unemployment. She stressed the rôle of women in recent strikes, and blamed communist parties for their neglect of the question: "*we have done hardly anything to win the masses of women workers*".[161] Nobody took up the challenge till, in the debate on "economic struggles" at the end of the session, a member of the communist fraction in Profintern recalled the resolution on women workers adopted by the fourth congress of Profintern; he admitted, however, that no member organization of Profintern had given effect to the recommendations.[162] A paragraph was included in the resolution of the session on economic struggles pointing out the striking discrepancy "between the present rise in the participation of women workers in economic disputes and the weak leadership of women workers by communist parties and by the revolutionary trade union movement", and demanding that this should be made good.[163] But these sporadic pronouncements did not remove the impression that the women's section enjoyed no great prestige in the hierarchy of Comintern, and that movements in other countries gained nothing from the determination to impose on them a central and uniform directive from Moscow.

161 *Protokoll: 10. Plenum des Exekutivkomitees der Kommunistischen Internationale* (n.d.), pp. 344–355.
162 *Ibid.* p. 832.
163 *Kommunisticheskii Internatsional v Dokumentakh* (1933), p. 907.

CHAPTER 74
FRONT ORGANIZATIONS

(a) The League against Imperialism

THE notion of an organized protest of subject peoples against the imperialist Powers was born in China. A League against Imperialism was formed in Peking in July 1924, and issued an appeal on behalf of oppressed peoples; and two months later, a "Hands off China" society was founded in Moscow, with corresponding societies in Berlin, London and elsewhere.[1] In July 1926 an International Association of the Oppressed Peoples held a conference in Canton.[2] These *ad hoc* activities centering on China were complemented early in 1926 by the foundation in Berlin in February 1926 of a "league against colonial cruelties and oppression", which was apparently designed to counter official propaganda for the restoration to Germany of her lost colonies.[3] This organization, of which the indefatigable Münzenberg was one of the promoters, also became involved in protests against imperialist policies in China.[4] The idea caught on. Leagues against Imperialism sprang up elsewhere, notably in Latin America. The German league originally planned an international conference to be held in Brussels in November 1926, and received favourable replies from several countries, including one from the central commitee of Kuomintang.[5] But the German group, according to Münzenberg who was evidently its moving spirit, "disposed of no international connexions or monetary resources". These were supplied by MRP, doubtless with the backing of Comintern.[6] But Calles, the Mexican president, eager to

[1] *Socialism in One Country, 1924–1926*, Vol. 3, pp. 686, 708.

[2] *Ibid.* Vol. 3, p. 628; according to K. Fuse, *Soviet Policy in the Orient* (Peking, 1927), pp. 274–282, the original Peking movement of July 1924 faded out after May 30, 1925, as being insufficiently radical.

[3] *Die Rote Fahne*, February 16, 1926.

[4] *Ibid.* March 14, 23, 1926; *Pravda*, March 26, 1926; for a general account of the organization see *ibid.* February 4, 1927.

[5] *Kommunisticheskii Internatsional: Kratkii Istoricheskii Ocherk* (1969), p. 275; *Internationale Presse-Korrespondenz*, No. 100, August 3, 1927, pp. 1629–1630.

[6] *Ibid.* No. 15, February 4, 1927, pp. 305–306. In this account Münzenberg did not mention MRP; the intention at this time was evidently to play down

strike a blow against United States imperialism, was also an unexpected and generous contributor to the funds of the congress.[7]

The congress met in Brussels on February 10, 1927. Vandervelde, the Belgian socialist Minister for Foreign Affairs, gave permission for the congress to be held there on condition that a list of delegates was supplied, and that the Belgian Congo was not mentioned.[8] Officially described as the founding congress of the League against Imperialism and for National Independence, it was a miscellaneous gathering. The 174 delegates, more than 100 of them from colonial and semi-colonial countries, represented a glittering variety of Left-wing organizations. Nobody officially represented any communist party.[9] No delegate from the Soviet Union attended the congress; the only organization in Moscow to take official cognizance of it was Krestintern, which sent a telegram of greeting.[10] Codovilla, Koenen and Lominadze were present, no doubt as "emissaries of Comintern",[11] but were not delegates and took no part in the proceedings. Most social-democratic organizations boycotted the congress as a communist device. But William Brown, the British secretary of IFTU, and

any link with Comintern. In his later account in *Solidarität* (1931), pp. 333–334, he referred to the "active assistance" of MRP, and did not mention the Berlin league founded in the previous year.

[7] Calles's intervention will be discussed in a later section of this volume.

[8] B. Gross, *Willi Münzenberg* (1967), p. 200; the Central African delegate spoke of the sufferings of the Negroes under French rule, but did not mention Belgium (*Das Flammenzeichen vom Palais Egmont* (1927), pp. 113–117). No Belgian delegate spoke at the congress; but a "Belgian resolution" was included in the record condemning Belgian in the same terms as British and French imperialism and not mentioning the Congo (*ibid.* p. 262).

[9] Several speakers emphasized that they were not communists; Ledebour remarked: "I am no communist, as you all know, but when communists pursue a practical revolutionary goal or action, I join them, and assume that our British and American friends, who are also no communists, are of the same opinion" (*Ibid.* p. 183).

[10] *Ibid.* p. 270; Trotsky observed that the league was "a translation of Krestintern into colonial language" (*Byulleten' Oppozitsii*, No. 15–16, September–October 1930, p. 6).

[11] M. Buber-Neumann, *Von Potsdam nach Moskau* (1957), p. 99; the author was present at the congress, and worked in the secretariat of the league (*ibid.* pp. 107–110). The statement in B. Gross, *Willi Münzenberg* (1967), p. 205, that Melnichansky represented the Soviet trade unions is a confusion with the second congress of the league in 1929 (see pp. 306–307 below). Nor is it likely that Lominadze represented KIM; a declaration to the congress by youth organizations were signed by secretaries of the British and French youth leagues, but not of Komsomol or KIM (*Das Flammenzeichen vom Palais Egmont* (1927), pp. 263–264).

Fimmen, secretary of the International Transport Workers' Federation, long a dissident figure in IFTU, both spoke in their personal capacities.[12] Davies, Cook's deputy at the head of the British Mineworkers' Federation, formally opened the proceedings, and Lansbury was elected president of the congress; Barbusse and Ledebour were other distinguished senior figures, Nehru the outstanding Asian delegate.[13] The Chinese delegation, twenty-five strong, included representatives of Kuomintang, of the Chinese trade unions, and of Chinese student organizations in several countries, but not of the CCP; except for the twenty-six Germans, it was the largest delegation. Katayama was the lone representative of Japan. The British delegation of fifteen comprised representatives both of the Labour Party and of the ILP, as well as Pollitt, described as a delegate of the Minority Movement. A small handful of United States delegates included Roger Baldwin, the secretary of the American Civil Liberties Union.[14] Anti-imperialism proved the most effective platform on which to unite leading personalities sympathetic to the Soviet Union but unwilling to undertake a commitment to communism. An attempt was made to mobilize the support of well-known French and German intellectuals. Besides Barbusse, who was present and was elected to the honorary presidium, Romain Rolland and Margueritte sent greetings to the congress.[15] Einstein sent greetings and was elected a member of the honorary presidium, in which capacity his signature appeared under the manifesto of the congress; and Toller the poet was among the delegates who spoke.[16] The congress lasted from February 10 to 15, 1927, and held ten

[12] *Ibid.* pp. 42, 185; Fimmen had credentials from the official Mexican trade union organization (*ibid.* p. 236).

[13] According to B. Gross, *Willi Münzenberg* (1967), p. 200, Roy and Codovilla in discussions in Moscow opposed the holding of the congress; the determining factor was Nehru's agreement to attend.

[14] For a complete list of delegates and of the organizations represented by them see *Das Flammenzeichen vom Palais Egmont* (1927), pp. 229–241. According to a report in *The Ninth Congress of the CPGB* (1927), p. 58, the CPGB sent "a strong delegation, including our late comrade MacManus, as part of the British delegation" to the congress, and "our delegation took an active part"; this part was presumably played behind the scenes, and left no trace in the record of the congress, which names no British communist other than Pollitt among the delegates. *Die Komintern vor dem 6. Weltkongress* (1928), p. 138, merely records that MacManus attended the congress "on the instruction of the party".

[15] *Ibid.* p. 271.

[16] *Ibid.* pp. 163–165, 241, 264.

sittings. There seems to have been no formal agenda, but successive orators mounted the tribune to denounce the particular forms of imperialism with which they were concerned; and the efficient secretariat produced a number of resolutions which were unanimously voted. When the official record of the congress was published, the speeches were arranged, not in the order in which they had been delivered, but in separate chapters relating to countries or regions. This produced one or two anomalies; all the British speeches were grouped in the chapter on China, though some British delegates also referred to other topics.[17]

When the congress met, the Chinese nationalist armies were at the peak of their success; the problems and embarrassments of the national revolution had scarcely begun to emerge. The liberation of China from the imperialist yoke was the first and major theme of the congress. Two resolutions were passed on China, one put forward by the Chinese delegation, the other jointly by the British, Chinese and Indian delegations, which included a demand for the withdrawal of British and Indian armed forces from China; and there was a Chinese–Indian declaration on the struggle against British imperialism.[18] Nehru brought the greetings of the Indian National Congress, and sponsored a resolution calling for "the complete liberation of India" and for action to prevent the despatch of fresh troops to China (a separate resolution apparently demanded the withdrawal of Indian troops from Mesopotamia).[19] The occupation of Nicaragua by United States marines in January 1927, as well as the sponsorship of the congress by the Mexican president, brought American imperialism into the forefront of the picture; and the failure of communism to strike roots into Latin America in no way militated against the design, which inspired the whole congress, of establishing a close alliance between the victims of imperialism and the policy-makers of Comintern. Of a bevy of Latin American delegates, several of them representing newly formed anti-imperialist leagues in Latin American countries, and

[17] The record is in *Das Flammenzeichen vom Palais Egmont* (1927); for the order of the speeches see the summaries of the sittings in *Internationale Presse-Korrespondenz*, No. 19, February 15, 1927, pp. 383–386, No. 20, February 18, 1927, pp. 400–402. For other accounts see *Labour Monthly*, No. 3, 1927, pp. 179–185; J. Nehru, *An Autobiography* (1936), pp. 161–164.

[18] *Das Flammenzeichen vom Palais Egmont* (1927), pp. 52–54.

[19] *Ibid.* pp. 55–62.

none of them avowed communists, the most distinguished was a former Mexican minister, Vasconcellos, who appeared as delegate of a Puerto Rican national party. In a fierce denunciation of United States imperialism, he took pains, however, to define his position:

> I am a socialist, others are liberals. The party which I represent has, for example, given me instructions to state clearly that they are not communists, not because they are reactionary, but because we in Latin America feel that we must solve our problems in our own way.... The question of anti-imperialism is not in Latin America the problem of a single party.[20]

Philips, a United States communist who worked in Latin America under the name of Gomez, addressed the congress on behalf of the American Anti-imperialist League; and the congress approved two declarations drafted jointly by the Latin American delegates and another submitted by the American Civil Liberties Union of New York.[21] Delegates from Egypt, Syria and Palestine, from South, North and Central Africa and from Indonesia, Indo-China and Korea, addressed the congress and submitted resolutions which were formally adopted or included in the records of the congress; and there was a resolution on the Negro question.[22]

The seventeen trade union delegates present at the congress were led by the energetic Fimmen. The neglect of non-European workers' movements by IFTU and by European social-democratic parties was a favourite theme; and appeals were drafted for "an active campaign to popularize the adoption of partial strikes and of the general strike in imperialist countries engaged in crushing the Chinese revolution and other national movements of oppressed peoples", and for the international unity of the trade union movement.[23] The delegate of an International Anti-Militarist Bureau at The Hague recalled that "the anti-militarist movement in Holland has for twenty years past struggled for the independence of Indonesia", and presented a resolution denounc-

[20] *Ibid.* p. 64. Vasconcellos, who met Chicherin in Berlin in December 1926, told him that he had resigned his post as Mexican Minister for Education "owing to his Leftism", that he was living in France, and would like to visit Moscow (*Dokumenty Vneshnei Politiki SSSR*, ix (1964), 573).

[21] *Das Flammenzeichen vom Palais Egmont* (1927), pp. 63–79, 256.

[22] Some of these resolutions will be discussed in a later section of this volume.

[23] *Das Flammenzeichen vom Palais Egmont* (1927), pp. 203–204.

ing "colonial oppression and the modern wars of imperialism".[24] A curiosity of the congress was a speech by a German professor named Goldschmidt, who exhibited a walking-stick once the property of Schopenhauer, who had received it from an Indian philosopher. The orator quoted Schopenhauer on the superiority of eastern over Christian culture, and commended a policy of "colonization in reverse" which would give the coloured races unrestricted access to "white" countries.[25] Münzenberg, summing up the proceedings at the last sitting, announced that the present congress would serve as a prelude to "a real world congress", which would found "a world league against imperialism and colonial oppression"; he added, however, that "the chief task at present is to support the Chinese revolution".[26] A general resolution on the struggle against imperialism ended with a call for strikes, especially of transport workers, to prevent the despatch of troops and munitions to countries where the struggle was in progress; China was evidently the country in mind.[27] Finally, the congress issued a manifesto signed by the president, the honorary presidents and all the delegates, containing an analysis of world-wide imperialism and ending with the motto: "Oppressed peoples and oppressed classes, unite!"[28] After the congress some of the delegates visited various European cities on a speaking tour organized by Münzenberg.[29] The congress had been designed to stimulate the foundation of leagues against imperialism in countries where they did not yet exist. But not much success attended these efforts. The CPGB delegation on its return home "took the initiative for the formation of a British section of the league at the earliest possible moment", but was said to have met with obstruction from Lansbury and from the

[24] *Ibid.* pp. 200, 261. The original text of the declaration, preserved in the Internationaal Instituut voor Sociale Geschiedenis, Amsterdam, contained a final paragraph calling for "a permanent struggle against all governments and the state idea, in order to make war impossible by the use of economic methods of struggle and to consummate the social revolution"; this passage was omitted from the official record.

[25] *Ibid.* pp. 205–214.

[26] *Ibid.* pp. 215–224.

[27] *Ibid.* pp. 174–176.

[28] *Internationale Presse-Korrespondenz*, No. 23, February 25, 1927, pp. 472–474.

[29] This was recalled many years later by Philips, who also remembered meeting Nehru and Haya de la Torre at the congress (*Survey*, lv (April 1965), 118).

Labour Party in general. A section was eventually formed at a meeting on July 22, 1927, and a provisional committee was elected, including Fenner Brockway as chairman and Pollitt and Saklatvala among the members.[30]

The campaign against imperialism continued to be an important weapon in the armoury of Soviet propaganda. The congress had drawn up elaborate statutes providing for group and individual members or associates, and for the appointment of a general council, an executive committee and an international secretariat.[31] The head of the secretariat was Chattopadya, an old Indian nationalist resident in Berlin, who had visited Moscow, but had been in eclipse during the period of Roy's ascendancy.[32] Nehru and Saklatvala were prominent participants in sessions of the executive committee of the league in Cologne on August 20–21, 1927, and in Brussels on December 9–10, 1927, both of which were occupied mainly with India and China. The December session expressed particular disappointment with the attitude of the Labour Party to India and its willingness to participate in the Simon commission. In addition to the resolution on India, resolutions were passed on Indonesia and Persia, and on the danger of war;[33] and a manifesto was issued a few days later protesting against the white terror in China after the Canton fiasco.[34]

In the winter of 1927–1928 the activities of the League against Imperialism were temporarily eclipsed by those of the newly founded organization of Friends of the Soviet Union.[35] But the campaign against imperialism was fanned by events in China, and was a key topic at the sixth congress of Comintern in July–August 1928. Bukharin, in his main report, deprecated the view of "some comrades" that the league was not "a specially viable institution", and that the Brussels congress had been simply "a great parade, a great political demonstration". But he added that

[30] *The Ninth Congress of the CPGB* (1927), pp. 58–59.

[31] A copy of the statutes, issued by the international secretariat in Berlin, is in the Internationaal Instituut voor Sociale Geschiedenis, Amsterdam.

[32] J. Nehru, *An Autobiography* (1936), p. 161.

[33] *Internationale Presse-Korrespondenz*, No. 87, August 30, 1927, pp. 1895–1896, No. 122, December 13, 1927, pp. 2789–2790; according to Roy, Nehru's father, Motila Nehru, who was present at the December session, explained that he was not in favour of total separation of India from Great Britain (*ibid.* No. 1, January 3, 1928, p. 3).

[34] *Ibid.* No. 126, December 28, 1927, pp. 2935–2937.

[35] See pp. 307–310 below.

"Münzenberg knows better than anyone the *organizational weaknesses* of the league".[36] Katayama thought that the main function of the league was "preparation of the struggle against war and for the defence of the Soviet Union". A leading official of MRP asserted that the Brussels congress, "on the one hand, sowed seeds of hope and courage in millions of the colonial population, ... and, on the other hand, attracted the attention of the bourgeoisie and of the social-democrats". But his claim that it had split the ranks of the social-democrats rested on slender foundations.[37] Complaints were made of the lukewarmness of Dutch members of the league; even Fimmen had said that the slogan of independence for Indonesia was unacceptable.[38]

During the proceedings of the congress in Moscow, the executive committee of the league met again in Berlin on August 18–19, 1928. Münzenberg made the principal report, and Ledebour, Maxton and Saklatvala were among the speakers. The resolutions, in line with the current Comintern campaign against social-democracy, were largely concerned with denunciation of the Second International and of the attitude of its recent congress on the colonial question. It was decided to convene a second congress of the League against Imperialism in July 1929 in Paris.[39]

[36] *Stenograficheskii Otchet VI Kongressa Kominterna* (1929), i, 56, 604. After the Brussels congress a sour comment had appeared in the journal of the KPD, deprecating talk about "political strikes and other mass action" by people who, like the British ILP, had no experience of such things, and expressing the view that the congress relied too much on "*propaganda* effect" and too little on preparation for action (*Die Internationale*, x, No. 6, March 15, 1927, pp. 186–187); the eighth IKKI of May 1927 in its resolution on China blamed communist members of the League against Imperialism for "insufficient activity" (*Kommunisticheskii Internatsional v Dokumentakh* (1933), p. 729).

[37] *Stenograficheskii Otchet VI Kongressa Kominterna* (1929), i, 305–306, iv, 157–161.

[38] *Ibid.* iv, 44, 405; Lozovsky at the seventh IKKI in November 1926 said that Fimmen "declared against the independence of Indonesia on the ground that an independent Indonesia would fall into the hands of a more powerful imperialism" (*Puti Mirovoi Revolyutsii* (1927), i, 544). No other evidence has been found of Fimmen's alleged declaration, which contradicted his normal attitude; Lozovsky was speaking just after the abortive insurrection in Indonesia, which will be discussed in a later section of this volume.

[39] *Internationale Presse-Korrespondenz*, No. 88, August 21, 1928, pp. 1659–1660, 1662; the Second International at its congress a few days earlier had spent some time denouncing the League against Imperialism (*Dritter Kongress der Sozialistischen Arbeiter-Internationale* (1928), ii, pp. vi, 107–108).

In the autumn of 1928 Münzenberg gave an optimistic account of the progress of the league in the colonial countries, and recorded a mass meeting held at Limehouse in London to protest against the acceptance by Attlee, the Labour MP for the constituency, of an invitation to join the Simon commission in India.[40]

The year 1929 witnessed a decline in the activities of the League against Imperialism. It no longer had the freshness of novelty; the major current campaign against war,[41] and the minor campaign against Fascism,[42] were both conducted independently of it; above all, the growing mistrust in Comintern of united front tactics, and the deepening rift in all countries between communists and social-democrats, did nothing to help an institution which depended on action in common by parties and individuals of the Left. At the session of the executive in Cologne on January 15–16, 1929, a strong attempt was made to enlist trade unions in the campaign. The Soviet trade unions formally adhered to the league, and sent a strong delegation to Cologne headed by Melnichansky. In addition to the familiar members of the British delegation (Maxton, Saklatvala and Bridgman), Cook, the president of the miners' federation, came to deliver the main report of the session on "the tasks of the trade unions in the struggle against imperialism". It was not altogether a success. Cook depicted the British Labour leaders as blockheads who did not understand what they were doing, but not as traitors; and he asserted that the method of influencing the masses must be judged in each country in the light of its particular condition, and not be subject to interference from outside. Melnichansky rejected both propositions, referring contemptuously to "the old story of 'non-intervention in the internal affairs of another country' ". Heckert, the German delegate, also attacked Cook; and Cook rejoined tartly that he was "not disposed to let the league be transformed into a Red International", and that "we cannot use German or Russian models". Herclet, the delegate of the CGTU, admitted that the league had little following in France, and that it was the affair of the PCF rather than of the trade unions.[43] The session passed a

[40] *Internationale Presse-Korrespondenz*, No. 132, November 27, 1928, pp. 2620–2621.

[41] See pp. 245–246 above. [42] See pp. 310–313 below.

[43] *Internationale Presse-Korrespondenz*, No. 6, January 18, 1929, pp. 106–109. The text of Melnichansky's speech is described as "a free translation",

resolution on the rôle of trade unions, and a special resolution on Latin America.[44] But it was only the British section of the league which showed some signs of life and activity; Great Britain was the country where united front tactics were still not dead. A manifesto of March 1929 protested against the police terror in India and demanded Indian independence.[45] Two months later, on the occasion of the forthcoming British general election, the British section appealed to all workers to vote only for candidates who endorsed the policies of the league, i.e. to reject Conservative proposals for a closed imperial tariff system, to withdraw the Labour members of the Simon commission, and to support the demand of all colonial peoples for independence.[46]

One further effort was made to galvanize the League against Imperialism into life at the second congress which met in Frankfurt on July 21–30, 1929. It was numerically larger than its predecessor, mustering 257 delegates from thirty-three countries, as well as numerous representatives of sympathizing organizations, including sixty members of an anti-imperialist youth congress which had met on the eve of the major congress.[47] But most of the distinguished independent figures who had appeared at the first congress were absent; and the attempt to conceal or play down Soviet and communist participation was not repeated. Maxton presided. Pollitt, representing the National Minority Movement, and Saklatvala were active in the British delegation. No less than eighty German delegates are said to have been present; but the very imperfect records of the congress make no mention of any contribution by them to the proceedings. Melnichansky, the delegate of the Soviet trade unions, played a leading rôle throughout the congress. The Brussels congress had taken place at the moment of the victorious advance of the Chinese

since no stenographic record was available; it does not appear to have been published elsewhere. Münzenberg did his best to gloss over the asperities of the debate in an account which called Cook's view of the reformist leaders "a utopia", and referred to the "illusions" of other speakers (*ibid.* No. 7, January 22, 1929, pp. 122–123).

[44] *Ibid.* No. 7, January 22, 1929, pp. 123–124; the influence of the league in Latin America had been stressed by speakers at the sixth congress of Comintern in July 1928 (*Stenograficheskii Otchet VI Kongressa Kominterna* (1929), i, 105, 235).

[45] *Internationale Presse-Korrespondenz*, No. 28, March 27, 1929, p. 620.

[46] *Ibid.* No. 46, May 28, 1929, p. 1106.

[47] The anti-imperialist youth congress was briefly reported in the bulletins of the main congress (see p. 306, note 50 below) and in *Pravda*, July 24, 1929.

revolutionary nationalist armies. The sensation of the Frankfurt congress was the attempt by the Kuomintang forces, whose victories had been celebrated in Brussels, to take over the Chinese Eastern Railway, and the prospect of a Soviet–Chinese war.[48] Maxton declared that the whole league was on the Soviet side in the conflict. Melnichansky demanded unequivocal support of the Soviet Union as the champion of the oppressed, and was followed in the same sense by Pollitt. The Latin American delegates contributed a picturesque episode by presenting a United States flag captured in Nicaragua in the previous year by the nationalist leader Sandillo.[49] A Chinese delegate claimed that the Chinese workers were against the war in Manchuria and were organizing armed resistance to Kuomintang. The only discordant note on this issue seems to have been struck by the delegates of the International Anti-Militarist Bureau whose views had been hailed with enthusiasm in the eclectic atmosphere of the Brussels congress more than two years earlier. They now declared that, while ready to join in resisting any attack on the Soviet Union, they did not believe in the overthrow of imperialism by military action, or support Soviet military and diplomatic policies in China.[50] Friction also occurred over the Indian question. Gupta, the delegate of the Indian National Congress, advocated boycotts, non-cooperation and refusal to pay taxes; these were criticized by Pollitt as inadequate and futile weapons in the struggle against British imperialism. Maxton demanded total independence for India, but was sharply reproved by Melnichansky for his failure to denounce the complicity of the Labour government in policies of repression, as illustrated in the Meerut trials.

While Melnichansky seems to have missed no opportunity of

[48] This will be discussed in a later section of this volume.

[49] *Pravda,* July 23, 1929.

[50] For reports of the congress see *Pravda,* July 23, 1929; bulletins issued by the press service of the congress, and press releases of the International Anti-Militarist Commission, preserved in the Internationaal Instituut voor Sociale Geschiedenis in Amsterdam, add further details. The speech of Lehning, the delegate of the Anti-Militarist Bureau, appeared in one of these releases, and the speech of the Chinese delegate was published in *Die Internationale,* xii, No. 15, August 1, 1929, pp. 477–480; otherwise no texts of speeches were published. Among the messages of sympathy received were one from De Valera enclosing a contribution of £20 from Fianna Fail, and one from Kenyatta, secretary-general of the Kikuyu Central Association, expressing the hope of being able to attend the congress.

attacking non-communist speakers, the acrimonious exchanges were played down in the scanty records of the congress. After a concluding speech by Münzenberg, the congress adopted, apparently by acclamation, a manifesto addressed to the "workers and peasants of China and the USSR and oppressed peoples and toilers of the world", which affirmed that an attack on the Soviet Union must be regarded as "an attack on the oppressed of the whole world". It also adopted resolutions on the danger of war, on China and on the rôle of the trade unions in the struggle against imperialism. While Münzenberg still made an effort to carry on the Brussels tradition of the league as an organization in which communists and non-communists could cooperate, regardless of their differing allegiances, in the struggle against imperialism, this conception of the united front was now obsolete in Moscow. Melnichansky laboured, with the full authority of Comintern behind him, to carry the split between the communist and the non-communist world to its logical conclusion; and unqualified support for the Soviet Union was the acid test of determination to fight against imperialism. The purpose and the moral of the congress were summed up, while it was still in progress, by a commentator in *Pravda*:

> With the sharpening of the class struggle, . . . non-communist elements in the League against Imperialism will have finally to reveal their political physiognomy, since the masses rising up for the struggle against imperialism will demand a clear answer to the question, who is their friend, who their enemy.[51]

The sequel was inevitable, and had perhaps been desired. Later in the year, Maxton, Nehru, Fimmen and Hatta all resigned their seats on the executive committee of the league.[52] Thereafter the league, having served its limited purpose, passed into oblivion.

(*b*) *Friends of the Soviet Union*

Preparations were made in good time to celebrate the tenth anniversary of the October revolution, and included invitations for large workers' delegations from foreign countries to attend the

[51] *Pravda*, July 23, 1929.

[52] B. Gross, *Willi Münzenberg* (1967), pp. 209–210. This account of the congress contains inaccuracies; Manuilsky does not appear to have been present.

festivities. At the end of September 1927 *Pravda* reported from London that the organizing committee of the British delegation had proposed to other delegations to hold a conference in Moscow during the celebrations, one purpose of which would be to consider measures of defence against the danger of war which threatened the Soviet Union.[53] The Soviet leaders fully grasped the potentialities of the occasion, which was described as a struggle for the fraternal *rapprochement* of the workers of capitalist countries with the victorious proletariat of the USSR.[54] On November 5, 1927, Stalin gave a six-hour interview to eighty members of the foreign delegations, including the German and the French[55] (the British delegation, travelling by sea, had not yet arrived). What was now officially called the World Congress of Friends of the Soviet Union met from November 9 to 13, 1927. Of 947 delegates from forty-three countries, 173 came from Germany, 146 from France and 127 from Great Britain. Lawther, the head of the British delegation, made the opening speech, again stressing the danger of war; and Rykov delivered a long report on the achievements of the Soviet Union. Bukharin, Voroshilov, Zetkin, Barbusse, Toller and Tomsky were among the other orators. The congress adopted a resolution praising the Soviet Government as the builder of socialism and the only government which represented the workers and the oppressed of all countries, and ending with a pledge "to prepare in our countries and by all means for the defence of the first workers' and peasants' republic". A further resolution denounced the military preparations of the imperialist powers.[56] Bukharin commented in his speech at the fifteenth party congress in the following month on the importance of the occasion. The delegations had comprised fewer communists and more social-democrats than previous workers' delegations; yet the attitude of the social-democrats had been the best. He looked forward to "bitter struggles with the social-democrats *for*

[53] *Pravda*, September 28, 1927.

[54] *Desyat' Let Profinterna v Rezolyutsiyakh* (1930), p. 188.

[55] Stalin, *Sochineniya*, x, 206–238.

[56] The congress was welcomed in a leading article in *Pravda*, November 10, 1927, and reported *ibid.* November 12, 13, 15, 1927, in *Internationale Presse-Korrespondenz*, No. 112, November 15, 1927, pp. 2477–2481, and in *Internationaler Bauern-Korrespondent* Special No. [4], December 1927, pp. 50–53. Totals of the number of participants varied slightly in different accounts; 927 delegates are classified by country, by trade union membership and by occupation in *Zeitschrift für Geschichtswissenschaft*, iv, No. 2, 1956, p. 357.

the soul of the working class, for mass influence on the working class".[57] It was a carefully guarded plea for the maintenance of united front tactics.

The task of the principal delegates on their return home was to found societies or committees of Friends of the Soviet Union in their respective countries; this was achieved during the winter of 1927–1928. A conference of the British society in April 1928 was attended by 233 delegates.[58] Early in May 1928 it was announced that, once more on British initiative, a conference of European committees of Friends of the Soviet Union would be held in Cologne on May 26–27.[59] The joint presidents were Lawther, Cannone (a representative of the French non-communist CGT) and Siewert (the principal organizer of the German workers' delegations to the Soviet Union in 1926 and 1927),[60] who was expelled from the KPD a year later as a Rightist. A declaration proposed by Lawther on the danger of imperialist war against the Soviet Union invited the workers to demonstrate on August 4 and 5, the anniversary of the outbreak of war in 1914 (the date chosen betrayed the British origin of the resolution). A resolution on trade union unity submitted by Cannone apparently (it was not published) failed to meet the usual dilemma of reconciling participation in non-communist unions with a strengthening of revolutionary unions; the Belgian delegation abstained from voting. A declaration on Fascism proposed by Tasca concentrated on Italian Fascism.[61] The conference also decided to set up a bureau in Berlin to issue a weekly information sheet, to maintain contact between Friends of the Soviet Union organizations in all countries, and to prepare for a second world congress.[62] Münzenberg claimed that the French society at this time had

[57] *Pyatnadtsatyi S"ezd VKP(B)*, i (1961), 652; according to *Kommunisticheskii Internatsional: Kratkii Istoricheskii Ocherk* (1969), p. 281, 22 per cent of the delegates were social-democrats.

[58] *The New Line: Documents of the Tenth Congress of the CPGB* (n.d.), p. 28.

[59] *Internationale Presse-Korrespondenz*, No. 46, May 15, 1928, p. 823.

[60] For these see pp. 401, 430–431 below.

[61] *Internationale Presse-Korrespondenz*, No. 51, May 29, 1928, pp. 934–935; for the declarations see *ibid.* No. 52, June 1, 1928, pp. 942–943, No. 55, June 8, 1928, pp. 1001–1002.

[62] *Ibid.* No. 54, June 5, 1928, p. 985; A. Tivel and M. Kheimo, *Desyat' Let Kominterna v Tsifrakh* (1929), pp. 370–372, in recording this conference, treats the organization as an offshoot of MRP.

more than 20,000 members, and the British society a similar number.[63]

During the summer of 1928 attention was diverted to the long and arduous sixth congress of Comintern. But on September 27, 1928, the international committee held a further meeting in Berlin; a congress of German Friends of the Soviet Union was held there on November 4, 1928; and, according to Münzenberg, congresses were planned in Prague, Brussels, Paris, New York, Buenos Aires and Mexico.[64] But another account, while affirming that "the organization of war against the Soviet Union is not something invented by panic-mongers", admitted that the delegations which had attended the Cologne conference in May 1928 had not all responded with equal fervour to the appeal.[65] The Friends of the Soviet Union movement had been inspired by the tenth anniversary of the revolution and by the danger, real or imagined, of war against the Soviet Union. It was a propaganda campaign rather than an organization, and after the end of 1928 was merged in the more durable League against Imperialism or in specific anti-war campaigns.

(c) *The Anti-Fascist Congress*

The example of the League against Imperialism was probably responsible for an anti-Fascist congress which took place in Berlin on March 9–10, 1929. The formal initiative appears to have been taken by an anti-Fascist committee in Berlin under the presidency of the French writer Barbusse. Münzenberg, past master in the art of mobilizing non-party support for communist causes, later recorded a decision of the executive committee of MRP to participate in the convening of the congress;[66] and the part played by him at the congress suggests that the idea had sprung from his fertile brain. In December 1928 IKKI set up a small commission under the presidency of Humbert-Droz to prepare for the congress; and the party central committee delegated Stasova to represent it. These choices indicated reluctance to

[63] *Stenograficheskii Otchet VI Kongressa Kominterna* (1929), i, 105.

[64] *Internationale Presse-Korrespondenz*, No. 113, October 5, 1928, pp. 2190–2191, No. 123, November 2, 1928, pp. 2434–2435, No. 124, November 6, 1928, p. 2465.

[65] *Ibid.* No. 122, October 30, 1928, p. 2419.

[66] W. Münzenberg, *Solidarität* (1931), p. 341.

give any undue prominence to Soviet participation. The division of authority resulted in a minor *contretemps*. Stasova journeyed to Berlin without informing the commission, and made the necessary arrangements with the Berlin committee, whereupon Humbert-Droz in dudgeon asked to be relieved of his function.[67] The congress was summoned by an announcement of February 1, 1929, which spoke of the populations of Italy, Poland, Lithuania and the Balkan countries living "under the yoke of Fascism". The brutal methods of Fascism were said to constitute "a standing threat to peace", and the aim of the congress was "to unite all sincere opponents of war against the permanent danger of war conjured up by Fascism". The support of "countless workers' organizations and anti-Fascist intellectuals" was claimed for the project, but no political parties were named.[68] Sponsorship in Moscow remained lukewarm; no notice was taken in the Soviet press of the initial announcement. The first response came from Vienna, where an anti-Fascist meeting attended by members of the Social-Democratic and Communist Parties and by non-party workers was held on February 10, 1929 — an example of united front tactics which hardly accorded with current Comintern procedures.[69] A list of organizations supporting the congress consisted mainly of French organizations, and international and *émigré* organizations centred in Paris.[70] Münzenberg hailed the approaching congress in an article which avoided any mention of parties, called Fascism "*an international danger for the international working class*", and recorded anti-Fascist demonstrations in many countries.[71] The Italian communist Silone took a tougher line, denouncing social-democrats who treated Fascism as an incidental episode, and "free-thinking" and "sentimental" people who protested against it on moral or ideological grounds. Fascism was essentially a product of capitalism:

> The struggle for the overthrow of Fascism must coincide with the struggle for the overthrow of capitalist society.... There is no separation between the anti-Fascist struggle and

67 J. Humbert-Dorz, *De Lénine à Staline* (Neuchatel, 1971), p. 368.

68 *Internationale Presse-Korrespondenz*, No. 10, February 1, 1929, p. 181.

69 *Ibid.* No. 15, February 15, 1929, p. 295.

70 *Ibid.* No. 20, March 1, 1929, p. 419.

71 *Ibid.* No. 16, February 19, 1929, pp. 309–310; for further anti-Fascist demonstrations see *ibid.* No. 22, March 5, 1929, pp. 465–466.

the class struggle; to strengthen the anti-Fascist struggle without strengthening the revolutionary class struggle of the proletariat is unthinkable.

Nevertheless, it was important, through the international congress, to win the support of "non-proletarian strata" for the tasks of the revolutionary proletariat.[72]

The congress held three sittings on March 9–10, 1929, concluding with a mass demonstration in the Busch Circus in Berlin, at which a choir sang revolutionary songs. Münzenberg was president of the congress and principal manager. Barbusse was the respected and eloquent proposer of the main resolution on "Fascism, Imperialism and Danger of War". Pieck brought to the congress the greetings of the KPD. Heckert played a prominent part in the proceedings and proclaimed that "he who leads the struggle against Fascism must equally lead the struggle against social-democracy". But communist participation was reduced to a minimum — in part, perhaps, for police reasons. Stasova was the only Soviet delegate named in the report; her speech, if she made one, was not mentioned. Three Soviet trade union delegates — none of them well-known names — had been refused entry to Germany and telegraphed their greetings. Two figures from the past, who emerged from obscurity to make their contributions to the denunciation of Fascism at the congress, were Karolyi, president of a short-lived Hungarian democratic republic in 1919, and Fan Noli, who had been head of an Albanian Government for six months in 1924. Max Hölz, a turbulent agitator who had been in and out of the KPD, had spent many years in prison, and had been awarded the Order of the Red Banner by the Soviet Government, made an unexpected entry at the last session with a dramatic, if not quite credible, story that he had been arrested and beaten by the police on his way to the meeting. Mussolini and Pilsudski, the Stahlhelm and the SPD Reichsbanner, were all targets of attack at the congress; Hitler and the National-Socialists seem to have escaped notice. The congress ended quietly; the chief of police had prohibited any outdoor demonstration.[73] The

[72] *Ibid.* No. 23, March 8, 1929, pp. 487–488.

[73] *Ibid.* No. 24, March 12, 1929, pp. 519–524; for Fan Noli see *Socialism in One Country, 1924–1926*, Vol. 3, p. 34 note 5. The congress was briefly reported by *Pravda*, March 10, 12, 1929, which named Barbusse, Münzenberg and Heckert, but mentioned no Soviet representative.

resolution declared that "reformism everywhere prepares the way for Fascism", and that "*the social-Fascist policy of the reformists leads directly to the victory of Fascist reaction*". It proclaimed bravely that the only way to destroy Fascism was "the violent overthrow and the complete destruction of the order of society whose consequence and expression Fascism is: of the rotting capitalist society". But it concluded more cautiously by describing the anti-Fascist struggle as "*an integral component*", not of the proletarian revolution, but of "*the world front of the proletariat against imperialism*".[74] A resolution on the trade unions described the way in which Fascist régimes, in Italy and elsewhere, had crushed the unions with the complicity of their corrupt reformist leaders, and the extension of that process to Great Britain and France.[75] A resolution was also passed to set up an "international anti-Fascist bureau" in Berlin.[76] But no record of such an institution has been found; and the slender enthusiasm displayed in Moscow for the congress was significant. The anti-Fascist congress of March 1929 was the last example in this period of a policy of cooperation with the radical Left which was now increasingly outmoded and rejected.

[74] *Internationale Presse-Korrespondenz*, No. 27, March 22, 1929, pp. 598–599.

[75] *Ibid.* No. 38, May 3, 1929, pp. 918–919.

[76] *Ibid.* No. 24, March 12, 1929, p. 523.